DATE DUE

Luminous Passage

Luminous Passage

The Practice and Study of Buddhism in America

Charles S. Prebish

UNIVERSITY OF CALIFORNIA PRESS

Berkeley / Los Angeles / London

University of California Press
Berkeley and Los Angeles, California

University of California Press, Ltd.
London, England

Library of Congress Cataloging-in-Publication Data

Prebish, Charles S.
Luminous passage : the practice and study of Buddhism in America / Charles S. Prebish.
p. cm.
Includes bibliographical references and index.
ISBN 0-520-21696-2 cloth; 21697-0 paper.
1. Buddhism—United States. 2. Buddhism—Canada.
I. Title.
BQ732.P736 1998
294.3'0973—dc21 98-20767

Printed in the United States of America
9 8 7 6 5 4 3 2 1

The paper used in this publication meets the minimum requirements of American National Standards for Information Sciences—Permanence of Paper for Printed Library Materials, ANSI Z39.48-1984.

Contents

Preface

There can be little doubt that both the practice and study of Buddhism in North America have grown enormously in the last quarter century. Fueled by a dramatic increase in ethnic Asian American Buddhist communities since the 1965 change in U.S. immigration laws and the continued expansion of the various Euro-American Buddhist communities, this growth has resulted in several million Buddhist practitioners now residing in North America. Although the expansion of the American Buddhist movement is likely not surprising to observers of the American religious landscape, the surge of scholarly interest in Buddhism in general, and in American Buddhism in particular, was surely unexpected. In 1975 there was *one* academic course on the American Buddhist movement; now there are many (and perhaps even dozens). A cursory glance at the bibliographies of the three earliest comprehensive books on Buddhism in America—Emma Layman's *Buddhism in America,* my *American Buddhism,* and Rick Fields's *How the Swans Came to the Lake*—reveals a dearth of scholarly sources on American Buddhism, because there were none at the time. Instead, these authors and I relied on the popular writings of American Buddhists and Buddhist sympathizers, on scholarly books about other aspects of Buddhism, and on general books about religion. More recent volumes show an entirely different circumstance. For example, the bibliographies included in *American Buddhism: Methods and Findings in Recent Scholarship* (edited by Christopher Queen and Duncan Ryūken Williams) and *The Faces of Buddhism in America* (edited by Kenneth Tanaka and me) present a wealth of important new writings on American Buddhism, highlighting the rich literature that has emerged in a short twenty-year span.

When *American Buddhism* was published in 1979, I did not foresee writing another book on the topic nearly two decades later. At that time I presumed to have a reasonable prescription for the ongoing development of the American Buddhist movement, noting in the conclusion that it could "participate fully in the American experience by emphasizing the unique qualities of freedom, equality, and justice held dear by so many Americans." I went on to suggest that it "would also be beneficial for American Buddhist groups to manifest their American nature in their holiday observances, art, music, ritual life, and so forth." No doubt this overly zealous projection was predicated on the assumption that American Buddhism had something definitive and integral to add to American religious life. The intervening years have demonstrated, I think, that while the assumption remains true, the suggestions as to how this contribution might be made are no longer apt. This being the case, by 1994 I had developed a plan to write another volume, one that would, I hoped, be more temperate in viewpoint, would revisit the expanding frontier of American Buddhism, and would try to capture and understand American Buddhism's vibrancy and its contribution to American religious life. In that regard, *Luminous Passage: The Practice and Study of Buddhism in America* can be seen as a companion volume to *The Faces of Buddhism in America,* which I coedited with Kenneth K. Tanaka, and which is also published by the University of California Press. It is my hope that, taken together, these two volumes will present a comprehensive picture of American Buddhism at the turn of the coming century.

More than anything else, this is a book about Buddhist communities, or *sanghas.* It does not intend to minimize the role of important Asian American Buddhist teachers, and now Western Buddhist teachers, or the seminal work they have done in developing American Buddhism; rather, it focuses on life within the communities that these individuals have founded and structured. It considers the various Buddhist practices and rituals and liturgies employed in these communities, as well as the manner in which American Buddhist communities have confronted the changing, shifting framework of American values and lifestyles. The book considers the legacy Buddhism will leave to the children of many American Buddhist pioneers. And it presents a first look at the role of technology in American Buddhism as new technological developments alter the very nature of the defining characteristics of the Buddhist *sangha.*

This book contains six chapters, each approaching one aspect of Buddhist community life in America. Chapter 1 presents an overview of American Buddhist history. Because this overall topic has been treated quite thoroughly in the general volumes on American Buddhism, with most of the specific lineages carefully documented in the publications of the respective Buddhist groups, this chapter intends only to familiarize and reacquaint the reader with the historical perspective of the American Buddhist movement. Chapter 2 focuses on developmental issues in American Buddhism. It considers first the variety of ways in which the American Buddhist landscape can be charted, highlighting several operative but conflicting theories. As a corollary of this charting process, it also considers the interaction between Asian American, Euro-American, African American, and Hispanic American Buddhists while also examining gender roles, the sexual abuse of authority, and minority sexual lifestyle choices as well as the impact of American Buddhism on the healing professions. And finally, this chapter examines the way in which social engagement is manifested in American Buddhist communities.

Chapter 3 moves outward from a consideration of historical and social issues into the diversity of American Buddhist communities, attempting to provide brief looks at different kinds of life in those communities. It examines communities from nearly all the Asian Buddhist traditions and tries to showcase the variety of practices employed by those communities. In at least one case, the community examined is most certainly a nontraditional *sangha*.

Chapters 4 and 5 extend the traditional Buddhist definition of *sangha* to include the scholars' community—with specific reference to the growing number of scholar-practitioners in American Buddhism—and the "cybersangha," a community that has no location in real geographic space but instead reflects the manner in which technology has allowed those who are isolated from existing communities to have a rich and full Buddhist life. Neither of these communities could have existed at the time of the Buddha, yet both contribute greatly to Buddhism's growth not only in the West but throughout the world.

Buddhism continues to develop into a truly global religion. Thus it is only appropriate to conclude the volume with some considerations about the future of American Buddhism at the millennium. Chapter 6 presents the reflections of the past twenty-five years of scholarship, from which a small number of common themes are extracted, each of which is likely to have an impact on the American Buddhism of the next century. However, as American Buddhism approaches the turn of the millennium, for the first time in Buddhist history every Buddhist sectarian lineage from each of the Asian Buddhist cultures is represented in one place and at one time. Perhaps the most critical issue is not how to develop some universally acceptable and probably presumptuous standard of acceptability, such as adaptation or acculturation or ethnicity, but instead to consider how American Buddhism might promote an ecumenical sense of itself that allows for and even encourages diversity, recognizing the integrity of each American Buddhist community irrespective of how it defines itself. Furthermore, since teachers and teachings now move freely from one part of the world to another, it might well be possible to see the entire world as a field of merit. Moreover, some of the mechanisms to support such an effort are already in place.

The field research for this project has been supported by a variety of grants and fellowships. The American Academy of Religion provided a research grant in 1994–95 that enabled me to visit Zen Mountain Monastery in Mt. Tremper, New York. The Research and Graduate Studies Office at the Pennsylvania State University provided funding in 1996–97 that allowed me to visit Buddhist communities in Washington, D.C., San Francisco–Berkeley, and Boston. In addition, a second grant from that office provided the occasion to examine Buddhist communities in Toronto, Montreal, and Halifax in fall 1997, thus adding a Canadian component to my fieldwork. In 1997–98 I was awarded a Rockefeller Foundation Humanities Fellowship that enabled me to spend the academic year at the Centre for the Study of Religion at the University of Toronto, where I was able to complete the manuscript for this book in a most ideal setting.

Many people contributed to this project in ways that I will never be able to adequately acknowledge. Damien Keown, my coeditor at the *Journal of Buddhist Ethics,* read every chapter and was a good enough friend to politely tell me when my ruminations and speculations ventured a bit too deeply into never-never land. Richard Seager, whose textbook on American Buddhism will soon be available, was a constant source of information, and a wonderful colleague with whom to share notes and ideas. Christopher Queen of Harvard University read the chapter on the academic study of Buddhism and offered many valuable suggestions for its final version. Mavis Fenn read a number of the chapters as well, sharing her gentle critique freely. Suwanda Sugunasiri, of the University of Toronto, was a wonderful help in arranging fieldwork opportunities for me in the Toronto Buddhist community, and in including me in the activities of this exciting Buddhist community. Through the steady stream of publications by Martin Baumann, who has studied Western Buddhism more thoroughly than anyone else, I was constantly reminded to look beyond the American setting for clues about how the globalization of Buddhism might have an impact on America. In addition, Baumann read the entire manuscript, offering an incredibly comprehensive and useful commentary. Paul Numrich, whose volume *Old Wisdom in the New World* has helped shaped the way we study immigrant Theravāda communities in North America, also read the entire manuscript with a keen and discerning eye, and provided many important suggestions. Each chapter was eventually read by Gwyn McVay, who not only corrected my Buddhist Hybrid English without complaint, but also offered many important suggestions on how to make my turgid writing style less impenetrable. At the University of California Press, both Douglas Abrams Arava and Reed Malcolm provided strong and continued support from the inception of the project to its completion. To Deke, who came to be known as the "Dharma Dog," and who proved that golden retrievers most assuredly have Buddha-nature, I am indebted for always knowing just when to startle me out of frustrated inactivity with either her ferocious bark or her gentle nuzzling. Finally, each time I came across some seemingly impossible hurdle in the preparation of the manuscript, my wife, Susan, would find some uncanny new way to convince me to write the whole problematic section over again, without wounding my sensibilities. Without her, this book might never have been completed.

CHAPTER 1

American Buddhism

A Brief History

Just before the publication of my book *American Buddhism* in 1979, I was fortunate to have a sabbatical year at the Graduate Theological Union in Berkeley, California. Nestled at the base of the Berkeley hills, this wonderful little consortium of seminaries and theological schools found itself at that time in the midst of a Buddhist explosion in the Bay Area. It was quite literally surrounded by Buddhists. Just above it was the Tibetan Nyingma Meditation Center; a few blocks below it was the Jōdo Shinshū–sponsored Institute of Buddhist Studies; and the Berkeley Zen Center wasn't much farther away. Across the bay in San Francisco, the city was virtually teeming with American Buddhist groups of all kinds. For a researcher investigating the development of Buddhism as an American religious phenomenon, it was a nirvana of sorts.

About the same time, the British Broadcasting Company was releasing a film series on world religions entitled *The Long Search.* Unlike most previous efforts at portraying on celluloid the vast diversity of humanity's religious yearnings, this series was narrated by a nonspecialist named Ronald Eyre, who described himself as a Yorkshire-born, London-based displaced theater director. As one might expect, his choices about where to go, whom to visit, and what to ask were highly eclectic and often eccentric. With regard to many of the religious traditions he was clearly a novice, and it showed—sometimes painfully so for the viewer. Nonetheless, the films were often breathtaking and exciting. From Hindu festivals on the banks of the Ganges, to the "Zen restaurant" in Tokyo, to the Baptist Temple of Indianapolis, the films debated and pondered critical questions surrounding our individual and collective search for fulfillment. As a result, many professors used these fine films in academic classes with great success, and some still do. When it was all over, the final film, called *Reflections on the Long Search,* allowed Eyre to share with his viewers what he had learned on his own long search as the project neared completion. He said that, irrespective of where he went and whom he interviewed, the questions he was asked most invariably began with the phrase "Just between you and me . . ." And this final segment concluded with our tired narrator making himself a cup of tea.

It might be fair to assume that in the early years of researching American Buddhism, inquiring scholars might have been asked questions phrased in this same manner. In my fieldwork, however, and in my academic classes as well, I got questions phrased quite differently, and I suspect I was asked them many more times than Ron Eyre's "Just between you and me . . ." The catch phrase I heard was: "Say, did you hear about the new Buddhist group in . . . ?" Not a day went by when someone didn't ask me whether I had information on the new Buddhist sitting group in some city or town, or a new ethnic Buddhist temple somewhere, or a new rinpoche or rōshi who had come to North America. In those early days of research on American Buddhism, it was even possible to keep track of all the groups, or at least almost all of them. However, charting the American Buddhist landscape was complicated by the fact that many of these groups were even more ephemeral than their early Indian Buddhist counterparts, some of which came and went leaving barely more than their names in some early Buddhist historian's records. It was also not at all unusual to find, in checking the status of a new American Buddhist group, recently discovered, that the group's telephone had been unceremoniously disconnected.

Within a decade, Don Morreale's book *Buddhist America: Centers, Retreats, Practices* would organize, list, and describe more than five hundred American Buddhist groups. Although the astronomical growth rate for American Buddhist groups was slowing at that time, it was still necessary to telephone first to make sure that the groups still existed. More importantly, there were so many groups in existence by the close of the 1980s that nobody could any longer keep all the centers and sects and teachers inside his or her head. That all of the Buddhist cultures and traditions and sects were simultaneously present in North America was no doubt the most important event in the history of Buddhism as a world religion, but a database was becoming necessary. Now, a decade later, that continually changing database is being created. Barry Kapke's "DharmaNet International" site on the World Wide Web not only lists American Buddhist communities, organized by sect and by state, but also offers a form for Buddhist groups to complete that is forwarded directly to Morreale, in order that he may include all groups in his recent and much-needed update, despite the fact that any print record will be outdated before it actually appears.

Later, we will see that there is a large and growing literature on the development of American Buddhism. Although there are still too few comprehensive volumes that examine the whole of the tradition, there are many fine articles, chapters, and books that examine aspects of American Buddhism in depth, both historically and thematically. In other words, while the earliest volumes attempted to span the entire Buddhist road map throughout North America, it is no longer necessary, or even desirable, for one book to do that. In that regard this chapter intends to provide an overview of American Buddhist history, identifying the significant appearance of each tradition and sect, commenting on the ongoing development of important traditions and teachers, highlighting the issues that informed then and continue to inform American Buddhism, and providing a new sense of where American Buddhism stands at the beginning of the millennium.

American Buddhism in the Nineteenth Century

Many current researchers in the academic field of Buddhist Studies consider the French scholar Eugène Burnouf to be the father of "Buddhology." Such being the case, it is only fitting that Thomas Tweed, in his book *The American Encounter with Buddhism, 1844–1912,* marks the beginning of the American encounter with Buddhism by two events: first, the appearance of Henry David Thoreau's 1844 rendering of Burnouf's French translation of the *Lotus-sūtra* into English for a transcendentalist magazine; and second, the publication of Edward Elbridge Salisbury's paper entitled "Memoir on the History of Buddhism," a Burnouf-influenced address read at the first meeting of the American Oriental Society on 28 May 1844.[1] According to Rick Fields, in less than a decade thereafter there would be more than twenty thousand Chinese in California, and by 1860 roughly 10 percent of Californians would be Chinese.[2] Nonetheless, the environment in which the new Buddhists in America found themselves was largely shaped by the individuals Tweed highlights, and by the Victorian mind-set they brought to their encounter with Buddhism. Nowhere is this expressed more explicitly than in Tweed's reference to an article published by Rev. Edward Hungerford (of Menden, Connecticut) in the *New Englander.* Tweed says:

> Hungerford, who embraced the Victorian Protestant worldview, suggested that Buddhism "looks only at the dark side of existence" and contradicts not only optimism but other fundamental beliefs and values as well. Further, it fails to manifest the usual characteristics of religion: "There is no great glowing future to which faith can lift its eye, no eternal progress to inspire aspiration. No God, no soul, no Saviour from sin, no love, no heaven!"[3]

In view of the above, it is hardly shocking that the Chinese immigrants who came to work in California after the discovery of gold at Sutter's Mill, and who began to lay track for the Central Pacific railroad in the 1860s, found themselves in a mostly hostile racial environment. Still, within a short time there were hundreds of Chinese temples up and down the California coastline. No doubt the religious practice in these temples was a highly eclectic blend of Buddhism, Taoism, and Confucianism, but there were at least a number of Buddhist priests in residence at these sites. Although an explicit and distinct Chinese Buddhism would not appear on the North American continent until later, by the time of the Chinese Immigration Exclusion Act of 1882 America was the site of more than simply an edifying discussion about Buddhism as a religious tradition. Images of various Buddhist figures like Śākyamuni, Amitābha, Bhaiṣajyaguru, Vairocana, Mañjuśrī, and Maitreya were present in the purely Buddhist temples, and Pure Land and Ch'an practices began to appear in the small but growing American Buddhist community.

With the passage of the exclusion act, the way was paved for a new group of immigrants from Asia to bring Buddhism to American soil. Louise Hunter, the author of *Buddhism in Hawaii,* asserts that as early as 1839 Jōdo Shinshū Buddhism was beginning to find its way into Hawaii, largely as a result of Japanese shipwrecks in Hawaiian waters.[4] The official entry of Buddhism into Hawaii does not occur, however, until 12 March 1889, when a young priest named Sōryū Kagahi arrived in the islands to investigate the welfare of his countrymen, who had by that time begun working in Hawaii but without any opportunity for spiritual guidance from the home church, Honpa Honganji.[5] This was, of course, a full decade prior to Hawaii's being granted status as an American possession in 1898. The first Japanese immigrants to settle on the mainland arrived in 1869. Settling near Sacramento, California, they served as a precursor for the arrival of Matsudaira Katamori, a Japanese feudal lord, who founded the short-lived Wakamatsu Tea and Silk Farm Colony. The U.S. census listed less than one hundred Japanese in the United States in 1870, and by 1890 the number had grown to barely over two thousand.[6] In other words, the Japanese presence was much slower to develop than the Chinese. The early Japanese settlers, unlike their Chinese predecessors, did attempt to adopt the American lifestyle of the time. They wore Western clothing, often studied English, and to a large extent left their Buddhism in Japan.

If the beginnings of America's encounter with Buddhism were marked by the two events indicated by Tweed, two further events must be cited as critical in the early formation of the Buddhist tradition in America: the development from the mid-1870s of the Theosophical Society and the so-called White Buddhists that patronized it; and the World Parliament of Religions, held in conjunction with the Chicago World's Fair (or Columbian Exposition) in 1893. The Theosophical Society was founded in New York in late 1875, as a collaboration between Helena Petrova Blavatsky, Colonel Henry Steel Olcott, and others. By the 1880s the society's publicly stated mission was: "to form the nucleus of a Universal Brotherhood of Humanity, without distinction of race, creed, sex, caste or color; to study the ancient and modern religions, philosophies, and sciences, and the demonstration of the importance of such study; and to investigate the unexplained laws of Nature and the physical powers latent in man."[7] Eventually, Olcott and Blavatsky left New York and traveled to India (arriving in February 1879) and Sri Lanka (arriving in May 1880). Blavatsky had considered herself a Buddhist since the mid-1870s, and Olcott apparently felt similarly. Nonetheless, on 25 May 1880 Olcott and Blavatsky made their Buddhist commitment formal by "taking refuge" and also taking the five vows of the laity. In his frequent visits to Sri Lanka, and in his travels throughout Asia, Olcott supported numerous Buddhist causes, not the least of which was the Bodh-Gaya Maha Bodhi Society, founded on 31 May 1891 with Olcott as its first director. In this regard he became associated with Anagarika Dharmapala, who was appointed first secretary of the organization, editor of its publication (called the *Maha Bodhi Journal*), and, more importantly, representative of the Buddhists of Sri Lanka at the World Parliament of Religions, which took place in 1893.[8]

Few would disagree that the World Parliament of Religions changed the religious landscape for the development of Buddhism in America.[9] Although the vast majority of participants were Christian, ample representation came from Hindus, Sikhs, Jains, and Buddhists as well. Especially significant for Buddhism was the fact that Anagarika Dharmapala delivered the concluding address of the opening ceremonies. If the Parliament was planned, as Rick Fields suggests, "as the spiritual expression"[10] of the Chicago World's Fair, Dharmapala placed it squarely in a Buddhist context by asserting that the Parliament "was simply the re-echo of a great consummation which the Indian Buddhists accomplished twenty four centuries ago."[11] By the third day of the Parliament, nearly all of the Japanese delegation had been introduced, including members of the Jōdo Shinshū, Nichiren, Tendai, Shingon, and Zen traditions. Included in this latter group was Shaku Sōen, a disciple of Imakita Kōsen of Engaku Temple. Although Sōen was not one of the more popular figures of the Parliament, he would later return to America in 1905 to promote Rinzai Zen. Perhaps more important to the development of Zen in America than the appearance of Sōen himself was that of three of his students: D. T. Suzuki, Nyōgen Senzaki, and Shaku Sōkatsu.

During Sōen's lectures at the Parliament, an extremely interested member of the audience was Paul Carus, editor of the *Monist* and owner of Open Court Publishing Company in LaSalle, Illinois.[12] Carus, like many of the Buddhist contingent to the Parliament, believed that Buddhism was better suited to healing society's ills than Christianity, and although Carus made friends with Dharmapala, it was Sōen that he invited to his home. That visit produced a most unusual and important offer: that Sōen remain at Open Court to help edit the publishing firm's new series of Asian books. Though Sōen declined, he did send D. T. Suzuki in his place. Suzuki remained at Open Court from 1897 until 1909, when he returned to Japan to pursue a career in Buddhist Studies. Suzuki's presence was one of the most fortuitous events in the early development of Zen in the United States. A few days after the Parliament concluded, another first for American Buddhism took place. Following a Theosophical Society–sponsored lecture in Chicago, Dharmapala administered the refuge ceremony to Charles Strauss of New York City. Rick Fields describes the event: "So it was that Charles T. Strauss of 466 Broadway, a New York City businessman, born of Jewish parents, not yet thirty years old, long a student of comparative religion and philosophy, found himself—in the words of Dharmapala's biographer—'the first person to be admitted to the Buddhist fold on American soil.' "[13]

Zen was not the only Japanese Buddhist tradition that made its appearance in America prior to 1900. In July 1898 two informal missionaries from Honpa Honganji in Japan arrived in San Francisco on a fact-finding tour. On the basis of their report, and because of the resistance of the Japanese immigrants to be converted to Christianity despite persistent conversion attempts, two priests were dispatched to the United States, arriving on 1 September 1899 and shortly thereafter establishing the Buddhist Mission of North America to support the roughly ten thousand Japanese then present in America. These two "official" missionaries, Revs. Shuei Sonoda and Kakuryo Nishimjima, became the first Buddhist clergy to enter America as permanent residents.

American Buddhism in the Twentieth Century

In his epilogue to *The Faces of Buddhism in America,* Kenneth Tanaka echoes Thomas Tweed in noting that

> Buddhism failed to become a more abiding presence in America following its initial entrance during the Victorian period, largely due to the absence in Buddhism of two qualities: optimism and activism. While other features of Buddhism appealed to certain elements of the Victorian ethos, such as its amenability to scientific worldview and the spirit of individualism, the pessimistic and passive Buddhist image dampened further growth.[14]

Although the growth of the American Buddhist movement was indeed slow in the initial decades of the twentieth century, by 1950 Buddhism had begun a period of much more aggressive expansion, and by the 1960s its increases had become explosive. Abetted by a more tolerant and pluralistic American society, an increasing ecumenicism in the aftermath of Vatican II, immigration reform in 1965, and the development of an openly assertive sense of optimism and activism in American Buddhist communities, the growth spurts of the 1960s and 1970s were consolidated in the 1980s and 1990s. Thus American Buddhism faces the turn of the millennium with a forward-looking vision.

There are at least two approaches that might be utilized in presenting an overview of American Buddhism throughout the current century. The first involves simply offering a developmental, historical timeline, noting the chronological details and offering a brief commentary on the significance of the various events. The second entails presenting a comprehensive traditional and sectarian record, tracing the ongoing development of the various American Buddhist communities according to their country of origin and sectarian affiliation. Each approach is somewhat problematic. With the former, there is a strong tendency to get lost in the sheer volume of information, thus losing the overall continuity of the historical progression. With the latter, in keeping Zen separate from Theravāda, for example, the records of each begin to look far more separate than they really are. Nonetheless, because of the rich diversity and depth in American Buddhist communities, I have opted for the second approach. I am hopeful that as the remaining chapters of the book unfold, the overall threads of the American Buddhist tradition, including those that make up its historical timeline, will become properly woven together.

American Buddhist Communities of Japanese Origin

Zen

A dozen years after his appearance at the World Parliament of Religions in Chicago, Shaku Sōen was visited at Engaku Temple in Japan by Mr. and Mrs. Alexander Russell of San Francisco. Of all the Zen masters in Japan at the time, Sōen seemed to be the only one engaged in teaching foreigners, and when the Russells invited him for an extended visit with them in the summer of 1905, he gladly accepted. During the slightly less than a year that the rōshi stayed with the Russells, he not only provided meditation instruction to their large family and engaged Mrs. Russell in *kōan* study, but also lectured in various cities, eventually becoming convinced that America was ready for Zen. In March 1906 Sōen was joined by D. T. Suzuki (1870–1966), who had by that time been at Open Court Publishing Company for almost a decade, and they set out across America by train. The rōshi lectured and Suzuki translated. Within a short time two of the Zen master's other students from Japan also joined him in America. The first of these was Nyōgen Senzaki (1876–1958). As a tubercular young monk, Senzaki appeared at Engaku Temple and was cared for as he recovered. Following a five-year stay, he moved on and founded a school known as Mentorgarten. When he arrived in America, he worked for the Russell family and, presumably, imagined himself raising money to support his school. Senzaki saw Mrs. Russell particularly as a great friend to Zen, and called her "the gate opener of Zen in America."[15] He was also instructed by his master not to "utter the 'B' of Buddhism"[16] for seventeen years—a promise he clearly kept. The second student to arrive, in 1906, was Shaku Sōkatsu (1869–1954). Prior to studying with Sōen, he too had been a student of Imakita Kōsen. Following a decade of rigorous practice, and a lengthy pilgrimage of sorts that took him to Burma, Sri Lanka, and India, he returned to Japan and began a small temple outside of Tokyo. When summoned to America by his master, Sōkatso took six of his own students with him. He lived in America between 1906 and 1908, and again from 1909 to 1910, but it was his student Sokei-an (1882–1945) who made the greater impact.

As noted above, D. T. Suzuki worked at Open Court from 1897 to 1909. Two years after returning to Japan he married Beatrice Lane, eventually moving to Kyoto to teach at Otani University. Suzuki had a prolific writing career, and also founded the well-known journal the *Eastern Buddhist* in 1927, which he edited with his wife. He returned to the United States in 1936, remaining until the beginning of World War II. His final stay on the North American continent was from 1950 to 1958, during which time he lectured at a number of universities, most notably Columbia. In addition, he became president of the Cambridge Buddhist Association, and the Zen Studies Society of New York was organized in 1956 in part to support his work. Suzuki retired from Columbia University in 1957 and died in 1966. Suzuki's contribution is especially significant in that he was not a Zen priest and never became a Zen master.

Nyōgen Senzaki worked at a variety of jobs in San Francisco, primarily in the hotel business. In 1916 he bought a hotel, but it failed and he sought other employment. Three years after Sōen died in 1919 and seventeen years after his arrival in America, Senzaki began to teach Buddhism, hiring halls from time to time and running what he called a "floating *zendō*." Near the end of the 1920s he established *zendōs* in San

Francisco and Los Angeles, remaining at the latter one until his death in 1958. He called the Los Angeles *zendō* the Mentorgarten Meditation Hall, and used it as a place for innovation—no Buddha statue in the *zendō, zazen* seated on chairs—and for the study of Japanese culture. During the World War II years Senzaki was interred at the Heart Mountain Camp in Wyoming along with about ten thousand other Japanese Americans. In 1945 he returned to Los Angeles, taking up residence in Little Tokyo and reestablishing his *zendō*. In 1949 he met Nakagawa Sōen Rōshi, with whom he had corresponded for many years, beginning what would be a fruitful relationship. In the 1950s he gained many disciples, most notably Robert Aitken, who would found the Diamond Sangha in Honolulu in 1959. In a stirring reflection on Senzaki, Louis Nordstrom says:

> Nyogen Senzaki had come to this country partly because he felt that Zen in Japan had begun to drift in the direction of decadence, and like Soyen Shaku before him, he hoped America would indeed prove to be the "happy field" of his teacher's dreams. He encouraged his students to be critical of all things Eastern and Oriental, thereby discouraging an unreflecting assimilation of dogma and mindless guru worship. What he hoped to bring about was a thoroughly international Buddhism, with an American base; a Buddhism that would transcend not only church and sect affiliation, but language affiliation as well.[17]

When Shaku Sōkatsu returned to Japan for the final time, he took five of his original six students with him, leaving behind only a lay disciple known as Shigetsu Sasaki. Sasaki had been primarily an artist (trained as a dragon carver) and writer. Unlike his predecessors, Sasaki moved to the East Coast, settling in New York. In 1919 he returned to Japan and completed his Zen training, and in 1928 was declared a rōshi. He returned to New York, and in 1930 launched the Buddhist Society of America (which was incorporated the following year, and renamed the First Zen Institute of America in 1945). Eventually he was ordained and took the name Sokei-an. Like other Zen teachers, Sokei-an was interned during the war, and his camp experience exacerbated problems with his already failing health. Following his release, in 1944 he married Ruth Fuller, an American widow who had supported his work since 1938. Nonetheless, his health had been irreparably damaged, and he died in May 1945. In 1935, Sokei-an had remarked, "It is an unhappy death for a Zen master when he does not leave an heir,"[18] and it was to be a foreshadowing of his own circumstance.

Three other Rinzai Zen rōshis should be mentioned before considering the other forms of Zen that began to appear in the United States after the mid-1950s: Eidō Tai Shimano Rōshi (b. 1932), Maurine Stuart Rōshi (1922–1990), and Kyozan Joshu Sasaki Rōshi (b. 1907). Now head of the Zen Studies Society in New York and of Dai Bosatsu Zendo in the Catskills, Eidō Tai Shimano Rōshi had been a young monk at Ryutakuji Monastery in Japan. In 1957 he was encouraged to go to America by Nyōgen Senzaki. He spent time in Hawaii studying English and serving as resident monk at the Koko-an Zendo, eventually deciding to go to New York, where he arrived on New Year's Eve 1964. While in New York, he met regularly with a group of interested *zazen* practitioners at the American Buddhist Academy and slowly built the group into a growing *sangha.* With the help of friends, he resurrected the Zen Studies Society, which had been dormant since D. T. Suzuki had returned to Japan in 1956. He eventually received Dharma transmission from Nakagawa Sōen Rōshi.

Canadian-born Maurine Stuart Rōshi also received Dharma transmission from Sōen Rōshi, but in an odd and informal manner. Sōen Rōshi had previously given formal Dharma transmission to five individuals, all male. In Stuart's case, he gave her the title of rōshi in an informal, private ceremony in 1982—one involving only himself and Stuart. Helen Tworkov reports that during the ceremony he said to Stuart, "Please tell everyone that Soen has made you a roshi."[19] Tworkov goes on to say:

> Stuart's transmission contradicted established ethics, but not the variegated dimensions of Soen's Zen, making its status all the more difficult to categorize. She accepted the title as an indication of genuine transmission but has never called herself Soen Roshi's dharma heir nor a holder of his lineage. Rather, her dharma transmission specifies for her a horizontal understanding between teacher and student independent of the vertical concerns of Zen genealogies. By Stuart's assessment, Soen intended this title to sanction her authority to teach Zen, which had not been legitimized by her training as a Zen student or her ordination in 1977 as a Rinzai Zen priest.[20]

Stuart Rōshi was the spiritual leader and president of the Cambridge Buddhist Association.

Prior to coming to Los Angeles in 1962, Kyozan Joshu Sasaki Rōshi had been resident monk at Shoju-an Rinzai temple in Japan, having attained his status as abbot in 1947. Upon arriving in the United States, he settled in Gardena, a Los Angeles suburb, utilizing the garage of his small house as a *zendō*. As his reputation and number of students grew, he expanded to found the Cimarron Zen Center in Los Angeles in 1966, and in 1971, the Mt. Baldy Zen Center. Now he also has major centers in Albuquerque and in Vancouver, British Columbia, as well as throughout the United States; for more than twenty years he has sponsored a summer seminar on Buddhism for scholars and practitioners—a program that for the last decade has been held at the Bodhi Manda Zen Center in Jemez Springs, New Mexico. Although trained in the Rinzai tradition, Sasaki Rōshi has concluded that the traditional *kōans* are not applicable in the Western environment, and has replaced them with more American counterparts.

One of the first books on American Buddhism noted:

> By the mid-1950s, Buddhism in America was on the brink of several new developments. First, new forms of Buddhism were appearing on the American scene, particularly Sōtō Zen, Zen that combined Rinzai and Sōtō techniques, and the beginnings of Tibetan Buddhism. Second, and by far the most important development in Buddhism since its entry to America, was the emergence of "Beat Zen."[21]

What followed Allen Ginsberg's first reading of his poem "Howl" at the Six Gallery in San Francisco has been more than amply documented elsewhere, as have the various excursions into Buddhism by Jack Kerouac, Philip Whalen, Kenneth Rexroth, Gary Snyder, and others. What is also documented but generally not often discussed is that for some of the Beats, Buddhism was more than just an expression of "lunatic Zen." Gary Snyder, for example, left graduate school at Indiana University and enrolled at the University of California at Berkeley to study Oriental languages. It was there that he and a few other like-minded friends began meeting in a study group at the Berkeley Buddhist Church, a Jōdo Shinshū–affiliated community with Rev. Enryo Imamura as its resident minister. Lest anyone question the seriousness of the endeavor, one of the participants in the group was Alex Wayman, then a young graduate student in Tibetan who would go on to pursue one of the most distinguished careers in Buddhist Studies in the twentieth century. Yet for Snyder, this intellectual pursuit of the intricacies of Buddhist philosophy was insufficient; he wanted the direct experience of Buddhism. To get it, he sailed to Japan in May 1956. Introduced to Isshu Miura Rōshi by Sokei-an's widow (Ruth Fuller Sasaki), Snyder served the rōshi for a year and then continued with Sesso Oda Rōshi when Miura Rōshi left for New York with Mrs. Sasaki. He continued in these studies for a decade, ending them only with his teacher's death in 1966.

Snyder was the exception. Most of the Beats, despite their identification with the spontaneity and antinomianism of Zen, understood less than one might have imagined. Although they attempted to replace what they rejected of American culture with Zen culture, the Beats' accuracy remains questionable. According to Theodore Roszak: "It is indisputable . . . that the San Francisco beats, and much of our younger generation since their time, *thought* they had found something in Zen they needed, and promptly proceeded to use what they understood of this exotic tradition as a justification for fulfilling the need."[22] Over against the Beats was the so-called Square Zen of Alan Watts. Born in England in 1915, and possessed of a huge appetite for reading of all kinds, Watts never attended university. He frequented the Buddhist Lodge in London, married into the Buddhist community, and moved to New York near the end of the 1930s. Nearly two decades later his essay "Beat Zen, Square Zen, and Zen" appeared in an issue of the *Chicago Review* devoted to Zen. Although neither his zeal for Zen nor his passion to make it seem like something Americans could do can be questioned, his misunderstandings may have been quite as severe as those of the Beats. Nonetheless, one well-known author referred to Watts as "the Norman Vincent Peale of Zen."

Certainly what emerged in the years following 1960 was a Zen explosion. Rick Fields aptly remarks: "As Eido Tai Shimano and others have observed, 1960 marked the point when American Zen turned from the intellectual to the practical. By the mid-sixties more than a score of Zen groups had appeared in the soil watered by Soyen Shaku, Sokei-an, Senzaki, D. T. Suzuki, and all the others, like mushrooms after a spring rain."[23] Apart from Zen's becoming practical, two more Zen traditions appeared. The first of these was one of the other traditional Zen schools of Japan: Sōtō.

Sōtō Zen began to appear on the American scene around 1950. In 1949, Soyu Matsuoka Rōshi founded the Chicago Buddhist Temple (now called the Zen Buddhist Temple of Chicago). Eventually, he left the organization in the hands of his disciple Richard Langlois, one of the very first American rōshis, and moved on to serve other emerging Sōtō communities, especially in California. Matsuoka Rōshi was followed shortly by Shunryu Suzuki Rōshi (1904–1971), who was to become perhaps the most well known Sōtō Zen master in North America. Suzuki Rōshi arrived in San Francisco on 23 May 1959 to become chief priest for the Japanese-American community at Sokoji Temple (also called the Sōtō Zen Mission) on Bush Street. The temple had been in existence since 1934, having been founded by Hosen Isobe, a Sōtō missionary who also founded temples in Hawaii and Los Angeles. Although he initially practiced *zazen* alone, within a short time a number of American students began to join him for early-morning periods of meditation, and in less than a year they had worked up a regular program, with Suzuki Rōshi offering lectures in English. The San Francisco Zen Center (SFZC) opened in 1961, and was incorporated the next year. Throughout, Suzuki Rōshi emphasized the primary Sōtō practice of *shikantaza,* "just sitting."

In 1967 the San Francisco Zen Center opened a country meditation center at Tassajara Hot Springs—also called Zen Mountain Center, Zenshinji Monastery—in the mountains near Carmel, California. By 1969, SFZC had outgrown its modest accommodation at Sokoji Temple on Bush Street and purchased its current headquarters at 300 Page Street. Within a short time the center had opened a series of satellite *zendōs*, and in 1972 it began Green Gulch Farm on land purchased in Marin County. Early on, Suzuki Rōshi was assisted by Dainin Katagiri Rōshi (1928–1990), who came to the United States from Japan in 1964. He assisted greatly in the years after 1969, and although he wanted to begin his own group, he was always persuaded to stay at SFZC. He eventually moved to Monterey and established a *zendō* in his home. A year after Suzuki Rōshi's death in 1971, Katagiri Rōshi moved to Minneapolis and began his own center (which is now well established). Beginning in 1967, Kobun Chino Sensei also assisted the head of SFZC while heading the Los Altos Zendo. Almost from the beginning Richard Baker Rōshi (b. 1936) was Suzuki Rōshi's closest student. He was ordained on the night before Tassajara's opening, and on 21 November 1971, in the Mountain Seat Ceremony, was installed as his teacher's successor. Within two weeks Suzuki Rōshi, who had been suffering from liver cancer for some time, was dead.

Helen Tworkov notes that in the 1960s nobody knew about Dharma transmission or asked for it; and she pointed out that Suzuki Rōshi never spoke of it.[24] In fact, when she first conceived the idea for her book *Zen in America,* there were only *seven* Americans whose qualifications to transmit Zen had been authorized by their Japanese teachers. Richard Baker was one of them. By 1983, SFZC operated, in addition to the three facilities mentioned above, the Green Gulch Grocery, Tassajara Bakery, Alaya Stitchery, and a vegetarian restaurant. It also had a scandal, reported extensively elsewhere, following which Richard Baker was forced to resign his position as abbot after more than a decade of service. About his experience at SFZC, he says:

Suzuki Roshi created the teaching and I created Zen Center. I don't care what other people think, it is correct to say that I may have created the illusion that Suzuki Roshi created Zen Center but basically, I did. Nothing like Zen Center would have existed if I hadn't been there to "translate," to make him accessible. And I overdid it. I created too much structure so that anything the students heard they thought was a teaching. But for me a good part of the teaching was creating the arms, the structure that allows a person to hear the teachings. When I came back from Japan, I knew why those people were there and how they got there. I orchestrated it. I was Suzuki Roshi's agent in a sense as well as his disciple. And I did all that because I felt that Zen Buddhism was going to be an enormously powerful, formative influence in the United States in the next decade.[25]

Zentatsu Richard Baker left SFZC, moving first to Santa Fe, New Mexico, in 1984 and then to Crestone, Colorado, in the Sangre de Cristo Mountains, where he now runs a new Buddhist organization known as the Dharma Sangha. In July 1987 Baker Rōshi transmitted the Dharma to Philip Whalen, one of the original Beat poets.

Another Sōtō organization begun in the 1960s is Shasta Abbey, initially referred to as "The Reformed Sōtō Zen Church." It was begun as a outgrowth of the Zen Mission Society in Japan as part of its Foreign Guest Department. More importantly, its founder and teacher was Jiyu Kennett Rōshi (1924–1996), one of the earliest Western women to be declared a rōshi. Born Peggy Theresa Nancy Kennett, she initially became involved in the Theravāda *sangha* in her native England. D. T. Suzuki's visits to England advanced her study of Zen. In 1960 she met Chisan Kōhō Zenji, abbot of Sōjiji Temple, and accepted his offer to study with him in Japan. She was ordained as a priest on 14 April 1962, and immediately encountered all the problems one would expect for a female British Zen priest in Japan. Nevertheless, in little more than a year she received Dharma transmission, and, shortly after the death of her teacher, acceded to his wish to establish a center in the West. She arrived in San

Francisco along with two disciples in November 1969, and subsequently founded Shasta Abbey in 1970 in northern California, which now continues after her death. In 1978 the name Zen Mission Society was changed to the Order of Buddhist Contemplatives, and the group was incorporated in 1983.

Along with Shunryu Suzuki Rōshi, one of the best known and most important Zen practitioners in America was Hakuyu Taizan Maezumi Rōshi (1931–1995), founder of the Zen Center of Los Angeles. He arrived in the United States in 1956 as a young monk who had come to the Los Angeles Sōtō Zenshūji temple, the headquarters of the Sōtō school in America. As the son of Hakujun Kuroda Rōshi, he was ordained in the Sōtō lineage at age eleven. While he took courses at Komazawa University and trained at Sōjiji Monastery, he also began *kōan* study in Tokyo with Kōryū Ōsaka Rōshi, a Rinzai master. With this unusual background he began his career in America, becoming friends with Nyōgen Senzaki and beginning to build a following of his own. Maezumi Rōshi completed his training in Japan and, in quite atypical fashion, received Dharma transmission from *three* masters: Hakujun Kuroda Rōshi, Kōryū Ōsaka Rōshi, and Hakuun Yasutani Rōshi. In so doing, he became a Dharma heir in all three Japanese Zen lineages that have been imported to America. By the time of his death, Maezumi Rōshi had built the Los Angeles Zen Center into one of the most important Buddhist communities in the United States, established an academic enterprise known as the Kuroda Institute, which attracts many of the most erudite scholar-practitioners to its programs, and conferred Dharma transmission to twelve of his students, all of whom have now begun their own *sanghas* throughout North America. One of his Dharma heirs, Bernard Tetsugen Glassman Rōshi, received *inka* from Maezumi Rōshi prior to his death. In his teachings, Maezumi utilized both the *shikantaza* meditation practice of traditional Sōtō Zen and the Rinzai practice of *kōan* study. This was not his own innovation, but rather the creative approach utilized by Daiun Harada Rōshi (1871–1961), a most important figure for American Zen despite his never having stepped foot on American soil.

Unlike traditional Zen, where introductions to the topics under discussion were not often given, Harada Rōshi gave rather explicit lectures at the beginning of his *sesshins* so his students knew precisely what to expect. His monastery, Hosshinji, was in a cold climate, just the way Harada Rōshi liked it. In the *zendō,* the *kyosaku* was aggressively used in an attempt to encourage his students to achieve *kenshō* (the religious experience of seeing into one's own nature). And the result was, in Rick Fields's words, "to modernize and demystify Zen."[26] In this environment, Hakuun Yasutani (1885–1973) was trained. An elementary school teacher by profession, he began training in *sesshins* in 1925, completed his *kōan* study in 1938, and received *inka* from the master in 1943. He is reported to have said:

> Rinzai and Soto Zen have their respective strong and weak points, but since strong points are liable to change into weak points and evils, by correctly learning each kind of Zen the strong points of both are taken in, and one is saved from the easily engendered short-comings and ill effects of both . . . Then, each may devise his characteristic methods of guidance without imitating anyone, in accord with the times and adapting to the country.[27]

Following the completion of his training, Yasutani Rōshi established a small temple outside Tokyo where his students lived in their own dwellings and maintained outside employment. At this temple he founded a Zen tradition known as Sanbo Kyodan—literally, the "Order of the Three Treasures"—which offered to serious lay practitioners the respect and training previously available only to those willing to undergo complete monastic commitment. Because of its unorthodox approach, the new tradition broke from the Sōtō school in 1954. Owing to Yasutani's spiritual training under Harada Rōshi, the lineage is also sometimes referred to as the Harada-Yasutani School of Zen. The full details of this lineage are carefully explained in Robert Sharf's article "Sanbokyodan: Zen and the Way of the New Religions."[28]

Yasutani Rōshi's first visit to the United States was almost an accidental event. In 1962 Nakagawa Sōen Rōshi canceled a trip to America because of his mother's illness, and suggested that Yasutani Rōshi replace him. His first *sesshin* was held in Hawaii, with an exhortation for the need to eliminate our laziness and experience *kenshō*. Many in attendance were likely not used to the combative atmosphere throughout, including periods of absolute silence and frequent use of the *kyosaku*. His first *sesshin* on the mainland was also held in 1962, in Los Angeles, assisted by Eidō Tai Shimano and Taizan Maezumi, neither of whom had yet attained the status of rōshi. Throughout the rest of his life Yasutani Rōshi was a frequent visitor to the United States. He died on 28 March 1973 in Kamakura. His work with Sanbo Kyodan in Japan was left to one of his

Dharma heirs, Koun Yamada Rōshi (1907–1989), and in America to Taizan Maezumi Rōshi and Eidō Tai Shimano Rōshi as well as two other teachers, Philip Kapleau and Robert Aitken.

Philip Kapleau (b. 1912) was a court reporter at the war-crimes trials in Tokyo in 1946. There he met D. T. Suzuki, and upon his return to the United States he began attending Suzuki's lectures at Columbia University. Kapleau returned to Japan in the 1950s to begin formal Zen practice. He first stayed at Ryutakuji Monastery and studied with Nakagawa Sōen Rōshi. After six months at Ryutakuji, he moved on to study with Harada Rōshi for three years. Because Kapleau was in failing health, Sōen Rōshi took him to Yasutani Rōshi, and in the midst of finally having his own living quarters and being able to negotiate his Zen training as a lay disciple rather than a monk, Kapleau recovered his health and attained *kenshō* within two years.

During his training with Yasutani Rōshi, the master allowed Kapleau to make notes on the *dokusan*—private encounters between master and disciple. These records, along with some of Yasutani's introductory talks at the beginning of *sesshins* and some additional materials, were collected into a book published in Japan in 1965 as *The Three Pillars of Zen*. By the time Kapleau received Dharma transmission from Yasutani Rōshi and prepared to return to America in 1966, the book (published in the United States as well) had made a huge impact. As Rick Fields notes:

> It was the first book written by a Westerner from within the Zen tradition, and the fact that Kapleau had convinced Yasutani-roshi to give him permission to use dokusan interviews along with the kensho experiences, made the book unique in any language. *The Three Pillars of Zen* made it clear that zazen was at the heart of Zen, and gave instructions on how to begin sitting. It made it possible for people who had never met a Zen teacher to begin practicing on their own.[29]

Philip Kapleau founded the Zen Meditation Center in Rochester, New York, in August 1966, and it quickly became one of the most energetic and active Zen centers in the United States. It currently has affiliates throughout the United States and Canada. In his zeal to make Zen truly American, and less exotic, Kapleau was one of the first teachers to promote Zen as an American religious practice, adopting Western clothing during *zazen,* chanting in English, and so forth. When Kapleau decided to translate the famous *Heart-sūtra* into English, Yasutani Rōshi protested vigorously, an event that eventually led to a break between the two men in 1967. Kapleau has now retired, but he left his own line of students, most notably Toni Packer (b. 1927), who has now gone independent and runs a non-Buddhist, non-Zen center of her own; Albert Low (b. 1928), who teaches at the Montreal Zen Center; and Michael Danan Henry (b. 1939), who now teaches at the Denver Zen Center and studies with Robert Aitken.

Robert Aitken (b. 1917) was a construction worker on Guam when he was captured by the Japanese in the early stages of World War II and detained near Kobe, Japan. During his little more than a year of internment, he engaged in many conversations with Reginald Blyth, an Englishman and friend of D. T. Suzuki, who was in the same camp. Upon release, Aitken returned to Hawaii to finish his education and begin married life. While studying briefly at the University of California at Berkeley, he met Nyōgen Senzaki. Though his initial training was with Senzaki, he was able to extend his training during a fellowship that allowed him to visit Japan as part of his graduate training in Japanese literature. He experienced his first *sesshin* at Engaku Temple in Kamakura in 1950, and soon afterward met Nakagawa Sōen Rōshi, who invited him to come to Ryutakuji, where he stayed for seven months. Upon the retirement of Yamamoto Gempo Rōshi as abbot of Ryutakuji, Sōen Rōshi was installed as the new abbot, with Aitken as a student. Aitken finally returned to Hawaii following a bout of dysentery. In addition, his marriage failed, and he came back to the mainland in 1956. Eventually, he remarried (to Anne Hopkins) and made several trips back to Japan but settled in Hawaii, where he and his wife opened a bookstore in the Chinatown section of Honolulu.

They began a sitting meditation group in 1959, which led to the formation of the Koko-an Zendo. They called their group the Diamond Sangha, and in 1961 Sōen Rōshi returned to lead two *sesshins*. Soon the *Diamond Sangha Newsletter* followed, and the Diamond Sangha became a pivotal link between the Zen tradition in Japan and that on the American mainland. Aitken also had the opportunity in the fall of 1961 to visit Japan and study with Yasutani Rōshi for an extended period. It was difficult balancing a career working for the University of Hawaii with an escalating involvement in Zen training, and in 1969 Aitken retired from the university and moved to Maui, where he and Anne started the Maui Zendo. With the blessing of both Nakagawa Sōen Rōshi and Yasutani Rōshi,

Koun Yamada Rōshi was invited to lead the Diamond Sangha, and he moved to Hawaii in 1971. By 1974 Aitken had received Dharma transmission from Yamada Rōshi. In the subsequent twenty years, Robert Aitken has had a prolific career as an author, Zen master, and activist, becoming very involved in the activities of the Buddhist Peace Fellowship. Moreover, he has become a noted authority on Buddhist ethics and the application of Buddhist values to the modern world. He has a long line of his own students, many of whom have gone on to create their own communities throughout the world. A wonderfully sympathetic and stirring profile of Aitken Rōshi is offered in Helen Tworkov's *Zen in America*.

No doubt one could fill many more pages extending and updating the ongoing historical development of the Dharma heirs of the above teachers and the establishment of the many specific communities they have founded. Much of that desired work, however, has been done by those individual communities themselves. Through their programs, publications, and World Wide Web sites, it is possible to stay up-to-date almost daily. Moreover, as I stated at the outset of this chapter, it is not my intention here to provide anything more than an overview of the major traditions and sects of the American Buddhist movement. Those interested in learning more about specific communities should consult the resources cited in chapter 5 below, as well as the bibliography.

Jōdo Shinshū

In North America, two of the traditional four denominations of Japanese Pure Land Buddhism are present: Jōdo Shū, founded by Hōnen, and Jōdo Shinshū, founded by his disciple Shinran.[30] Although there are ten sects of Shinshū Buddhism in Japan, only two of these are found on American soil: Nishi Honganji (or the "Western School") and Higashi Honganji (or the "Eastern School"). Tetsuden Kashima estimated in 1977 that the former school represented 75 to 90 percent of the Japanese Buddhists in America, and noted that it is the Nishi Honganji that incorporated as the Buddhist Churches of America (profiled in chapter 3 below).[31]

Originally established as the Young Men's Buddhist Association (*Bukkyō Seinen Kai*), within but one church in San Francisco, by the time the group was renamed as the Buddhist Mission of North America in 1914, it had many churches. U.S. census figures show that between 1900 and 1910 the Japanese population in the United States tripled (from 24,326 to 72,157).[32] It is likely that as many as two-thirds of these Japanese immigrants came from prefectures that were dominated by Jōdo Shinshū. Nonetheless, despite their location on the American mainland, the Buddhist Mission of North America was still considered to be a "district" of the home temple, Honpa Honganji, in Kyoto, and the sign outside the original North American facility verified as much; it read: "Honganji Branch Office." When Rev. Koyu Uchida became the fourth director (*kantoku*) of the organization in 1905, he changed the name to the Buddhist Church of San Francisco and allowed other affiliated organizations to call themselves Buddhist churches. Presumably, the change was an attempt to make the Buddhist population appear less foreign and exotic, since the term "church" was normative for American religious organizations of the time. Still, there was a significant amount of anti-Japanese sentiment in the early years.

By the tenth anniversary of its presence in America, Jōdo Shinshū had more than twenty churches (and branch fellowships) operating, and the need for a headquarters building was apparent. Under Uchida's guidance, a facility was constructed in San Francisco in 1914 at a cost of over thirty thousand dollars, and a constitution was drawn up for the newly named Buddhist Mission of North America (BMNA), with representatives present from all twenty-five churches then operating. As a result, Uchida's title was changed from director to bishop (*sōchō*). Uchida returned to Japan in 1923, one year before the Japanese Immigration Exclusion Act brought Japanese immigration to a complete standstill. By this time there were well over 100,000 Japanese present in the United States.

Uchida was replaced as bishop by Rev. H. Sasaki and then Rev. Kenju Masuyama in 1930. Many changes and innovations occurred during the tenure of Masuyama. An endowment foundation had been started earlier, with a goal of raising $500,000 by the time of the BMNA's thirtieth anniversary. Knowing that most of the ministers had difficulty speaking English, and that there was a growing number of second-generation Japanese Americans, or Nisei, Masuyama facilitated the organization of a training center in Kyoto, known as Wakoryo, to train new ministers for this need. By the early 1930s there were thirty-three churches operating, with fifty-nine ministers, as well as a Young Women's Buddhist Association (YWBA), a Sunday school, and a scouting program. But there were also a significant number of what Kashima calls "intraracial conflicts" between the older Issei community and the newer, English-speaking Nisei generation.[33] Partly as a remedy, in 1934 the organization was restructured into six main departments: Sunday School, Education, Young Men/Women Buddhist Association, Social Work, Publication, and Propagation-Research; and ministers broadened the use of English equivalents for Buddhist terminology.

The outbreak of World War II had potentially catastrophic implications for the BMNA. Following the creation of the War Relocation Authority on 18 March 1942, the evacuation of all citizens of Japanese ancestry was ordered, and by 6 June 1942 over 100,000 persons had been interned. Donald Tuck notes:

> The majority of the evacuees confessed the Buddhist religion; the largest number of religiously oriented Japanese-Americans affiliated with the BMNA. Official statistics recorded 61,719 Buddhists or 55.5 percent of those interned in the relocation camps. Of those who indicated a religious preference, 35,327 (48.7 percent) claimed American birth, while the foreign-born calculated as 26,372 or 68.5 percent.[34]

It was during the period of internment that the decision to change the name from the BMNA to the Buddhist Churches of America (BCA) was made at the Topaz Relocation Center in Utah. Once the War Relocation Authority announced that all the relocation camps would be closed by 2 January 1946, BCA members began to resettle, but not all members returned to the West Coast. Many choose to move to the Midwest or the East Coast, thus laying a fertile foundation for later BCA expansion. Those who did go back to the West Coast worked diligently at reestablishing previous churches, and by 1960 BCA was clearly developing an aggressive expansion. A publication program was begun, with the monthly publication *Horin* in Japanese and the *American Buddhist* in English. Between 1962 and 1974 more than $300,000 was raised from a "Sustaining Membership Program," designed to lessen the need for borrowing or soliciting funds. The modern headquarters project on Octavia Street in San Francisco was finally completed in 1971, when the organization was preparing for its seventy-fifth anniversary celebration—an event marked by the publication of the *Buddhist Churches of America 75th Anniversary Commemoration Volume*.

Buddhist Churches of America also operates two major educational centers: the American Buddhist Academy in New York City; and the Institute of Buddhist Studies (IBS) in Berkeley. The IBS offers an M.A. degree in Buddhist Studies, but more importantly, it provides all the requirements for ordination in Shin Buddhism. It also publishes the important Buddhist Studies journal *Pacific World.*

In the period between 1980 and the present, BCA has experienced a decline in membership and number of ministers, as well as a general concern for the difficulties associated with remaining a largely ethnic Buddhist community. This has been a serious concern for the organization (which is discussed at length in chapter 3, utilizing the new work of Tetsuden Kashima, Kenneth Tanaka, and Alfred Bloom).[35] Despite the difficulties noted, BCA will celebrate its centennial in 1999.

Sōka Gakkai

In Japan, more than thirty sects developed that were based on the teachings of Nichiren Daishōnin (1222–1282), the son of a fisherman who founded one of the major schools of Japanese Buddhism.[36] Formerly a Tendai priest, Nichiren tried to harmonize Buddhism into one holistic tradition that would serve all people during the period of the decline of the Dharma, known as *mappō.* He concluded that the *Lotus-sūtra* was the most complete of all Buddhist teachings, the essence of the text being revealed in the title itself: *myōho-renge-kyō.* Eventually, Nichiren inscribed a scroll called the *Gohonzon* with the letters *Nam-myōho-renge-kyō,* or "Homage to the *Lotus-sūtra.*" His disciples would engage in a practice called *gongyō,* in which they sat in front of the *Gohonzon* and recited the title of the text (known as the *daimoku*) with reverence, as well as other portions of its contents.

Three Nichiren sects have appeared in the United States: (1) the Nichiren Shū, which has attracted primarily Asian Americans in the western United States for a number of decades, and which is called the Nichiren Buddhist Church of America; (2) Sōka Gakkai International–USA, formerly called Nichiren Shōshū of America, a group with more than sixty community centers and a diverse, multiethnic membership; and (3) Nichiren Shōshū, a layman's group with six American temples run by Japanese priests, which broke off from the group now called Sōka Gakkai International–USA in 1991. These three groups now have more than 300,000 disciples on American soil.

I trace the early history of the development of Sōka Gakkai in chapter 3 below. It made its first appearance in the United States in 1960 when its third president, Daisaku Ikeda, visited briefly. Three years later, in 1963, it opened its headquarters in Los Angeles, under the direction of Masayasa Sadanaga, a close disciple of Ikeda. Quick to acculturate to America, Masayasa Sadanaga changed his name to George Williams and began a determined proselytizing campaign aimed at the recruitment of membership. Nichiren Shōshū of America (NSA) held its first U.S. convention in Chicago in 1963, with fifteen hundred delegates. The following year, when it began publication of a newspaper known as the *World Tribune,* it had thirteen chapters, and by middecade it was reporting one thousand conversions per month. The first temple opened in Los Angeles in 1967, quickly followed by others in Hawaii and Washington, D.C., and in 1968 the organization opened an "American Joint Headquarters" in Santa Monica, California. In the next five years George Williams was relentless in presenting NSA seminars on college and university campuses, tallying more than eighty by 1973. Emma Layman reports that by 1974 there were student groups of NSA members on more than sixty campuses.[37]

NSA continued its drive to fully acculturate to American society, changing the name of its meeting halls, formerly called *kaikans,* to "community centers" and staging an elaborate American Bicentennial celebration in New York in 1976. By that time an American membership of more than 200,000 had been reported,[38] and NSA was operating more than 250 chapters, with major centers in Los Angeles, San Diego, Santa Monica, San Francisco, Seattle, Phoenix, Portland, Philadelphia, Washington, D.C., Toronto, Mexico, and several other sites. The *World Tribune* was publishing three times per week, with a subscriber base of sixty thousand readers, and a more substantial periodical called the *NSA Quarterly* had begun publication.

Jane Hurst suggests that NSA's success in converting non-Asians can be traced to three basic factors: (1) its utilization of the *Lotus-sūtra* as the basis for a religious practice based on each individual's power to change his or her life; (2) its social dynamic and the energy of the proselytizing group, focusing on the recruitment of laity; and (3) an attraction for the discontented members of society and the insistence that Nichiren's Buddhism was the "true Buddhism."[39] My own suspicion is that NSA's early success was based on a combination of recruitment through the technique known as *shakubuku* and a carefully structured top-down organizational configuration that involved all members in the organization's activities. In addition to the general director, there was a board of directors that supervised a series of "territories," which were further subdivided into "areas." Each area had a director, as well as supervisors for each of the area's divisions: Men's Division, Women's Division, Young Men's Division, and Young Women's Division. Further subdivisions broke the organization down into "communities," "chapters," "districts," "senior groups," "groups," and "junior groups."[40] The early growth rate was stunning, with roughly seventy-five hundred new members per month being reported in 1969. Whereas in 1960, 96 percent of all members were Asian Americans, by 1970, 41 percent were Caucasian, 30 percent Asian American, 12 percent black, and 13 percent Latin American.[41] The largest age group consisted of those between twenty-one and thirty, and the highest proportion of membership was represented by housewives (27 percent).[42]

Sōka Gakkai International (SGI) was founded in 1975 with Daisaku Ikeda as honorary president. Shortly thereafter, much of the Nichiren Shōshū priesthood was demonstrating against Ikeda and militantly calling for his removal as president of the parent Nichiren Shōshū organization. He was ousted from the presidency in 1979, and assumed a new role as active president of SGI. Cooperation between the two groups diminished throughout the 1980s, and in 1991 all interaction ceased when the high priest Nikken Shōnin excommunicated all Sōka Gakkai members. The implications of this action were staggering, because all Sōka Gakkai members were denied access to priestly functions, to the Head Temple (and the original *Gohonzon),* and to all other Nichiren Shōshū temples—even those in the United States. As such, SGI-USA has become a Buddhist community composed entirely of lay members. There are obvious consequences. The Nichiren Shōshū priesthood has lost millions of members throughout the world, along with the huge financial support they provided. In many respects, the split has provided SGI-USA with only minimal distress. Even before the split with the priesthood, SGI had been transforming itself into a highly democratic organization. The newest general director, Fred Zaitsu, was limited to a three-year term, and SGI-USA is now directed by a "Central Executive Council" with members appointed to one-year terms. Women play an active role, too, with several women serving as vice–general directors of SGI-USA.

In recent years, President Ikeda has worked aggressively for the promotion of world peace, or *kōsen-rufu*. As a result, SGI-USA was granted status as a nongovernmental organization of the United Nations (NGO), and has begun a program (known as "UN 50") to celebrate the fiftieth anniversary of the United Nations. The organization also began Soka University of America in 1987, modeled on its Japanese counterpart. This university has a variety of programs, including one leading to an M.A. in second- and foreign-language education. In addition, in 1993 SGI-USA founded the Boston Research Center for the 21st Century to explore various peace-related issues and promote cross-cultural dialogue. In her recent essay "Nichiren Shōshū and Sōka Gakkai in America: The Pioneer Spirit," Jane Hurst concludes that "Nichiren's Buddhism is the most successful of the twentieth-century Buddhisms imported to America."[43]

Other Japanese Traditions

Although the history of the development of Japanese Buddhist traditions in North America is largely one of Zen lineages, the various Pure Land groups, and the proponents of Nichiren's Buddhism, one must also mention that the esoteric or Vajrayāna tradition of Japanese Buddhism, known as Shingon, appeared quite early. In 1912, the Koyasan Buddhist Temple was founded in the Little Tokyo area of Los Angeles. For the most part, the use of mantras and mudras has been eliminated from the practice, and the temple follows the BCA pattern of holding a Sunday service, maintaining a Sunday-school program, and serving as a community center for its adherents.

American Buddhist Communities of Chinese Origin

In his essay "Chinese Buddhism in America: Identity and Practice," Stuart Chandler notes that by the 1880s the Chinese population in the United States had reached about 100,000 but that by 1920, in the aftermath of the Chinese Immigration Exclusion Act of 1882, only 61,639 Chinese were left, and most of those were elderly men.[44] Following the 1965 amendments to the Immigration and Nationality Act of 1952, the Chinese population grew overwhelmingly, numbering 921,000 in 1990.[45] Nonetheless, when the initial books on American Buddhism were being written, with barely an exception the only Chinese Buddhist group mentioned in any detail was one that was then called the Sino-American Buddhist Association. In her remarkably complete and insightful case study of Hsi Lai Temple, Irene Lin is quick to point this out, noting at the beginning of her paper: "The paucity of studies on Buddhism of Asian Americans also extends to the general ignorance about Chinese religions in America."[46]

In Chandler's recent study cited above, he locates nearly 150 Chinese Buddhist organizations in the United States, classified by state:[47]

Alabama 2
California 68
Colorado 2
Connecticut 1
Florida 3
Georgia 1
Hawaii 9
Illinois 4
Indiana 1
Iowa 2
Louisiana 2
Maryland 3
Massachusetts 2
Minnesota 1
Nevada 1
New Jersey 2
New York 25
Ohio 2
Pennsylvania 4
Washington 6
Wisconsin 1

It is difficult to predict with precision how many of the nearly 1 million Chinese in the United States are exclusively Buddhist, because, as Lin points out, "Chinese culture does not view religious traditions as mutually exclusive. A person can belong to different religious organizations simultaneously and appeal to one or another or even many."[48] This dilemma is further exacerbated by the fact that Chinese Buddhism itself is highly eclectic and often includes various aspects of all five traditional Chinese schools (i.e., Ch'an, *Vinaya,* T'ien-t'ai, Tantric, and Ching-t'u). The majority of Chinese Buddhism in the United States is dominated by four groups and their various branches: the Dharma Realm Buddhist Association (formerly the Sino-American Buddhist Association), the Buddhist Association of the United States, the Institute of Chung-Hwa Buddhist Culture, and Hsi Lai Temple.

Dharma Realm Buddhist Association

Venerable Tripiṭaka Master Hsüan Hua (1908–1995) arrived in the United States in 1962 to meet the spiritual needs of some of his students who had founded the San Francisco Buddhist Lecture Hall. On Chinese New Year's Day in 1968, Hsüan Hua said, "This year the Dharma Flower will bloom in America—a five-petalled flower."[49] On 1 December 1968, the Sino-American Buddhist Association was formed with a board of directors, Hsüan Hua as chairman, and a stated mission to promote the Buddhadharma in the West. The following year, five of his students accompanied him to Keelung, Taiwan, where they received the three full platforms of *śrāmaṇera, bhikṣu,* and bodhisattva precepts. They returned as the first ordained members of his lineage in the United States, and began to lead a life in accord with the regulations of the *Vinaya.*

In 1970 they renovated a building in San Francisco's Mission District and renamed it Gold Mountain Monastery. That year, the Buddhist Text Translation Society was founded, and began publishing a journal known as *Vajra Bodhi Sea.* More importantly, four more of Hsüan Hua's disciples traveled to Taiwan for ordination, and the following year Hsüan Hua conducted the first formal ordination ceremony in the United States. Before middecade, the Bodhi Dhamma Center in Seattle had become their first branch temple, followed in 1976 by the opening of the Gold Wheel Temple in Los Angeles. That same year the Sino-American Buddhist Association purchased a 237-acre site in California's Ukiah Valley and began to construct the City of Ten Thousand Buddhas. In 1977 they founded the Dharma Realm Buddhist University within the city. The City of Ten Thousand Buddhas now comprises over 488 acres and more than sixty buildings.

The 1970s marked a period of extensive growth for the Sino-American Buddhist Association. With financial help from C. T. Shen, the International Institute for the Translation of Buddhist Texts was formed in 1974, serving not only as a publisher for Buddhist texts, but as a training facility for translators. A bilingual elementary school was also begun in 1974, followed by a secondary school in 1976. In 1976 the association's Institute for World Religions was founded, with the Roman Catholic cardinal Yu Bin as its first director. The institute offered not only educational programs, but also activities in the living Buddhist traditions and in interfaith dialogue, some of which are held in conjunction with the Berkeley Buddhist Monastery, where the institute relocated in 1994.

The Sino-American Buddhist Association was renamed as the Dharma Realm Buddhist Association in 1984, but the rigor of the Buddhist practice maintained by the organization did not change. Although Hsüan Hua was quoted as saying, "I have come to America to create Patriarchs, to create Buddhas, and to create Bodhisattvas,"[50] he didn't alter the basics of his training program for monks and nuns, which often ran from 4 A.M. until 10 P.M. Currently, in addition to the City of Ten Thousand Buddhas and Gold Mountain (Sagely) Monastery, the organization boasts eight additional monasteries and hermitages in the United States, two in Canada, and a temple in Malaysia, as well as a book-distribution center in Taiwan.

Buddhist Association of the United States

The Buddhist Association of the United States (BAUS) was founded in 1964 by C. T. Shen (b. 1913). An electrical engineer by profession, he opened an international trading company in Shanghai in 1947, moving to Hong Kong two years later. In 1952 he came to the United States and, along with a number of business partners, began a prosperous shipping company. In 1973 he was awarded an honorary Litt.D. degree by Saint John's University in New York, and eventually retired from the shipping business in 1980 to devote all his energies to Buddhist activities.

An ardent lay devotee, Shen wanted North America Buddhists to have locations for regular Dharma assemblies. Thus in 1969 he and his wife donated a property in the Bronx, New York, to the BAUS upon which the group could establish the Temple of Great Enlightenment. The following year he started Bodhi House on Long Island, New York; this latter site has been used not only by Chinese Buddhists in America, but also by a variety of Buddhist groups and individuals, including the sixteenth Karmapa of Tibetan Buddhism. In 1980 he donated 125 acres of land in Putnam County, New York, near Carmel, upon which the BAUS established Chuang Yen Monastery. In addition to a landscape designed to approximate the Pure Land, the monastery houses the largest Buddha statue in the Western Hemisphere, a thirty-seven-foot likeness of Vairocana Buddha. Surrounding the huge Buddha figure, a "Hall of Ten

Thousand Buddhas" is currently being constructed as a facility that will accommodate two thousand people. The monastery also has a "Kuan-Yin Hall," completed in 1985, a dining hall, housing for monks, and an activity center known as the Tai-Hsu Hall.

In addition to the monastery, Shen founded the Institute for the Advanced Study of World Religions in 1971 at the Stony Brook campus of the State University of New York. Now located at Chuang Yen Monastery, it hosts the Woo-Ju Memorial Library, named after Shen's wife, which boasts more than seventy thousand volumes on Buddhist topics. Many scholars, myself included, have been afforded access to what is arguably one of the finest libraries for Buddhist Studies in North America. The monastery runs an active series of ongoing programs, including a Sunday-morning meditation and a book-discussion group.

Institute of Chung-Hwa Buddhist Culture

The Institute of Chung-Hwa Buddhist Culture is now the institutional home of the Ch'an Meditation Center, which began as a meditation group within the BAUS's Temple of Great Enlightenment (see above) in 1976. By 1978, with a rapid growth in membership, the group moved into an apartment in Woodside, New York, and in 1987 moved into a three-story building in Elmhurst, New York, its current location.

The Institute of Chung-Hwa Buddhist Culture is the creation of Master Sheng-Yen (b. 1930), a Shanghai native who became a monk at age thirteen. He moved to Taiwan following the Communist takeover and in 1963 embarked on a six-year retreat in the mountains. Following his retreat, Master Sheng-yen addressed himself to the decline of Chinese Buddhism, and sought to revive the tradition of proper education for monks and nuns by studying in Japan, where he received M.A. and Ph.D. degrees in Buddhist literature. In 1975 he received transmission from Ch'an Master Tung-chu of the Ts'ao-tung (or Japanese Sōtō) lineage, and three years later received transmission from Ch'an Master Ling-yuan of the Lin-chi (or Japanese Rinzai) lineage. In 1978 he became abbot of Nun Ch'an Monastery, and first visited the United States at the invitation of the BAUS. He founded the Chung-Hwa Institute of Buddhist Studies in Taiwan in 1985 as a Buddhist graduate school. It has become an extremely important institute for the promotion of Buddhist Studies, and periodically sponsors international conferences.

Despite his demanding schedule, Master Sheng-Yen also serves as the resident teacher of the Ch'an Meditation Center in New York. The center offers an extensive program of meditation workshops (for both beginners and advanced students) as well as Ch'an retreats. There are weekly sitting meditation groups, Ch'an classes that center around Sheng-Yen's Dharma talks, and a Sunday open house. The organization has also begun a publishing venture known as Dharma Drum Publications to distribute Master Sheng-Yen's books, and to publish a quarterly magazine called *Ch'an Magazine* and the *Ch'an Newsletter,* published eight times per year.

Hsi Lai Temple

Unquestionably the newest, largest, and most important expression of Chinese Buddhism in America is Hsi Lai Temple in Hacienda Heights, California, a project of Fo Kuang Shan in Taiwan, built at a cost of over $30 million.[51] Completed in 1988 on a twenty-acre site, the temple—whose name is usually translated as "Coming to the West," highlighting the fact that Bodhidharma is presumed to have brought Buddhism to China from the West—originally housed about fifty monks and nuns, but that figure has more than doubled following a 1990 change in U.S. immigration law. (The temple is profiled in more detail in chapter 3 below.) The brainchild of Master Hsing-yün, a retired abbot of Fo Kuang Shan, Hsi Lai Temple not only houses a Buddhist university and university press, but also serves as the world headquarters of the Buddha's Light International Organization. This latter unit now has more than one hundred regional chapters, and functions as a vehicle through which Master Hsing-yün's disciples can "take refuge" and become lay devotees, thus attaining membership status in Hsi Lai Temple. Hsi Lai Temple currently maintains branch temples in Austin, Dallas, Denver, New York, San Diego, and San Francisco.

The functional role of Hsi Lai Temple as a cultural center for Chinese American Buddhists is discussed below, but it is important to note here that it has moved beyond its ethnic community ties in extending outreach activities to the non-ethnic-Chinese community, including Euro-Americans. Moreover, it has promoted an ecumenical approach in bridging the sectarian gap by inviting Theravāda, Mahāyāna, and Vajrayāna practitioners to its programs. Irene Lin suggests that the way in which Hsi Lai Temple balances its multiplicity of roles will determine its future in America.[52] In reflecting on the entirety of the Chinese Buddhist tradition in America, Chandler concludes: "The apparent opposites of stability and transformation are occurring in tandem, indicating that Chinese Buddhism will enjoy a long-lasting and fruitful life in the United States."[53]

American Buddhist Communities of Korean Origin

Zen (S'ŏn)

When most Americans think of Zen, they immediately assume an association with the Japanese forms of the tradition. In the case of Korean Zen (or S'ŏn), it is more the product of the Chinese Ch'an tradition than Japanese Zen, because the Chinese-Korean connection largely bypasses the Japanese developments. In 1935, while Korea was occupied by the Japanese, the celibate S'ŏn monks merged with the Kyo school, forming a new unit called the Chogye school. Once independence from Japan was gained in 1945, the remaining celibate monks reestablished their own group, known as the Tae-go order.

A number of Korean Zen teachers visited the United States in the years after 1960. The first of these was Kyung Bo Sunim, who toured in 1964, visiting many Buddhist groups. He studied at Temple University from 1965 to 1969, earning a Ph.D. for his dissertation on the early history of Korean Zen. He later became dean of the Buddhist College of Dongguk University; although he was a frequent visitor to America, he set up no teaching organization on this continent. Also noteworthy in this regard is Ku San Sunim (1909–1983), a Zen master who took ordination at age thirty-one. He received Dharma transmission from Hyobong Sunim, and went on to serve as abbot of several monasteries. He visited the United States in 1972 to attend the dedication of the Korean Buddhist Sambhosa (or "Temple of the Three Treasures") in Carmel Valley, California. He returned to the United States several times, particularly to visit Los Angeles, which Rick Fields has identified as "the largest Korean city in the world next to Seoul."[54] The first Korean teacher to stay in America is Seung Sahn. To some degree, his approach was informed by the environment of Korean Buddhism after the Korean War. Mu Soeng is of the opinion that "Zen master Seung Sahn's personality especially was shaped by these ecclesiastical skirmishes of the 1950s and 1960s and his personality in turn shaped the culture of Buddhism he brought to America in 1972."[55]

Seung Sahn was born in 1927 of Christian parents. Following the war, he studied at Dongguk University, but he eventually became disenchanted with scholarship and in 1948 became a Buddhist monk. He received Dharma transmission from his teacher Ko Bong on 25 January 1949, becoming the seventy-eighth teacher in the lineage. He spent five years in the South Korean army during the Korean War but returned to monastic life afterward, replacing his ill master as abbot of Hwa Gae Sah Temple in Seoul in 1957. Before coming to the United States, he spent nearly a decade in Japan and Hong Kong founding temples.

Upon arriving in America, Seung Sahn settled in Providence, Rhode Island, took a job in a laundry repairing washing machines, and began to learn English. Within a short time he was attracting students from nearby Brown University, and with their help he founded the Providence Zen Center, which now serves as the main locus of what has become known as the Kwan Um School of Zen. The style of Zen practiced by the Kwan Um School and its affiliate temples is unusual in that it fits neither the Korean S'ŏn model nor the traditional Japanese form. Instead, it utilizes Pure Land and Hua-yen practices, chanting, and a rigorous daily practice of prostrations along with the expected meditation practice. As his fame grew, Seung Sahn became a sought-after speaker, traveling throughout the world and proselytizing for his unique brand of Korean Zen.

Seung Sahn's innovations are quite unusual, too. He has permitted lay students to wear traditional Korean monk's robes, and has begun to ordain American lay students as monks and nuns, despite the Chogye order's traditional stance on celibacy for monks and nuns. Additionally, he has routinized the approach to *kōan* practice during retreats and widened the path of entry to bodhisattvahood. He has given Dharma transmission to a number of students, now known as "Zen masters":

Zen Master Su Bond—a student of Seung Sahn's since 1974. He was ordained as a monk in 1983, and transmitted in 1992. Prior to his death in 1994, he was abbot of a temple in Los Angeles, and helped construct the school's Providence and Cambridge centers.

Zen Master Soeng Hyang (Barbara Rhodes)—a student of Seung Sahn's since 1972. She is the head Dharma teacher of the Kwan Um School of Zen, and the guiding teacher of centers in Florida, Illinois, and Colorado. She was transmitted in 1992, helped found the Providence Zen Center, where she lived for seventeen years, and was instrumental in beginning the center's Buddhist-Christian dialogue.

Zen Master Dae Kwang—a student of Seung Sahn's who received transmission in 1996. He is abbot of the international Kwan Um School of Zen, and guiding teacher of the Providence Zen Center.

Zen Master Wu Bong (Jacob Perl)—Seung Sahn's first American student in 1972, and a former student of Shunryu Suzuki Rōshi. Born in Poland, he helped begin the first center in that country in 1978. He was given authority to teach in 1984.

Zen Master Wu Kwang (Richard Shrobe)—a student of Seung Sahn's since 1975. He was transmitted in 1993, maintains a private psychotherapy practice, and heads the Chogye International Zen Center of New York.

Zen Master Dae Gak—a monk since 1993 who was transmitted in 1994. Having practiced Zen for nearly three decades, he founded a retreat center known as Furnace Mountain on five hundred acres in Kentucky in 1986. He also has a Ph.D. in clinical psychotherapy and has maintained a private practice for a quarter century.

Zen Master Ji Bong (Robert Moore)—founder of the New Haven Zen Center. He was formerly a music professor, and was transmitted in 1997.

In addition, Seung Sahn has conferred the title of Dharma Master (or Ji Do Poep Sa Nim) on more than a dozen other students. Moreover, two individuals, Zen Master Bo Mun (George Bowman) and Dharma Master Lincoln Rhodes, have been identified as emeritus teachers.

The Kwan Um School of Zen now has more than two dozen branches throughout the United States. The best known of these are the Providence Zen Center, which serves as head temple of the international organization; the Cambridge Zen Center; Dharma Sound Zen Center in Washington, D.C.; and Furnace Mountain. In recent years, Seung Sahn's health has waned, increasing the activity of his students in carrying out the mission of the Kwan Um School of Zen.

Another prominent Korean monk residing in North America is Samu Sunim (b. 1941).[56] He arrived in the United States in 1967, working as a night-shift parcel sorter in New York and founding the Zen Lotus Society. In 1968 he moved to Montreal, and then to Toronto in 1972. Following a three-year retreat in his basement flat, begun in 1974, he declared that he had received Dharma transmission from his teacher in a vision, and began calling himself a Zen master.[57] In 1979 he purchased the property in Toronto on which the Zen Buddhist Temple was founded, and formed branches in Ann Arbor (in 1981) as well as Chicago and Mexico. His centers publish the journal *Spring Wind.* Because of his quick wit, interest in cross-cultural exchange, and appreciation for art, he has become a sought-after speaker at many of the Buddhist events that have begun to appear on the Buddhist landscape in North America.

Wŏn

Wŏn Buddhism is a modern form of Korean Buddhism started by Sot'aesan, originally born as Chungbin Pak (1891–1943). The school attempts to see the Buddha-nature in all things, and utilizes a meditational practice involving a black circle, representing the *Dharmakāya,* on a white background. As a result, this school is sometimes referred to as the "round" or "circular" school. It is not an exclusively monastic tradition, as monks are allowed to marry. Since 1953 it has been very active in Korea, claiming more than 500,000 disciples and two hundred temples by 1975, and four hundred temples today. It has developed a number of branches in the United States, most notably in Philadelphia.

In the United States the Wŏn Buddhist Church is active primarily in missionary work for Korean adults and children, spiritual training programs, and educational institutions. The temple in Philadelphia also began publishing a journal known as *Won Buddhist Studies,* edited by Bokin Kim, the first issue of which (1996) contains the papers from an international conference held at the Philadelphia site in 1995. In addition, an "Institute of Won Buddhist Studies" has been founded, with a distinguished staff of academic scholars.

American Buddhist Communities of Vietnamese Origin

The two influential teachers most often associated with Vietnamese Buddhism in the United States are Thich Thien-An (1926–1980) and Thich Nhat Hanh (b. 1926). Ven. Thich Thien-An came to the United States in 1966 to serve as visiting professor at UCLA, planning to return to Vietnam the following year. He had been trained in the Lin-chi tradition of Ch'an Buddhism, only later adopting a more ecumenical approach.

Responding to the urgings of his American students for him to stay and teach, he delayed his return to Vietnam and in 1967 began to teach from a small rented house in Hollywood. As his students grew in number, he founded the International Buddhist Meditation Center in 1970 in Los Angeles, followed three years later by the University of Oriental Studies (now directed by his disciple Ven. Dr. Karuna Dharma). The approach in both of these organizations was highly ecumenical, using as teachers Shingon scholars, Theravāda monks, Tibetans, and Koreans.

In his practice community Thich Thien-An ordained both monks and nuns, who maintained celibacy, wore robes, and had shaved heads—all in keeping with the orthodox tradition—but he also ordained lay disciples, often married ones, who wore robes only for center functions and did not engage in the traditional head-shaving practice. After the fall of Saigon in 1975, Thich Thien-An became active in bringing Vietnamese refugees to the United States. In so doing, he was thrust into a role that included fund-raising, job procurement, and assisting in acculturation. Ven. Thien-An died on 23 November 1980, following a short bout with cancer.

Thich Nhat Hanh now lives in exile in Plum Village in France, head of an international network of *sanghas* known as the Community for Mindful Living. Long active in the movement to end the war in Vietnam, he had been instrumental in founding Van Hanh University in Saigon. He first visited the United States in 1966, as a spokesman for monks who supported reconciliation in Vietnam. Shortly thereafter his book *Vietnam: Lotus in a Sea of Fire* was published, in which he coined the phrase *engaged Buddhism,* now the driving force behind many Buddhist organizations throughout the world. The basis of engaged Buddhism is the Tiep Hien Order (or Order of Interbeing), an ethical program of fourteen disciplines designed to protect the practitioner and the planet.

Nonetheless, Thich Thien-An and Thich Nhat Hanh are hardly the only two significant individuals in the development of Vietnamese Buddhism in North America. In a recent study, A. W. Barber and Cuong T. Nguyen note that in 1995 there were approximately 160 Vietnamese Buddhist temples and centers in North America.[58] These semi-independent temples generally offer the same mix of Buddhist practices that Chinese temples do: Ch'an and Pure Land. Unlike Chinese Americans, among whom it is difficult to identify the number of Buddhists, the majority of those Vietnamese arriving in the United States after 1975 are Buddhists. The temple is central to Vietnamese Buddhist practice, but within the Vietnamese communities of North America meditation seems a less predominant practice than that of gaining merit (*puṇya*). The temple remains the place where traditional and cultural values are engendered, and where children get both Dharma instruction and visions of Vietnam. Barber and Nguyen note that Vietnamese Buddhism may well be the least popular form of Buddhism in North America, and that when one observes the services at a Vietnamese temple, one "hardly sees any Westerners."[59]

American Buddhist Communities of South and Southeast Asian Origin

Emma Layman notes in the beginning of her presentation of Theravāda Buddhism in America that "until the latter part of 1966 there was no formally organized American center devoted to presentation of the Theravada viewpoint and providing a setting for ceremonial observances in the Theravada context."[60] She goes on to link the growth of Theravāda Buddhism in North America to a fivefold series of events that include: (1) the establishment of the Washington Buddhist Vihara; (2) the beginning of the Buddhist Society in Denver (later moved to San Jose, California, and renamed the Stillpoint Institute); (3) the establishment of the Wat Thai in Los Angeles; (4) large numbers of Americans undertaking meditation training in Burma (now Myanmar) and Thailand; and (5) an increasing presence of Theravāda monks as campus lecturers and meditation instructors.[61] To a large extent she is correct, although we shall see that she overlooked what was perhaps the most significant event in the development of Theravāda in America.

As early as 1964, Madihe Pannaseeha Thera, a visiting emissary from Sri Lanka, noticed that there was much interest in Buddhism in the United States but no center available for presenting the Theravāda viewpoint. The following year Ven. Bope Vinita Thera was sent from Vajirarama Temple in Sri Lanka to take up residence in what came to be known as the Buddhist Vihara Society in Washington, D.C. In 1967 Ven. Vinita Thera was succeeded by Mahāthera Dickwela Piyananda, and later Mahāthera Henepola Gunaratana took up residence in the *vihāra*.[62] The organization maintained close ties with the parent Sāsana Sevaka Society in Sri Lanka, eventually establishing a permanent residence from which it could conduct services, celebrate Buddhist festivals, and publish the *Washington Buddhist*. In many respects the Wat Thai fulfilled a similar funcuon on the West Coast, where five Thai monks, in 1972, began to establish an extensive series of programs for both Asian and non-Asian Buddhists.

What Layman overlooked was the major change for Buddhism in the United States instigated by the 1965 amendments to the Immigration and Nationality Act of 1952. Because her work was published in 1976, it is likely that she was simply too close to the historical event to understand or even see the implications of this legislation. Paul Numrich, however, writing twenty years later, was not. In *Old Wisdom in the New World: Americanization in Two Immigrant Theravada Buddhist Temples,* he notes that between 1961 and 1970 there were 6,313 immigrant admissions from Thailand, Laos, and Kampuchea. Between 1971 and 1980 the figure jumped to 105,770; between 1981 and 1990, to 613,887.[63] Utilizing figures from the 1990 census, Numrich lists the number of U.S. residents from Theravāda Buddhist countries at that time:

Laos	149,014
Kampuchea	147,411
Thailand	91,275
Sri Lanka	10,970
Myanmar	6,177

When considering the above total (404,847) in the light of what he calls "census undercounting," which he believes is typical in figures for racial and ethnic minorities, Numrich postulates a conservative estimate of between 500,000 and 750,000 Theravāda Buddhists in the United States in 1990, the vast majority living in urban environments.[64]

In Asia, Theravāda temples serve the twofold function of monastic residence and religious center for the local Buddhist community. In the United States, where the number of monks and nuns is minimal, the temple may house monastic residents infrequently, having no more than one or two in permanent residence. Nonetheless, Numrich counted 142 Theravāda Buddhist temples in the United States in 1996, all of them except the Washington Buddhist Vihara built after 1970; this number is confirmed and analyzed in Don Morreale's *Complete Guide to Buddhist America*:[65]

Thai	55
Kampuchean	34
Laotian	34
Burmese	11
Sri Lankan	8

The Theravāda Buddhist experience in the United States has fostered at least three ecumenical organizations, created largely as an expression of the ethnic diversity of the Theravāda communities.[66] These include the Buddhist Sangha Council of Southern California (BSCSC), the American Buddhist Congress (ABC), and the Buddhist Council of the Midwest (BCM). The BSCSC was formed in 1980, claiming to be "the first permanent cross-cultural, inter-Buddhist organization in the United States."[67] Ven. Dr. Havanpola Ratanasara has served as its president since its inception. In 1983 it opened a "College of Buddhist Studies," also with Ven. Dr. Ratanasara as president. The ABC was founded in 1987, with Ven. Dr. Ratanasara as its executive president. The BCM began in 1985, having arisen out of informal meetings of the Chicago-area Buddhist clergy and laity.

A highly interesting phenomenon emerging from Numrich's study of Theravāda communities in the United States is the notion of what he calls "parallel congregations," in which one location supports two communities—one ethnic, and the other consisting of non-Asian converts. This development is discussed in chapter 6 below. Contrasted with the presence of largely ethnic Theravāda communities, however, is the development of the *vipassanā* movement. It is clearly Theravāda in origin, but almost exclusively a Euro-American Buddhist phenomenon.

The leader of the *vipassanā* movement was Mahāsi Sayādaw, a Burmese monk who devised a methodology for eliminating the *samatha,* or "calming," practice in Theravāda meditation and moving directly into the "insight," or *vipassanā,* phase.[68] His teaching method was brought to the United States primarily by Joseph Goldstein, Jack Kornfield, Sharon Salzberg, and Ruth Denison. Goldstein and Kornfield had met during the first summer of Naropa Institute in 1974 and discovered that they were doing similar things in their teaching of "insight meditation"; their collaboration was sealed, and the American *vipassanā* movement was launched. The Insight Meditation Society, founded in 1975 and located in Barre, Massachusetts, is profiled in chapter 3 below. The various centers affiliated with this initial venture constitute a formidable network for *vipassanā* training on the North American continent. It is now becoming quite clear that the ethnic Theravāda communities no longer occupy the subsidiary position they did when Numrich completed his research, and that, combined with the *vipassanā* programs being offered, they present an extensive, growing presence on this continent.

American Buddhist Communities of Tibetan Origin

Gelug

The Tibetans were one of the latest of the Asian Buddhist communities to arrive in the United States.[69] The earliest notable figure to appear was the Gelug teacher Geshe Ngawang Wangyal (1901–1983), who arrived in this country in February 1955. He was born in Astrakhan (USSR), to Kalmuck-Mongolian parents. He joined the monastery at age six. As a young man, his root guru was Agvan Dorjiev, a well-known Buryat lama, who advised him to go to Tibet. Following his teacher's advice, he began training at Drepung Monastery, receiving his *geshe* degree in 1938. When the Chinese entered Kham in 1951, Geshe Wangyal left, eventually settling in the United States. He also eventually brought Geshe Lhundrup Sopa, Lama Kunga, and two other lamas to America.

Geshe Wangyal settled in Freewood Acres, New Jersey, where he served a Kalmuck refugee community brought to the United States by the Tolstoy Foundation; taught at Columbia University; and founded the Lamaist Buddhist Monastery of America (Labsum Shedrub Ling, renamed the Tibetan Buddhist Learning Center in 1986). Within a short time Geshe Wangyal had attracted Robert Thurman, Jeffrey Hopkins, and Christopher George, three Harvard students interested in Buddhism. They learned Tibetan and in turn taught the other lamas English. Thurman wanted to take ordination, but Geshe Wangyal refused, suggesting that if Thurman truly desired to do so, he could go to India and consult the Dalai Lama—which is exactly what Thurman did, becoming the first Western student to be ordained by the Dalai Lama. He studied at Namgyal Monastery but later returned to lay life, finishing his doctorate at Harvard in 1972. Thurman now serves as Jey Tsong Kha Pa Professor of

Buddhist Studies at Columbia University. Hopkins entered the Buddhist Studies program at the University of Wisconsin, received his Ph.D., and began his teaching career at the University of Virginia, where he founded a graduate program in Buddhist Studies. Geshe Sopa (b. 1923) joined Sera Monastery at age eighteen, following nine years of local monastic training in his home province of Tsang. A brilliant scholar, he was on the committee that administered the *geshe* examinations to the Dalai Lama. He fled Tibet in 1959 and earned his *lharampa geshe* degree while living in a refugee community in 1962. Staying first in the United States with Geshe Wangyal, he was appointed professor at the University of Wisconsin in 1967. While at the University of Wisconsin (from which he has recently retired) he founded the Deer Park Buddhist Center in 1975, and serves as abbot of Ewam Monastery. Lama Kunga founded the Ewam Choden Tibetan Buddhist (Sakya) Center in Kensington, California (discussed below).

The Tibetan Buddhist Learning Center is one of the premier Gelug communities in the West. In fulfilling its mission of promoting an understanding of Tibetan Buddhism in the West while supporting the religious practice of the Kalmuck community it represents, it has combined a program of Buddhist text translation with traditional Tibetan Buddhist training. In addition, it has been host to the Dalai Lama on numerous visits, beginning in 1979. The center houses three buildings: a schoolhouse (which also accommodates the resident monks), a rectory (where the executive director, Joshua Cutler, and his wife, Diana, reside), and a large temple.

The Tibetan Buddhist Learning Center is not the only important Gelug center in the United States. In 1987 Lama Thubten Zopa founded Osel Shen Phen Ling in Missoula, Montana. Born in 1946 in Nepal, Lama Zopa studied at Dungkar Monastery until 1959, when he fled Tibet. Like many exiled Tibetans, he studied at the Young Lamas' School in Dalhousie, India. He later studied with Lama Thubten Yeshe, jointly founding a center in Nepal. After Lama Yeshe died in 1984, he became head of the Foundation for the Preservation of the Mahayana Tradition, which supervises more than fifty Buddhist centers worldwide. Osel Shen Phen Ling sponsors not only meditation practice, but also a prison program. In addition, the Dalai Lama's personal monastery (Namgyal) founded a North American branch in Ithaca, New York, in 1992. It also houses an "Institute of Buddhist Studies" staffed by both Tibetan monks and

Western scholars. As such, it provides a systematic study of Tibetan Buddhism in a monastic setting, with courses taught in English.

Sakya

Not long after Geshe Wangyal had arrived in New Jersey, Deshung Rinpoche traveled to the University of Washington to work on a research project sponsored by the Inner Asia program and directed by Professor Turrell Wylie. He arrived in 1960, along with H.H. Jigdal Dagchen Sakya, and stayed more than twenty-five years. In 1986 he returned to Tharlam Monastery in Nepal, where he died the following year. The University of Washington was a lively place during Deshung Rinpoche's stay, and he worked with some of the brightest and most active scholars of Buddhism of the time, including Leon Hurvitz, Edward Conze, and Agehananda Bharati. Deshung Rinpoche, however, did not engage in Dharma instruction during his tenure in America. Instead, he suggested other individuals who might be invited to do so.

One of the very earliest Sakya centers in the United States was founded by Lama Thartse Kunga, originally brought to the United States in 1962 by Geshe Wangyal. Trained at Ngor Monastery in Western Tibet, he established the Ewam Choden Tibetan Buddhist Center in 1971. The center offers Tibetan language training, seminars, and meditation instruction. Like many Tibetan centers in the United States, Ewam Choden maintains close ties with the Tibetan community in India.

Not long after the founding of Ewam Choden, the Sakya Monastery of Tibetan Buddhism was founded in 1974 in Seattle by H.H. Jigdal Dagchen Sakya, H.H. Ngawang Trinley Sakyapa, and Deshung Rinpoche. Sakya Monastery embraces a nonsectarian approach to the teachings of Tibetan Buddhism and is the international seat of this approach. It has hosted lamas from all four traditions, including, in addition to Sakya lamas, the Dalai Lama (Gelug), Kalu Rinpoche (Kagyu), and Dudjom Rinpoche (Nyingma). The monastery possesses an extensive library, maintains a series of academic and cultural activities, and runs a rigorous program of practice and training. The principal practice of the monastery is meditation on the Bodhisattva Avalokiteśvara (Chenrezi), and the Mahākāla Pūja is conducted at the end of each month.

On the other coast are two additional important Sakya facilities: the Sakya Center for Buddhist Studies and Meditation (Sakya Sheidrup Ling) in Cambridge, Massachusetts, and the Sakya Phuntsok Ling Center for Tibetan Buddhist Studies and Meditation in Silver Springs, Maryland. The former center was founded in 1980 on Deshung Rinpoche's first visit to Cambridge, although the spiritual head is considered to be H.H. Sakya Trizin, or "holder of the throne of Sakya." In middecade a retreat center was purchased in Barre, Massachusetts, from which many teachers have conducted a wide variety of empowerments. The latter center was founded in 1986, also with H.H. Sakya Trizin as spiritual head. It functions as an urban meditation center, utilizing many approaches in addition to the Vajrayāna (and including both Mahāyāna and *vipassanā*).

Nyingma

The earliest and best-known Nyingma teacher in the United States is Tarthang Tulku Rinpoche. Born in 1935, in the Golok region of eastern Tibet, he was educated at Tarthang Monastery. He left for Sikkim in 1958, eventually traveling to India, where he taught at the Sanskrit University in Varanasi. He arrived in the United States in 1968, settling in Berkeley the following year. At first he worked with only a small group of students, establishing the Tibetan Nyingma Meditation Center (or Padma Ling) in March 1969. The organization's first public activity was an exhibition of Tibetan art, held at the California College of Arts and Crafts in 1970. That same year Tarthang founded Dharma Publishing, and one year later a small fraternity house in Berkeley was purchased to serve as a home base for the young community. In November 1972 the Tibetan Nyingma Meditation Center was visited by Dudjom Rinpoche (1904–1987), the supreme head of the Nyingma lineage, who blessed the center and offered a variety of Tantric initiations.

Within a short period of time Tarthang Tulku had expanded Dharma Publishing, and in 1973 founded Nyingma Institute. Two years later he began the highly ambitious project of establishing Odiyan Retreat Center on nine hundred acres in Sonoma County, and in 1975 he started the Tibetan Aid Project and Tibetan Relief Foundation to assist in the resettlement of Tibetan refugees. In the ensuing years Tarthang has continued his expanding projects, as well as maintaining a rigorous writing schedule that has resulted in the publication of many books on various aspects of Nyingma practice.

More recently, another Nyingma teacher, known as Sogyal Rinpoche, has become extremely active and popular on the North American continent. As a youngster he was identified as a reincarnation of Tertön Sogyal, a master of the Dzogchen practice. Sogyal Rinpoche was brought up at Dzongsar Monastery, and when his root guru, Jamyang Khyentse Rinpoche, died, he continued his studies with Dudjom Rinpoche and Dilgo Khyentse Rinpoche. He studied philosophy in India and then comparative religion at Trinity College, Cambridge. In 1973 he accompanied the Dalai Lama on a European tour, and then served as Dudjom Rinpoche's translator on an American tour.

Sogyal established his first center in London in 1975 (Dzogchen Orgyen Chöling) and another in Paris shortly thereafter. In 1981 he founded the Rigpa Fellowship, which now has a major center in Santa Cruz, California. He has focused a significant portion of his teaching on death and dying, and is the author of the highly acclaimed volume *The Tibetan Book of Living and Dying.*

Another Dzogchen teacher who has attracted much recent attention is Lama Surya Das, born Jeffrey Miller in New York in 1950. Following his graduation from the State University of New York at Buffalo in 1971, he traveled in India and Nepal, studying with a variety of teachers. It was there that the name Surya Das was given to him by the Hindu teacher Maharaj-ji (Neem Karoli Baba). Eventually, Surya Das studied with Lama Thubten Yeshe, Kalu Rinpoche, H.H. Gyalwa Karmapa, and other Tibetan teachers, as well as the *vipassanā* masters S. N. Goenka and A. Munindra. In 1980 he entered a Nyingma retreat center in France and completed two three-year retreats under Dudjom Rinpoche and Dilgo Khyentse Rinpoche. At that time he became a lama in the Dzogchen tradition. In March 1991 Lama Surya Das founded the Dzogchen Foundation to provide Western students with access to Dzogchen teachers and teachings, and to explore ways in which Dzogchen can enhance Western culture. The Dzogchen Foundation is located in Cambridge, Massachusetts, and Surya Das uses it as a base from which he maintains a vigorous teaching and writing program. His quick wit and familiarity with American cultural patterns have made him a highly sought-after speaker.

Kagyu

There can be little doubt that the most famous Tibetan Buddhist in the West has been Chögyam Trungpa Rinpoche (1939–1987).[70] Born in

Geje, in eastern Tibet, he was recognized as the eleventh Trungpa Tulku at eighteen months of age and enthroned as supreme abbot of the Surmang monasteries by Gyalwa Karmapa. He became a novice monk at age nine, and received full ordination in 1958. Eventually he was forced to flee Tibet, traveling to India, where he studied English with Freda Bedi (Sister Kechog Palmö). In 1963 he received a Spaulding Fellowship to study comparative religion, philosophy, and art at Oxford. Near the end of the decade he, along with his friend Akong Rinpoche, founded Samyê-Ling in Scotland as the first Tibetan meditation center in the West. Following a debilitating automobile accident, in 1969 he gave up his monastic vows; he married Diana Pybus the following year. That same year he moved to the United States to take up residence at Tail of the Tiger (later renamed Karmê-Chöling) in Barnet, Vermont. Within a decade he had built an impressive international network of religious centers, organized under an umbrella organization known as Vajradhatu, and a series of secular ventures, organized as part of the Nalanda Foundation.

Following his death in 1987, responsibility for his complex community fell to Ösel Tendzin (Thomas Rich; 1944–1990), Trungpa's Vajra Regent. The first Westerner to receive empowerment in the Karma Kagyu lineage, Tendzin died of AIDS slightly more than a decade following his empowerment. Responsibility then fell to Trungpa's eldest son, Mipham Rinpoche, who now administers the renamed Shambhala International organization.

Trungpa was strongly influenced by H.H. Sixteenth Gyalwa Karmapa (1923–1981), who was recognized early as the new incarnation of the head of the Karma Kagyu lineage, and was ordained at age seven by Tai Situ Rinpoche and Jamgön Kongtrül of Palpung. A year later he was enthroned at Palpung by Tai Situ. In 1957, when the Tibetan situation was quite desperate, he began sending lamas out of Tibet, and he himself followed in 1959. He was instrumental in helping to spread the Karma Kagyu lineage throughout the Western world. The North American seat of H.H. Gyalwa Karmapa was established at the Karma Triyana Dharmacakra, founded in Woodstock, New York, in 1978. Located in the Catskill Mountains, it has housed several resident teachers, a Karma Kagyu institute, and a bookstore, and maintains a highly active schedule of events throughout the year.

Also noteworthy is Kalu Rinpoche (1905–1989), born in Kham and recognized as an incarnation of Jamgön Kontrül Lodö Thaye. Following a highly productive monastic career in Tibet, in the early 1970s he began to visit North America and Europe. In 1972 he established his chief North American center, Kagyu Kunkhyah Chuling, in Vancouver, British Columbia. As early as 1976 he began supervising three-year retreats for Westerners in France. Kalu Rinpoche's death was mourned throughout the world, for he had often been referred to as "a modern Milarepa."

Nondenominational American Buddhist Communities

Having surveyed the major American Buddhist communities originating from the various Buddhist traditions in Asia, it is important to note that a growing number of *sanghas* are appearing that claim no specific cultural or sectarian affinity other than their commitment to Buddhist ideals and practices. Rather than being admittedly syncretistic, they are simply eclectic, drawing freely from the enormous diversity of traditions I have outlined in this chapter. In the last decade these communities have been growing faster than the more traditionally affiliated Theravāda, Mahāyāna, and Vajrayāna *sanghas*. Some of them, too, have become quite well known throughout the world.

The Buddhist Peace Fellowship (BPF), a community of "meditating activists," is profiled in chapter 3. It was founded in 1978 by Robert and Anne Aitken, along with a few friends from within the Maui Zendo. This beginning American concern of theirs for "socially engaged Buddhism" quickly spread to the mainland and began to attract a group of American Buddhist practitioners from a variety of traditions. Soon Gary Snyder, Joanna Macy, Alfred Bloom, Jack Kornfield, and others were working together to promote human rights throughout the world, and within a short time were publishing an influential journal called *Turning Wheel.* Today the BPF maintains more than a dozen chapters, and works cooperatively with the International Network of Engaged Buddhists (organized in Thailand in 1989 by Sulak Sivaraksa and others). It boasts an impressive number of social programs and has been a genuine model of cooperative Buddhist ecumenicism.

Also highly visible is the Friends of the Western Buddhist Order (FWBO), a unique community founded by Bhikshu Sangharakshita, which seeks to reinterpret Buddhism in a fashion that takes modern changes in industry, technology, communications, ethics, and the like into consideration. It tries to draw out of traditional Buddhism an essence that is useful to Westerners without undermining the integrity of Buddha's teachings. In this way, Sangharakshita has tried to develop a Western Buddhist lifestyle.

Born in South London in 1925 as Denis Lingwood, Sangharakshita was eventually stationed in India during World War II as a member of the Royal Signal Corps. He stayed on in India, becoming a Buddhist novice in 1949 and taking full ordination the following year. He studied widely with a variety of teachers from the several Buddhist traditions, eventually founding the Monastery of the Three Vehicles. By the mid-1950s he was working with Dr. Ambedkar among the untouchables. He returned to England in 1964, founding the Western Buddhist Order (WBO) three years later, and the FWBO in 1968. Throughout his career Sangharakshita has been a prolific author, with more than a dozen books to his credit.

The FWBO does not distinguish between the traditional Buddhist designation of monastic and lay disciples, but rather offers ordination to men and women as a lifelong commitment to live in the Buddhist tradition. While there are no formal rules, all FWBO members adhere to a traditional set of ethical precepts designed to address all activity in body, speech, and mind. Ordination is generally conferred by a senior FWBO member serving as preceptor, following a number of years of preparation by the adept.

The FWBO maintains communities throughout the world, including U.S. centers in New Hampshire, Maine, and Montana as well as Boston, San Francisco, and Seattle. These centers provide meditation classes for beginners, and retreats for more experienced students. The FWBO emphasizes the importance of right-livelihood businesses and supports an extensive network of social-service projects.

Another nondenominational group is the Community Meditation Center of Los Angeles. Founded in 1982 by Shinzen Young, it uses a variety of Buddhist techniques from many traditions in trying to help its members cope with living a Buddhist life in the midst of a challenging urban environment. Its founder was born into a Jewish family but became fascinated with Japan at an early age. He eventually earned a Ph.D. in Buddhist Studies at the University of Wisconsin. But unlike his academic colleagues, he went to Japan and took ordination as a Shingon monk, living near Mount Koya and learning the rigorous techniques of the Japanese Vajrayāna tradition. Upon returning to the United States, he was able to draw upon his own monastic experience as well as his extensive knowledge of all the Buddhist traditions.

Some of the nondenominational Buddhist communities have a markedly academic purpose, such as the College of Buddhist Studies, founded in 1983 as a project of the Buddhist Sangha Council of Southern California. Because southern California is home to so many different varieties of American Buddhism, it provides a wonderful opportunity for individuals to study and practice in a highly ecumenical environment, learning from both ethnic American Buddhists and Euro-American scholars. There are perhaps as many kinds of nonsectarian American Buddhist communities as there are individual groups, and it has been my purpose here to attempt to highlight only a few of these, each emphasizing a different approach, as a demonstration of the diversity and richness of the American Buddhist endeavor.

Scorecards

Don Morreale's *Complete Guide to Buddhist America,* an updated and expanded version of his earlier *Buddhist America: Centers, Retreats, Practices,* lists more than one thousand Buddhist meditation centers in the United States and Canada. If one added to this list the many Buddhist centers of nonmeditative traditions, the total would rise considerably. It is clear enough that it would take an entire volume, or even multiple volumes, to adequately delineate the historical development of each tradition and center now practicing on American soil. (As I stated at the outset of this chapter, a comprehensive historical treatment of the American Buddhist movement is not the goal of this book.) Nonetheless, Morreale offers some interesting bits of information about the growth of American Buddhism during the second half of this century.[71] Of the more than one thousand centers listed in his new volume, only about 2 percent were founded between 1900 and 1964. By 1975, the number of centers had increased fivefold, and between 1975 and 1984 the total doubled, and doubled again between 1985 and 1997. Theravāda and Vajrayāna centers have doubled in the last decade, while Mahāyāna groups have tripled.

Moreover, Morreale has included a new category of center that claims no sectarian identification—creatively termed "Buddhayāna"—as a signal of the growing trend toward Buddhist ecumenicity, and identified by Morreale as "poly-denominationalism." This latter group has shown an almost tenfold increase in the last decade. In charting *sangha* size, Morreale offers the following:

Size of sangha	*Number of centers*
0–25	435
26–50	244
51–100	138
101–200	106
201–500	96
500+	43

In addition, more than one hundred centers offered information about their mailing lists. While the majority of respondents reported small numbers of mailings, some did not:

Size of mailing list	*Number of centers*
1,000–2,000	23
2,000–4,000	8
4,000–10,000	7
20,000–30,000	2

To be sure, the above data, while interesting and impressive, suggest that a large-scale sociological study remains a desideratum for American Buddhism. At best, our speculations about the number of Buddhists in the United States and Canada are just that.

In the 1970s, I often suggested to my students, with some degree of seriousness, that they look for Buddhist groups in the United States in the Yellow Pages. Now I tell them to look in *Tricycle: The Buddhist Review* as well. As an example, in that publication's fall 1997 issue I found more than 150 entries. Many, such as the New Orleans Zen Temple, Providence Zen Center, Karmê Chöling, Zen Mountain Monastery, Kanzeon Zen Center, San Francisco Zen Center, Nichiren Order of North America, Palden Sakya Center, and numerous others, had major listings. Yet there was much more than merely center listings. One could find Dharma merchandise of all sorts, from bamboo flutes to *zafus* and *zazen* benches.

And ads for Buddhist journals, universities, and bookstores proliferated. One could even plan which Dharma events to attend based on the published teaching schedules of famous Dharma teachers such as Thich Nhat Hanh, Lama Surya Das, Lama Zopa Rinpoche, and others. Perhaps most interesting of all was the full-page advertisement for the Buddhism in America conference, which was to take place in May 1998 in San Diego. Following the highly successful "first" conference held in January 1997 in Boston (and discussed in chapter 6 below), this conference, according to the ad, would feature an impressive list of Dharma professionals, who would be presenting keynote speeches, workshops, panels, discussions, and performances. Learning about the Dharma has become a cottage industry in North America, supported by the members of the many centers presented in this chapter.

In 1950 my father took me to my very first major-league baseball game between the Chicago Cubs and the St. Louis Cardinals. We arrived at Wrigley Field well before game time so we could watch the players as they shagged fly balls against the backdrop of the vine-covered outfield wall and took batting practice. To my six-year-old's eyes, it was a sports miracle. But I couldn't keep from continually asking my father, "Dad, who is that guy?" or "Dad, what position does that guy play?" After enduring my incessant barrage of questions for what must have seemed like an eternity, or a *kalpa,* my father reached into his pocket and produced a fold-open scorecard, where all the players' uniform numbers were listed along with their positions, and upon which one could even keep the box score if one chose to do so. My father simply said, "Son, you need a scorecard to tell who the players are," as he thrust the scorecard into my eager hands. Now, almost fifty years later, it seems that American Buddhism is like that too. As in baseball, the players occasionally move from team to team, and sometimes entire teams move to different cities. Baseball endures as the American pastime—and now some of the major-league players are Buddhists.

CHAPTER 2

Shaping the *Sangha*

Developmental Issues in American Buddhism

In the midst of the explosive growth that American Buddhism was experiencing in the 1970s, prominent Buddhist teachers from the various traditions often visited colleges and universities. My own university classes certainly benefited from the frequent appearance of these teachers, who could explain Buddhist practice far better than I might ever hope to do. Yet the visit that impressed me the most during that period, and the one that was most meaningful to the small Buddhist community that was growing up alongside the Pennsylvania State University campus, was not from a famous Buddhist teacher. Instead, it was from an Englishwoman named Freda Bedi (1911–1977), who late in life decided to make a full commitment to Buddhism by first taking novice ordination from Gyalwa Karmapa in 1966 and then the full *bhikṣuṇī* ordination in Hong Kong in 1972. After her ordination she was known as Sister Kechog Palmö. Following an Oxford education, she had married an Indian named Baba Bedi, and lived the majority of her adult life in India. She was active in the Indian independence movement, and eventually worked with Tibetans who fled to India after 1959. In that regard, she became principal of the Young Lama's School in Dalhousie, and was tutor to many lamas who later came west (Chögyam Trungpa among them).

Because she was highly literate and thoroughly conversant with Western customs, she was frequently sent on speaking tours both to call attention to the plight of Tibetans following their Holocaust and to raise funds for the Tibetan refugee program in India. Her Penn State visit, which lasted two days, was part of a whirlwind tour of the United States. My first responsibility as Sister Palmö's host was to take her, and a young American Buddhist monk from San Antonio who was traveling with her, to breakfast. Although the community in which Penn State University is located can hardly be called unsophisticated, it is somewhat rural, and as we walked into the favorite campus restaurant of many local residents, we attracted stares from the diners. After all, how often could they expect to see a large, maroon-robed, bald-headed woman and a young similarly dressed fellow enter their quiet little eatery? Throughout breakfast, and whenever we went anywhere else during her visit, we got the same surprised stares.

Yet Sister Palmö was an incredibly engaging woman and a highly poised speaker. In my classes, she deftly answered all my students' probing questions, inviting them to stay after class for continued conversation about things Buddhist. In her public talk to the community, she encouraged members of the audience to ask anything and everything they wanted to know about what must have appeared to them a highly exotic tradition. No question was too simple for a respectful and complete answer, and even the more difficult queries were handled with aplomb. My students in particular were fascinated, and before she left our community for her next stop, five of my most serious pupils asked her if they might "take refuge." She was delighted, and invited them to appear at 7 o'clock the next morning at her hotel room. There she conducted an impromptu refuge ceremony and provided each student with a certificate attesting to his or her new "Dharma name."[1] That she insisted on blessing every room of my home before she left continues to be a treasure for my family.

Following her visit to Penn State, Sister Palmö was giving a series of lectures in Washington, D.C., and before she left, we tried to find suitable accommodations there for her and the young monk. The most logical place at the time seemed to be the Washington Buddhist Vihara because it offered a somewhat monastic setting—and, I presumed, would offer free lodging as a courtesy. I should have remembered my monastic regulations more effectively, for the Buddhist *Vinaya* tradition prohibits monks and nuns from sharing the same dwelling, and the head monk pointed that fact out to me immediately upon hearing my request. Thus the young monk stayed at the *vihāra,* but Sister Palmö stayed in a hotel. I never saw her again, as she died not long afterward.

Although I did not think about it at the time, my short visit with this remarkable woman highlighted several critical issues in the general development of Buddhism in the West, and each has specific application to the growth of Buddhism as a North American religious tradition. Her status as a European woman who had assumed a monastic career foreshadowed a variety of critically important developmental issues that are currently being discussed throughout Buddhist communities on this continent.

An Overview of Issues in American Buddhism

When Kenneth Tanaka and I edited *The Faces of Buddhism in America,* we organized the book into two sections: (1) "American Buddhist Traditions in Transition"; and (2) "Issues in American Buddhism." Although there was considerable content overlap in the chapters presented in the "Issues" section, five general areas of concern emerged (each of which consisted of a variety of components): (1) ethnicity; (2) practice; (3) democratization; (4) engagement; and (5) adaptation. It is important to recognize that these five areas are profoundly interpenetrating, mutually influencing one another. For convenient cross-referencing with the above-named volume, I have retained those categories in this book. In his epilogue to *The Faces of Buddhism in America,* Tanaka suggested that the optimism and activism that were lacking in Buddhism at the turn of the last century, and that limited its initial growth on the North American continent, have clearly found a voice in the various American Buddhist traditions of the latter portion of the current century, and for that reason he drafted his reflections within that framework. Without disputing Tweed's initial notions about Buddhist optimism and activism in the previous century, or Tanaka's conclusions in this century, I have chosen to situate my own consideration of the five issues between two different contextualizing factors: at the beginning, we must address the question of how Buddhist identity is determined; and at the end, we must consider the degree to which ecumenicity might play a role in providing a unifying instrument for the exceedingly diverse spectrum of Buddhist traditions now present in North America.

Who Is a Buddhist?

In her 1976 volume *Buddhism in America,* Emma Layman devotes an entire chapter to the question "Who are the American Buddhists?"[2] She considers the question of how many Buddhists there are in America; the geographic diffusion of Buddhism in America; the personal characteristics of Buddhists in America, their educational and occupational status, and their "personality factors"; American versus Asian Buddhists; and, in the case of converts, previous religious affiliation. What she does not consider is precisely how one determines who is an American Buddhist. Three years later, in *American Buddhism,* I suggested that one of the traditional ways of identifying Buddhists in Asian countries—their taking refuge—was perhaps an insufficient and even misleading approach when applied to the American scene. My search for specificity in this determination had been fueled by a passage in Holmes Welch's classic book *The Practice of Chinese Buddhism, 1900–1950,* in which the author suggested that it was unacceptable to ask a Chinese person if he/she was Buddhist and then assume that an affirmative response was a guarantee of an exclusively Buddhist person—the reason being that the same person might just as easily also indicate that he/she was Taoist and Confucian. For Welch, the determining factor was a positive response to the questions "Have you taken the three refuges?" and "Do you practice the five layman's vows?" Unfortunately for overly zealous researchers, even two decades ago American Buddhists defined themselves in a variety of quite radically disparate ways. Some organizations identified members as those who attended religious service, or engaged in meditation sessions, or were financial contributors, and so forth. To be sure, it was a murky issue.

Just who is a Buddhist continues to be an important issue today, and since American Buddhism has become an interesting phenomenon to empirical sociologists of religion, the desire to provide accurate quantification has complicated the issue. Basing their conclusions on their 1990 study, Barry Kosmin and Seymour Lachman reported in *One Nation under God: Religion in Contemporary Society* that the Buddhist population in America amounted to 0.4 percent of the total population (or roughly 1 million people).[3] When Robert Thurman in the mid-1990s told researchers from *ABC Nightly News with Peter Jennings* that there were 5 to 6 million Buddhists in the United States, it was obvious that he was guessing.

In her essay "Who Is a Buddhist? Charting the Landscape of Buddhist America," Jan Nattier frames the issue well:

> One issue that must be faced at the outset in any study of American Buddhism is precisely who is to be included within the category of "Buddhist." Is it enough merely to call oneself a Buddhist, or are other features—certain be-

liefs, certain ritual practices (such as meditation or chanting), or perhaps even active membership in a specific organization—required as well? Though these questions may arise in the study of any religious tradition, they are particularly acute in the case of religions that are so new or small in a given region that very few people have any first-hand familiarity with them. To take a not uncommon example: if a college sophomore buys a book on Zen by Alan Watts, reads it, likes it, and subsequently begins to think of himself as a Buddhist—but without ever having encountered any form of "Buddhism" beyond the printed page—should he be included within the scope of a study of Buddhism in North America?

Many scholars, and an even larger number of Buddhists, would probably reply in the negative. Yet just as one senses that an all-inclusive stance will net more "Buddhists" than we may have had in mind, there are difficulties with more exclusive approaches as well. Criteria of belief or ritual practice quickly begin to resemble standards of orthodoxy, for one cannot require these elements for inclusion without specifying *which* beliefs and *which* practices are meant.[4]

Nattier goes on to tell us that although "official membership" in some Buddhist group might solve the problem, Americans are, in her opinion (one with which I concur), "notorious non-joiners," and in her search to steer a middle course between "uncritical inclusiveness and arbitrary exclusiveness" she turns to a sociological study by Rodney Stark and William Sims Bainbridge: *The Future of Religion*.[5] Stark and Bainbridge put a new spin on typologies, adding to the traditional Weberian categories of church and sect a third: "cult." They apply this new term in a very specific way so as not to highlight the negative sense of that term in the popular media. Further, they subdivide the term "cult" into "audience cult," requiring nothing more than a minimal commitment on the part of the advocate (such as occasional event attendance), and "client cult," in which the participant has direct interaction with a group member. Significantly, no renunciation of prior religious affiliations is required, nor does a "community" necessarily result from one's involvement. While Nattier points out some limitations of the model, and suggests that some expansion of the model is necessary when considering Buddhist groups, she sees the typology as a reasonable antidote to the problems noted above, concluding that "the researcher can decide, on the basis of the parameters of a given line of inquiry, how narrowly or how broadly to draw the lines."[6]

Not everyone agrees. Martin Baumann, for example, has said of Nattier's suggestions, "To my mind it is highly questionable whether such an approach is useful at all; secondly it becomes increasingly outdated; thirdly the subsequent criticism and refinement of the typology then would have to be taken into account, which Nattier at no point does. This part is not really convincing and—honestly—does it tell us in the end, who is actually a Buddhist according to the model and who is not?"[7] My solution in 1979 was regarded as highly controversial at best, and obviously incorrect at worst. Nonetheless, in the light of Nattier's useful discussion, I am convinced that it remains correct and workable. My suggestion was a Buddhist appropriation of Agehananda Bharati's definition of a mystic:

Here is what I regard as a thoroughly operational definition of a mystic: *A mystic is someone who says "I am a mystic,"* or words to that effect, *consistently,* when questioned about his most important pursuit. Further, his statement must be an *etic* statement—that is to say, it has to have a general widely applicable meaning, and must not be a term used only by a group of people in a manner peculiar to them, *emically,* that is.[8]

I went on to explain how one would apply this definition in a Buddhist context:

If we define a Buddhist as someone who says "I am a Buddhist," when questioned about "his most important pursuit," we not only abandon our attachment to a ritual formulary that is neither workable nor widely followed, but we also provide more than a modicum of freedom for the American Buddhist groups—a freedom in which they can develop a procedure that is consistent with their own self-image and mission . . . In other words, what appears initially as an outrageous definition of Buddhist affiliation serves the double purpose of providing a new standard and a simple method of professing Buddhist commitment while at the same time imposing a renewed sense of seriousness on all Buddhist groups.[9]

During the initial summer of Naropa Institute, one excited and interested woman, probably a fledgling would-be Buddhist, questioned Chögyam Trungpa, following one of his fabled evening lectures, about what she had to do to be considered a Buddhist. He smiled broadly and said, "When you go into the hospital, on the admitting form, write 'Buddhist' on the dotted line where it asks for religious affiliation." Once one begins to look beyond the simple delineation of identifying who is Buddhist and starts, as Nattier says, "charting the landscape," the task ahead becomes significantly more complicated.

Ethnicity

The most recent attempt to quantify the American Buddhist population is found in Martin Baumann's 1997 article "The Dharma Has Come West: A Survey of Recent Studies and Sources," in which he estimates that there are 3 to 4 million Buddhists in the United States, of which 800,000 are "Euro-American."[10] In view of Baumann's data, it is clear that Asian Americans make up the vast majority of Buddhists in the United States. In recent years the relationship between Asian American Buddhists and non–Asian American Buddhists has become extremely tense and complex. Kenneth Tanaka summarizes the issue well:

> This division has also contributed to the simmering debate concerning the question, Who represents the true American Buddhism? Some Asian American Buddhists are offended at the suggestion that white Buddhists are the sole contributors to the creation of American Buddhism, while ethnic Buddhists are seen as having played virtually no role in it. Such perception, in their view, ignores the contributions made by the Asian American Buddhists with much longer history, some entering their second century on American soil. What is often implied, according to Asian American critics, is that Buddhism becomes truly American only when white Americans become seriously involved. This form, then, is called "American Buddhism," distinguished from simply "Buddhism in America," as practiced by Asian American Buddhists.[11]

The most recent debate about ethnicity in American Buddhism was precipitated by an editorial in *Tricycle: The Buddhist Review,* published in its issue of winter 1991. Helen Tworkov wrote that "if we are to affirm true pluralism we must accept that one person's practice is another's poison." But, she added, "the spokespeople for Buddhism in America have been, almost exclusively, educated members of the white middle class."[12] Tworkov continued the argument: "Meanwhile, even with varying statistics, Asian-American Buddhists number at least one million, but so far they have not figured very prominently in the development of something called American Buddhism."[13] Her editorial provoked a letter of response from Ryo Imamura, an eighteenth-generation Jōdo Shinshū priest, but the letter never appeared in *Tricycle,* although it was later printed in its entirety in the *Sangha Newsletter* (the newsletter of the Wider Shin Buddhist Fellowship),[14] along with Tworkov's original editorial, her rejoinder, and newsletter editor Diane Ames's introduction to the controversy.

Since the publication of Tworkov's editorial, many articles have appeared in the popular and scholarly literature addressing the issue of how to speak of the two different kinds of Buddhism alluded to above. These articles seem to fall into two camps. The first of these camps emerged in response to and in support of my 1993 article "Two Buddhisms Reconsidered."[15] I had originally coined the phrase "two Buddhisms" in 1979[16] to delineate one form of Buddhism that "places primary emphasis on sound basic doctrines, shared by all Buddhists, and on solid religious practice" from another that seemed "to emerge shortly after radical social movements." At that time, I considered the former group conservative and stable, while I characterized the latter as "flashy, opaquely exotic, and 'hip.' " In "Two Buddhisms Reconsidered," I redefined the former group as representing "the Buddhism practiced by essentially Asian American communities." My intention was to find a way for Asian American immigrant Buddhists and American Buddhist converts (mostly, but not exclusively, of European American descent) to find a respectful and mutually enhancing way of relating, and to find a way for scholars interested in studying these communities to properly and accurately refer to the communities.

Interestingly, between 1979, when I coined the term "two Buddhisms," and December 1992, when Rick Fields used it in a telephone conversation, I never heard the phrase again. In the aftermath of that conversation, I wrote:

In the interim, only the descriptive language had changed, reflective perhaps of a concern for being politically correct. One Buddhism now referred exclusively to ethnic Asian-American Buddhist groups in America, to some extent considered highly "fundamentalist" or "dogmatic" or "devotional" by its rivals. The other Buddhism included mostly members of European-derived ancestry, deemed "intellectually arrogant" or "purely enlightenment-seeking" or even "White Buddhists" by its seemingly adversarial ethnic Buddhist counterparts. Needless to say, ethnic Buddhist groups apparently felt that they represented the various "true lineages" and authentic heritage of Buddhist teaching, while the newer form of emergent American Buddhism felt it had made innovations that were both necessary and important for Buddhism's successful move to the West. At best, the above is hardly reflective of Buddhist tolerance and compassion, and at worst, symptomatic of an inferred racism on each side. Unfortunately, it wouldn't be going too far, I think, to submit that all of the above claims are to some extent true.[17]

In an effort to move beyond the stalemate, I went on to suggest that while generalizations about American Buddhism are probably either impossible or foolish, we might reconsider these "two Buddhisms" in a way that not only added other critical issues into the mix, but also moved beyond the limits of a perhaps restrictive twofold typology. To do that, I utilized Peter Williams's then-recent book *American Religions: Traditions and Cultures*. Williams identifies three categories to describe the way Asian religions impact on America: (1) "ethnic religions" practiced by Asian immigrants and, to an extent, by their descendants; (2) "export religions," popular among well-educated, generally intellectual Americans; and (3) "new religions," developing in consonance with the process outlined by Jacob Needleman and others, often as revolutionary outgrowths of religions cited in the first two categories. This threefold typology is largely an extension of Robert Redfield's categories of "great traditions" and "little traditions." The great traditions are the religions of books and scholars. The little traditions, less historically grounded, are popular expressions of the great traditions, transmitted mostly through family values and community practice. Williams's approach is useful in understanding Buddhist groups such as Buddhist Churches of America as "little tradition" manifestations of an "ethnic religion," while categorizing Zen and Tibetan groups as "export religions," part of the "great tradition," and typifying an "elite Buddhism in America." To some extent, one may presume that Williams links the success of ethnic religions to the degree to which they make the transition from past to present, to their ability to become Americanized—a process he knows is no simple task.[18] It didn't take long for others to enter the fray.

The fall 1994 issue of *Tricycle* was devoted to the topic "Dharma, Diversity, and Race." One of the most interesting articles, "Confessions of a White Buddhist," was written by Rick Fields. He had initially used the term "white Buddhist" in the first edition of *How the Swans Came to the Lake,* and here he returned to the same theme. Eventually, he expanded his discussion of ethnic Buddhism in the essay "Divided Dharma: White Buddhists, Ethnic Buddhists, and Racism," published in *The Faces of Buddhism in America*. Here he spends considerable time explaining what he calls "a classificatory bramble," concluding:

> The reality, in any case, revealed a landscape of complex and bewildering variety: what might be called American Tibetan Buddhists, American Japanese Zen Buddhists, American Korean Buddhists, American Burmese (or Vipassana) Buddhists on one side; and immigrant Asian Buddhists and their often native-born bicultural children: Japanese American Buddhists, Korean American Buddhists, Vietnamese American Buddhists, Burmese American

Buddhists on the other. But even this attempt as a rough classification is problematic: the largely Japanese American Buddhist Churches of America (BCA), for example, includes thoroughly acculturated fourth-generation Japanese Americans, as well as at least a scattering of white Americans. In fact, five out of sixty BCA ministers are white Americans. In what sense, then, can this be considered an "ethnic" or immigrant Buddhism?[19]

By the time Fields had completed his critique of a plethora of terms such as "Euro-American" and the like, he had even rejected the phrase "Western Buddhism" because it didn't distinguish between the different national styles of the various countries that now are home to Buddhist traditions. The dexterity of his name shuffling is impressive, but his point, when he finally offers it, seems perhaps a bit too tidy: "Such a Buddhism would continue to provide a safe haven for ethnic Buddhist communities from a beleaguered Asia, as well as an experiential crucible for creative and effective adaptations, and would give all of us the chance to create a truly liberating, multicultured, many-hued, shifting, shimmering Pure Land of American Buddhism."[20]

One year later, Jan Nattier published an article in *Tricycle* that was far more explicit and sophisticated in its approach to the varieties of Buddhism in America.[21] She went on to develop the argument more thoroughly in "Who Is a Buddhist?" Her motive is extremely clear: "The notion of 'two Buddhisms' . . . is clearly inadequate to the task, primarily because it fails to account for the full spectrum of racial and ethnic diversity in Buddhist America."[22] For explaining how religions move into new locations and cultures, Nattier postulates a threefold typology:

1. Import religion—a "demand-driven transmission" in which a religion is sought out in an active fashion by the recipient. With specificity for Buddhism, this is labeled "Elite Buddhism."
2. Export religion—a missionary-driven transmission, in which individuals encounter Buddhism through the proselytizing effort of a particular Buddhist group. With specificity for Buddhism, this is labeled "Evangelical Buddhism."
3. Baggage religion—the religion of immigrants to North America whose motivation for travel was not evangelical. With specificity for Buddhism, this is labeled "Ethnic Buddhism."

Nattier cites a striking similarity between her typology and that developed by Catherine Albanese in *America: Religion and Religions*—one that consists of a tripartite division into "meditative," "evangelical," and "church" forms of American Buddhism. Satisfied that she has provided both the means to determine who is a Buddhist in America and the typology for classifying such Buddhists, Nattier remarks:

> In sum, by studying Buddhist groups in North America in terms of the types of transmission that have led to their formation, we can identify patterns that would be impossible to see by other means. These patterns obtain above all, of course, in the initial period of transmission, and there is much research to be done on the adjustments that take place as each form of Buddhism evolves over subsequent generations.[23]

What is especially confusing is that whereas Nattier finds the terms "white Buddhist" and "Euro-American Buddhist" obviously inadequate, she has little if anything to say about the individuals who employ those terms, yet offers a serious, extended critique of the "two Buddhisms" theory. Nowhere in my "Two Buddhisms Reconsidered" does the phrase "Euro-American Buddhist," utilized first in an American Buddhist context by Thomas Tweed, ever appear; and "white Buddhist" occurs only in the quoted citations of others. Nor does Nattier apparently read the enhancement of the "two Buddhisms" notion by the addition of Peter Williams's threefold typology—one that has far more in common with Nattier's than it has differences. Perhaps if "Two Buddhisms Reconsidered" had been better titled (possibly as "Two Buddhisms/Three Sources"), a clearer understanding would have been reached. To be sure, each approach has its advocates and adversaries, but it seems clear that none of the approaches described above has found a consensus.

An elegant consensus may be found, I think, in Paul Numrich's *Old Wisdom in the New World: Americanization in Two Immigrant Theravada Buddhist Temples*. Part of a recent spate of publications on ethnic Buddhist groups in North America that includes such works as Penny Van Esterik's *Taking Refuge: Lao Buddhists in North America* and Janet McLellan's *Many Petals of the Lotus: Asian Buddhist Communities in Toronto,* these volumes are giving us the tools to better categorize and understand the interaction between Asian American and non-Asian Buddhists in North America. After dismissing the various phrases previously employed—"ethnic" and "occidental" (Ellwood), "Asian immigrants" and "Caucasian Americans"

(Prebish), and "Asian-American" and "Euro-American" (Tweed)—Numrich settles on "Asian immigrants" and "American converts."[24] Numrich's choices are far more comprehensive than they initially appear to be, although he recognizes the limitations of his designations:

If we push these analytical categories far enough we will find that they are not "pure." I am describing generalized groups whose representative constituents manifest both significant similarities among themselves and significant dissimilarities with the general membership of the other group. Admittedly, each group includes a range of religious attitudes and behaviors. For instance, we will find some Asians who think a lot like American converts and some Americans who sometimes behave like Asian Buddhists (ritually speaking, that is).[25]

Numrich's simple arrangement has an added bonus: the category of "American converts" includes *all* Americans who might embrace the Buddhist tradition (such as African Americans and Hispanic Americans, among others), thus bypassing the general critique of terms such as "Euro-American," while the category of "Asian immigrants" covers all the various traditions imported or exported without distinctions that might reflect value judgments.

Numrich's work is particularly valuable for another reason. His research on Theravāda temples and their maintaining what he calls "parallel congregations" demonstrates that Asian ethnic and non–Asian American Buddhist communities are not nearly so separate as one might think. His starting point is that "the assumption seems to be, as Nattier puts it, that ethnic-Asian and American-convert groups have 'precious little contact,' as well as 'little in common.' "[26] The results of his fieldwork, primarily with Wat Dhammaram in Chicago and Dharma Vijaya in Los Angeles, are extremely well documented in his book, and are highly suggestive of a growing movement toward the inclusion of two communities, one of Asian immigrants and one of American converts, within numerous Theravāda temples in the United States. Furthermore, he carefully draws out the implications of this movement toward parallel congregations on at least three fronts: (1) the temples themselves; (2) the development of Theravāda Buddhism in America; and (3) the scholarly investigation of the immigrant Theravāda Buddhist movement in America. The most striking finding of Numrich's study is that "in such temples, under one roof and through the guidance of a shared clergy, two ethnic groups pursue largely separate and substantively distinct expressions of a common religious affiliation."[27] Their separateness, though, begs the question of how these communities might cooperatively participate both within their own temple and in the larger American Buddhist community. One potential solution is provided by Diana Eck:

> The impulse toward preservation among immigrant Buddhists and the impulse toward transformation among new Euro-American Buddhists may, in time, converge. It is not enough to preserve a religious or cultural heritage; that heritage must also nourish a new generation in a new environment. Many immigrant Buddhist communities are finding that the social life of the temple is not enough and that meditation classes are, in fact, attractive to young people. And Euro-American Buddhist communities are finding that meditation programs are not enough and that the social life of a gathered community is, in fact, important to young people as they come to identify themselves as part of the community.[28]

Practice

There is no disagreement among researchers that Asian immigrant Buddhist communities and American convert communities engage in significantly different expressions of Buddhist practice. The general consensus is that American converts gravitate toward the various meditation traditions of Japanese or Korean Zen, Vajrayāna, and *vipassanā,* while Asian immigrants maintain practices coincident with ritual activity or Pure Land observance, depending on the nature of the parent tradition of their community, and usually encompassing the Theravāda, Chinese, Japanese, and Vietnamese Buddhist traditions. With the exception of those American converts who have taken up the practices of Sōka Gakkai, there is an almost completely exclusive focus upon meditative practices. More than a few observers of the American Buddhist tradition have remarked that American converts treat Buddhism as if it were a "onefold path," focusing on meditation and little, if anything, else. In a very real sense, meditation continues to be seen in America as an all-pervasive activity, offering a complete spectrum of solutions to life's ills—from getting high without the risks of drugs to finding a way to cultivate peace.

It would not be going too far, I think, to suggest that Buddhist meditation, and the tradition associated with it, have become their own subculture. And it is a subculture that has spawned an enormous popular literature. When I wrote *American Buddhism,* I could find very few books on meditation, popular or scholarly, to include in the bibliography. Even as recently as 1990, Peter Harvey, in his *Introduction to Buddhism: Teachings, History, and Practices,* was able to extend his useful and reliable bibliography of scholarly books on meditation only to two pages. In this volume, on the other hand, I decided to omit popular books on meditation lest the bibliography become longer than some of the individual chapters. If one surveys any of the popular Buddhist magazines that are targeted for American converts, such as *Tricycle* and *Shambhala Sun,* one finds that the advertisements for books on meditation are more than plentiful. In a recent issue of one of these publications, the inside front cover advertises a book entitled *Complete Enlightenment,* by Master Sheng-Yen, with Ayya Khema's *Who Is My Self: A Guide to Buddhist Meditation* and Pabongka Rinpoche's *Liberation in the Palm of Your Hand: A Concise Discourse on the Path to Enlightenment* among titles on the facing page. Flip to the rear inside cover and one finds Sharon Salzberg's *A Heart As Wide As the World: Living with Mindfulness, Wisdom, and Compassion.*

In addition to the literature, the meditation subculture has created a fertile ground for the establishment, by various teachers from the traditions emphasizing meditation, of a seemingly unending lecture/teaching circuit in North America, whereby students of these famous practitioners can get instruction directly from the acknowledged masters. In many cases the schedules of these teachers are published in the magazines noted above, as well as on the Internet. Occasionally the availability of these important teachings gives rise to an unfortunate by-product—the granting by students of a kind of personal status upon those colleagues who have accumulated an extensive collection of teachings. Many years ago, as an expression of disdain for this practice, two well-known scholars perpetrated a mild hoax in one of the communities simply to highlight the foolishness of this "politics of enlightenment." At that time it was ordinary for participants in some Tibetan empowerment ceremonies to be given maroon "protection cords" to be worn after the completion of the ritual. The two scholars went to a local yarn store and bought lime green cords, which they each wore, quietly, in place of their more traditional protection cords. When questioned about these unusually colored cords, each related that the cords had been offered by a very famous rinpoche who had bestowed an especially portentous empowerment on them. Within days the community was buzzing with news of their heightened importance.

Some of the individuals currently active in teaching these meditative traditions have done little to suggest that a more balanced approach to Buddhist practice might be beneficial, and in so doing they have actually expanded the gap between the meditative and nonmeditative communities. In his introductory essay to Don Morreale's *Buddhist America: Centers, Retreats, Practices,* Jack Kornfield writes:

> As Buddhism comes to North America, a wonderful process is happening. All of us, as laypeople, as householders, want what was mostly the special dispensation of monks in Asia: the real practice of the Buddha. American lay people are not content to go and hear a sermon once a week or to make merit by leaving gifts at a meditation center. We, too, want to *live* the realizations of the Buddha and bring them into our hearts, our lives, and our times. This is why so many Americans have been drawn to the purity of intensive Vipassana retreats, or to the power of Zen *sesshin,* or even to the one hundred thousand prostrations and three-year retreats of the Vajrayana tradition.[29]

This one-pointed focus on meditation on the part of many American convert communities and teachers has, however, created conflict and concern in some of the Asian immigrant communities. Not long ago, one such Shin practitioner noted: "White Buddhist centers rise and fall dramatically like ocean waves whereas Asian temples seem to persist uneventfully and quietly through generations. White practitioners practice intensive psychotherapy on their cushions in a life-or-death struggle with ego whereas Asian Buddhists just seem to smile and eat together."[30] In other words, rather than promoting mutuality and support for each other, irrespective of the practices employed by any specific community, American Buddhists are allowing a growing chasm to emerge, one that also reinforces some of the ethnic distinctions cited above. Moreover, American converts who have joined nonmeditative traditions are trapped in a very uncomfortable, perhaps even untenable, position between the two extremes.

The conflict between the various forms of practice in American Buddhism also tends to undermine the applicability of these practices to Western psychotherapy. Buddhists are quick to point out that the importance and efficacy of mind is mentioned in the very first verse of the famous *Dhammapada,* but there seems little agreement on how this idea might apply to a Buddhist psychotherapy. To be sure, meditation is being used in various therapeutic contexts, as books like William Alexander's *Cool*

Water: Alcoholism, Mindfulness, and Ordinary Recovery, Jon Kabat-Zinn's *Wherever You Go, There You Are,* and Sogyal Rinpoche's *The Tibetan Book of Living and Dying* attest, and psychotherapists like Diane Shainberg have incorporated meditation into individual and group therapy. Yet Ryo Imamura, in his essay "Buddhist and Western Psychotherapies: An Asian American Perspective," published in *The Faces of Buddhism in America,* has shown that meditation is not the only constructive approach that might be utilized in incorporating Buddhist practice into psychotherapy.

In an interesting short article entitled "The Future Is in Our Hands," which appears in Arnold Kotler's edited volume *Engaged Buddhist Reader,* Stephen Batchelor ponders: " 'What is your practice?' Many Buddhist practitioners would assume that this question is about the kind of meditation they do, for they tend to answer, 'I practice vipassana,' or 'dzogchen,' or 'shikantaza.' Such responses reflect a widespread view that practice is essentially a matter of spiritual technique."[31] Batchelor's assessment that in the West most Buddhists define what they do almost exclusively in terms of meditation is certainly correct. However, even if one expands the notion of practice to include the nonmeditative traditions in Buddhism, one still falls short of a genuine understanding of what constitutes a truly *balanced and complete* Buddhist practice. Irrespective of whether one is a faithful and consistent practitioner of one or more of the various forms of meditation, or engages in daily recitation of the *daimoku* in Sōka Gakkai, or worships in front of one's family altar and attends temple services at least once weekly in the Pure Land traditions, or engages in ritual observances in Theravāda, what one is doing represents but a tiny fragment of one's time—a brief moment in the overall fabric of one's daily experience of the world.

Yet Buddha spoke of a threefold training that includes not simply spiritual practice, but also the ethical training that supports it, and the wisdom that emerges from it. Most often the ethical training is described in terms of the practice of precepts, or *śikṣā.* This is significant, because precepts are not practiced in a specific, temporally defined portion of one's day. Properly observed, precepts apply to the totality of one's experience. They infuse our lives in every moment. Thus, in the broadest sense, precepts *are* practice in a far more comprehensive fashion than any single spiritual endeavor. Batchelor is one of the few scholar-practitioners who have come to identify the application of ethics and spiritual practice as interpenetrating, complementary factors. He says, "Ethics, from this perspective, is seen as a set of values and precepts that support one's practice."[32] The problem, in general terms, is how Buddhist ethical guidelines can be applied to daily life; and in specific terms, what adaptations must be made to accommodate the experience of Buddhist life in the West.

It is important to realize that Buddhist ethical guidelines, both for the monastic order and for the laity, were preached with specific application to sixth-century B.C.E. India. They emerged not as an excursus on theoretical ethics by the Buddha, but rather in response to serious breaches of conduct on the part of his followers. However, rather than presuming the early *sangha* to have been an indolent, immoral group—which they clearly were not—we should be grateful for the indiscretions of these practitioners, for as I. B. Horner maintains, their indiscretions have provided us with a clear glimpse into the ethical concerns that shaped the early community.[33] Of course these fell into two categories: *Vinaya* and *śīla,* the former representing "an externally enforced code, incumbent on all monks and nuns, that is as much concerned with *pariśuddhi* or complete purity of the community, individually and *organizationally,* as it is with the ethics of conduct"; and the latter representing "an internally enforced ethical framework around which *any* Buddhist practitioner might structure his/her life."[34] In the earliest Buddhist traditions, there were two obvious ways of updating the Buddhist ethical tradition to reflect changing times and circumstances. The first involved the creation of *Vinaya* commentaries, and the various sects of early Buddhism preserved a rich heritage of these texts.[35] The second, in the Theravāda tradition, involved amendments, decisions taken outside the text (called *pālimuttaka*) that were appended as an expression of new situations not previously encountered. Unfortunately, in most Buddhist countries the commentarial tradition on matters of *Vinaya* ceased rather early, and *pālimuttaka* decisions (made through a consensual process called *katikāvata*) seem not to have been applied since the thirteenth or fourteenth century.

As a remedy for this dilemma, I suggested as early as 1979, in *American Buddhism,* that the Buddhist tradition in the West should once again employ the traditional mode of commentary composition and new ethical decision-making as a means of not only squarely facing the complex ethical arena of practicing Buddhism in the modern West, but also revitalizing the ethical framework of Buddhism generally. I said:

What I am suggesting . . . is that both the monastic and lay ethical dimensions of Buddhism need to be reconsidered, and this has special relevance for America. Buddhism in America appears to need, on the one hand, a revitalized ethical system, emphasizing the laity and informed by modern advances in the human and physical sciences. Further it must more actively incorporate those formulations in the traditional doctrines that are still relevant—or might be made relevant—in the modern world. I have in mind here a return to the practices known as the Brahmavihāras or the "divine abodes." These four practices, usually identified as *love* (matrī), *compassion* (karuṇā), *sympathetic joy* (muditā), and *equanimity* (upekṣā), when explicated in their totality, are the highest expression of the Buddhist ethical domain. And they have clear application to American religious experience.[36]

The response, consistent and uniform, and generally expressed at either "Dharma talks" or professional presentations, has been manifestly negative. To an American Buddhist audience that was largely unfamiliar with the internal mechanisms of the Asian Buddhist *sangha,* my suggestion sounded like heresy. Nevertheless, within a decade, when Rick Fields delivered a paper titled "The Future of American Buddhism" at a conference at the Graduate Theological Union in Berkeley in 1987, in which he presented eight features that he felt would be critical to the ongoing development of American Buddhism, all eight points were either directly or indirectly related to issues of Buddhist ethics, with the final one, on the necessity of lay precepts, citing my earlier work as its referent. Fields does not suggest any sources where one might find these new ethical insights that might inform American Buddhism, but it is not unreasonable to simply look at many of the traditional Buddhist texts from a new perspective. I would point to such traditional texts as the "short tract" (*Sīlakkhandhavagga*) of the *Dīgha Nikāya* as well as the *Maṇgala-sutta, Metta-sutta, Sigālovāda-sutta,* and *Milindapañha* of the Theravādin tradition, and the *Brahmajāla-sūtra, Śikṣāsamuccaya, Bodhicaryāvatāra, Bodhisattvabhūmi,* and *Upālipariprcchā-sūtra* of the Mahāyāna tradition for these ethical insights.

More recently, Numrich has identified three hermeneutical principles of *Vinaya* adaptation, which, while case-specific to the Theravāda temples he investigated, might be more broadly applied beyond the *Vinaya* to general notions of *śīla* and to other American Buddhist traditions. These include: (1) minor modification, in which only lesser rules are modified; (2) practicality, allowing for such adjustments as driving cars; and (3) consensus, reviving a judicious use of the *katikāvata* procedure to allow decisions that are "outside the text" (or *pālimuttaka*).[37] In a 1989 meeting with the Sangha Council of Southern California, the Dalai Lama is reported to have said, "Therefore in certain vinaya rules, when it comes to [a] clash between existing situations, sometimes a change can be undertaken. But these things depend entirely upon particular circumstances in a particular individual. We cannot change the basic rule."[38]

To sum up: If the American Buddhist tradition is to affirm the suggestion of Batchelor and others that precepts are an integral aspect of Buddhist practice, and of a Buddhist lifestyle that fosters awareness of and respect for all living beings, then a new and modern ethical literature must necessarily be created. However, if that literature is to meaningfully address the conflicts and ambiguities that result from colliding with a modern world that the earliest tradition never imagined, and engaging that confrontation in a fashion that is truly transcultural and transnational, then it is essential for that new literature to reflect what Harold Coward has called "the reciprocal relationship between text and tradition in Buddhism."[39] The new American Buddhist ethics will thus be both current and textually supported.

Democratization

Whereas Asian Buddhism was, for the most part, primarily hierarchical and highly authoritarian, the forms of American Buddhism that are developing in the latter portion of this century are clearly undergoing a process of democratization. Unfortunately, and perhaps ironically, this democratization was hastened by a series of scandals that rocked many American Buddhist communities. In an interesting article in *Time* magazine about the collective American Buddhist community, David Van Biema notes: "Beginning in 1983 the community discovered to its horror that a probable majority of U.S. teachers, both foreign-born and American, had abused their authority by sleeping with the disciples." He goes on: "The result, in many schools, was a radical democratization, with leadership often subdivided to prevent abuse, and even a certain amount of government by consensus."[40] This radical democratization is being manifested in three essential aspects of American Buddhist communities. First, it can be observed in changing patterns of authority in the various Buddhist *sanghas,* highlighted by a reevaluation of the nature of the relationship between the monastic and lay communities. Second, democratization can be witnessed in changing gender roles in American Buddhism, and especially in the prominence of women. Finally, it can be seen in the manner in which individuals pursuing a nontraditional lifestyle, particularly with regard to sexual preferences, are finding a meaningful role in American Buddhist communities. As a result of this process of democratization, American Buddhism has been able to move away from the hierarchical pattern of Asian Buddhism and toward an egalitarian approach that is more consistent with American democratic trends.

Changing Patterns of Authority

In chapter 5 below, I point out that the term *sangha* originally referred exclusively to the community of monks, called the *bhikṣu-sangha.* Somewhat later, when women in Buddhism turned to the homeless life, their community was known as the *bhikṣuṇī-sangha.* Although Buddha sometimes used the term "*sangha* of the four quarters" to describe his community, it was clear from the context that he was referring to the *monastic* members only. Eventually, as the role of laymen (*upāsakas*) and laywomen (*upāsikās*) grew, the fourfold *sangha* of monks, nuns, laymen, and laywomen came to be identified with the *sangha* of the four quarters. Nonetheless, despite the interdependence of the two communities, it is clear that the monastic goal of liberation (and arhatship) is higher than the laity's goal of merit (*puṇya*), and that an essential inequality of religious status forms the basis of the authoritarian hierarchy that permeates the Asian Buddhist tradition.

Studies of the Buddhist monastic tradition in various Asian countries are too plentiful to mention, but nearly all such books and articles reveal the importance of the monastic unit for the surrounding community and the degree to which its monks and nuns were venerated for their effort and, often, for their erudition. In other words, the ideal lifestyle for Buddhist practitioners was that of the monastic. In the United States, however, the monastic lifestyle has never been the ideal. This was noted quite early in the American Buddhist literature: "Buddhism in the 1960s was still searching for a lifestyle consistent with its pursuits in America. In the first place there was virtually no monastic saṃgha present, and there were almost no Buddhist monks or nuns in residence. Thus Buddhist community meant *lay* community, and, to a large extent, *city* community."[41] Nearly twenty years later, the situation has not changed appreciably, although there are now a preponderance of monks and nuns living in

American Buddhist communities, some of which are essentially monastic in nature. Thus in 1995 I wrote:

In the nearly two decades that I have been writing about Buddhism in America, I have consistently argued that since the vast majority of Buddhists in this country were members of the laity, for Buddhism to be truly American, it would need to address the dilemma of tailoring the *major emphasis* of Buddhist practice to lay rather than monastic life . . . Most practitioners, for an enormous variety of entirely valid reasons, cannot make the full and complete commitment to the rigorous practice associated with the monastic life. That doesn't mean we *ignore* the monastic tradition, or *exclude it from American Buddhist life,* but rather that we provide the context for all Buddhists in America to practice in a fashion appropriate to their choice of approach. In so doing, we would simply be following, and perhaps adapting, an Asian Buddhist model predicated on the notion that there have always been more members of the laity than members of the monastic tradition, but that both endeavors needed to be affirmed and endorsed for the successful development of Buddhist religious life.[42]

Curiously, when the recognition of the normative status of lay Buddhist life in America was first argued in the late 1970s, there was more than a small amount of resistance, well intentioned and cognizant of the fact the Asian Buddhist paradigm was being quite literally turned back upon itself. Now this admission is commonplace and routine—resulting, I suspect, from the large number of American Buddhists who championed that recognition. Although concerned about how to work out the details of such a lifestyle, Rick Fields, in his paper "The Future of American Buddhism," says, "American Buddhism will be primarily a lay Buddhism. Strategies for balancing the demands and distractions of lay life with the demands and disciplines of strong practice will remain a challenge for American Buddhists."[43] A year later, Jack Kornfield said:

How can we *live* the practice in our American lives? Our practice will emphasize *integration,* not a withdrawal from the world, but a discovery of wisdom within the midst of our lives. North American Buddhists have already begun to develop means to integrate and live the practice as householders, as family people, as people with jobs who still wish to partake of the deepest aspects of the Dharma—not through running away to caves, but by applying the practice to their daily lives.[44]

Almost a decade later, when interviewed by *Time* magazine, Kornfield was far more direct: "American people don't want to be monks or nuns . . . They want practices that transform the heart."[45] And support for such a position was widespread. In 1992, *Tricycle* editor Helen Tworkov observed: "Just now, ours is not predominantly a Buddhism of removed monasticism. It is out of robes, in the streets, in institutions, workplaces, and homes."[46]

This emphasis on the lay life notwithstanding, substantial numbers of monastic institutions have developed on American soil, and within virtually all of the traditions discussed in chapter 1 above. Nowhere is the difficulty of such a monastic lifestyle highlighted better than in Paul Numrich's *Old Wisdom in the New World,* as he frankly discusses the difficulties of the monks in Chicago's Wat Dhammaram and Los Angeles's Dharma Vijaya. As an antidote, a number of creative alternatives have been launched as experiments within some American Buddhist communities, most reflecting what Lama Surya Das calls the "in-between *sangha.*" As early as 1970, Shunryu Suzuki Rōshi remarked:

> Here in America we cannot define Zen Buddhists the same way we do in Japan. American students are not priests and yet not completely layman. I understand it this way: that you are not priests is any easy matter, but that you are not exactly laymen is more difficult. I think you are special people and want some special practice that is not exactly priest's practice and not exactly layman's practice. You are on your way to discovering some appropriate way of life.[47]

One of the recent attempts to find a workable alternative to the traditional lay vs. monastic bifurcation was put into practice at the Zen Center of Los Angeles, where many serious students of Taizan Maezumi Rōshi engaged in an intermediate lifestyle, marrying and holding outside jobs while negotiating the full course of training incumbent on a Zen monk. As the Dharma-heirs of Maezumi Rōshi moved on to begin forming their own Zen communities, many of them utilized this pattern with much success. In the Theravādin tradition, Numrich has identified a similar approach in the temples he studied, noting that a number of lay disciples have taken ordination as an *anagārika,* which means they follow a celibate path about midway between those of the traditional lay and monastic *sanghas*. Numrich suggests that these intermediary ordination experiments have arisen for two primary reasons:

> First, they provide ceremonial rites of passage for Americans converting to Buddhism, both at their initial conversion and in subsequent rededications

to the demands and responsibilities of their new faith . . . The second reason for such lay "ordinations" of American converts to Buddhism stems from the typical American reticence to take the full vows of the monastic order, particularly the celibacy vow.[48]

Many of these experiments in American Buddhist communities have eschewed the celibacy issue. Seung Sahn, whose Korean community was cited in the previous chapter, has created a class of "bodhisattva monks" who do not follow the *Vinaya* explicitly, omitting, among other things, its celibacy rule. Rick Fields refers to this sort of quasi-monastic *sangha* as a "kind of halfway house between monastic and lay life, . . . which recognizes the importance of lay Buddhist practitioners of American Buddhism."[49]

Until quite recently, the problem of Buddhist lifestyle and changing patterns of authority was exacerbated by the fact that, unlike its Asian counterpart, American Buddhism was a city movement. The early pattern for American Buddhist communities was to first establish a city center and then, as the center grew and became stable, to develop satellite country centers. To some extent, the members of many infant American Buddhist city centers communicated more effectively with city-centered members of *other Buddhist sectarian groups* than with country-centered members of *their own community*. Harvey Cox, in general terms, has said as much:

The religion of *homo urbanitas,* the dweller in the city, is a special kind of religion. Regardless of his or her past, once the city really makes its impact on the psyche, any city person's religion begins to have more in common with that of other city people than it does with the faith of people of his own tradition who still live, either physically or spiritually, in the countryside or small towns.[50]

Now, a quarter century after Cox wrote that, his statement is no longer true. The general explosion of information-exchange technology, and the widespread accessibility of the Internet, have changed the shape of how and where American Buddhist communities define themselves and engage in Buddhist practice. In chapter 3 we will see that Zen Mountain Monastery, like many such communities, maintains a huge computer database including a file for each of its *sangha* members, irrespective of residential location. No doubt American Buddhism is still largely a city movement. The fall 1997 issue of *Turning Wheel,* for example, is devoted to the topic "Buddhists in the City," and the feature story of the November 1997 issue of the *Shambhala Sun* is titled "Zen on the Street," but equally, rural Buddhist communities are now a lively part of the communication and dialogue.

Are the various Buddhist lifestyles, as described above, working? Not everyone thinks so, and some writers have rather pointed suggestions in the way of remedy. In her much discussed book *Buddhism after Patriarchy,* Rita Gross remarks:

> Traditional Buddhism's heavy reliance on its monastic institutions, which are preponderantly male at present, is responsible, more than anything else, for the superficial impression that Buddhism is a highly patriarchal religion. This male dominance, almost male monopoly, at the heart of traditional Buddhism also produces that familiar ache experienced so often by every religious feminist—of being on the outside looking in.[51]

But it is not only the monastic tradition that draws the focus of Gross's displeasure. Just as she would argue for an androgynous reconstruction of the monastic tradition, she notes: "The androgynous reconstruction of lay Buddhism must take into account . . . rather different problems. The first is that Buddhism offers very weak models for meaningful lay Buddhist life and must forge new paths in the West and in the modern world, even without reference to the questions and issues raised by feminism."[52] For Gross and others, the solution to the problem involves a reconstruction of the patterns of authority in Buddhist communities, not effecting an abandonment of the monastic tradition and its authority, but rather including that tradition fairly in a broad-based pattern of democratization—one that welcomes the laity and women as equal partners in the exercise of determining and administering guidelines for the Buddhist lifestyle in American communities. This pattern eliminates the previously unquestioned authority of the monks, and holds all individuals in positions of authority accountable for proper actions. Gross sees this middle way as a "natural hierarchy," neither completely authoritarian nor completely egalitarian. As she says:

> The more accurate picture of "natural hierarchy" is the mandala structure of center and fringe, in which the parts are organically connected, mutually interdependent and in constant communication . . . Natural hierarchy has much to do with recognizing that not everyone is equally good at everything

and, therefore, communities flourish when people can find their niche at which they are most comfortable, most productive, and most able to contribute to society. Natural hierarchies are also fluid hierarchies, in a sense that no one is always in the center and most people will be in the center at some point. In some situations I will be in a middle position, in other situations in a bottom position, and in others at the top of the current hierarchy. Sometimes I serve, and sometimes I direct, depending on what needs to be done and on my abilities, achievement, and training. All roles are valuable as learning experiences.[53]

Natural hierarchies become unnatural, and dysfunctional, when they become perverted by irrelevant issues, such as absolute authority or gender, or when they become reified into static pyramids. Whether or not the concept of natural hierarchy offers the solution for successfully altering the traditional patterns of authority in American Buddhism remains to be seen, and Gross is aware of this. But it is certainly one creative possibility.

Changing Gender Roles

Stories about Buddha's reluctance to begin an order of nuns are legion in the scholarly Buddhist literature devoted to the development of the early *sangha.* Articles and books about the contribution of Buddhist nuns, or *bhikṣuṇīs,* to the growth of the Buddhist tradition are not. Until the publication of I. B. Horner's *Women under Primitive Buddhism: Laywomen and Almswomen* in 1930, not much had been written about women in Buddhism. More recently, there has arisen a small but continually growing corpus of scholarly literature on women in Buddhism. It includes such works as Tessa Batholomeusz's *Women under the Bo Tree: Buddhist Nuns in Sri Lanka* (1994), Kathryn Blackstone's *Women in the Footsteps of the Buddha: Struggle for Liberation in the Therīgāthā* (1998), Anne Klein's *Meeting the Great Bliss Queen: Buddhists, Feminists, and the Art of the Self* (1995), Diana Paul's *Women In Buddhism: Images of the Feminine in Mahāyāna Buddhism* (1979), Miranda Shaw's *Passionate Enlightenment: Women in Tibetan Buddhism* (1994), Liz Wilson's *Charming Cadavers: Horrific Figurations of the Feminine in Indian Buddhist Hagiographic Literature* (1996), and several others. However, there has been a huge profusion of popular books on the role of women in Western—and, more specifically, North American—Buddhism. Of special note and importance are a number of edited anthologies in which leading Western Buddhist women speak to the needs of female practitioners on both the monastic and lay levels. These include, but are not limited to, Sandy Boucher's *Turning the Wheel: American Women Creating the New Buddhism* (1988), Marianne Dresser's *Buddhist Women on the Edge: Contemporary Perspectives from the Western Frontier* (1996), Lenore Friedman's *Meetings with Remarkable Women: Buddhist Teachers in America* (1987), and Karma Lekshe Tsomo's *Sakyadhita: Daughters of the Buddha* (1989) and *Buddhism through American Women's Eyes* (1995). There is even a good bibliography available through the Internet,[54] and a very helpful guide written by Sandy Boucher (called *Opening the Lotus: A Women's Guide to Buddhism*) that includes a "Directory of Women Teachers" in the United States and worldwide.

In his paper "The Future of American Buddhism," Rick Fields notes that two specific tendencies have emerged from a feminist critique of traditionally male forms of Buddhism: first, a tendency to "critique forms of practice from the vantage point of a 'woman's spirituality' "; second, a strong movement to recover the full *bhikṣuṇī* lineage and, correspondingly, to have Western nuns play a leading role in teaching Westerners.[55] This is especially significant because in the Tibetan tradition the nuns' ordination was never introduced from India, and in the Theravādin tradition the nuns' lineage died out no later than the thirteenth century. While there is currently an increase in the number of Theravādin nuns in Asia, the chief locations from which to receive the full nun's ordination remain Taiwan and Korea, which have preserved the ordination lineages intact, although a first nuns' ordination in the United States was held in 1988.[56]

Although I pointed out earlier that the monastic tradition represents only a tiny portion of American Buddhist communities, many American Buddhist women see the role of nuns as instrumental in cultivating gender equality in American Buddhism. The penultimate chapter of *Buddhism through American Women's Eyes* presents an interesting and arousing discussion of the nuns' monastic experience, highlighted by the perceptive personal reflections of Karma Lekshe Tsomo, Eko Susan Noble, Furyo Schroeder, Nora Ling-yun Shih, and Jacqueline Mandell. Covering five different traditions, the chapter concludes with an inspiring conversation in which viewpoints and perspectives are discussed. Many other American Buddhist women might be included in the discussion too. Can one make a substantive case for the attractiveness of the nun's lifestyle in the West?

Thubten Chodron, who lives in Seattle and has been a Buddhist nun since 1977, says:

I believe it is important to present a variety of lifestyle options for Western Buddhists. While some think that the monastic model is stressed too much in Asia, we must be careful not to swing to the other extreme and present only the lay model in the West. Because people have different dispositions and tendencies, all lifestyles must be accepted in the panorama of practitioners . . . As Buddhism comes to the West, it is important to preserve the monastic lifestyle as a way of practice that benefits some people directly and the entire society indirectly. For those who find strict ethical discipline and simplicity helpful for practice, monasticism can be wonderful.[57]

In somewhat more explicit terms, Rita Gross makes the same compelling claim:

One can make a rather strong case for the attractiveness of the nuns' lifestyle, especially in post-patriarchal Buddhism. Even in patriarchal Buddhism becoming a nun was often a woman's best refuge from harsh and abusive domestic situations. Contrary to outsiders' impressions of the limitations of being a nun, most nuns stress the freedom inherent in their lifestyle. Freed of energy-draining, conflict-ridden family relationships, they can develop themselves fully and be available freely and as needed to provide service and support. The emphasis is not on losing an immediate family and a primary relationship, but on taking on a much wider, more inclusive network of relationships that will be healthier and less prone to conflict. Furthermore, nuns live in a supportive community of like-minded and like-spirited companions. Such a community can be very attractive to those living in a society in which alienation and loneliness are the widespread norm. Nuns live a lifestyle dedicated to study and spiritual discipline (though in some contemporary still-patriarchal contexts, these are sub-standard). The opportunity to pursue these goals single-mindedly in a community dedicated to such vocations sometimes seems almost utopian. Finally, especially in Western Buddhism, in which monastics may have to undertake some of their own support, nuns may be able to develop and perfect their competence in arts, crafts, and other skills in a supportive community environment.[58]

The degree to which male Buddhist practitioners and teachers welcome such women remains the challenge of changing gender roles in American Buddhism. Yet it is an important challenge, because the changing of gender roles in American Buddhism, and the elevation of females to positions of prominence in their respective communities, seem to be coincident with the emergence of a number of outstanding and influential female teachers in the various traditions, some of whom are lineageholders or rōshis. Moreover, almost all of these female teachers are now or have been monastics.

The growing community of female teachers is significant in that it bridges the gap between the small *sanghas* of monastic members and the overwhelmingly larger number of female lay practitioners in American Buddhism. Few would contest the necessity of spiritual authority in Buddhism; nor would most Buddhists challenge the necessity of a top-down rather than bottom-up orientation for the successful recognition of leadership figures. The changing of gender roles in American Buddhism, however, requires that women achieve spiritual authority and discharge the proper duties associated with its attainment. As Rita Gross indicates, "There is no question that Buddhism cannot become postpatriarchal until women wield authority in Buddhism—however that comes to be defined and structured eventually in Western Buddhism. That is one of the reasons why I claim that the presence of female gurus is so crucial as the central issue for Western Buddhist women."[59] Diana Eck's CD-ROM *On Common Ground* also points out that the female teachers in American Buddhism are creating new organizational forms, enabling them to network with themselves and other women Buddhists worldwide. They have planned retreats especially for women, as well as conferences on women and Buddhism. They have also become prolific authors, aiming the focus of their books to American Buddhist women. There is even a journal called *Kahawai: A Journal of Women and Zen* and a *Newsletter on International Buddhist Women's Activity*.

Sandy Boucher identifies two generations of American Buddhist women teachers.[60] In the first generation she includes Maurine Stuart, Jiyu Kennett, Ruth Denison, Ayya Khema, Prabhasa Dharma, and Charlotte Joko Beck. These women have more than two decades of training and activity in American Buddhism, and all studied with Asian Buddhist teachers. The second generation includes Toni Packer, Yvonne Rand, Sylvia Boorstein, Barbara Rhodes, Thynn Thynn, Sarah Grayson, Christina Feldman, Pema Chödrön, Tsultrim Allione, Arinna Weisman, Julie Wester, Sarah Harding, and others. They continue to carry on the work of the first-generation teachers and make Buddhist practice more accessible to American Buddhist women. It is clear that many if not most American Buddhist women share a sentiment expressed by Sandy Boucher:

> It was important to me when I first began practicing to have a woman teacher, for several reasons. First, as a feminist activist, I was used to working with women and trusting women. It felt natural to seek the guidance of a spiritually seasoned woman. Then also, having had experience with male authority figures all my life, I did not want to have to deal with yet another, no matter how wisely or gently he told me what to do.[61]

As these American Buddhist women teachers are carving out what Rick Fields referred to as a "women's spirituality," can one offer any generalizations about these important women? Lenore Friedman responds:

> Actually, [one can offer] very few. If anything, it is their diversity that has struck me most. Some of them knew as children that there was a reality beyond the world of the senses. Others were jostled into awareness much later. Almost all of them live in the world, with children and families. In some cases, the husbands have practices of their own; in others not. Some of the children practice, others don't. All these teachers are insistent that everyday life is our essential spiritual arena.[62]

In trying to generalize how the two generations of women teachers in America have affected American Buddhism, Boucher highlights an interesting interpenetration between the two groups. The more recent group of women teachers has brought an insistence on equality, a strong critique of male hierarchical patterns of authority, an identification of misogynist texts and practices, and a concern for eliminating sexist language from Buddhism. This view has been facilitated and enhanced by the patience and spiritual perspective of the earlier group. Collectively, they have begun to bring about an American Buddhism that is more open to women's needs, more receptive to women's spiritual leadership, and less dependent on formerly hierarchical, male-dominated Buddhist social institutions.[63]

Nontraditional Lifestyles

Amid the huge variety of lifestyle choices available in modern America, none are more visible than the nontraditional, alternative sexual preferences of gay, lesbian, bisexual, and transgendered people. Nonetheless, there is very little literature in Buddhism that addresses these communities. The two most useful scholarly articles are Leonard Zwilling's "Homosexuality As Seen in Indian Buddhist Texts,"[64] and José Cabezón's "Homosexuality and Buddhism."[65] On the general, popular level one can learn much from David Schneider's *Street Zen: The Life and Work of Issan Dorsey.*[66] But the issue remains largely muddled and unclear in terms of Buddhism's ethical stance on these lifestyles.

Quite recently, Roger Corless's "Coming Out in the *Sangha:* Queer Community in American Buddhism"[67] creatively explored the existing material, with Corless finding scriptural references where he could. He points out that since the *Vinaya* precepts largely assumed heterosexuality, both homosexuality and homoeroticism were basically ignored. He does note, though, that the Tibetan writer sGam po pa (1079–1153) explicitly prohibits homosexuality in his commentary on the third precept (i.e., "false conduct with regard to sensuality") and that Śāntideva's *Śīkṣāsamuccaya* identifies a special hell in which male homosexuals are reborn. Because the above article was completed early in 1997, Corless didn't report on the Dalai Lama's remarks to a private meeting with a small group of gay and lesbian Buddhists in San Francisco on 11 June 1997. At the meeting—precipitated by a letter from Steven Peskind, coordinator of the Buddhist AIDS Project—the Dalai Lama "expressed his strong opposition to discrimination and any form of violence against gay and lesbian people and voiced support for full human rights for all, regardless of sexual orientation."[68] However,

> Reading the Tibetan text of Lam Rim ethics, he noted that the traditional teachings, dating back to the Indian Buddhist philosopher Ashvaghosha, assert that sexual misconduct for *all* Buddhists, heterosexual and homosexual, is determined by "inappropriate partner, organ, time, or place." Inappropriate partners include men for men, women for women, women who are menstruating or in the early stages of nursing, men or women who are married to another, monks or nuns, and prostitutes "paid for by a third party and not oneself." Sex with the "inappropriate organs" of the mouth, anus, and "using one's hand" also constitute sexual misconduct for all Buddhists. Inappropriate places include Buddhist temples and places of devotion. Proscribed times are "sex during daylight hours" and "sex more than five consecutive times" for heterosexual partners.[69]

There was lively discussion, but little consensus. Nonetheless, José Cabezón is quoted as having remarked, "It is wonderful to see a religious thinker of the caliber of His Holiness the Dalai Lama grappling with the issues of sexual ethics and especially the rights and responsibilities of gay and lesbian people in such an open, empathetic, and rigorous fashion."[70] The discussion continued on the scholarly level at the 1997 annual meeting of the American Academy of Religion, at which time the Gay Men's Religious Issues Group sponsored a panel on the topic "Buddhism from Gay Perspectives."

Perhaps because what Corless calls the "queer community" is so prominent in America, and in the midst of the expansiveness of the AIDS crisis (highlighted by the death of several Buddhists, including Ösel Tendzin and Issan Dorsey), Buddhism has been prompted to take a stance on this issue. Corless says:

> The stimulus for taking a position other than neutrality is usually attributed to Robert Aitken Rōshi, who asked Richard Baker Rōshi, in the course of a queer caucus at San Francisco Zen Center, what was being done to make Zen practice available to the gay community. Aitken Rōshi is supposed to have said, "If you are not in touch with your sexuality, you are not practicing Zen," and "You can't do zazen in the closet."[71]

Corless points out that a number of Buddhist groups have emerged that support gay, lesbian, and bisexual Buddhists. The Gay Buddhist Fellowship in San Francisco, for example, was formed as an exclusively gay male organization, and had a mailing list of about four hundred people in August 1994; while the Dharma Sisters, also in San Francisco, and formed for lesbian and bisexual women, had a mailing list of about one hundred in August 1994. It is now not uncommon for American Buddhist centers to run retreats exclusively for gays or lesbians, or gays and lesbians together. In trying to isolate the motives and characteristics of queer Buddhist groups, Corless extracts points from the mission statement of one of these groups, concluding that the main issues include: (1) creating a safe environment in which to practice; (2) creating an environment in which practitioners of various Buddhist paths can meet, share viewpoints, and be mutually supportive; (3) providing a community that is socially and psychologically supportive; (4) offering compassion through social action; and (5) offering a place to explore the degree to which Buddhism does, or does not, meet members' spiritual needs.[72]

Engagement

In the first chapter of Kenneth Kraft's edited volume *Inner Peace, World Peace: Essays on Buddhism and Nonviolence,* Kraft describes the circumstances surrounding the first meeting of Dr. Martin Luther King, Jr., and Thich Nhat Hanh in 1966. Later, shortly before Dr. King was assassinated, he nominated Thich Nhat Hanh for the Nobel Peace Prize. To a large extent, the emergence of what has come to be known as "socially engaged Buddhism" owes not only its visibility, but also its very existence, to Thich Nhat Hanh. By this I do not mean to say that Buddhism had never been socially active in its early history, but rather that, as Kraft notes, "because Buddhism is not perceived to have been socially active in Asia (at least in comparison to Christianity's role in the West), Western Buddhists have had to reassure themselves that their adopted tradition really sanctions the sociopolitical engagement to which they are drawn."[73] And the view of social passivity was pervasive, too. Joanna Macy, a longtime Buddhist activist and one of the early advocates of the Buddhist Peace Fellowship, which was formed in 1978 and is profiled in chapter 3 below, has said: "I found that the texts which had been gathered and translated into the anthologies of Buddhist thinking by nineteenth-century Western scholars had been done by people who had already decided that Buddhism was world-rejecting and passive."[74] It was this prevailing viewpoint cited by Macy that Thomas Tweed suggests contributed heavily to Buddhism's failure to make deep inroads into American culture following its initial entrance to the United States during the Victorian period.[75] A century later, utilizing not only Buddhist values but also American forms of protest and active social involvement, socially engaged Buddhists have aggressively employed boycotts, hospice work, tax resistance, ecological programs, voter mobilization, prison reforms, letter-writing campaigns, and a host of other techniques to actively inject sanity into our dialogue with our planet and each other.

Although the term "socially engaged Buddhism" seems to have emerged from the French words *engagé* and *l'engagement,* Donald Rothberg points out that Nhat Hanh was actually using this phrase as a cover term for three Vietnamese ideas emphasizing awareness in daily life, social service, and social activism. The first Vietnamese notion, *Nhân Gian,* actually means "Buddhism for everybody"; the second, *Nhâp Thê',* is translated as "going into the world"; and the third, *Dâ'n Thân,* means "getting involved."[76] Rothberg feels that this citation of the three Vietnamese bases for socially engaged Buddhism is significant not only because it captures the association of the term with "the social, political, economic, and ecological affairs of the non-monastic world," but also because of its more general sense of "including the everyday contexts of families, interpersonal relationships, communities, and work."[77] In other words, socially engaged Buddhism has application to a wide variety of general human-rights issues such as nonviolence and environmental concerns, but also to the lives of individual Buddhists living "in the world."

In the United States, a large portion of the work of socially engaged Buddhism has been coordinated by the Buddhist Peace Fellowship. Working with individual Buddhist communities from virtually all the American Buddhist traditions, it has sponsored an impressive number of programs in its twenty-year history. Interest in the work of socially engaged Buddhism has been so great that in 1986 Arnold Kotler founded Parallax Press in Berkeley as a vehicle for publishing and disseminating materials relevant to the movement. While the staple product of Parallax Press remains the prolific writings of Thich Nhat Hanh, it also boasts a wide range of other authors and editors, including Allan Hunt Badiner, Catherine Ingram, Claude Whitmyer, Joanna Macy, Stephen Batchelor, Susan Murcott, Maha Ghosananda, Sulak Sivaraksa, and the Dalai Lama. The press also serves as a resource for information on retreats, public lectures, and other issues relative to socially engaged Buddhism. Parallax Press is by no means the only publishing outlet for work on socially engaged Buddhism, and a substantial literature, both scholarly and popular, has emerged in the last decade. Of special note are *Engaged Buddhism: Buddhist Liberation Movements in Asia,* edited by Christopher Queen and Sallie King; *The Social Face of Buddhism* and *Beyond Optimism: A Buddhist Political Ecology,* both by Ken Jones; and *The Attentive Heart: Conversations with Trees,* by Stephanie Kaza; as well as a host of articles in *Tricycle, Turning Wheel, Inquiring Mind,* the *Journal of Buddhist Ethics,* and a number of other pertinent journals.

Donald Rothberg, in his essay "Responding to the Cries of the World: Socially Engaged Buddhism in North America," has been instrumental in providing an interpretive framework for understanding socially engaged Buddhism in terms of the traditional three trainings of ethics (*śīla*), meditation (*samādhi*), and wisdom (*prajñā*). He suggests that a number of socially engaged Buddhist activists have worked to extend the traditional principles of *śīla* into a more carefully developed social ethics. In so doing he draws on the work of Robert Aitken, Ken Jones, Sulak Sivaraksa, and Thich Nhat Hanh. Quite important to the attempt is the notion of extending the traditional five precepts in accord with a supplementary series of fourteen precepts constructed by Nhat Hanh as part of the Tiep Hien Order, a community of activist-practitioners founded in 1964. These principles can be summarized as follows:

1. Do not be idolatrous about or bound to any doctrine, theory, or ideology, even a Buddhist one.
2. Do not think the knowledge you currently possess is changeless absolute truth.
3. Do not force others to adopt your views, whether by authority, threat, money, propaganda, or even education.
4. Do not avoid contact with suffering or close your eyes to suffering.
5. Do not accumulate wealth while millions remain hungry.
6. Do not maintain anger or hatred.
7. Do not lose yourself in distraction, inwardly or outwardly.
8. Do not utter words that can create discord or cause your community to split apart.
9. Do not say untruthful things for the sake of personal advantage or to impress people.
10. Do not use the Buddhist community for personal gain or profit, or transform your community into a political party.
11. Do not live with a vocation that is harmful to humans or nature.
12. Do not kill. Do not let others kill.
13. Possess nothing that should belong to others.
14. Do not mistreat your body.[78]

In explaining the use of meditative practices for socially engaged Buddhism, Rothberg draws on the work of Robert Aitken, Joko Beck, and Jon Kabat-Zinn in demonstrating how to apply a meditative mind-set to ordinary activities such as driving, bathing, cleaning, and so forth. But he also shows how to bring meditation into social service, emphasizing such innovative techniques as those described by Joanna Macy in her "Despair and Empowerment" workshops. And he uses the work of John Wellwood and of Stephen and Ondrea Levine to indicate how meditative practice can be extended into interpersonal relationships and family practice. Wisdom too can be used for its ability to offer informed Buddhist analysis of complex social problems, infused with not only the skillful means (*upāya*) that provide the basis to apply wisdom, but also the compassion (*karuṇā*) that informs it.

Of course the greatest challenge for socially engaged Buddhism in the West is organizational. It is far less developed in its organizational patterns and strategies than its Christian or Jewish counterparts. As such, it has much to learn from the many experiments in interfaith dialogue, such as the Society for Buddhist-Christian Studies. Nonetheless, an exciting array of activities can now be documented in the records of the individual American Buddhist communities actively pursuing socially engaged Buddhist programs. These activities are highlighted in the many books on the subject, and now even in the CD-ROM project *On Common Ground,* which vividly portrays such projects as the San Francisco Zen Center's Hospice Volunteer Program, the Hartford Zen Center's Maitri AIDS Hospice, the Upaya Community's "Being with Dying" program, Zen Mountain Monastery's meditation program in the New York state prisons, and others. While the socially engaged Buddhist movement in the United States represents perhaps a radical revisioning of traditional Buddhist approaches to societal issues, it is a nonetheless creative revisioning, and as it gains in maturity, it promises to permeate the American Buddhist environment.

Adaptation

Perhaps the one issue that dominated the early comprehensive books on American Buddhism was *adaptation,* or, as it is sometimes referred to, *acculturation* or *Americanization.* On the very first page of her introduction to *Buddhism in America,* Emma Layman asked, "Is there a characteristically American style of Buddhism?" Three pages later, she went on:

> Now that Buddhism in the United States is no longer considered a religion just for Asians, American Buddhists are directing their attention to how they may fashion an *American* Buddhism. They also are trying to apply Buddhist principles in finding answers to the problems of American society. How successful they are in making such applications will possibly determine in part the future of Buddhism on the North American continent.[79]

After almost three hundred pages of text, Layman still waxed uncertain when she said, "Looking at the various forms in which it manifests itself, it is clear that Buddhism in America does not really have an American style, but appears as an Oriental anachronism in a Western society."[80] My own book *American Buddhism* addressed the same issue in questioning whether we were witnessing "Asian Buddhism transplanted onto (but not necessarily into) American soil, or whether we have a new cultural amalgam that we should properly identify as 'American Buddhism.' "[81] At that time, I presumed that we were witnessing what Donald Swearer had called, in a different context, "Buddhism in transition," and I intended to document the journey in my book. Although Rick Fields's *How the Swans Came to the Lake* did not focus appreciably on Asian American Buddhist groups, instead choosing to emphasize the Tibetan and Zen traditions among American converts, the issue of adaptation or acculturation was no less visible in his work. Even those early works that are case-specific to an Asian American Buddhist tradition consider the topic. Tetsuden Kashima, in his *Buddhism in America: The Social Organization of an Ethnic Religious Institution,* for example, devotes most of his chapter titled "The Future" to a consideration of the Americanization of the Buddhist Churches of America.

In examining the adaptation of Buddhist traditions to America, most scholars have searched for parallels by looking backward in history to Asian Buddhism's numerous transitions from one culture to another. The one most often cited is Buddhism's journey from Indian culture to Chinese culture sometime around the fall of the Han Dynasty in 220 C.E. These two cultures were radically different from one another, and, as a result, Buddhism tried to find doctrines within Taoism that were similar to those of Buddhism and by means of which Buddhism could be explained to the Chinese. This process resulted in many approximations, and it was not until the time of Kumārajīva, around 400 C.E., that China was graced by Buddhists who were sufficiently bilingual, and sufficiently grounded in Buddhist ideals and doctrines, that significant steps could be taken toward the accurate Sinicization of Buddhism. However, Jan Nattier, in her essay "Who Is a Buddhist?" has insightfully noted that by the late fourth century C.E., Chinese Buddhists began to "*remove* elements of Chinese influence that now seemed incongruous with Buddhist values, and to introduce previously overlooked elements that were now viewed as central to the Buddhist tradition."[82] Buddhism's travel through South, Southeast, and East Asia simply repeated the paradigm. However, as Kenneth Tanaka points out:

> The cross-national transmissions of Buddhism in the past have flowed typically from a highly developed to a less developed society as, for example, in its transmission from China to Korea, Japan, and Vietnam, and from India to Tibet and Central Asia . . . The United States in the 1990s however is the dominant country on earth from the standpoint of its economic, popular cultural, military, and technological influences.[83]

This world domination complicates the process considerably, as does America's secularized, highly pluralistic society, in which Buddhist and other religious groups vie for religious consumers in what Robert Greenfield has called the "spiritual supermarket." Nonetheless, I was so sure that Buddhism in the United States owed its potential success to its ability to acculturate and adapt that I concluded *American Buddhism* by saying:

> Throughout this study, I have made much of the fact that there is a singular relationship between Buddhism's degree of acculturation in its new American environment and its potential role in American religious life . . . Needless to say, American Buddhist groups would be able to participate fully in the American experience by emphasizing the unique qualities of freedom, equality, and justice held dear by so many Americans. It would also be beneficial for American Buddhist groups to manifest their American nature in their holiday observances, art, music, ritual life, and so forth. To date, this has remained an unfulfilled dream for Buddhists in this country.[84]

I am no longer so certain that this viewpoint is correct, or even applicable to the Buddhist situation in North America.

During the fall of 1994, the Institute of Buddhist Studies in Berkeley sponsored an ongoing lecture series entitled "Buddhisms in America: An Expanding Frontier." Most of the papers from this series were collected into the book that was eventually called *The Faces of Buddhism in America.* Why was there a switch in title on the path from conference to book? Presumably, it was more effective to present American Buddhism as one whole with many faces rather than as many American Buddhisms celebrating their diversity together. This issue appears again and again in the literature. In the "issues" portion of the CD-ROM *On Common Ground,* one of the subdivisions is called "Two Buddhisms or One?" and it contrasts the Buddhism of Asian Americans against that of Euro-Americans. Perhaps a more appropriate query would be: "One Buddhism or many?"

Much to my good fortune, I was able to spend the academic year 1997–98 at the University of Toronto in the Centre for the Study of Religion. Toronto is perhaps as diverse as any city in North America, having the largest Buddhist population in Canada as well as a wonderful array of Buddhist temples. If one walks from the Centre several blocks to the west, and then heads south, one encounters within a very short time the huge and sprawling Chinatown of Toronto. It is an exciting and diverse area, host to Canadian Buddhists and Canadian Buddhist groups from throughout Asia. In much the same fashion in which scholars in the United States are questioning the adaptation of Buddhist groups to American culture, scholars in Canada are asking similar questions about Canadian Buddhist groups, especially with regard to Asian Canadian ethnic Buddhists.[85] On the other hand, if one begins the same walk from the Centre but continues west *without* turning south, over the next several miles one passes through nearly a dozen ethnic neighborhoods whose residents practice one or another denomination of Christianity. Yet while these largely Canadian ethnic Christian communities are somewhat interesting to scholars, a concern for their adaptation or acculturation seems not to be an issue. One could make a similar case for the United States; Paul Numrich, in the final chapter of his *Old Wisdom in the New World,* called "Americanization," examines the adaptation strategies of the temples he studied, and utilizes the work of Winthop Hudson, William Warren Sweet, H. Richard Niebuhr, Sidney Mead, R. Steven Warner, and Catherine Albanese to reinforce his case.

Nevertheless, the "soil" metaphor endures. Lenore Friedman invokes it in the introduction to *Meetings with Remarkable Women.* After pointing to the fact that Buddhism in the United States is at a crossroads, she says:

> So Buddhism has been transplanted to American soil. It has been watered and fertilized by rich, ancient Asian traditions that have helped strengthen its roots and young stems. But the terrain and climate here are different, and different nourishment seems needed now. For Buddhism to be truly established in America, it will need to move away from reliance on inherited forms and to look instead to the very ground on which it is growing. In other words, who are *we,* the current generation of Buddhist practitioners? What do *we* most need to deepen our understanding? In what unique and perfect form would the Dharma flourish *here, now?* In some places there has already been a shaking-free from Asian forms and a collective searching for more authentic, indigenous ones . . . This is the stage we have arrived at now. American Buddhism is in the process of finding its own nature. It must be said that the process is a tumultuous one.[86]

The more authentic, indigenous forms of American Buddhism that Friedman postulates clearly resemble the sort of "Americanization" process that has often been the editorial topic of *Tricycle's* editor, Helen Tworkov. One cannot help but wonder if, as Jan Nattier pointed out with regard to Buddhism's acculturation to China, American Buddhism may eventually *remove* some of the distinctly American elements now finding their way into the tradition.

Some North American Buddhists are concerned about the implications of modifying or altering the Buddhist tradition in the name of adaptation. Victor Sōgen Hori, a Canadian Rinzai priest and academic professor, has written two articles that are highly critical of the Americanization process: "Sweet-and-Sour Buddhism" and "Japanese Zen in America: Americanizing the Face in the Mirror."[87] Hori critically evaluates the ritual life, methods of teaching and learning, social organization, and meditation practice in Japanese and American Zen. He does it within the amusing, if perhaps somewhat irreverent, comparison of Zen in America to Valentine's Day in Japan. In addition, his "insider's" viewpoint as a longstanding Zen priest is especially useful in exploring the experiential implications of Zen, both in Japan and in the West. In the end, he concludes:

> The call for an Americanization of Buddhism is unnecessary. Every attempt by Americans to comprehend Zen intellectually and to implement it in practice has already contributed to its Americanization. What Americans have been practicing for the last several decades is already Americanized Zen. Pouring wine into a new bottle immediately made it a different wine, although it is an ongoing process. In the long slow process of acculturation, the host culture and the guest religion change each other. The wine changes the bottle into which it is poured; the object changes the lens through which it is viewed.[88]

What emerges from Hori's analysis is an awareness that American Zen has created, in addition to its distinct practices, a series of enterprises that Japanese Zen never imagined: residential communities, businesses, farms, hospices, publishing companies, Dharmacraft cottage industries, and the like. As such, it is hard not to wonder if these latest innovations represent a new kind of Zen practice in America or simply a distraction from Zen practice.

In his treatment of adaptation in the epilogue to *The Faces of Buddhism in America,* Kenneth Tanaka acknowledges that in some cases the qualities of American individualism and secularism can give rise to a sense of impatience with, and possibly even arrogance toward, ancient forms of Buddhism. Nonetheless, he tries to interpret this inclination in a positive way, proposing that it "may be the sign of an active and serious engagement to make sense of a foreign religion in a new culture."[89] In so doing, he suggests that the urgency for aggressive adaptation has fostered what he calls "diffuse affiliation" and "eclectic tendencies" in American Buddhism. "Diffuse affiliation" suggests that individuals may have association with a variety of Buddhist forms in their religious quest. Thus, not only may the current affiliation of an individual not necessarily be his/her final affiliation, but an individual may also maintain concurrent affiliation with more than one Buddhist organization. Diffuse affiliation is also witnessed among American Dharma teachers who have received training authorization in more than one tradition. The most publicized expression of diffuse affiliation, as Tanaka points out, is Rodger Kamenetz's book *The Jew in the Lotus,* in which he coined the term "JUBU" to refer to individuals holding a Jewish-Buddhist dual affiliation. "Eclectic tendencies" refers to such accommodations as Seung Sahn's blending of Zen with Korean folk Buddhism, or, in a more extreme example, the practice of some *vipassanā* teachers to claim no association with the Theravāda tradition or even with Buddhism. For Tanaka, these are not poor or inappropriate choices; they are simply a reflection of the highly pluralistic nature of American Buddhism.

Ecumenicism

In chapter 1 we traced the historical development of the Buddhist tradition in North America, noting in the process that our era marks the first time in the history of Buddhism that all its forms, from all the various Buddhist traditions, have been present in one place at one time. To a large extent, the possibility for that auspicious circumstance emerged from the secularism and its concomitant pluralism that typified American culture in the 1960s. In making that argument, I relied heavily on the suppositions of Peter Berger, carefully delineated in *Sacred Canopy: Elements of a Sociological Theory of Religion.* Berger maintained that pluralistic conditions created a "market situation" in which monopolies could no longer take their client communities for granted. Furthermore, one of the byproducts of pluralistic situations is ecumenicity, in which religious communication and collaboration occur among religions and within religions.[90] By application, I simply postulated that this environment allowed Buddhism to find a fruitful pathway into American culture.

In this chapter we have seen that American Buddhism has grown within a developmental framework in which the serious issues of ethnicity, practice, democratization, engagement, and adaptation have necessitated a careful self-examination on the part of individual American Buddhist communities. Resulting from that self-reflection is the generally accepted notion that an internal American Buddhist ecumenicity is now required for the continued harmonious growth of the tradition on American soil. In each of the sections of this chapter, it is possible to discern—in fact, easy to see—the need for cooperative and ecumenical discussion between American Buddhists of all traditions and all sectarian communities. Indeed, it is a necessity perceived by the Buddhist groups themselves. Thus on 10–17 July 1987, a "Conference on World Buddhism in North America" took place, sponsored by the Zen Lotus Society in Ann Arbor, Michigan. Conceived by Ven. Samu Sunim, and with ample assistance from Professor Luis Gómez (who served as co-coordinator), the conference comprised a wide variety of talks, panel discussions, and meetings held in an effort to bring together representatives of the Buddhist traditions in America to work together toward common goals. In the end, the attendees developed a carefully conceived "Statement of Consensus"[91] for implementation.

In chapter 6 we will review the conclusions about the future of American Buddhism offered by many researchers over the past quarter century. Invariably, each stresses the necessity of an ecumenical attitude on the part of each Buddhist group. In 1976, the author of the earliest comprehensive book on Buddhism in the United States said that ecumenicism

> is taking several forms: (1) establishment of nonsectarian or intersectarian churches and monasteries; (2) intersectarian sharing of resources, for example, Sunday School materials and visual aids; (3) exchange of priests and ministers on occasion; (4) integration of meditational-type approaches into ceremonial-type churches; and (5) joint services involving different sects and/or non-Buddhist groups. In each of these ways Buddhists of different sects do get together in comfortable interaction, coexistence, or union.[92]

More than twenty years later, Lama Surya Das, the closing speaker at the "Buddhism in America Conference" held in Boston on 17–19 January 1997, emphasized that American Buddhism must be ecumenical in the future.

The underlying assumption seems to be the hope that an ecumenical attitude, implemented in the proper way, will function as a protective umbrella under which the issues of ethnicity, practice, democratization, engagement, and adaptation may be addressed in a constructive and productive fashion. To some extent, we have seen some preliminary attempts at implementing this approach. In *Old Wisdom in the New World,* Paul Numrich described three such ecumenical organizations: the Buddhist Sangha Council of Southern California, the American Buddhist Congress, and the Buddhist Council of the Midwest. In addition to the organizations identified by Numrich, one also finds the Buddhist Council of Northern California, the Northwest Buddhist Association, the Texas Buddhist Association, and the Buddhist Coalition of New England. These organizations have created a forum through which issues of interest to all American Buddhists can be profitably addressed. Equally noteworthy is the Buddhist Council of Canada, a similar organization facilitated largely through the tireless effort of Suwanda H. J. Sugunasiri in Toronto. There is little doubt that more organizations of this type will appear on the North American Buddhist landscape in the near future.

Blooming

At the outset of this chapter, I described the visit of Sister Kechog Palmö to Penn State University. During her short stay with us, I planned a dinner at my home at which my professional colleagues in the Religious Studies Department might have a more relaxed and intimate occasion to meet Sister Palmö and learn a bit about Tibetan Buddhism. With the exception of Garma Chen-chi Chang, who had lived a portion of his teenage years as a monk in a Tibetan monastery, I was quite sure none of my colleagues had ever met a Buddhist nun before that evening. The odd juxtaposition of traditions led to some amusing circumstances. Traditionally, Buddhist monks and nuns eat two meals per day, with the latter of these meals taken before noon. As an expression of caring and politeness, the director of Penn State's Eisenhower Chapel spent nearly an hour trying to convince Sister Palmö to eat the dinner that had been prepared for the other guests. I am not sure he ever understood her choice not to partake, or the emphasis of the monastic regulation that governed her decision. Another of my colleagues was interested in the elaborate rituals of Tibetan Buddhism, comparing them to parallels in the Christian tradition that he understood and respected. But when he began asking her about the meditative tradition in Tibetan Buddhism, he seemed unable to fathom why someone might journey so deeply within in order to search for religious enlightenment. In the absence of a compassionate deity who provided salvation by grace, he was clueless, trapped in an ontology-theology stalemate. The most fruitful exchange of the evening involved a discussion of comparative ethics, and the suggestion that Western Jews and Tibetan Buddhists seemed to get along so well because, among other things, they understood the horror of having experienced a genocidal Holocaust.

By the end of the evening my Religious Studies colleagues were surely perplexed, having many more questions than they had at the beginning, but Sister Palmö told each of them that she had had a "simply delightful evening." However, neither Sister Palmö nor my erudite colleagues were present to witness what for me was the most amazing event to occur during her visit. The following morning when my family arose, despite the fact that it was quite late in the fall, and we had experienced the first so-called killer frost of the season, a huge rhododendron in my front yard was in full bloom with dozens of enormous, multicolored flowers that lasted for weeks.

CHAPTER 3

Seeking American Buddhist *Sanghas*

North American Buddhist Communities

In 1975 I was invited to return as a summer faculty member for the second tumultuous year of Naropa Institute in Boulder, Colorado. One of the most interesting innovations in the Buddhist Studies curriculum was the addition of a series of programs called "modules," in which students would study together in a series of courses, meditate together, share meals, and live in close proximity in anticipation of promoting an intense and ideally holistic immersion in the Buddhist experiential tradition. Reginald Ray and I were to share the teaching in a seminar entitled "Indian Buddhism," in conjunction with meditation training supervised by Lodrö Dorje (Eric Holm). Since Ray and Lodrö Dorje were long-standing members of the community then called Vajradhatu, I was the lone "outsider" of the group, and my presence was therefore met with more than a little suspicion by the students. My eagerness, at the outset of our seminar, to jump right into a consideration of the primary textual material on the life of the Buddha simply exacerbated uneasiness among the module participants about my status. I was a *professor.* Strike one! I was *not* a disciple of Chögyam Trungpa Rinpoche. Strike two! And I am quite sure that nearly every member of the module was privately wondering not only *what* strike three would be, but how quickly I would strike out.

Halfway through the ten-week experimental program, we gave the participants a written examination. After the test, I walked back from the classroom to the main administration building with some of the students.

Along the route, one of the students asked with hesitancy, "Tell me, Dr. Prebish, are you Buddhist?" When I replied in the affirmative, and filled in a little personal history about having taken refuge and so forth, the questioner relaxed a little and asked a bit more about my "practice." I explained that I was doing four hours per day of sitting meditation, with an all-day sit every weekend. By the time I explained that I had done a few monthlong solitary retreats involving sixteen hours of daily meditation, I had achieved instant status and acceptance. Not a single person asked me whether I had actually accomplished anything constructive or attained anything valuable in those long hours spent on the meditation cushion. I accrued respect the way a long-distance runner amasses conditioning by "banking" a lot of training miles. Years later, Robert Thurman would joke in his lectures to American Buddhist communities and conferences about being honored to be amid an audience of practitioners who had logged so many hundreds of thousands of meditation hours. In my case, my authenticity as a module leader was never questioned again, and I noticed during the next class session that a number of students had actually begun taking notes.

This episode should not be taken as a critique of Naropa Institute; the ensuing years have demonstrated its growth and maturity in providing a vital, and accredited, alternative to traditional education. Moreover, I experienced similar incidents at other Buddhist centers in the 1970s. While on sabbatical in Berkeley in 1978, students who attended my *Vinaya* seminar at Nyingma Institute manifested the same initial distrust of someone who was perceived to be *merely* a professor. As I mentioned in chapter 1, by the 1970s nearly all Buddhist traditions and sects present in Asia had found their way onto, and into, American soil. Amid the hundreds of Dharma centers and affiliate branches concentrated in the cities and dotting the countryside, there were plentiful opportunities for curious and interested Americans to become temporary "Dharma-hoppers," sampling the cornucopia of Buddhist treats available, but also occasionally settling into one special community. And while this often less committed group of spiritual seekers and sympathizers did not undermine the pursuits of the serious American Buddhists of the period, they did create an atmosphere of chaos that made it difficult for all but the most stable Buddhist communities to endure. Because of this instability, many Buddhist groups disappeared almost as quickly as they appeared on the scene.

As the proliferation of Buddhist groups began to subside in the 1980s, it became possible to begin to locate, identify, and classify the most stable groups. Don Morreale's *Buddhist America: Centers, Retreats, Practices,* published in 1988, represents an admirable first effort at cataloguing the American Buddhist landscape.[1] In writing *American Buddhism,* I made some extremely difficult choices in deciding which groups to study. Of the eight groups I chose, all continue to survive, and some have prospered. Nichiren Shōshū of America has been transformed into the important Sōka Gakkai International–USA. The San Francisco Zen Center has been rocked by scandal and the resignation of its abbot, Richard Baker Rōshi, but continues to be one of the most important Zen centers in North America. Hsüan Hua (leader of the Sino-American Buddhist Association), Chögyam Trungpa Rinpoche (leader of Vajradhatu), and Jiyu Kennett Rōshi (leader of Shasta Abbey) have all died. The Tibetan Nyingma Meditation Center can still be found nestled in the Berkeley hills. And the Washington Buddhist Vihara and Buddhist Churches of America continue as significant ethnic Buddhist organizations. As we approach the end of the twentieth century, the choice of which American Buddhist groups to focus upon has become even more difficult as the current landscape has become increasingly wide and varied. For the sake of continuity, we will revisit some of the above groups, while also having a glimpse at some others that have emerged in the last quarter century to lead the ongoing growth of the American Buddhist movement. I hope this tour will reflect the diversity of ethnic-Asian and American-convert traditions and the wide scope of practices in American Buddhism, as well as the depth of the commitment of American Buddhists to leading moral and fulfilling lives amid often confusing and sometimes excruciating outside pressures.

Zen Mountain Monastery

Before 1995, my only association with Taizan Maezumi Rōshi or his students was through courteous, professional acquaintances I maintained with members of the Kuroda Institute, one of the divisions of the Zen Center of Los Angeles (ZCLA). Of course I had read much of the popular literature about his best-known students—primarily Bernard Tetsugen Glassman Rōshi of the Zen Community of New York, Dennis Genpo Merzel of the Kanzeon Sangha in Utah and Europe, Jan

Chozen Bays of the Zen Community of Oregon, and John Daido Loori of Zen Mountain Monastery—but in midsummer 1995 I had no idea whatsoever of what to expect as I drove the twenty miles from Kingston, New York, to Mt. Tremper, where I would meet the abbot of Zen Mountain Monastery (ZMM). When I was introduced to Abbot Loori by the monastery's chief of operations, Geoffrey Shugen Arnold, I was rather stunned to notice a prominent tattoo on Loori's forearm as we bowed first and then shook hands. Equally surprising was the abbot's absolute lack of formality with me and his willingness to spend hours personally taking me on a tour of ZMM's facilities. Early in my stay, I discovered that Abbot Loori and I shared a common professional background in food chemistry and a strong interest in computers. He was a kind and sharing host, answering all my questions with far more aplomb and candor than I would have imagined possible from someone of his stature and position.

Zen Mountain Monastery is a residential retreat center, an American Zen Buddhist monastery and training facility for both monastic and lay practitioners of both genders that is the nucleus of an umbrella organization known as the Mountains and Rivers Order (MRO).[2] In addition to maintaining a media company known as Dharma Communications, the MRO also has a number of centers and affiliates in the eastern United States and abroad. Mt. Tremper, New York, home to the monastery's 230 acres of property, is located in the gently sloping foothills of the Catskill Mountains, and has long been thought to be a sacred space. The monastery is bordered on two sides by forest preserve and on two sides by the Esophus and Beaverkill Rivers. Much of the land remains wilderness and serves as a nature sanctuary for the many species of local wildlife.

The main house of ZMM, which seems to be continually undergoing restoration, was built nearly one hundred years ago by a Catholic priest and Norwegian craftsmen, and in 1995 the state granted it the status of a historic landmark. It is a huge, four-story structure, built from natural bluestone and stately white oak, and serves as the focal point for much of the organization's activities. In the main house are the *zendō,* kitchen and dining hall, training offices, library, Buddha Hall, dormitories, and private rooms. In addition, one finds nearby a series of cabins and A-frames for residential housing, two hermitage sites, an outdoor chapel, a graveyard, and the abbacy. A short walk takes one to a separate building in which the extensive technical facilities and offices of Dharma Communications are housed.

Abbot Loori, the spiritual leader of ZMM, is one of twelve successors to Hakuyu Taizan Maezumi Rōshi, founder of the White Plum Sangha. Before his death on 14 May 1995 at age sixty-four, Maezumi Rōshi founded six temples in the United States and Europe that are formally registered with the headquarters of Sōtō Zen in Japan.[3] Having been ordained in the Sōtō lineage at age eleven, he received Dharma transmission from Hakujun Kuroda Rōshi and *inka* from both Kōryū Ōsaka Rōshi and Hakuun Yasutani Rōshi. As such, he was a Dharma heir in three Zen lineages. Maezumi Rōshi arrived in Los Angeles in 1956, and eleven years later founded the Zen Center of Los Angeles, which continues as one of the most influential Zen groups on the North American continent, with more than fifty affiliate groups in North America and Europe. The White Plum Sangha, named after the rōshi's father, Baian Hakujun Daisho, was formed as a means of promoting harmony among the rōshi's Dharma successors.[4] This group includes Bernard Tetsugen Glassman Rōshi (who received *inka* and succeeds Maezumi Rōshi as spiritual head of the organization), Dennis Genpo Merzel (now Genpo Rōshi, having received *inka* from Glassman Rōshi in October 1996), Charlotte Joko Beck, Jan Chozen Bays, Gerry Shishin Wick, John Tesshin Sanderson, Alfred Jitsudo Ancheta, Charles Tenshin Fletcher, Susan Myoyu Andersen, Nicolee Jikyo Miller, William Nyogen Yeo, and John Daido Loori.[5]

John Daido Loori came from a Catholic background, and worked in the food industry as a chemist who analyzed natural flavors so that they could be synthesized as food additives. But it was his lifelong interest in photography that led him to Zen. He studied under Minor White, from whom he also learned meditation, and eventually continued his Zen studies in New York and then at UCLA, finally taking ordination in 1977.[6] With only a small amount of cash, in 1980 he purchased the acreage on which ZMM resides. He continues his interest in photography, having had about three dozen one-man shows and periodically conducting photography workshops across the continent. He has also taught his craft at a variety of places, including Naropa Institute and the Synechia Arts Center in Middletown, New York. Additionally, the computer technology he learned as part of his work in the food industry has informed his Buddhist practice in a useful way, for it is the basis of Dharma Communications, which he founded as a compassionate expression of Zen educational outreach. In fact, as we walked along one of the trails on the way to the abbacy, with Abbot Loori puffing on a cigarette, he told me that his students initially thought his interest in and use of computers was a bit eccentric for a Zen abbot. Then he smiled and said, "It kind of blew away their overly romantic image of Zen." However, as we shall see, Dharma Communications is one of the most efficient and successful publishers of Buddhist materials on the continent, and a place where practitioners can learn how to cultivate both mindfulness and compassion in front of a computer. At the abbacy, he showed me the database he maintains for the Mountains and Rivers Order, with a personal file for every community member, wherever they might currently reside. In other words, Abbot Loori was one of the very first American Buddhists, if not the first, to appreciate how computer technology might enable American Buddhist communities to extend far beyond the geographic, real-space location of any one particular *sangha.*

Abbot Loori is a permanent resident of the community, which gives him a wonderful opportunity to develop a strong student-teacher relationship with practitioners in residential training. Trained in both the *kōan* style of Rinzai Zen and the quiet sitting practice (*shikantaza*) of Sōtō Zen, he continually tries to promote right action on the part of his students and approaches all daily experiences as occasions for cultivating awareness. As he demonstrated almost all of ZMM's ample hardware to me, it was also clear that Loori heartily endorsed a hands-on approach. He wasn't quiet or withdrawn in personal matters either, aggressively expressing his discontent when he couldn't find a book in his well-stocked library.

Loori's penchant for reading and study is reflected not only by the various programs sponsored by ZMM, as we shall see, but also by his own writing: he is a prolific author. His most recent book, *The Heart of Being: Moral and Ethical Teachings of Zen Buddhism,* is his fifth volume. The book is significant in that it attempts to offer a modern interpretation of the traditional precept ceremony called *jukai,* and it resonates well with the abbot's powerful concern for a morality in which individual and global ethics interpenetrate. During the past fifteen years he has also written *Mountain Record of Zen Talks, Eight Gates of Zen, Still Point,* and *Two Arrows Meeting in Mid-Air.*

Two other teachers assist Abbot Loori in running ZMM. Each is a "Dharma holder" with extensive residential training. The vice-abbess of

ZMM is Bonnie Myotai Treace. She is a former director of Dharma Communications and has lived in the residential training setting for more than a decade. She coordinates all the affiliate groups of the MRO and works especially with the Zen Center of New York City. Like the vice-abbess, Geoffrey Shugen Arnold has lived in residential training for more than a decade and not only serves as chief of operations for the monastery, as noted above, but also is the training coordinator and supervises the new prison *sangha* program (see below).

As a comprehensive training center for both lay and monastic practitioners, ZMM offers a wide variety of programs that include, in addition to a daily routine of meditation, introductory weekends of Zen training; weeklong *sesshins,* or intensive periods of silent meditation retreat; and special retreats focusing on selected areas such as Buddhist Studies, Zen arts, and the like, all designed to promote direct realization through practice. Because Abbot Loori is aware that many Western practitioners of Zen begin their training with no more than a modicum of background in Buddhism, he has devised a training program known as "The Eight Gates of Zen," designed to provide what he calls a "training matrix." The eight "gates" include, in order: (1) *zazen;* (2) the student-teacher relationship developed through face-to-face training; (3) academic study; (4) liturgy; (5) precepts; (6) art practice; (7) body practice; and (8) work practice. Each "gate" is fully explained in Loori's above-mentioned *Eight Gates of Zen.* Taken together, they address all the aspects of an individual's life, providing the basis for actualization in daily life.

The most popular program at ZMM is the "Introduction to Zen Training Weekend," in which those in attendance are given extensive instruction in *zazen* and body practice, participate in the liturgy of the community, and have wide opportunity to ask questions about Zen practice. The retreat is a requirement for all potential MRO students, and a prerequisite for *sesshin* attendance. Quite often, too, students at weekend retreats are afforded the occasion of asking their questions directly to Abbot Loori in a face-to-face meeting. In addition, there is a scholarship program to assist financially limited students who are interested in attending weekend training programs or *sesshins,* and there is a children's program on the Sundays following the Zen Training Weekends.

Some students at ZMM desire a more complete and intensive immersion in Buddhist teachings and Zen practice. For these students, it is possible to enter into a residency period, generally ranging from one week to one year, but with the possibility of staying for much longer periods as well. The residential training program is integrated into the overall seasonal practice of ZMM, in which spring and fall are devoted to intensive periods of practice called *Ango,* while winter and summer allow one the opportunity to tailor a creative, individual practice that integrates the morning monastic practice with an afternoon program designed in a more individualized fashion in consultation with the training staff. For students participating in the general residential program, a monthly weeklong *sesshin* is required, while students pursuing a long-term residency often *begin* their training program with a monthlong retreat. In this way, students learn to eat together, work together, and discuss the Dharma together on a daily basis. One should not infer from the above that the atmosphere at ZMM is overly solemn or unpleasant, as anyone sharing lunch with the residential students will quickly learn.

Like the Zen Center of Los Angeles, ZMM accepts a variety of Buddhist lifestyles in which members of the lay *sangha,* monastic *sangha,* and quasi-monastic *sangha* live together in the same community. To be sure, this provides the potential for much creative tension as individuals try to develop a distinctly American style of Zen practice and community life. Nonetheless, having benefited from difficult lessons learned at the ZCLA, Loori has been extremely careful in designing rules and guidelines for those in residency, which are directed toward developing the highest moral standards and minimizing the potential complications of interpersonal relationships in a practice setting.

Distributed throughout the calendar year are a series of ZMM topical special retreats, generally led by MRO community members, individuals in John Daido Loori's extended Dharma family (such as Jan Chozen Bays and others), various practitioners of Zen arts, and scholars. Thus an incredibly rich and varied series of opportunities for learning and growth are almost continuously available, juxtaposed against each other in a manner that inhibits rigidity and fixed patterns of thought. It is not at all unusual to have a retreat on Zen archery followed by one addressing gay and lesbian spirituality, or a retreat on landscape photography followed by a weekend focusing on the *Heart-sūtra.* Whether one is interested in exploring weeds and wildflowers or learning to cope with the loss of a child, ZMM can provide both the occasion and the opportunity for experiencing these aspects of Buddhist and American life in a retreat setting. Needless to say, providing a continuous stream of consequential retreats led by individuals with impeccable credentials is a scheduling nightmare—which, however, seems to disturb nobody and is simply woven back into the community's collective Buddhist practice.

Combined with its other activities, ZMM is a leader in instituting programs of Buddhist social engagement—a feature that is quite typical of communities associated with the Dharma heirs of Maezumi Rōshi. ZMM's program is called Right Action, and is considered to be an active expression of the bodhisattva's concern for both wisdom and compassion. The two chief expressions of this approach are the ZMM Prison Program and the Zen Environmental Studies Center (ZESC). The ZMM Prison Program began in 1984 in response to a request from an inmate in a New York state correctional facility to start a practice group there. Following a court battle, resolved by the New York State Supreme Court, the first Zen prison practice group was formed.[7] Currently, senior ZMM students make weekly visits to a number of prisons, where they lead the developing prison *sanghas* in meditation and liturgy, and give Dharma talks. In addition, they supervise weddings, memorial services, and precept-taking, and they even offer Dharma combat. As a result of its instrumental role in developing this program, not only has ZMM become an invited adviser on Buddhist affairs for the New York State system of corrections, but it has also begun a National Buddhist Prison Sangha comprising a national network of Buddhist practitioners who volunteer their time in a variety of ways consistent with Buddhist values. The ZESC began in 1992 as a means of integrating the monastery's concern for environmental education, protection, research, and recreation. Within the monastery's more than two hundred acres, opportunities abound for camping, boating, rock climbing, bird-watching, learning to understand deep ecology, and cultivating a proactive environmental activism. ZMM even has a "Green Dragon Council" to protect the monastery grounds.

The centers and affiliate groups of Zen Mountain Monastery (the Society of Mountains and Rivers Order—SMR) include the Providence Place Zendo in Albany, New York; the Burlington, Vermont, *zendō;* a series of New Zealand affiliates, which provide nonresidential locations for lay practitioners; and a major city center known as the Zen Center of New York City. Quite early in the study of American Buddhism it was noted that the general pattern in American Buddhist communities was for each organization to first establish a city center, only later opening satellite centers in the rural countryside.[8] Despite its association with the

White Plum Sangha (which emerged from the urban-based ZCLA), the Zen Center of New York City is one of the first American Buddhist expressions of the reverse process: an affiliate city center created *after* the establishment of a major center in a rural setting. The Zen Center of New York City is also called the Fire Lotus Zendo, and serves as a training center for both the monastic and lay communities. Readily accessible to those living throughout the city, it sponsors sitting meditation six days per week (Saturday is excluded), one-day intensive meditation periods each month, and a variety of one-day workshops. Abbot Loori and his senior training staff play an active, continual role in this ZMM city center, and it is a most convenient location for those isolated from ZMM or in the beginning stages of Zen practice.

Dharma Communications (DC) is a nonprofit educational corporation that functions as the "educational outreach arm" of ZMM. Yet it is more than that; it is an occasion for its staff members to engage in the active pursuit of right livelihood. Run by residential monastics as well as resident and nonresident Zen lay practitioners, it provides a wide range of Dharma publications, in virtually all media forms, as well as an extensive listing of Dharma crafts and supplies. Although Dharma Communications has much to offer the reading, viewing, and listening interests of the general American Buddhist community, its publications are especially useful to individuals in Abbot Loori's community who cannot attend workshops or retreats, and to those who might be housebound or inmates. Because of its mission, its pricing is almost always significantly lower than that of other Buddhist publication enterprises. Dharma Communications is organized into seven chief areas: (1) the *Mountain Record* journal; (2) DC Press; (3) DC Video; (4) DC Audio; (5) DC Interactive Multimedia; (6) Dharma Telecommunications; and (7) The Monastery Store. Virtually all of the operation of Dharma Communications is orchestrated from one small building near the ZMM main house. Nonetheless, the technological capability housed in that small building is overwhelming. Daido Loori has an equally impressive computer and multimedia facility housed in the abbacy, from which he constantly contributes to the publication program of DC.

Currently edited by Pat Jikyo George, *Mountain Record* is a quarterly publication, offering slightly more than one hundred pages in each issue and usually including a half dozen or more articles (sometimes devoted to a single topic) in addition to regular features, which consist of an editorial, a photo gallery, a media review, *sangha* news, and a host of information about upcoming retreats and programs. It is available by subscription as a conventional print journal, but an abbreviated version, minus the articles, is offered as an electronic journal on the World Wide Web. The fall 1996 edition of *Mountain Record* marked the fifteenth anniversary of the journal, making it the oldest consistently published journal of any Zen center in the United States.

DC Press is a traditional publishing house focusing primarily on books that inform Zen practice. In addition, it serves as a distributor for other selected titles on Buddhism published by other presses. In addition to the DC Press–produced books of John Daido Loori, books by members of Abbot Loori's Dharma family, such as Glassman Rōshi, Genpo Rōshi, Charlotte Joko Beck, and others are featured. Zen titles are organized into categories of modern masters, ancient masters, Dōgen studies, *kōan* studies, and Zen art. The rest are categorized according to history, academic studies, sūtras, right action, body practice, and children's books. Collecting the nearly 150 titles advertised would yield an impressive personal library by any standard of measurement.

As of midsummer 1997, DC Video had produced sixteen videotapes in its Mountain Light Video Library. These videotapes, addressing virtually all aspects of Zen training, are produced entirely by Dharma Communications and are offered for sale on an individual basis or through a subscription program. In addition to the above, DC has produced two important videos of tribute to Maezumi Rōshi (*Now I Know You* and *On Life and Death*) and a plethora of others on such topics as Zen home practice, ecology, daily work, intimacy, and eating. DC Audio also offers a subscription program and tapes for individual purchase. In addition to Abbot Loori's discourses on history, practice, morality, precepts, giving, sexuality, and even the Internet, audiotapes by other noted authorities such as Robert Thurman (on ethics) and Ken Cohen (on Taoist healing imagery) are available. Discourses by Loori's two chief disciples, Bonnie Myotai Treace and Geoffrey Shugen Arnold, can also be purchased on audiotape. One of the most interesting and forward-looking aspects of Dharma Communications is the project of DC Interactive Multimedia, which is producing an interactive CD-ROM on Zen meditation practice in which a built-in electronic interface will allow end-point users to communicate with live meditation instructors. Only one step removed from the CD-ROM project is Dharma Telecommunications, which offers not only an electronic bulletin board service, but also an online E-mail opportunity for practitioners to participate in "Questions for Cybermonk," available through the center's World Wide Web site. The Monastery Store offers everything one could imagine for Zen practice and Buddhist home furnishings, from *zafus* to meditation gongs. One can even purchase T-shirts emblazoned with the emblem WAKE UP!

It is by no means unusual for an American Buddhist community to publish books and audiotapes by its teacher. The Tibetan Nyingma Meditation Center began Dharma Publishing in 1969 and has built this operation into an impressive, important enterprise in its short three decades of existence; in the early 1970s Chögyam Trungpa's seminars were recorded and sold commercially by Vajradhatu Recordings, which has now grown into Vajradhatu Publications and Kalapa Recordings. But Dharma Communications is much more than a copy of those other publishing ventures. It is perhaps the most comprehensive community-based Buddhist publication effort in North America, and is a leader in applying communications technology to the problem of effectively serving an extended, largely nonresident *sangha*. In so doing, DC offers a complete program for Buddhist living that encompasses each of the eight gates of Zen discussed by its teacher.

Zen Mountain Monastery is by no means the largest Zen community in America, although the thousands of entries in Daido Loori's *sangha* database are an impressive testament to the work of ZMM in redefining how we think about Buddhist communities in real space when we have sophisticated new communication technology at our command. Yet it is in the quiet but eloquent manner in which Abbot Loori addresses the issues of Buddhist practice, education, work, relationships, ethics, aesthetics, social engagement, outreach, and concern for children that his community is making its impact on American Buddhism. Loori has developed a readership among academic scholars of Buddhism too, largely because of his aggressive commitment to the above issues. It is not an attainment based on the high-profile, even flamboyant approach utilized by some American Buddhist teachers, but rather one earned by a quiet, persistent attitude that reveals the naturalness of his method. His special commitment to ecological issues and the protection of the environment, as well as the obvious and strong moral values demonstrated by the residents of ZMM, sets his teaching apart as exemplary. In this he is like the other members of the White Plum Sangha, who have collectively made a more profound and constructive impact on American Zen than have the students of any other Zen master.

In one of his Dharma discourses, titled "Precepts and Environment," Abbot Loori commented near the outset of his talk:

> When we look at the Precepts, we normally think of them in terms of people. Indeed, most of the moral and ethical teachings of the great religions address relationships among people. But these Precepts do not exclusively pertain to the human realm. They are talking about the whole universe and we need to see them from that perspective if we are to benefit from what they have to offer, and begin healing the rift between ourselves and the universe.

After describing the ninth of the "ten grave precepts," he goes on:

> In another incident, the fellow who owned the house that is now the monastery abbacy had beavers on his property. They were eating up his trees so he decided to exterminate them. A neighbor told him that they were protected, so he called the DEC. The rangers trapped and removed the animals. When we moved into the house, however, a pair of beavers showed up and immediately started taking down the trees again. In fact, they chomped down a beautiful weeping willow that my students presented to me as a gift. I was supposed to sit under it in my old age, but it was now stuck in a beaver dam, blocking up the stream. With the stream dammed, the water rose and the pond filled with fish. With the abundance of fish, ducks arrived. That brought in the fox and osprey. Suddenly the whole environment came alive because of those beavers. Of course, they didn't stay too long because we didn't have that much wood, so after two seasons they moved on. Nobody was taking care of the dam. The water leaked out and the pond disappeared. It will be like that until the trees grow back and the next pair of beavers arrive. If we can just keep our fingers out of it and let things unfold, nature knows how to maintain itself. It creates itself and defines itself, as does the universe. And, by the way, the weeping willow came back, sprouted again right from the stump. It leans over the pond watching me go through my cycles these days.[9]

During my visit in the summer of 1995, Abbot Loori and I walked past that tree on the way to the abbacy. Once inside, he immediately showed me his computer facilities. He wanted to demonstrate all the sound and visual capabilities of his system, and how everything could be integrated into various multimedia presentations. There we were: two grown men, both past fifty, both former chemists, both Buddhists, and having spent thousands upon thousands of hours in sitting meditation. If anyone had peeked in on us that morning, they would certainly have seen two little boys totally engrossed in exploring sounds and sights and images as if nothing else in the world mattered. We were two adult men with the open hearts of little children. I had come to ZMM to talk about American Zen with John Daido Loori, and without my having realized it along the way, he had me doing Zen instead.

Buddhist Peace Fellowship

In December 1996 I traveled to the San Francisco Bay area to visit Buddhist communities in conjunction with the preparation of this book. While there, I had also hoped to get some photographs that might be utilized in this volume or in *The Faces of Buddhism in America*. In the past, I had always found Buddhist communities more than willing to accommodate such requests, and to be especially hospitable as well. Since I had not planned to visit the Buddhist Peace Fellowship until later in the day, I drove to a nearby Buddhist facility and asked a young man at the entrance if I might take a few photographs. He said he wasn't authorized to make such a decision but would get someone who was. The next person who came out also could not provide authorization, but eventually I was told by a person in charge that photographs would not be allowed. Rather surprised, I wondered if perhaps I had not explained myself properly, so I tried again. This time I was very specific about who I was, why I wanted to take the snapshots, and how they would be used. I also mentioned that I surely didn't think a photograph in a scholarly book on American Buddhism could harm the community and, quite the contrary, imagined that it might spark a little extra interest. At that point I was told quite clearly, again, that no photographs would be allowed under any circumstances, and it didn't matter who I was or why I wanted them. As I left, it occurred to me that I had come pretty close to actually being thrown out of the place—something that had never happened to me in more than a quarter century of visiting Buddhist sites in the United States. Shortly thereafter, as I entered the Berkeley headquarters of the Buddhist Peace Fellowship, it seemed strangely ironic that I had experienced my first truly unpleasant experience in American Buddhism immediately prior to visiting an organization that promoted peaceful relations and gentle causes.

The Buddhist Peace Fellowship, with more than four thousand current members, began in 1978 in Hawaii at the Maui Zendo as a project jointly founded by Robert and Anne Aitken, along with Nelson Foster and a few of their Zen friends. Within a short time, this first American expression of socially engaged Buddhism was joined by a rather eclectic collection of Dharma friends that included Gary Snyder, Alfred Bloom, Joanna Macy, Jack Kornfield, and a number of other, mostly Euro-American practitioners. The group was ecumenical from the start; most of the members of the infant Buddhist Peace Fellowship (BPF) lived in Hawaii or the San Francisco Bay area, and it took a year to build the membership roll to fifty. To maintain a network of contact, the group began a newsletter, largely facilitated by Nelson Foster, which eventually grew into the journal *Turning Wheel.* By the end of the 1980s, not only had the group grown to several hundred members and moved its base of operations to Berkeley, but it had actively promoted human rights in Bangladesh, Vietnam, and Cambodia and also worked to free imprisoned monks who belonged to Vietnam's Unified Buddhist Church. Shortly thereafter, the BPF hired a part-time coordinator and began forming its first chapters. Editorial responsibility for the newsletter passed on to Fred Eppsteiner (editor of *The Path of Compassion: Writings on Socially Engaged Buddhism*) and later to Arnie Kotler (who went on to found Parallax Press in 1986). It also became a vehicle for documenting some of the rapid growth in American Buddhist communities.

Alan Senauke, currently the national director of the BPF, was ordained as a Sōtō Zen priest in 1989 and now lives at the Berkeley Zen Center with his wife and two children. In a short article titled "History of the Buddhist Peace Fellowship: The Work of Engaged Buddhism," published on the BPF World Wide Web page, he acknowledges the pivotal role that Thich Nhat Hanh's peace efforts have played in the work of the fellowship. In 1983, the BPF and the San Francisco Zen Center sponsored Thich Nhat Hanh's first retreat for Western Buddhists at Zen Mountain Center (at Tassajara Hot Springs). Longer BPF-cosponsored tours by Thich Nhat Hanh took place in 1985, 1987, and 1989. Eventually, near the end of the decade, Thich Nhat Hanh's lay *sangha* in the West shared office space in Berkeley with the BPF and the growing Parallax Press.

The BPF is a totally nondenominational group that describes itself as comprising "meditating activists." It offers a simple, fivefold statement of purpose:

1. To make clear public witness to Buddhist practice and interdependence as a way of peace and protection for all beings.
2. To raise peace, environmental, feminist, and social justice concerns among North American Buddhists.
3. To bring a Buddhist perspective of nonduality to contemporary social action and environmental movements.
4. To encourage the practice of nonviolence based on the rich resources of traditional Buddhist and Western spiritual teachings.
5. To offer avenues for dialogue and exchange among the diverse North American and world sanghas.[10]

Membership in the BPF does not require active status in any Buddhist organization, and is available for a low yearly stipend, which supports the work of the group and entitles members to a subscription to *Turning Wheel*. Today the BPF has sixteen chapters spread across the United States (currently coordinated by Diana Winston). While most are on the West Coast, primarily in California and Washington, there are also chapters in New York City; Buffalo, New York; Yellow Springs, Ohio; DeKalb, Illinois; and the Research Triangle area in North Carolina. It also has affiliates in Australia, Bangladesh, India, Thailand, Japan, and the United Kingdom. Senauke notes that the membership base of the BPF is largely among the Euro-American Buddhist population, but indicates that the BPF works extensively with ethnic Buddhists and people of color who embrace Buddhism as members try to move beyond their own residual insensitivity.

The BPF "seeks to awaken peace where there is conflict, bring insight to institutionalized ignorance, promote communication and cooperation among sanghas, and in the spirit of wisdom, compassion, and harmony, offer practical help wherever possible."[11] With this mission statement, the BPF is able to work with virtually any Buddhist community or Dharma center, and with Christian and Jewish groups as well.

In addition to its peace efforts in the United States, focusing largely on weapons control and nonviolence, the BPF has devoted much international effort to promoting peace in Asia. A significant portion of that effort concentrated on effecting the release of Aung San Suu Kyi after six years of "house arrest" in Burma, and securing low-interest loans for right-livelihood projects with Tibetan exile communities living in India and Nepal. The international work of the BPF is organized as part of its association with the International Network of Engaged Buddhists (INEB), organized in February 1989 in Thailand by peace activist Sulak Sivraksa and others. The INEB now has groups in thirty-three countries, working toward the promotion of socially engaged Buddhism in an atmosphere of inter-Buddhist and interreligious cooperation, identifying itself as supporting "grassroots Dharma activism around the world."

To date, the primary areas of INEB concern have been human rights, nonviolence, the environment, women's issues, alternative education, and the integration of spirituality and activism. During its first seven years of existence, the INEB promoted these issues by holding an annual winter conference, and now schedules conferences in alternate years. The INEB's vision and strategy are clear enough:

1. Creating a variety of working groups to explore ways in which Buddhism can be applied in the search for new global paradigms.
2. Furthering INEB's resources to disseminate information on urgent action and human rights campaigns, training workshops, and for our understanding of this interdependent world.
3. Helping to develop workshops and qualified trainers at the grassroots level in various countries and regions.[12]

The INEB works closely with another of Sulak Sivaraksa's programs, founded in Thailand in 1995 and known as the Spirit in Education Movement. This program promotes an alternative, experiential education that addresses issues such as deep ecology and consumerism. In addition, the INEB runs an information network and has developed an extensive publishing program for the production of books and pamphlets. To stimulate a continually fresh flow of ideas, the INEB began a project known as Think Sangha, which in 1992 emerged out of a small circle of activists called the Buddhism and Social Analysis Group, which sought to network with many scholar-activists in producing Buddhist models for effective social action. Functioning like a think tank but based on a Buddhist *sangha* model, this group has held international meetings as a means of calling attention to its attempt to integrate Buddhist moral values into real-world activities in a fashion that moves beyond the abstract. The group's vision of *sangha* is forthrightly stated, too: "Our sense of 'sangha' is a community of people who interact, challenge, and support one another in the spirit of transformation."[13]

The most ambitious program of the BPF is its project called Buddhist Alliance for Social Engagement (BASE). It is predicated on its proponents' manifesting the bodhisattva's vow to save all beings through an active, aggressive agenda of social and personal transformation. The BASE program, first developed in the San Francisco Bay area but now spreading to other locations, revolves around six-month cycles of part-time or full-time commitment. In many respects, the program of training, meditation, and service mirrors the life of a Buddhist monk or nun in Asia but reflects the American Buddhist preference for a nonmonastic lifestyle. BASE participants may enroll full-time (working thirty hours per week in a placement, and thus becoming eligible for financial support) or part-time (working fifteen hours per week in a placement while they maintain their regular, outside employment), or they may work on a "job as placement" basis (for those who are already engaged in social-action work or who participate in the training component of the BASE program). The initial BASE training effort had eight participants, who combined social work with a rigorous Buddhist practice program.

The BASE program focuses on four major components: (1) social action (*sevā,* in Pali); (2) retreat and training (*paññā*); (3)commitment (*adiṭṭhāna*); and (4) community (*sangha*). The social action component requires fifteen to thirty hours of work each week in a service or social-justice organization. Program organizers attempt to match candidates' skills, backgrounds, and interests closely with the organization in which participants are placed. To date, placements have involved hospice work with the Zen Hospice Project, support work at the Women's Cancer Resource Center, working at a local San Francisco health clinic for homeless persons, providing assistance to Bay Area antinuclear and environmental groups, and working in one of the urban community garden projects in the Bay Area.

The core of the BASE program is its retreat and training component. Training revolves around:

1. Comprehensive study of the roots of engaged Buddhism and its current manifestations.
2. General Dharma teachings and practice.
3. Applications of Buddhist practice to the daily experience of social action.
4. Buddhist-based group dynamics.

The retreat aspect of the program includes:

1. Twice-weekly gathering of meditation/study/discussion on issues of socially engaged Buddhism.
2. Monthly retreats (1–5 days).
3. Opportunity for dialogue and study with activists and thinkers.
4. Mentorship with local Buddhist activists providing ongoing spiritual guidance and support.[14]

The commitment aspect of the program requires each BASE participant to take on a full six-month obligation to the program, during which time the volunteer will work diligently at Dharma study, Buddhist practice, and social action. Finally, the *sangha,* or community, component provides a contextual basis in which to frame these three areas of work. In this respect, all participants in the BASE program are linked to the entire Bay Area Buddhist community, construed as broadly as possible.

Like most stable Buddhist communities, the BPF publishes a journal, known as *Turning Wheel.* It is offered on a quarterly basis, with individual issues corresponding to the seasons. Currently edited by Susan Moon, it is organized into three primary parts. The first section consists of "regular departments," which include letters; Buddhist readings; columns on ecology, Buddhist activists in history, family practice, and the like; news from the chapters; announcements and classifieds; and a director's report. The second section, the heart of the journal, includes a series of articles on a particular theme. Recent thematic issues have focused on sexual misconduct, home and homelessness, family, hatred, cities, health and health care, and weapons. Additionally, *Turning Wheel* ran a special feature on the BASE program in its winter 1996 issue, in which Diana Winston and Donald Rothberg wrote extended statements, with several other participants writing brief statements, about their experiences in the program. The third section features reviews of books on topics of interest to the BPF. Books can range from the critically important *Engaged Buddhist Reader,* edited by Arnold Kotler, to the pleasant but highly pertinent *That's Funny, You Don't Look Buddhist: On Being a Faithful Jew and a Passionate Buddhist* by Sylvia Boorstein. The journal's prose is also interspersed with occasional pieces of art and poems, all credited in the table of contents. Although it can hardly rival more popular Buddhist publications, having a circulation of only about six thousand, *Turning*

Wheel is one of the most balanced and equitable Buddhist publications in print. It cuts across tradition and sectarian barriers in its attempt to stimulate useful dialogue and social activism—a continuing testament to the mission of the BPF. The BPF also maintain an Internet discussion group (bpf-ineb) that addresses all aspects of socially engaged Buddhism; although the list is administered by Alan Senauke, it is unmoderated.

By any standard of assessment, the Buddhist Peace Fellowship is a most unusual Buddhist community. It owes allegiance to no one teacher or tradition, draws freely from the Theravāda, Mahāyāna, and Vajrayāna schools of Buddhism, emphasizes free choice of Buddhist lifestyle, and has no elaborate Dharma center or temple that functions as its home base of operations. In fact, its facility, located on the very outskirts of a Berkeley schoolyard, has been rather purposefully excluded from this discussion. Surely any first-time visitor would be shocked, as I was, upon entering its cramped and humble quarters. It is perhaps best to identify the site as a creative exercise in utilitarian space management. Yet to spend one more word on the national headquarters of the BPF would entirely miss the point of the remarkable and crucial work marshaled by this selfless group of Buddhist activists. With merely the help of some up-to-date information-exchange technology, the BPF is making a powerful impact for peace from this tiny office. And in so doing, the BPF is incredibly efficient in demonstrating the full extent of what a nontraditional *sangha* can accomplish when wisdom and compassion are combined with healthy doses of energy and motivation.

When I visited the BPF late in the morning on 18 December 1996, Alan Senauke's welcome was warmer and friendlier than I had any right to expect from someone with such a frenzied schedule. After showing me around the BPF office and introducing me to the various staff members in residence, we compared schedules for the day and made plans to meet at his home for tea in the afternoon. Following a quick tour of some of the prominent Buddhist locations in Berkeley and a visit to the Institute of Buddhist Studies, I arrived at Alan Senauke's home alongside the Berkeley Buddhist Zen Center. In no time at all we were sitting in his study, tea in hand, talking about a wide variety of topics ranging from the BPF's mission to our abiding concern for the ways in which Buddhist ethics might apply to modern American society. Once I noticed the computers in his study, our discussion shifted to the way in which technology was changing the manner in which we shared information and communicated with Buddhists in other communities and on other continents. Although the *Journal of Buddhist Ethics,* which I coedit, is essentially a scholarly, academic journal, whereas the BPF uses the World Wide Web to promote its mission as a fellowship of meditating activists, we were unable to avoid conspiring a bit on how these two well-known resources might mutually reinforce one another in publicizing common causes and concerns for all Buddhists. Although we had never previously met, the two hours flew by. We talked about our children and families, how our respective lives as scholar-practitioner and priest-scholar were received in the communities in which we resided, and what projects we hoped to develop in the future. In the midst of our rambling conversation, Alan's family returned home and, following a brief introduction, treated me with the warmth, kindness, and consideration that one might imagine for a long-standing friend. It was a remarkably more pleasant conclusion to my day than the beginning had been. When it came time for me to leave, Alan asked if I would like to see the Berkeley Buddhist Zen Center *zendō* before I departed. Alan's warm hospitality, and the photographs of the *zendō* that I took, remain my best memories of that trip.

Sōka Gakkai International–USA

Although Penn State University is rather isolated from Pennsylvania's major urban areas, prompting Indiana University basketball coach Bobby Knight to once (almost correctly) remark, "You can't get there from anywhere," local residents are fond of calling the area Happy Valley. One should not assume, however, that students who attend Penn State are any less sophisticated or intellectually gifted than their big-city counterparts. And when I arrived in Happy Valley in the early 1970s, its students showed the same hunger for meaningful, and often alternative, spirituality that was sweeping campuses across the country. A large part of that seeking and questing brought students to the study and practice of Buddhism, and the little community in central Pennsylvania that served as home to Penn State University was awash with Zen groups, *Tibetan Book of the Dead* study groups, and the like. But by 1975 it also had another informal group that I had never encountered before, whose followers claimed association with Nichiren Shōshū of America, a reasonably new American Buddhist group affiliated with the practice of Sōka Gakkai Buddhism in

Japan. I was immediately suspicious of this informal group for two primary reasons. First, it didn't fit either of the two stereotypes I had by that time developed for American Buddhism in the mid-1970s: Asian American ethnic Buddhists, or counterculture meditative types who followed some Zen rōshi or expatriate Tibetan guru. Second, they didn't practice the sort of "canonical" Buddhism that I had during my graduate studies come to think of as "proper" Buddhism. Instead, these practitioners were clean, and polite, and career oriented. They knew just where they were going and how they were going to get there. It was odd, and even a little threatening, because I surely didn't understand either them or their Buddhism.

At the time, Sōka Gakkai was where I felt furthest from the Buddhism I had studied or practiced, and my ambivalence toward this new group was apparent in two anecdotes I reported in *American Buddhism*. The first recounted the history of a young man who, after dropping out of Harvard University, embarked on a rather disappointing spiritual odyssey and was led back to the university only after discovering the "True Buddhism" of Nichiren Shōshū and the liturgical chanting that seemed to immediately put his life back on track. The second, and more dramatic, outlined the personal testimony of a local resident and student of mine, who explained in great detail to one of my classes the specific material benefits he obtained as a direct result of his chanting *Nam-myōhō-renge-kyō*.

As researchers often do, I conveniently omitted some of the accounts—those that might have painted a clearer, more objective, and even more accurate picture of this organization. Thus I omitted the story of another of my students named William Aiken. Inquisitive, articulate, and respectful, he had discovered Nichiren Shōshū like many of its other followers, and he was just as serious. He never manifested any bizarre behavior; he studied diligently, and left the university with degree in hand. Nearly two decades later he reappeared in my life when he telephoned one day, asking me if he might lecture at my seminar on American Buddhism. I was a little surprised that he remembered me, and thoroughly surprised that he knew what I was currently teaching. I didn't have to wait long for the explanation: his son was now attending Penn State, and since he was coming to visit his son, he thought he, as a long-standing American Buddhist practitioner, might also share some of his experiences with my students of American Buddhism. It was too good an opportunity to pass up. If he gave a weak performance, it would reinforce my old stereotypes, and if he gave a good performance, my students would benefit.

Following some preliminaries about Sōka Gakkai International–USA (SGI-USA), he went on to give a well-structured, informative, entirely lucid presentation of his organization's history, development, goals, and practices, and of how his personal involvement had made an immense and fulfilling difference in his life. He answered questions from the class astutely, thoroughly, in what I have come to recognize in the intervening years as his quiet but engaging manner. Bill Aiken is now a vice–general director of SGI-USA, and with his assistance I have come to know Virginia Straus and other staff members of the Boston Research Center for the 21st Century, a center devoted to peace-related issues founded by Sōka Gakkai International's president, Daisaku Ikeda, in 1993. As a result of my ongoing dialogue with Bill Aiken, Virginia Straus, and other SGI-USA members, I have discovered an entirely different Buddhist community than the one I thought I knew, and was alienated from, in the 1970s.

SGI-USA is one of three major American Buddhist organizations based on the teachings of Nichiren Daishōnin (1222–1282), a Japanese fisherman's son who founded a major school of Buddhism. Having first become a Tendai priest, he took the name Rencho and sought a way to harmonize Buddhist teachings into a single whole that would serve all people and not just the elite of Japanese society. By 1253 he had concluded that one Buddhist sūtra—the *Lotus-sūtra*—was the highest of all Buddhist teachings, and that the title itself, *myōhō-renge-kyō,* revealed the substance of the text's message. He adopted the name Nichiren (Sun-lotus), began to advocate chanting the title of the sūtra as the primary Buddhist practice, and disparaged the other forms of Buddhism as being insufficient for providing the highest truth in a period of decline (known as *mappō*). Although exiled as a result of his continual suggestions that Japan's then-current ways would lead to its eventual downfall, Nichiren persevered, ultimately gaining followers and disciples. Near the end of his life, Nichiren inscribed a scroll, known as the *Dai-Gohonzon,* which he regarded as the highest object of respect. This scroll contains the Chinese characters of what he considered to be the true invocation (*Nam-myōhō-renge-kyō*). His faithful followers would sit in front of the *Gohonzon* and engage in a practice known as *gongyō,* reciting the title of the text (known as the *daimoku*) reverentially, as well as a portion of the second chapter of the *Lotus-sūtra* (titled *Hōben,* and describing the inherent Buddha-nature in all sentient beings) and the entirety of the sixteenth chapter (titled *Juryō,* or the teaching that Buddhahood is attained from within rather than externally). The essence of Nichiren's teachings involves the interpenetration of faith, practice, and study, in which practice and study go hand in hand to deepen one's faith, while deepened faith allows more effective practice and study.

Nichiren left a large number of treatises and letters, many written during his periods of exile, and several hundred of these items have been preserved. Jane Hurst has organized what the Nichiren Shōshū priesthood considered to be his most important teachings into the helpful chronological chart shown in table 1.

Table 1 *The Five Major Writings of Nichiren Daishōnin*

Date	Writing	Thesis
16 July 1260	*Risshō Ankoku Ron (On Securing the Peace of the Land through True Buddhism)*	Declared that practice of a true life philosophy is the basis for securing happiness and attaining world peace
February 1272	*Kaimoku Shō (The Opening of the Eyes)*	Identified *Honzon* in terms of Person-Nichiren Daishōnin, the True Buddha
25 April 1273	*Kanjin-no Honzon Shō (On the Supreme Object of Worship)*	Declared the establishment of the true object of worship, the *Gohonzon,* in terms of law
10 June 1275	*Senji Shō (The Selection of the Time)*	Designated the time for the proper teaching, *Nam-myōhō-renge-kyō,* to be propagated in the time of *mappō*
21 July 1276	*Hō-on Shō (Requital for the Buddha's Favor)*	Stressed the importance of appreciation; clarified the Three Great Secret Laws (*sandai hiho*)

Hurst goes on to say:

This chart clearly outlines Nichiren's major teachings. In the *Kaimoku Shō,* Nichiren identifies himself as the True Buddha of the age of *Mappō,* the third and final stage of Buddhism, during which Śākyamuni Buddha's transient teachings have fallen away and the True Teachings are now available. There are Three Great Secret laws (*sandai hiho*) which pertain to the age of *Mappō.* One is the true object of worship, the *Dai-Gohonzon,* the *Hommon-no-*

Honzon. The second is the *Hommon-no-Kaidan,* the high sanctuary of True Buddhism, to be built in the age of *Mappō.* The third is the *Hommon-no-Daimoku,* the true invocation, *Nam-myōhō-renge-kyō.*[15]

In addition to engaging in personal practice, practitioners of Nichiren Buddhism are expected to work for world peace, a practice known as *kōsen-rufu.* One year following his death, Nichiren was given the title Daishōnin, or "great sage." More than thirty Nichiren sects developed, three of which (including SGI-USA, as noted above) have appeared in North America.

The three Nichiren groups in the United States are the Nichiren Shōshū, which has six temples on American soil run by Japanese priests, who supervise a variety of layman's groups, known as *hokkeko;* the Nichiren Buddhist Church of America, popular in the western United States among Asian Americans; and Sōka Gakkai International–USA, a layman's group with more than sixty community centers and a multiethnic membership. Collectively, these three groups claim well over 300,000 members. Because she has studied these communities for more than two decades, Hurst is perhaps the scholar most likely to be able to explain their success, especially with regard to non-Asians. She argues:

> The success of Nichiren Buddhism as an American religion spreading to non-Asians can be traced to three factors. First, Nichiren Buddhism has a strong practice center on the *Lotus Sūtra* at its core. This practice, with its emphasis on the individual's power to change his or her life for the better, resonates with the ethos of American culture and is so easily accessible to American practitioners. Second, Nichiren Daishōnin's Buddhism was spread to the United States starting in 1960 by the energetic, proselytizing layperson's group Soka Gakkai, later called Soka Gakkai International (SGI). Thus it is also a dynamic social movement. Third, the Buddhism founded in Nichiren's name has always carried the characteristics of its founder: stubborn insistence that its understanding is True Buddhism and that other Buddhist interpretations are wrong, a confrontational response to criticism, and a proud outsider status that attracts the disaffected.[16]

Irrespective of whether one affirms Hurst's postulates for the success of Nichiren Buddhism in America, its expansive growth in a short period remains an impressive testament to its appeal and the organizational skill of its U.S. groups.

Founded as the Value Creation Education Society (or Sōka Kyōiku Gakkai) by Tsunesaburo Makiguchi in 1930 in Japan, the organization installed Makiguchi as its first president in 1937. Makiguchi (1871–1944) worked diligently with his disciple Josei Toda (1900–1958) to promote and expand the horizons of the organization. Both Makiguchi and Toda were jailed for their refusal to compromise their beliefs and accept Shinto, which had been the state religion. Makiguchi died in prison, but Toda was eventually released in 1945 and installed as the second president of Nichiren Shōshū Sōka Gakkai on 3 May 1951. Following Toda's death in 1958, his closest disciple, Daisaku Ikeda (b. 1928), became the third president in 1960.

In 1960 Daisaku Ikeda became the first official of Sōka Gakkai to visit the United States, and by 1963 an American headquarters had been established by Masayasa Sadanaga, a Korean-born close disciple of Ikeda, who later changed his name to George Williams in an attempt to resonate more fully with the developing American character of the organization.[17] The organization's membership grew steadily throughout the 1960s, a trend largely attributable to an aggressive recruitment technique known as *shakubuku.* By the early 1970s Nichiren Shōshū of America (NSA), as it was then called, had a carefully implemented top-down organizational structure, with chapters in most major urban areas and an aggressive and impressive community outreach. Its commendable tolerance and openness made it especially popular with minority groups of all kinds, including the gay and lesbian communities. In their book *A Time to Chant: The Sōka Gakkai Buddhists in Britain,* Bryan Wilson and Karel Dobbelaere note:

> There is, then, an implicit permissiveness in Nichiren Shōshū Buddhism. Not only are there no objective criteria for judging conduct, but such judgments would be contrary to the spirit of the faith . . . Obviously, in practice, some patterns of behaviour are regarded as less than wholesome, less than satisfactory, if that can be said without becoming judgmental . . . Nonetheless, the emphasis on the individual and the need for him to take responsibility for his own life suggests that decisions and judgments about such matters are entirely his own affair. There is no community-supported social ethic with respect to concrete issues of this kind.[18]

In other words, as Wilson and Dobbelaere declare later in their work, "The majority of Nichiren members, like the majority of the public, adopt a situational ethic, in which circumstances, motives, goals, and intentions are taken into account in appraising good and evil."[19] The 9 January 1970 issue of *Life* magazine cited a membership of 200,000 for the group, and while this figure may be overstated, it is not excessively so.

Most early observers of Nichiren Shōshū of America found the NSA celebration of the American Bicentennial to be a very unusual and strategically clever activity, culminating in a "Spirit of '76" show staged on 4 July 1976 in Shea Stadium in New York City between games of a Mets doubleheader. In fact, Ikeda states very clearly that the organization's objectives include "working for peace by opposing all forms of violence and contributing to the welfare of humankind by pursuing humanistic culture and education."[20] His statement is mirrored in the published guidelines of SGI, which claim that the goals of its adherents are:

- To work for the prosperity of society by being good citizens who respect the culture, customs, and laws of each country;
- To promote humanistic culture and education based on the fundamental, humane principles of Buddhism; and
- To join our efforts for world peace, for instance, with those of the United Nations by supporting the spirit of its charter, thereby helping achieve our ultimate goal of the abolition of nuclear arms and universal renouncement of war.[21]

Although Sōka Gakkai claimed a membership of about 8 million families in Japan by 1990, all was not well within the organization. In order to rebuild Sōka Gakkai after World War II, Josei Toda had solicited the cooperation of the Nichiren Shōshū priests by vesting in them all ritual responsibility for weddings, funerals, and ceremonies. In addition, they maintain the head temple (Taiseki-ji) at the foot of Mount Fuji. Not long after the founding of Sōka Gakkai International, a long-smoldering conflict between the priesthood and the lay organization erupted into open confrontation and struggle. By 1980, many Nichiren Shōshū priests were demonstrating against Sōka Gakkai and calling upon SGI to remove Daisaku Ikeda from his new position as president of the organization. Following more than a decade of serious unrest, punctuated by charges and countercharges from each camp, Nichiren Shōshū in the early spring of 1991 "withdrew its recognition of President Ikeda as the sole person charged with the guidance of overseas members and revoked its existing policy of not recognizing any organization of overseas followers other than SGI."[22] The practical result of this action was that all Sōka Gakkai members were effectively excommunicated and thus denied access to all ritual functions performed by the priesthood. Additionally, SGI would no longer be allowed to sponsor pilgrimages to Taiseki-ji. Yet the SGI organization proved to be profoundly resilient, as is highlighted in Hurst's appraisal of the impact of the split:

To Soka Gakkai members, the split with the priesthood seems to be much less upsetting. The only ritual change in the way Soka Gakkai members practice Nichiren's Buddhism is that in their daily silent prayers they offer gratitude to Nikko Shōnin and Nichimoku Shōnin, the first successors to Nichiren, and no longer to the successive Nichiren Shōshū High Priests. Even before the excommunication occurred, Soka Gakkai had begun changing the character of the organization from an authoritarian paradigm with President Ikeda at the head—a lay version of the priestly authority structure—to a more democratic consensus-based organization.[23]

Currently, Sōka Gakkai International has grown into an association of seventy-six constituent organizations located throughout the world, with members in more than 120 countries. SGI-USA maintains a national headquarters in Santa Monica, California.

As noted above, SGI-USA has more than sixty community centers. They are located in approximately two-thirds of the fifty states, as well as the District of Columbia, Guam, and Puerto Rico. As one might imagine, the organizational structure is somewhat complicated. The basic organizational unit of SGI-USA is known as a "district." The districts are composed of smaller segments known as "units" and "groups." Moving upward, organizationally and geographically, one can identify larger units known as "chapters," "headquarters," "territories," and "joint territories," which encompass the regional and national design of SGI-USA. Administrative authority is generally based on length of practice and capability to teach others within the unit. Within the local units, activities are structured according to age and gender, and thus one finds a men's division, women's division, young men's division, and young women's division. Many activities are scheduled for the youngest members, emphasizing study groups, performance groups, and the like. This organizational structure is based on the parent unit in Japan.

As with any religious community, it is difficult to know with precision why people become involved in SGI-USA. The national organization maintains that "the majority of people who practice the Buddhism of Nichiren in the SGI-USA are introduced through a friend or an acquaintance who wants to share the benefits of their practice with others. A smaller number follow up on a newspaper or magazine article or a radio or television interview."[24] The former technique of aggressive *shakubuku* seems to have virtually evaporated in the 1990s, as Hurst confirms:

Recruitment is now based on preexisting relationships or social networks as well as social outreach. *Shakubuku* has been replaced theoretically by propagation based on putting the philosophy and ideals of Buddhism into action through changing one's own life and through secular activities for peace, culture, and education. This is seen by SGI as an expanding circle of compassion based on an interfaith model.[25]

Unfortunately, there is no North American counterpart to the useful sociological study carried out in the United Kingdom by Bryan Wilson and Karel Dobbelaere. And while such a study remains a desideratum on this continent, their findings with regard to the attraction of SGI and Nichiren's Buddhism are useful. Utilizing a well-constructed questionnaire, and with a 62 percent return from those individuals sampled, they have constructed a chart that maps not only the initial attraction of members, but also members' current attraction (see table 2).[26]

Table 2 *The Initial and Subsequent Attraction of SGI (%)*

Characteristic	Initial attraction	Current attraction	Change	Those whose initial attraction persisted[a]
Quality of members	37	14	−23	35
Practical benefits	19	18	−1	54
Character of organization	16	17	+1	64
Personal happiness and confidence	14	19	+5	68
Intellectual satisfaction	8	11	+3	75
Ethical motivation	3	18	+15	100
Social involvement	3	3	0	47
Total whose initial attraction persisted				53

[a]Indicates the proportion of those initially citing each characteristic as the source of what attracted them who persisted in citing that item as the source of their current attraction.

SGI-USA also maintains a "Culture Department," founded in 1990 and made up of members whose occupations involve academia, law, education, medicine, and the arts. The Culture Department sponsors a large variety of outreach programs intended for SGI-USA's own membership and the community in general. Some of these programs have been taken on the road as traveling exhibitions.

Because of his strong interest in world peace, President Ikeda has worked tirelessly in support of the United Nations Charter. In so doing, SGI has become an official nongovernmental organization of the United Nations. As a result, SGI-USA has played an integral role in working with various United Nations institutions, and in 1995 it sponsored a year-long series of activities to commemorate the fiftieth anniversary of the United Nations. This program, known as "UN 50," was highlighted by major events in San Francisco and New York.

As part of its educational mission, SGI-USA publishes a weekly newspaper, the *World Tribune,* and a monthly magazine, the *Seikyo Times.* It also maintains a bookstore near the national headquarters in Santa Monica. In addition, the SGI-USA World Wide Web page offers a mail-order online catalogue from which books, prayer beads, altar accessories, videos, and similar items can be purchased directly.

SGI-USA also maintains an educational institution known as Soka University of America. Founded in 1987 by President Ikeda and located in Calabasas, California, it is modeled on Japan's Soka University.[27] Soka University of America offers a variety of curricula including an M.A. program in second- and foreign-language education, a program in English as a second language for students from Japan, and noncredit foreign-language classes for American students. It also houses the Pacific Basin Research Center, as well as a botanical preserve and nursery. Soka University of America is in the midst of a twenty-five-year program that it hopes will establish it as a center for the study of Pan-Pacific cultures.

SGI-USA also supports the Boston Research Center for the 21st Century (BRC) in Cambridge, Massachusetts, founded in 1993 to promote dialogue between various scholars and social activists on peace-related issues. The center's executive director is Virginia Straus, a former urban-policy aide during Jimmy Carter's presidency. The BRC has sponsored a variety of conferences: on nonviolence (in 1993), the global ethic (at Columbia University in 1994), religion and ecology (a three-part conference series in 1997), and Buddhism in America (cosponsored with the Harvard Buddhist Studies Forum in 1997). In addition, the BRC has held a number of shorter programs and lectures, as well as a symposium titled "The Future of Democracy," which it cosponsored with the Fletcher School of Law and Diplomacy of Tufts University. The center has published two books, *A People's Response to Our Global Neighborhood* and *The United Nations and the World's Religions: Prospects for a Global Ethic;* moreover, a number of BRC programs are available on audiotape. The BRC also publishes a useful and informative newsletter.

The above information notwithstanding, if one mentions Sōka Gakkai in an audience of American Buddhists, one gets an immediate free-association response: "Chanting!" And with such high-profile celebrities as Tina Turner, Herbie Hancock, and Patrick Swayze also professing a commitment to Sōka Gakkai, SGI-USA's primary religious practice of chanting the *daimoku* is becoming widely known beyond American Buddhist circles. Why is this single practice so important among Sōka Gakkai practitioners? White and Dobbelaere explain:

> Chanting the *daimoku,* however, is the vital practice which effects release for the individual of his Buddha potential. Whilst the *sūtra* chapters purport to explain, or at least to indicate, the significance of *Nam-myōhō-renge-kyō,* it is chanting the invocation which is held to affect both the subjective state of consciousness of the believer and the objective circumstances of the environment in which he lives . . . In this Buddhist conception of salvation, chanting is important not only for producing material benefits and more spiritual attitudes of mind, but also because it is credited with changing the individual's destiny . . . By chanting *Nam-myōhō-renge-kyō* "the shackles of one's karma are progressively weakened until they are finally severed completely" . . . As we have already seen, chanting is believed to have its own internal potency, but it is in relation to the object of worship, the *Gohonzon,* that its operation is seen as most effective. It is this which leads the individual to acquire the capacity to observe his life in perspective and to glimpse his Buddha-nature at work.[28]

White and Dobbelaere argue that for British Buddhists, chanting and *gongyō* are the primary practice, while study and teaching others, although significant, are lesser priorities. Despite the lack of supporting empirical evidence, it appears that the same is true for members of SGI-USA. A similar argument can easily be made for the practice of pilgrimage to the sacred site of Taiseki-ji in Japan to worship at the original *Gohonzon*—a practice that, although important, attracted only about 27 percent of the British sample and was not a high priority when compared with chanting.[29] It is certainly difficult to quantify the regularity of chanting on the part of practitioners, but it is not unreasonable to assume that more than half of SGI-USA practitioners indeed manage to perform the roughly thirty-minute *gongyō* in both morning and evening, and that the regularity of practice becomes much more stable in long-standing members.

At the most basic level, Sōka Gakkai has not benefited from the invariably adverse publicity associated with reports of people chanting the *daimoku* purely for material benefits. Unfortunately, such reports dominated the early literature on the organization in America. More recently, this image has diminished. In the first article on Sōka Gakkai in *Tricycle* magazine, its author reports, "I had friends who started off chanting for cheaper drugs and free money. Like them, I treated the *Gohonzon* as a pimp. I wanted to see if chanting would work."[30] Nonetheless, if one reads further, the author describes a finally mature attitude: "But in front of the *Gohonzon* . . . I am left where I began; by myself, at my altar, conscious of a larger truth—that the Great Assembly of bodhisattvas described in the *Lotus Sūtra* is a reality taking place now, at every moment of our lives."[31] While it should be no surprise to learn that the two most frequent goals for chanting among British Buddhists were improved careers and better relationships, high percentages of this survey group also chanted for attitudinal changes, a better future, self-awareness, and similar issues. My informal questioning of American practitioners has produced a remarkably similar, if unscientific, response.

Does chanting work? Are the goals of chanting achieved for its proponents? No doubt it would be just as presumptuous to assume that it did *not* work as it would to believe all the positive testimony I have collected in the past two decades. It might be fairer to argue that irrespective of whether specific goals are attained, in very many cases strong and positive subjective changes can be witnessed in the behavior of individuals engaged in this Buddhist practice. In this way, attainment might be likened to the benefits of rituals and practices in other religious traditions. At the very least, it is *not* a passive activity. Coupled with the positive expectation of the practitioner, it allows him or her to proceed into the world with an attitudinal shift that is necessarily beneficial and productive. When projected outward from a current membership of more than 300,000, the potential impact of SGI-USA for implementing a Buddhist vision of wholeness and peace in America becomes highly significant.

The implementation of that vision, however, is not without hurdles to be surmounted. In chapter 6 I will examine a number of recent conferences devoted to the topic of the American Buddhist movement. One of them, held in Boston in January 1997, made it very clear that from one perspective—and a popular one at that—American Buddhism meant *meditative* Buddhism. In the final keynote address of the conference, the American lama Surya Das pointed to a variety of items that he felt would characterize the American Buddhism of the future millennium. He described a tradition that, among other qualities, was lay-oriented, promoted gender equality, affirmed social engagement, maintained an egalitarian approach to the Dharma, and was inquiry-based, simplified, and psychologically astute. All of these qualities might easily be found within SGI-USA. But he also argued that such a tradition would be *meditation-based,* thus effectively eliminating both SGI-USA and Buddhist Churches of America (addressed below). In many respects he was only mirroring Jack Kornfield's comments of a decade earlier, in which Kornfield identified the real practice of the Buddha with meditation.[32] In those terms, it would be possible to valorize the *sangha* of Zen Mountain Monastery as a community of meditators who also happened to place a great value on an active and aggressive process of social engagement in Buddhism. It would also be possible to take a similar position for the Buddhist Peace Fellowship as a *sangha* of meditating activists. Yet one fears that these individuals would not recognize the value and validity of SGI-USA as a *sangha* of chanting American Buddhists who are as committed to social engagement and other critical American Buddhist endeavors as any of the Buddhist groups emphasizing meditative practice.

Despite my own thirty-year involvement in meditative practice, I felt oddly alienated by what seemed to be the prevailing attitude of meditational superiority manifested in the sessions that I attended at the Boston conference. Although this was unplanned, I found myself increasingly in the company of Robert Eppsteiner, SGI-USA's director of public and academic affairs; Virginia Straus, executive director of the BRC; and Karen Nardella, events coordinator of the BRC. Although I suspect they were privately disappointed to have been summarily excluded from active participation in this major event, not a single word to that effect was uttered by them throughout the weekend. Instead, we discussed a wide variety of issues that we believed were relevant to the ongoing development of American Buddhism in the next century—primarily the role of the scholar-practitioner (to be discussed in chapter 4 below) and of the Internet (to be discussed in chapter 5). By the time the Harvard Buddhist Studies Forum took place in May 1997, cosponsored by the BRC, I was eager to see my new friends again. The conference (described in chapter 6 below) was exciting, with a wide variety of papers on American Buddhism. Following the session of Saturday, 24 May, a buffet dinner was scheduled at the BRC facility adjacent to the Harvard campus. As the conference participants were milling about prior to the dinner, a woman approached me and asked if I knew her. Upon my confessing that I didn't, she identified herself as Amy Morgante, a former student of mine of from Penn State. Following her graduation, she had moved ahead into the mainstream of her life, marrying and beginning a family, *and* coming to work as the publications coordinator for the BRC. To cover my embarrassment over my lapsed memory, I related to her the story of Bill Aiken that I mentioned at the outset of this chapter. In the midst of my spontaneous but nervous storytelling, Virginia Straus appeared and asked when Penn State would be sending its next batch of graduates to assume leadership positions in SGI-USA. Although spoken in jest, her comment reminded me of those times not so very long ago when I would have dismissed such a request at once. Now, impressed by the maturity of what I'd been learning, I promised myself to stay on the lookout.

Buddhist Churches of America

In *American Buddhism,* I chose Buddhist Churches of America as the first group to present in the portion of the volume devoted to case studies of American Buddhist communities. I chose it for that position simply and primarily because it had the longest history of any Buddhist group on American soil. It had recently celebrated its seventy-fifth anniversary on this continent, and at the outset of the chapter I cited President Gerald Ford's congratulatory message to the group on that fortuitous occasion. In the end, however, I concluded that although the Shin tradition in America had a fine chance of becoming masterfully transnational, most of what I had found hinted and even suggested that such a result was unlikely. The basis for that conclusion was the yardstick of acculturation, which I applied rather indiscriminately to all Buddhist groups presented in my study. I presumed that for Buddhist groups to take root and blossom in America, they must abandon their ethnic heritage and become "fully American," whatever that odd term might have meant at the time. In other words, I neither anticipated nor understood what Paul Numrich was later going to call "parallel congregations" (see chapter 6 below). Equally, I had no appreciation of how ethnic Buddhist communities contributed generously to the rich diversity that was developing in American Buddhism. Unfortunately, I began to properly learn about the contributions of ethnic American Buddhist groups only *after* the publication of

American Buddhism, with my most recent lessons having been precipitated in an odd way.

In 1992 I received a telephone call from Rick Fields, with whom I had compared notes on American Buddhism during the first summer of Naropa Institute in 1974. We had communicated only minimally in the intervening years, so his call caught me somewhat by surprise. He was inquiring as to whether I might be willing to write an article for the then fledgling magazine *Tricycle* on the relationship of, and potential division between, ethnic American Buddhism and Euro-American Buddhism. As an early subscriber to *Tricycle,* I was delighted, so when the formal invitation was later offered, I eagerly accepted. Although I had not written much on American Buddhism in the years immediately prior to this invitation, I still maintained a thorough network of informants, and my initial inquiries quickly led me to Ryo Imamura, an eighteenth-generation Jōdo Shinshū priest who also happened to be a psychology professor at Evergreen State College in Washington. Imamura, it seems, had become disturbed by Helen Tworkov's editorial "Many Is More," published in the winter 1991 issue of *Tricycle.* In that editorial, Tworkov said: "The spokespeople for Buddhism in America have been, almost exclusively, educated members of the white middle class. Meanwhile, even with varying statistics, Asian-American Buddhists number at least one million, but so far they have not figured prominently in the development of something called American Buddhism."[33] In a spirit of open exchange and debate, Imamura wrote a letter to the editor (dated 25 April 1992) outlining his dissent. It said:

> I would like to point out that it was my grandparents and other immigrants from Asia who brought and implanted Buddhism in American soil over 100 years ago despite white intolerance and bigotry. It was my American-born parents and their generation who courageously and diligently fostered the growth of American Buddhism despite having to practice discreetly in hidden ethnic temples and in concentration camps because of the same white intolerance and bigotry. It was us Asian Buddhists who welcomed countless white Americans into our temples, introduced them to the Dharma, and then often assisted them to initiate their own Sanghas, when they felt uncomfortable practicing with us . . . We Asian Buddhists have hundreds of temples in the United States with active practitioners of all ages, ongoing educational programs that are both Buddhist and interfaith in nature, social welfare projects . . . everything that white Buddhist centers have and perhaps more. It is apparent that Tworkov has restricted "American Buddhism" to mean "white

American Buddhism," and that her statement is even more misleading than one claiming that Americans of color did not figure prominently in the development of American history.[34]

This letter was never printed in *Tricycle*. Nor was my related article, "Two Buddhisms Reconsidered," nor one on a similar topic by Patricia Wong Hall. Eventually, I learned that Ryo Imamura's father, Enryo Imamura, had been the resident minister of the Berkeley Buddhist Church for many years, and it was this Jōdo Shinshū temple that was often a gathering place for "Beat Buddhists," including the later-famous Gary Snyder. Over the years, Ryo and Gary Snyder became friends, and it was in this context that Ryo kept Snyder informed about his letter-writing debacle with *Tricycle,* as well as that journal's rejection of my article (which Snyder had by that time read). Following the exchange of a series of letters between the three of us, Snyder resigned from the board of advisers of *Tricycle* (in a letter dated 18 June 1993), citing its rejection of Ryo's letter and my article as his basis for doing so. In the process of these discussions, and as a result of my continuing conversations with Ryo Imamura, I learned far more about the contributions of Jōdo Shinshū to American Buddhism than I had known previously.

Whether motivated by Snyder's little-known resignation from the board of advisers or not, *Tricycle* eventually addressed the issue. The fall 1994 issue was devoted to the topic "Dharma, Diversity, and Race." It contained a variety of articles by black poet bell hooks, Japanese Scottish Shin practitioner Addie Foy, Japanese Canadian Zen priest Victor Sōgen Hori, and other people of color. Sandwiched between these features was Rick Fields's "Confessions of a White Buddhist," at least some portion of which might fairly be called a Pure Land apologetic. Nonetheless, Fields's concluding words make a good beginning point for a reconsideration of the contribution of Buddhist Churches of America to the American Buddhist movement: "If we could drop all our self-striving for enlightenment we could see what is right in front of our eyes and nose: with nothing to define and no one to define it, a many-colored, multicultured, pluralistic Pure Land with room enough for all."[35]

The history of Buddhist Churches of America has been amply documented in American Buddhist literature, and capsulized in chapter 1 above.[36] By the time Revs. Shuye Sonoda and Kakuryo Nishijima arrived in San Francisco on 1 September 1899, as the first official missionaries of Honpa Honganji, there were ten thousand Japanese immigrants in the

United States.[37] Tetsuden Kashima points out that as early as 1877 a Protestant mission church was established in San Francisco, not only to aid those immigrants who had converted to Christianity while in Japan but also to proselytize among new immigrants in America.[38] Thus it cannot be blindly assumed that all Japanese immigrants were Buddhists, and that Revs. Sonoda and Nishijima had a ready-made congregation waiting for their arrival. They were preceded, however, by Revs. Eryu Honda and Ejun Miyamoto, who had visited San Francisco the previous year on a fact-finding tour and had established the *Bukkyō Seinen Kai* or Young Men's Buddhist Association (YMBA), which eventually became the Buddhist Church of San Francisco. By 1914, with many Shin "churches" in existence, the overall Buddhist organization was renamed the Buddhist Mission of North America (BMNA), a title that would remain until the organization took its present name, Buddhist Churches of America, in 1944.

Whereas legislation had been passed in California (the Anti-Alien Land Laws of 1913 and 1920) to restrict farmlands managed by the Japanese, the Japanese Immigration Exclusion Act of 1924 was designed to completely stop further Japanese immigration. Despite these attempts to limit Japanese immigrants, by 1931 there were thirty-three churches affiliated with the BMNA. Although the churches proliferated, and a Young Women's Buddhist Association (YWBA) was created to mirror its male counterpart, there was an obvious problem in meeting the needs of the English-speaking Nisei members of the temples. Because the temples were largely oriented toward the Issei, who also controlled the policy and decision making of the temples, and with a Japanese-speaking clergy, there were few growth opportunities for the youthful members of the temples. But because the temples were beginning to create Sunday "Dharma schools" for the children, they needed an English-speaking clergy to properly administer these programs. In 1929 a foundation was established for the propagation of American Buddhism, and when Rev. Kenju Masuyama was appointed *sōchō,* or "bishop," in 1930, he began an aggressive program to find English-speaking Nisei candidates for the BMNA ministry. Rev. Masuyama's English-language ministerial program never had a chance to fully develop, as it was truncated by the outbreak of World War II.

By the beginning of the 1940s, most Japanese immigrants had accepted their status in North America as permanent. As Kashima notes, however, it was not an easy allegiance:

This is not to say that the Issei ever felt at home or at ease in America. This was an adopted country, but they knew that the adoption was only one-way; America had often indicated to them their impermanent status. But the familial ties with the American Nisei, the economic ties to their occupations and farmlands, the social ties to the community, the psychological ties, binding the group together through suffering and endurance of anti-Japanese prejudice, were all factors in keeping them in America.[39]

The horrifying record of Japanese American internment during World War II is widely known. Because the San Francisco BMNA residents were incarcerated at the Topaz Relocation Center in Utah, the headquarters of the organization was reestablished there. Between February and April 1944, a number of meetings for ministers and lay representatives were held under the guidance of Bishop Ryotai Matsukage, eventually resulting in a decision (finally approved at a meeting on 29 April) to change the organization's name from the Buddhist Mission of North America to Buddhist Churches of America (BCA), and to incorporate in California. By mid-June an election of officers had been held, and a board of trustees, including two representatives from Topaz and each of five other camps, was in place. Before the last of the relocation camps had been officially closed (on 2 January 1946), BCA's articles of incorporation were already in place.

The West Coast was reopened for resettlement by Japanese Americans in January 1945, and by fall 1945 the BCA national headquarters had been reestablished at the Octavia Street location in San Francisco that had been home to the BMNA since 1937. Resettlement occupied most of BCA's efforts in the initial months and years following the war, but by the mid-1950s most previous temples were recovering, and by 1960 new Shin congregations had been formed in Chicago, Cleveland, Detroit, Minneapolis, and Washington, D.C.[40] Thirty years later, BCA could boast sixty-one temples.[41] Bishop Matsukage died in June 1948. He was replaced by the former minister of the Fresno Buddhist Church, Enryo Shigefuji, who was elected by the BCA ministers, representing a change from the previous mode of appointing bishops. In addition to beginning study classes in Berkeley, Bishop Shigefuji promoted the publication of two newspapers, *Horin* (begun in 1956) and the *American Buddhist* (started in 1957). A special-projects fund was also started in 1956. Upon the death of Bishop Shigefuji, Shinsho Hanayama succeed him, serving until 1968. It was during the tenure of Bishop Hanayama that BCA established the Institute of Buddhist Studies (on 1 October 1966), first located at 2717

Haste Street in Berkeley; the institute became associated with the Graduate Theological Union in 1985 and moved to its current location on Addison Street in Berkeley in 1987.

Following Bishop Hanayama's retirement in 1968, BCA selected Kenryu T. Tsuji as its new bishop, marking the first time a Canadian-born Nisei would head the organization. Bishop Tsuji was elected for a three-year term. While he was in office the election rules were modified, with Bishop Tsuji being reelected twice for five-year terms. In 1981 he was succeeded by Bishop Seigen Yamaoka, who was reëlected in 1986. The current bishop is Hakubun Watanabe. The clear intent during this succession of bishops and the concurrent developmental growth in BCA was for the organization to retain

the ideas of Buddhism at its core. The aim was to make Buddhism more acceptable, more understandable, more inclusive of all Buddhist thoughts, as well as less sectarian, less restrictive in membership, and more adaptable to the changing needs of the Nisei and Sansei. The Buddhists in America desired to lift, for the Nisei and their children, the veil of foreignness cast over their religion by the language and customs of the Issei. The predominant language was to be English, not Japanese, and the changes would aid in conveying the religion to the Nisei and Sansei.[42]

Perhaps the simplest manner of measuring the success of that intent is to examine some of the demographic data collected by leading Shin researchers. In 1977 Tetsuden Kashima provided the following statistics:[43]

Table 3 *BCA Membership Statistics, 1931–1972*

	1930	1936	1942	1960	1972
Family membership	11,852	14,388	n/a	10,000	14,008
Estimated total membership	35,000	43,164	46,289	50,000	43,476

Alfred Bloom updates Kashima's data with more recent information, citing 21,600 families and approximately 65,000 members in 1977, and 16,925 families and about 50,775 members in 1995.[44] Bloom further indicates a decline in ministers, ranging from a peak of 123 in 1930 to 71 in 1981, and a decline in Dharma-school enrollment, from a high of 7,500 in 1940 to 3,045 in 1993.[45]

It would be overly simplistic to argue that the decline in membership, number of ministers, and Dharma-school enrollment has resulted purely from BCA's lack of engaging in systematic proselytizing, both inside and outside the Japanese American community. By 1973, for example, BCA had an organizational and legislative structure quite similar to that of other developing Buddhist communities in North America.[46] In addition, BCA has had both direct and indirect financial support from the Buddhist Promoting Society (or *Bukkyō Dendō Kyōkai*) launched by Rev. Dr. Yehan Numata in December 1965. Rev. Numata, the founder of Japan's Mitutoyo Manufacturing Company, began a variety of projects on a worldwide basis, funded with his own assets. In spring 1982 he reestablished the publication of *Pacific World* (briefly published between 1925 and 1928) as the journal of the Institute of Buddhist Studies (IBS). Moreover, upon celebrating the fiftieth anniversary of Mitutoyo Corporation, he established the Numata Center for Translation and Research in Berkeley under the direction of Rev. Seishin Yamashita, and endowed chairs at a variety of North American and European universities including the University of California at Berkeley and the IBS. He has also erected Jōdo Shinshū temples in Washington, D.C.; Düsseldorf, Germany; and Mexico City. In trying to unravel the perplexing problem of overall BCA decline, Kashima presents three interesting chapters in his book *Buddhism in America* that address the problem in detail: "Evolution of the American Priesthood"; "The Role of the Buddhist Church in the Ethnic Adjustment of the Japanese American"; and "Pressure on the American Buddhist Church toward Denominationalism."[47] Although comprehensive in scope, none of these is as explicit as Alfred Bloom's succinct explanation:

> In the immigrant situation, the family system and its coordinate respect for authority supported the cohesiveness of the family and the ethnic community as a whole, stressing social responsibility and obedience to the law . . . There is, consequently, a disposition to be conformist, unquestioning, and prudent. This tendency has given rise to the terms *quiet Americans* or *model minority* which, though seemingly positive, have negative implications and undermine a Japanese American critique of society . . . Despite the popularity and seeming interest in, and attraction to, Buddhism by non-Japanese, Buddhist temples established by the immigrants have few members of other races. In such circumstances racial homogeneity, reinforced by language and culture, has made it difficult for outsiders to enter the Buddhist tradition . . . The appeal to be Shin simply because one is Japanese or out of some family loyalty has proven inadequate to stem the loss of adherents or to maintain the vitality of the community. Consequently, in contemporary America, Shin Buddhism is attempting, through such facilities as the Institute of Buddhist Studies,

gradually to develop its own well-defined form and position within the environment of Western culture.[48]

More recently, some creative and unusual suggestions have been offered that not only stress the possibility of adapting Jōdo Shinshū for a wider, Western, audience but also attempt to integrate the Shin religious practice of expressing faith in the saving grace of Amida Buddha into a more integral, less otherworldly framework more in step with American culture. In their article "Adapting the Jōdo-Shinshū Teaching for the West: An Approach Based on the American Work Ethic," Gordon L. Fung and Gregory Fung argue that the key to developing an American audience for Jōdo Shinshū is based on understanding the interrelationship of Shin's teachings about "self-power" (*jiriki*), "other power" (*tariki*), and faith (*shinjin*) in the context of what they term the "American work ethic."[49] For them, the American work ethic comprises three essential elements: (1) individual choice; (2) individual action; and (3) individual reward. They consider the possibility of combining Shin teaching and the American work ethic, and come to the following conclusions:

> A. The concept of (1) individual choice may be addressed by extrapolating from classical Jōdo-Shinshū teaching . . . In the present context it can be understood from the standpoint of individual choice that each of us can choose between virtuous actions and non-virtuous actions. Moreover, the classical discussion is firm evidence that choosing virtue over non-virtue is the appropriate decision for all Jōdo-Shinshū practitioners, new and old. The concept of post-*shinjin* activity done in gratitude to Amida and for the benefit of all further emphasizes the idea that there is a role for deliberately choosing a virtuous path in everyday decisions . . . For Jōdo-Shinshū teaching in America, an elaboration of this approved form of individual choice would provide direct and useful instruction for the beginning practitioner.
>
> B. With respect to (2) individual action it is evident that our knowledge of past activities are in the description of the deeds of these various models . . . Using the role-model approach, individuals may study how one who has fully accepted Amida's compassion resolves and carries through with actions that benefit all . . . These case studies would serve as additional guidelines for those trying to make decisions and act on the compassionate principle of benefitting all mankind. Using the model of the American Work Ethic, each individual action is the culmination of having made the decision to pursue a plan of action based upon the evaluation of options.

C. In the area of (3) individual rewards we can again look to the life of Shinran and others as the recipients of Amida's unconditional compassion . . . In each effort to better apply those principles is received the reward of a deeper experience with respect to demonstrating to one's self that Amida's teachings apply to present day circumstances.[50]

How does all this work to make Shin attractive to Americans? The authors go on to say:

For Jōdo-Shinshū in America, further elaboration on this form of individual reward for individual actions is necessary to provide a complete understanding of Jōdo-Shinshū for an American audience. Initiating such contact speaks directly to the propensities of the American Work Ethic, where choice, action, and rewards are so everywhere evident. As empathy is a significant aspect of compassion, it becomes clear that the message of Jōdo-Shinshū must begin to empathize with the different cultural context of present day American audiences. Appreciating the foundations of this American point of view as in part defined by the American Work Ethic is a first step in that empathetic appreciation. Through a thorough understanding of their bias towards individual choice, action, and rewards, it becomes clearer how the message of Jōdo-Shinshū teaching must be adapted in order to be accepted by Americans.[51]

Though the above argument is undeniably interesting, I think it is also unconvincing. Apart from sounding too much like a thinly veiled Shin apologetic designed to make the Pure Land tradition sound like American Christianity or Judaism, and while seriously underestimating the complexity of American religiosity, it fails to suggest how Shin bridges the experiential gap from sympathetic understanding to eager participation and conversion. A more informed vision of BCA's future in America necessarily lies elsewhere.

Just prior to the turn of the millennium, BCA will celebrate its centennial. It continues to face an obviously uncertain future, not altogether different from the one about which I commented in 1979: "As the issei (first generation) members of the congregation die, Buddhist Churches of America cannot seem to decide whether to follow the general wishes of the nisei members (second generation) and Americanize more fully, or honor the wishes of the clergy (and many young members) and reassert their Japanese heritage."[52] More importantly, those closest to the situation, and most informed, seem to be gradually gravitating to the conclusion that acculturation or adaptation holds the key to BCA success in

America. Tetsuden Kashima, whose 1977 sociological study remains our most reliable source of data on BCA, sees this uncertain future in terms of two interpenetrating series of challenges.[53] The first emerges from internal sources, and includes: (1) a decreasing, changing membership; (2) the almost exclusively Japanese American ethnic identity of the membership; (3) economic problems encountered by the member BCA temples; (4) finding the proper techniques for teaching Shin Buddhism in America; and (5) problems within the BCA ministry. Juxtaposed against the internal challenge is the external one, which Kashima links to America's developing civil religion. Robert Bellah offers a seductive argument for civil religion as a reasonable umbrella under which all Buddhists, even ethnic American Buddhists, might stand. This argument is furthered by historians of American religion as well, such as C. Conrad Cherry and Martin Marty. As a sociologist, Kashima is, not surprisingly, somewhat persuaded by Bellah's seminal work on this topic, but he eventually concludes that, because Buddhism continues to find itself outside the mainstream religious traditions in America and the symbols common to them, it does not benefit from the collective religious consciousness that forms the foundation of America's civil religion. Despite Bellah's claim that "the publicly institutionalized civil religion must remain as symbolically open or empty as possible,"[54] intending not to exclude groups who did not share in overspecific symbols, Kashima rightly points out that for Buddhists, the presumed separation of church and state does not obtain. But in the end Kashima accedes, stating in 1993:

> The BCA should strengthen its effort to maintain a strong Buddhist sangha in America by de-emphasizing its ethnic character. Because the Constitution decrees a separation of church and state, each American is guaranteed the right to practice any religion that an individual desires. But the reality of the situation for religious freedom is muted by the existence of America's civil religion. A covert and subtle influence toward making Buddhism conform to Judeo-Christian tenet and belief is pervasive and strongly felt. Whether and how this external challenge is recognized and met by BCA will affect its future.[55]

Two years later, Alfred Bloom was more direct in arriving at the same conclusion:

> Shin Buddhism is at a crossroads in the West. We must encourage our youth, not simply to replicate the past that we knew, but to chart new paths in the

new age. Through the youth we must enter the information age and begin to think of Shin Buddhism without borders, beyond ethnic and language differentiations. We must become an educating community that opens the minds of our members, our youth, our world.[56]

And in 1997 Kenneth Tanaka continued the same argument in "Issues of Ethnicity in Buddhist Churches of America," an address he delivered at the Harvard Buddhist Studies Forum. Collectively, these three Shin scholars seem to invest their trust for the future of BCA in a combination of interreligious dialogue and borrowing, and a climate of productive religious pluralism.

In the fall of 1994, the Institute of Buddhist Studies devoted that year's Numata Lecture Series to the topic "Buddhisms in America: An Expanding Frontier." Carefully organized by Kenneth Tanaka, it offered more than a dozen lectures by well-known scholars on various aspects of American Buddhism. On Monday, 12 September, I was to give the keynote lecture, entitled "The Development of American Buddhism: Two Overviews." It was to be a rather loosely structured "then and now" retrospective that would set the stage for the specific topics of the remaining speakers. Following our return from a leisurely dinner in one of the many restaurants near the IBS, Tanaka suggested that I "hang out" for about forty-five minutes prior to my lecture while he went into the room in which the lecture would be held and led a Shin service. On any other occasion I would have joined the service as a quiet spectator, but I was more than a little uneasy about delivering the first of a series of lectures on what I believed to be the newest subdiscipline of Buddhist Studies. And while I believed strongly in my position, I wasn't at all sure that many others shared my conviction. Nonetheless, during the time between Tanaka's departure and my beginning, I couldn't help but steal a glance or two at the Shin congregation gathered at the IBS. It was almost exclusively Japanese American, although an occasional Caucasian face could be glimpsed. Soon my wait was over, and my lecture began. Looking around the room of approximately 150 attendees, I saw an incredibly diverse group of listeners, mostly Caucasian, many of whom I could identify with specific non-Shin American Buddhist communities. I began a sort of makeshift mental scorecard that, by the end of my lecture, included Zen practitioners from at least two lineages, several *vipassanā* practitioners, a disciple of Chögyam Trungpa Rinpoche, and a Chinese nun. It was what my former mentor Richard Robinson called "a Buddhist zoo." But it was fun; the questions were exciting, and the dialogue was warm and filled with a special kind of collective Buddhist sharing. Although held in a Shin-supported institute, this was no purely ethnic gathering. It was as effective an ecumenical outreach program as one could imagine—one that joined the ethnic Japanese American and Euro-American Buddhist communities in a manner that was very profound and mutually enhancing.

When the lecture was over and I headed off for a couple of drinks with several members of the audience, I kept thinking back to the books and articles by Tetsuden Kashima and Alfred Bloom on Shin Buddhism and BCA that I had been reading. Although each author cited BCA efforts to include non-Japanese ministers in the community—dating back to Alex White, who, in 1940–41, became the first pioneer in this effort, and several women ministers such as Sunya Pratt, June King, Rebecca MacDonald, and others—the overall recruitment of non-Japanese ministers has not been effective. Creative experiments were employed, too, with varying degrees of success. Rev. Kenneth O'Neill began an outreach program in the early 1970s, extending Jōdo Shinshū beyond the "regular" temple membership, but it was discontinued in 1982. Later, Rev. Koshin Ogui created a parallel organizational structure in the Cleveland Buddhist Church, with services conducted in Japanese for the Japanese American community and in English for the non-Japanese. Despite the success of the program in Cleveland, Rev. Ronald Nakasone noted that "no other temple within the BCA has been as successful in bringing non-Japanese into the Jodo Shinshu fold."[57] To summarize: in nearly one hundred years on American soil, BCA has not attracted a significant membership or clergy from beyond the Japanese American community. Thus one wonders whether Bloom and Kashima are asking BCA to be something it is not, will likely never be, and possibly should not be. Perhaps it would be more constructive for BCA, without isolating itself, to continue to offer a meaningful and comprehensive experience of Shin Buddhism in America for those who wish to partake of it, irrespective of ethnic heritage. During the evening described above, BCA was fine just the way it was: an important and integral bit of fabric in the weave of American Buddhism.

Hsi Lai Temple

In the previous section on Buddhist Churches of America, I pointed out that the *Bukkyō Dendō Kyōkai,* or Buddhist Promoting Society, funded by Rev. Dr. Yehan Numata, endowed a series of chairs at various universities throughout the world. During fall 1993, when I held the visiting Numata Chair in Buddhist Studies at the University of Calgary, my major academic responsibility was to teach a graduate seminar on American Buddhism. Although most of the students in the seminar had only a modicum of training in Buddhist Studies, they were a talented and inquisitive group of individuals, and, given the rich Buddhist tradition that had developed in southern Alberta, I looked forward to the semester.

Despite the fact that there were fewer academic resources on American Buddhism available then, during the first several weeks the seminar moved ahead at a brisk pace, using Rick Fields's *How the Swans Came to the Lake* as one of the primary textbooks. Within a month I began coaxing my students into finalizing plans for their research papers, and set aside an hour of class time for each student to share his or her topic with the group. This sophisticated version of show-and-tell went smoothly enough at the outset. One student planned a paper titled "Zen and the Art of John Cage"; another was working on "Nichiren Shōshū: The Success of an American Oral Subculture"; a third proposed "Searching for the Buddha: Imagination and Landscape in Canadian Buddhist Identity." Just as I was about to congratulate myself for evoking such a group of inspiring topics, one student suggested "Hui Shan and the Possibility of Pre-Columbian Transpacific Contacts." Stunned, I blurted out: "Why did you choose that?" He indicated that he was not especially interested in American Buddhism at all, but that the course fit his schedule properly, so he intended to make his research as painless as possible; and he added that he felt this to be a much better choice than studying some current Buddhist groups that he thought were mostly crazy anyway! As a strong proponent of the value of studying the current Buddhist situation in North America, I wasn't terribly excited by the prospect of reading thirty-five pages devoted to the theory that a Chinese Buddhist monk named Hui Shan, along with a group of five fellow monks, in 458 C.E. journeyed to a country called Fu-sang, which was eventually presumed (by Joseph de Guignes in 1761) to be Mexico.

This student's choice of topic was an important wake-up call, though. While other students were interested in visiting the Chùa Bát Nhã Vietnamese Pagoda in Calgary or the Jōdo Shin community just to the south in Lethbridge, this student reminded me that there was a long and important Chinese Buddhist tradition on this continent that had been far too often overlooked, and especially so by me. In *American Buddhism* I included a chapter on the Sino-American Buddhist Association, an extremely rigorous group associated with Ven. Tripiṭaka Master Hsüan Hua, who arrived in San Francisco in 1962. In 1976 this group began construction on a monastery called the City of Ten Thousand Buddhas on a 237-acre tract of land in Talmage, California. In 1984 the organization changed its name to the Dharma Realm Buddhist Association, and the group continues today, despite the death of its leader. My reasons for including this group in my book had far less to do with its ethnic Chinese character than with its monastic and intellectual emphases, each of which cut against the grain of the American Buddhism of that time. And my chapter reflected that bias.[58] Had I looked around a little more carefully, I would have discovered many more Chinese Buddhist organizations in the United States. Stuart Chandler, for example, has recently identified approximately 125 such groups,[59] not the least of which is Chuang Yen Monastery, near Carmel, New York, long patronized by C. T. Shen, who for many years was a major contributor to my university. However, there is no doubt whatsoever that Hsi Lai Temple, identified as the largest monastery in North America, is the most dynamic Chinese Buddhist organization in the Western world.

Irrespective of the Hui Shan episode described above, it is widely known that the Chinese were the earliest Asian group to settle in North America. Within a decade of the discovery of gold at Sutter's sawmill, there were 13,000 Chinese in America, and barely two decades later there were more than 60,000 Chinese present.[60] By the time of the Chinese Immigration Exclusion Act of 1882, there were more than 100,000 Chinese in the United States, with more than a half dozen temples as well, although the temples were not exclusively Buddhist.[61] Within four decades of the passage of the immigration act, the Chinese population had reduced itself to about 60,000. Like many Asian groups, the Chinese benefited enormously from the 1965 amendments to the Immigration and Nationality Act of 1952, as well as further amendments in 1981 and 1990. As a result, the Chinese population in 1990 had risen to about

921,000, an increase of approximately 450 percent of the pre-1965 figure.[62] In addition, the Chinese immigrants seem to have divided into two rather different categories: professionals (called "Uptown Chinese" by Peter Kwong in his book *The New Chinatown*) and manual/service workers (called "Downtown Chinese" by Kwong).[63] The Uptown Chinese generally do not settle in Chinatowns, while the Downtown Chinese do, according to Kwong. A similar finding is noted by Ronald Takaki, who identifies a distinction between a largely undereducated working class and a more highly educated professional class.[64] Later, we will see that this distinction affects the mode of practice in the Chinese Buddhist community.

Unlike Buddhist sectarian traditions from other Asian countries, Chinese Buddhism is far more eclectic. In Japanese Buddhism, for example, there are strong institutional issues and issues of orthopraxy separating the Zen and Pure Land traditions. Equally, the *Vinaya* emphasis of Theravāda is very different than the Tantric practices of Tibetan Buddhism. In Chinese Buddhism, one can find all of the above. Thus it is not unusual to find emphasis on recitation of the *nien-fo* as an expression of homage to O-mi-t'o Fo (Amitābha Buddha) combined with meditation and sūtra study. Irene Lin points out that the vast majority of studies of American Buddhism are "largely based on European American experiences and encounters with Buddhism."[65] Thus she finds only minimal references to Chinese Buddhist organizations in encyclopedias of American religions, with complete studies of Chinese Buddhist groups totally lacking.

Hsi Lai Temple, in Hacienda Heights, California, is the largest overseas project of Fo Kuang Shan, the largest Buddhist center in Taiwan. Founded in 1967 by Master Hsing-yün (the forty-eighth patriarch of the Lin-chi School of Ch'an Buddhism), Fo Kuang Shan has established branches in Argentina, Australia, Brazil, Canada, Costa Rica, England, France, Germany, Hong Kong, India, Japan, Malaysia, Paraguay, the Philippines, Russia, Switzerland, and the United States. Planning for Hsi Lai Temple began in 1978, and construction began in 1986. The temple's completion marked the culmination of a more than two-year struggle, during which time six public hearings were held before the local city council granted a building permit for the construction of the temple. Nearly every imaginable negative racial and religious stereotype was considered during the long process.[66] It was built on a twenty-acre site, eventually including a floor area of 102,432 square feet. Completed in November 1988, it was built at a total cost in excess of $30 million, financed largely by donations from patrons in Taiwan, Malaysia, Hong Kong, and the United States.

The Chinese words *hsi lai* are generally translated as "coming to the West," suggesting that Buddhism is coming to the West from the East. Irene Lin offers an interesting slant on this notion, saying, "Hsi Lai can be alternatively read as 'coming from the West,' depicting the Dharma having come from the West and now returning to the West,"[67] highlighting the fact that Bodhidharma brought the Dharma to China from the "West" (i.e., India). In any case, the temple uses the traditional architecture of ancient Chinese monasteries, employing construction materials from Italy, Japan, Korea, Taiwan, Thailand, and the United States. With the grounds presumably structured in the shape of a leaf from the Bodhi tree (i.e., roughly triangular), the temple includes the Bodhisattva Hall and shrine (housing images of the five great bodhisattvas: Samantabhadra, Kṣitigarbha, Maitreya, Avalokiteśvara, and Mañjuśrī), the Buddha Hall and shrine (housing images of Amitābha Buddha, Bhaiṣajyaguru, and Śākyamuni Buddha), classrooms, auditoriums, a library, a museum, a gift shop, meeting and conference rooms, a requiem pagoda, administrative offices, and living quarters for the monks and nuns. In addition, an Avalokiteśvara theme garden and Arhats theme garden have been added. The temple now serves as the monastic unit of the International Buddhist Progress Society, a nonprofit organization incorporated in California.

Hsi Lai Temple maintains on its World Wide Web page that it was built "to serve as a spiritual and cultural center for those interested in learning more about Buddhism and Chinese culture," and that the objectives of the temple are:

- To nurture Buddhist missionaries through education.
- To propagate Buddhism through cultural activities.
- To benefit society through charitable organizations.
- To edify the populace through Buddhist practices.[68]

Lin gives a slightly different perspective, noting that "Hsi Lai's stated goal is threefold: to offer a spiritual and cultural center for the United States, to provide Westerners a place for learning about the Dharma, and to facilitate the exchange of culture between East and West."[69] For Lin, the first of the three goals she cites is met by the presence of the completed temple and its many facilities; in addition, the temple now has a number of branch temples (in Austin, Dallas, Denver, New York, San Diego, and San Francisco). The second goal is subsumed under the monastic organization and staff of monks and nuns who serve the temple; originally staffed by about fifty monks and nuns who were selected and sent from Fo Kuang Shan, with the 1990 change in the immigration law the temple now has a staff more than double this figure. The third goal is fulfilled through the efforts of the Buddha's Light International Association (BLIA), a lay organization established by Fo Kuang Shan that operates in more than fifty countries worldwide.

Following his retirement as abbot of Fo Kuang Shan, Master Hsing-yün became founding president of the BLIA. A Los Angeles branch was established at Hsi Lai Temple on 31 March 1991, and the following year, Hsi Lai Temple became the world headquarters for the BLIA, with more than twenty thousand BLIA regional delegates in attendance. There are now more than one hundred regional chapters, with a complex organizational framework. Significantly, it is through the BLIA that many individuals "take refuge," becoming lay disciples of Master Hsing-yün. This is important because it is the lay disciples of Master Hsing-yün who are official members of Hsi Lai Temple. The BLIA now claims to rank as the fourth largest social club in the world, behind the Rotary Club, Lion's Club, and United Way. Just as SGI-USA sees itself as promoting the Dharma through lay activity, the BLIA maintains a similar stance, with four clearly stated objectives:

- Follow and propagate the Buddha's teaching, venerate the Triple Gems, work for the welfare and awakening of the world.
- Promote living dynamic Buddhism, build the Buddha's Light Pure Land, actualize the humanistic Buddhist approach, with benevolence and compassion towards all.
- Abide by the Buddhist precepts and harmonize the Five Vehicles, practice the Three Teachings and perfect the human character.
- International involvement in cultural and educational events, have an open mind and treating others with mutual respect.[70]

How these stated objectives are facilitated varies, to some degree dictated by socioeconomic status. While the principal form of Buddhist activity in Chinese Buddhist organizations is the devotional recitation known as *nien-fo,* done irrespective of the status of the practitioner, Stuart Chandler suggests that organizations with high numbers of well-educated members generally manifest three additional emphases: (1) study of Buddhist scriptures; (2) consideration of the compatibility of Buddhist practice with a scientific and technological worldview; and (3) a "come and see for oneself" attitude.[71] Irene Lin believes the BLIA to be a high expression of Hsi Lai Temple's emphasis on a "this-worldly" life and an expression of Master Hsing-yün's hope to create a Buddhist Pure Land here on earth. She says, "In tangible ways, Fo Kuang Shan can be viewed as the eastern Pure Land and Hsi Lai Temple, the Western Pure Land—sacred, prosperous, and serene."[72]

Since summer 1994, Hsi Lai University has been in session within the facilities of Hsi Lai Temple. Offering undergraduate and graduate degree programs in Buddhist Studies, Hsi Lai University functions as a private, postsecondary school of theology under the authorization of the California superintendent of public instruction. By sending a number of monks and nuns to pursue graduate training in religious studies at major American universities, it is in the process of developing its own highly trained faculty. In addition, it has used some of the leading Buddhist Studies scholars in its rapidly expanding curriculum. In its educational program Hsi Lai University is seeking not only to improve mutual understanding between East and West, but also to develop a strong mutuality between Buddhist study and practice. Regarding its educational philosophy, it states:

> Hsi Lai University is a non-profit institution which actively promotes cultural recognition and understanding between East and West through exchange programs and conferences. The University also seeks to foster mutual understanding and respect among various religious groups through sponsorship and participation in conventions and dialogues. Hsi Lai University is a pioneering effort among Chinese and American Buddhists, preparing men and women for the many facets of spiritual life and leadership.[73]

And the link to monastic practice is equally clear:

> Hsi Lai University is a functioning monastery and part of a Buddhist community with temples and centers around the world. Opportunities are ample throughout the year for students of the University to become immersed in religious practice. They are encouraged to combine their experience with their studies to construct the foundation for lifelong intellectual and spiritual furtherance. There are several avenues by which a student may enter monastic life. A student may enter monastic training as an ordained bhiksu

(monk) or bhiksuni (nun), as a novice, or as a layperson intending to enter the sangha (monastic community) by receiving full ordination.[74]

The university is building an impressive library, which now houses more than fifty thousand volumes and has a solid commitment to continuing its program of acquiring Buddhist literature in all the canonical languages. Hsi Lai University Press was founded in 1994, intending initially to publish the collected works of master Hsing-yün. It also publishes a number of periodicals.

In his interesting essay "Chinese Buddhism in America: Identity and Practice," Stuart Chandler identifies six constellations in the overseas Chinese diaspora community in America: (1) Buddhist Chinese Americans; (2) American Chinese Buddhists; (3) Buddhist American Chinese; (4) American Buddhist Chinese; (5) Chinese Buddhist Americans; and (6) Chinese American Buddhists.[75] These categories reflect an interpenetrating complex of ethnic, religious, and cultural factors that suggests that, as Evelyn Kallen maintains (in a slightly different context), ethnicity as an expression of a "bio-cultural-territorial isolate frame of reference"[76] is no longer sufficient for understanding immigrant communities that have come to the United States from other parts of the world. Instead, Kallen uses the term "new ethnicity" to describe a more dynamic circumstance in which "a sense of rootedness or belongingness" is combined with an attempt to "alter the established distribution of power, privilege, and prestige so as to gain economic, political, and cultural rights/advantages."[77] Irene Lin maintains that in the recognition of "new ethnicity,"

Hsi Lai Temple provides the context for post-1965 Chinese Americans to construct their identity, characterized by heterogeneity, hybridity, multiplicity, fluidity, and situation . . . Hsi Lai serves as a multicultural resource for Chinese Americans. It is a cultural carrier in preserving traditional Chinese culture; a cultural broker in bridging Chinese subculture and American culture; a cultural entrepreneur in helping to define a new Chinese American identity . . . Hsi Lai Temple provides an instance of religion serving to revive and construct Chinese culture and identity for the Chinese Americans, ensuring relevance to their differential situations. Furthermore, Hsi Lai furnishes an example of how Buddhism has been revitalized to accommodate the needs of modern industrial society and to adapt to the culturally pluralistic environment.[78]

Were this all that it did, the accomplishments of Hsi Lai Temple would be noteworthy enough. It does far more, however, in extending its sphere of influence.

At least two other efforts of Hsi Lai Temple are noteworthy. First, it is extending its Buddhist activities beyond the ethnic Chinese community into the non–ethnic Chinese community and the community of Euro-Americans. Additionally, in conjunction with the Sangha Council of Southern California and other Buddhist organizations, it has begun engaging in outreach activities to other ethnic-Asian Buddhist groups. In some of its activities of this nature, Hsi Lai Temple has bridged both the ethnic and sectarian gaps, inviting Theravāda, Mahāyāna, and Vajrayāna groups to participate in the same activities. In this respect, without undermining its own primary mission, it can be seen as having developed a secondary mission as a Pan-Buddhist organization, wholly ecumenical in its efforts, with the supplementary benefit of having *Hsi Lai News* as a useful vehicle of extensive communication and publicity. Second, in the absence of formal diplomatic relations between the United States and Taiwan, Hsi Lai Temple has allowed the Coordination Council for North American Affairs, a veritable Taiwanese embassy, to use its reception hall for various events. In this way, it has functioned as a highly visible cultural center, celebrating both Chinese and American holidays, with generally, but not always, satisfactory results.

In attempting to summarize the Chinese Buddhist tradition in the United States, taking into account all of the information presented above, Chandler says:

> First, while the Chinese have the longest history of any Asian Americans and were the first to build temples in the United States, the present Chinese Buddhist organizations are quite young; the vast majority have been established only within the past twenty-five years. Second, partially as a function of their relatively short history, Chinese American Buddhist organizations have very few non-Chinese participants or masters. One can say that, as a whole, the tradition is American Chinese rather than Chinese American. Third, the emphasis on "Chinese" is a conscious choice. Many of the people who participate in these organizations became active Buddhists only after having come to the United States. The Buddhist groups act as an important link back to cultural China. Fourth, while the Buddhist tradition serves as a source of stability for a community whose members are undergoing a radical shift in their sense of identity, its transplantation to fresh soil is also regarded as an opportunity for the renewal of the authentic Buddhist message.[79]

Although Chandler's phrase "authentic Buddhist message" will prove troublesome for those who recognize and support both the diversity and integrity of all the imported Buddhist traditions in America, I cannot help being reminded, again and again, of how very impressed I was two decades ago when studying the way of life engendered by the monastic community of Ven. Hsüan Hua. Stories still circulate about the eleven-hundred-mile bowing journey for world peace of Bhikṣu Heng Ju and Bhikṣu Heng Yo (later described in the book *Three Steps, One Bow*), the rigorous personal discipline of the monks and nuns, and the powerful emphasis on textual erudition established by Master Hua. The *sangha* of Hsi Lai Temple evokes the very same awe and reverence today. Yet Hsi Lai Temple has enormously expanded the scope of what can be offered. The Dharma Realm Buddhist Association remains an important, but essentially isolated, unit. Hsi Lai Temple has created what the author of the most comprehensive study of its community and mission calls "a 'plausibility superstructure,' which incorporates numerous substructures—namely a religious organization, an ethnic community, a de facto embassy, a social relief center, a cultural center, and a school. Through religion, these substructures serve diverse roles in creating and maintaining different aspects of the Chinese American identity."[80] In this way, Hsi Lai Temple moves beyond virtually all of the other ethnic Asian American Buddhist communities in providing an integral and holistic American Buddhist identity for its *sangha* members.

Each year the American Academy of Religion (AAR) holds its annual meeting during the weekend before the Thanksgiving holiday. Over the past twenty years or so, this huge conference has become the congregating locale of choice for North American scholars of Buddhism. The Buddhism Section of this organization annually presents five panels devoted to Buddhist issues, and cosponsors a number of other panels in conjunction with related units. At the 1996 AAR annual meeting, held in New Orleans, the Buddhism Section and East Asian Religions Consultation jointly sponsored a panel entitled "Buddhist Precepts in Asia." Included among the scholarly presentations of those in attendance, and preceding T. Griffith Foulk's interesting and entertaining "response," was a paper called "From the Chinese *Vinaya* Traditions to Ch'an Regulations: Continuity and Adaptation." It was delivered by Ven. Yifa Shih, a Buddhist nun from Hsi Lai Temple, who was representing Yale University, where she was completing her graduate education. It was a quiet yet brilliant paper, one that immediately rekindled my appreciation for the richness of the Buddhist monastic disciplinary literature. Following her presentation, I stood in the background and watched this remarkable Buddhist nun deftly and confidently field questions and inquiries about the Chinese *Vinaya* tradition and about Hsi Lai Temple. Immediately upon my return to Penn State, I added Hsi Lai Temple to my list of World Wide Web bookmarks.

Insight Meditation Society and Spirit Rock Meditation Center

Gil Fronsdal comments in his essay "Insight Meditation in America: Life, Liberty, and the Pursuit of Happiness" that "arguably the most significant event for the introduction of *vipassanā* to America occurred when Jack Kornfield and Joseph Goldstein taught summer meditation courses at the Naropa Institute in 1974."[81] Although Naropa Institute was featured quite early in such popular magazines as *Time,* the description of it that I have always thought most fitting was Robert Greenfield's: "The crown jewel of the empire is Naropa Institute, a Buddhist university at which some of the intellectual heavies of Western civilization have agreed to teach."[82] Greenfield was correct, too. In the midst of the eighteen hundred students who attended Naropa Institute in 1974, that first year's faculty boasted such luminaries as Gregory Bateson, John Cage, Allen Ginsberg, Herbert V. Guenther, Ram Dass, and many others. Nonetheless, in 1975, when Anchor Press/Doubleday issued *Loka: A Journal from Naropa Institute,* edited by Rick Fields, Joseph Goldstein was not mentioned at all, while Jack Kornfield appeared only as the interviewer (under his monastic name of Sunno Bhikkhu) of Achaan Chā. Yet Fronsdal is absolutely correct in his assessment.

Naropa Institute in 1974 was thrilling but claustrophobic, exciting but emotionally challenging: a place where it was hard to maintain any stability at all. As students jumped around from poetry workshops to *thangka* painting classes to dance classes to Chögyam Trungpa's now-fabled evening lectures, it was virtually impossible to cultivate any calmness or insight. At this breakneck speed, I could barely get my Sanskrit students to sit still long enough to recite their grammatical paradigms, let alone read the passages from the *Laṅkāvatāra-sūtra* that I had planned. Nor were they shy about telling me they wanted to read the *Vajracchedikā-sūtra* instead. The meditation classes supervised by the students of Chögyam Trungpa didn't seem to help, either. The students emerged from their sessions of sitting, *zafus* in hand, and immediately raced off to some other class, workshop, lecture, or bar. Many of them were like spiritual jumping beans, temporarily trapped in a meditation-hall-shaped jar and anxious for their release. The stimulation of it all was highly contagious, and had I not been able to steal away to the loft of my rented summer house for a few hours each day of quiet *satipaṭṭhāna* meditation, I would have been just as out of control as many of the students.

Not everyone seemed to be so consumed, though. Over time, I noticed that a small group of students consistently appeared to be much calmer, slower, and more deliberate than the rest. After several weeks of observing these people, singly and collectively, I finally mustered up enough courage to ask what they were doing that allowed them to be so calm, as if on a quiet island surrounded by a very turbulent ocean. The answer of course was uniform: *vipassanā.* Each person queried credited his or her gentle sanity to either Joseph Goldstein or Jack Kornfield. Before I left Naropa Institute in 1974, I made a point of getting to know these two *vipassanā* teachers at least a bit, and their friendliness and openness reflected their students' high praise. Not surprisingly, I remember these meetings more intensely than they do.

Before the founding of the Buddhist Vihara Society in Washington, D.C., in 1966, there was very little *vipassanā* training available in the United States. Now and again, Theravāda monks who were visiting the United States would offer brief meditation instruction in the course of their travels, usually on college campuses. By the time the Washington Buddhist Vihara Society had established a permanent residence on 16th Street N.W. in 1968, under the direction of two mahātheras, Ven. Dickwela Piyananda and Ven. Henepola Gunaratana, regular meditation training was available to a small but steady stream of interested Western students.

Beginning in the early 1970s, *vipassanā* training was systematically brought to the United States by four primary teachers: Joseph Goldstein, Jack Kornfield, Sharon Salzberg, and Ruth Denison. The common link in their teaching is that each had studied in Asia with the leading teachers of this twentieth systematization of the ancient Buddhist method of meditation. The leader of the *vipassanā* movement was Mahāsi Sayādaw (1904–1982), a Burmese monk who eschewed the traditional preliminary *samatha,* or "calming," practice and moved directly to "insight," or *vi-*

passanā, practice, cultivated during intensive periods of practice. In addition, many of the traditional Theravāda practices, such as various rituals and merit-making, were eliminated from the training, as was the usual emphasis on doctrinal study. In so doing, Mahāsi Sayādaw and his colleagues not only simplified the training, but made it more readily available to both a lay audience of practitioners and an essentially non-Buddhist Western audience. In other words, *vipassanā* training became highly accessible.

Goldstein studied under Mahāsi Sayādaw and his students Anagārika Munindra and U Pandita; Salzberg studied under the above three teachers, and also under S. N. Goenka, a student of U Ba Khin; Kornfield studied with Mahāsi Sayādaw and Achaan Chā; and Ruth Denison studied in Burma with U Ba Khin. They each returned to the United States, and collectively set out to offer *vipassanā* training, almost completely stripped of its association with the Theravāda tradition; a Western audience was far more interested in the therapeutic benefits of the training, such as stress reduction, than in the religious trappings of Theravāda. As such, *vipassanā* is now taught in a variety of settings—schools, clinics, and even prisons—with no acknowledged connection to the Buddhist tradition at all. While there is now a much larger network of independent *vipassanā* teachers active on American soil, numbering perhaps as many as seventy-five, this section will focus on the work of the early importers of the tradition to America.

Founded in 1975 as a nonprofit organization for the intensive practice of insight meditation, the Insight Meditation Society (IMS) is located about two miles north of Barre, Massachusetts, in a former Catholic seminary and boys' school on an eighty-acre wooded site. Purchased collectively by Goldstein, Kornfield, Salzberg, and Jacqueline Schwartz, the complex now serves as the permanent home of IMS. The center is located about an hour's drive from Worcester and two hours from Boston. Its continual growth has recently caused the directors to cease the practice known as "Yogi runs," in which transportation to and from Worcester was furnished for retreatants. Fortunately, one of the community members has begun a commercial van service, aptly named Brahma Chariots, which keeps IMS accessible.

IMS sponsors retreats for both beginning and experienced meditators, which consist of daily meditation instruction and nightly Dharma talks, along with individual and group interviews with the various teachers.

These retreats present an extremely rigorous routine, with the daily schedule generally beginning as early as 5 A.M. and concluding around 10 P.M. The entire routine involves alternating periods of silent sitting and walking meditation. In addition, retreatants usually live in austere single rooms (with no male-female room sharing), and all meals are vegetarian. Along with the program of group retreats, three categories of individual retreat are offered to experienced meditators: (1) self-retreats; (2) work retreats; and (3) long-term practice. These individual retreats are open to anyone who has previously completed a teacher-led retreat. Self-retreats are limited in length so as not to exceed the longest teacher-led retreat the meditator has completed; moreover, the practitioner maintains silence and observes the five precepts during the entirety of the retreat. Work retreats are designed to provide an opportunity to integrate mindfulness practice with work activity; open only to experienced students, these retreats combine meditation practice with five hours of various work activity in an appropriate IMS department. Finally, long-term retreats exceed 118 days of practice; they are supported by a scholarship program that reduces fees after the eighty-eighth day. In 1997, IMS sponsored about two dozen retreats, ranging from two-day weekend retreats to an eighty-four-day retreat from late September to mid-December. The topic for each retreat varies, and the staff of teachers is rotated accordingly. Costs range from $95 for a two-day weekend retreat to $2,250 for the eighty-four-day retreat.

There are several categories of teachers at IMS, including senior Dharma teachers, associate Dharma teachers, and visiting teachers. In addition, Gloria Ambrosia serves IMS, where she has taught since 1990, as "resident teacher." Senior Dharma teachers have recently included Ajahn Amaro, Ruth Denison, Christina Feldman, Joseph Goldstein, Narayan Liebenson Grady, Ven. Henepola Gunaratana, Jack Kornfield, Michele McDonald-Smith, Larry Rosenberg, Sharon Salzberg, Rodney Smith, Steven Smith, Christopher Titmuss, and Carol Wilson. Although they are obviously not continuously in residence at IMS together, each has trained extensively under the guidance of one or more Asian Buddhist teachers. In addition, Christina Feldman and Christopher Titmuss are cofounders of Gaia House in England. Ruth Denison founded a desert retreat center called Dhamma Dena in Joshua Tree, California, and another center in Germany. Ven. Henepola Gunaratana founded a monastic center in West Virginia known as the Bhavana Society. Jack Kornfield founded Spirit Rock Meditation Center, described below. Larry Rosenberg serves as resident teacher of the Cambridge Insight Meditation Center (see below), and Steven Smith is the primary teacher of the New Zealand Vipassana Sangha and the Blue Mountain Meditation Center in Australia. Associate Dharma teachers have included Steven Armstrong, Anna Douglas (a founding teacher at Spirit Rock), Jose Reissig, Sharda Rogell, and Marcia Rose (a resident teacher at IMS from 1991 to 1995). In 1984 Jack Kornfield started a four-year program to systematically train teachers for the *vipassanā* program, and now both IMS and Spirit Rock have instituted a program for certifying teachers. Largely as a result of the ethical breaches, sexual abuses, and abuse of power by various American Buddhist teachers, both Asian and Western, in the various traditions, the teachers at IMS and Spirit Rock have formulated an "Insight Meditation Teacher's Code of Ethics."[83]

In June 1995 Jack Kornfield told Gil Fronsdal, "We wanted to offer the powerful practices of insight meditation, as many of our teachers did, as simply as possible without the complications of rituals, robes, chanting and the whole religious tradition."[84] To a large extent, these American *vipassanā* teachers have presented the training in a context almost wholly removed from association with the Theravāda tradition. Psychologist Daniel Goleman, who has been strongly influenced by the *vipassanā* movement, reflected that fact in his book *Vital Lies, Simple Truths,* in which he states: "The Dharma is so disguised that it could never be proven in court."[85] In the Buddhism in America Conference, held in Boston in January 1997 (cited above), medical doctor Jon Kabat-Zinn said as much regarding his work in stress reduction at the University of Massachusetts Medical Center. Although no statistics exist regarding the formal psychological training of the various IMS and Spirit Rock *vipassanā* teachers, my suspicion is that more than half might boast certifiable credentials in psychology. Kornfield even makes a rather explicit appeal for the combination (if not the consolidation) of the two disciplines in his article "Meditation and Psychotherapy: A Plea for Integration."[86]

Jack Kornfield moved to California in 1981, where he eventually founded Spirit Rock Meditation Center on 412 acres of land in western Marin County. Located near the town of Woodacre, the center is little more than a half hour's drive from either the Golden Gate Bridge or the Richmond Bridge. The land was purchased from the Nature Conservancy in 1988 (the group used the proceeds from the land sale to help preserve rain forests in South America). A meditation hall, administrative office, and caretaker's quarters were added in 1990, with a kitchen–dining hall added four years later. The community estimated that by the end of 1996, more than seven thousand individuals had assisted in the development of Spirit Rock.

Based on the classical teachings of Buddhism, and emphasizing the same approach to the practice of insight meditation as IMS, the center hosts daylong retreats along with a number of continuing classes that explore the relationship of meditation to daily life in a complex, modern society. Spirit Rock thus provides the occasion for looking inward and outward: outward into a world challenged by environmental, economic, political, and psychological dilemmas; and inward through the practice of *vipassanā*. The vision for the Spirit Rock approach is clear:

> We actually see Spirit Rock as a living *mandala* (a circle) whose central inspiration is the Dharma, the deepest truth of life, beyond words and concepts. The outer expressions of the mandala are both reflections of the Dharma and paths leading back to the Dharma. The outer expressions, which are interdependent and support one another, include our programs and trainings in retreats, wise relationship, study, hermitage, service, and spiritual practices, in the world.[87]

The center is run by a paid staff of about a dozen full- and part-time workers. The residential retreats are staffed by volunteers, whose work is supported solely by donations (or *dāna*). Decisions are handled by a board of directors, which oversees an interconnected series of committees devoted to such issues as finance, scholarships, events, ethics, and the like. Interestingly, Spirit Rock goes farther than IMS in presenting its teachings in a truly nonsectarian environment.

Because Spirit Rock is a community in the midst of development, its residential retreats, which last up to three weeks, are held at other retreat facilities, usually located in nearby Santa Rosa or San Rafael. In addition, it has designed programs and retreats that specifically address the needs of its constituent groups. Thus there are retreats for men, women, families, gays and lesbians, people of color, and singles; Spirit Rock has also presented special-interest programs on health care, art, service, and work.

Although many of the teachers at IMS also offer *vipassanā* instruction at Spirit Rock, the Spirit Rock community has its own complete staff that, at the time of this writing, included fourteen people: Guy Armstrong, James Baraz, Sylvia Boorstein, Eugene Cash, Debra Chamberlin-Taylor, Howard Cohn, Anna Douglas, Gil Fronsdal, Robert Hall, Jack Kornfield, Wes Nisker, Mary Orr, John Travis, and Julie Wester. Wes Nisker is the founding editor of the *vipassanā* journal *Inquiring Mind,* which has played an influential role in promoting the worldwide *vipassanā* movement. Unlike their Asian counterparts, American *vipassanā* teachers at IMS and Spirit Rock place much emphasis on the practice of loving-kindness (*mettā*) in conjunction with meditation training. They see this amalgam as an effective way of combining social awareness with deepening a meditator's concentration. Additionally, along with mindfulness practice *(sati),* ethics (*sīla*) and generosity (*dāna*) are also stressed.

It is very difficult to collect any demographic data on IMS and Spirit Rock because, unlike the majority of other *sanghas* investigated in this chapter, these two communities do not make formal distinctions between members and nonmembers. As Gil Fronsdal comments:

> This [lack of formal distinctions] is in large part because they [IMS and Spirit Rock] are primarily retreat centers providing classes and retreats where anyone is invited to learn and practice meditation. They are not churchlike community centers where the full range of people's daily spiritual needs and expressions are met. Rather than being based on membership dues, Spirit Rock and IMS are financed by charging fees for retreats and classes offered and by donations.[88]

There is some concern that the *vipassanā* movement appeals largely to the so-called baby boomer generation, thus driving the average age of the participants well beyond forty; however, its more recent popularity in schools, hospitals, and prisons will keep its numbers growing.

Also associated with the IMS and Spirit Rock in the *vipassanā* movement are two additional centers: the Cambridge Insight Meditation Center (CIMC); and the Vipassana Metta Foundation, on Maui. The CIMC was founded in 1985 as a nonprofit, nonresidential urban center for *vipassanā* practice. Located in the heart of Cambridge, Massachusetts, it draws practitioners from the entire Greater Boston area. Unlike IMS and Spirit Rock, however, membership is an important part of the CIMC program. In addition to revenue-producing programs and retreats, membership (currently a suggested $240 per year, which also accords reduced fees for classes and retreats) contributes a significant portion of the center's operating budget. The CIMC maintains a substantial library, which includes audio- and videotapes as well as reference materials. A number of cottagelike facilities (called *kuṭī* in Pali), consisting of sleeping quarters, bathroom, kitchenette, and practice space, are available for individual practice at reasonable rates. The center also makes every effort to accommodate the needs of people with disabilities and those who are environmentally sensitive. The founder of the CIMC is Larry Rosenberg, who continues as one of four main teachers (the other three being Narayan Liebenson Grady, Michael Liebenson Grady, and Sarah Doering). The CIMC occasionally benefits by drawing upon the staff of the Barre Center for Buddhist Studies (see below). Throughout the year, the CIMC sponsors a series of classes, drop-in groups, and community events such as the Refuge and Precepts Taking Ceremonies.

The Vipassana Metta Foundation developed from the *vipassanā* retreat community on Maui. The basic mission of the Vipassana Metta Foundation is to provide a residential lay community for men and women that focuses on a practice-oriented style of living. Its primary teachers are Kamala Masters, an Asian American woman living on Maui who studied with Anagārika Munindra; and Steven Armstrong, who spent five years as a monk in Burma, training rigorously with U Pandita, and later was a staff member at IMS. The community sponsors regular weekly sitting periods combined with Dharma instruction, occasional "days of mindfulness," a number of weekend retreats, and an annual monthlong silent *vipassanā* retreat in August. Like their counterpart teachers at IMS, Spirit Rock, and the CIMC, Steven Armstrong and Kamala Masters maintain an aggressive schedule of teaching *vipassanā* on a worldwide basis.

Like many American Buddhist *sanghas,* IMS has helped to develop an academic component of its community in order to allow its practitioners to combine both study and practice in a mutually reinforcing environment. With that in mind, the Barre Center for Buddhist Studies (BCBS) was founded in 1989. It is located on ninety acres of wooded land, about one-half mile from IMS. Primarily through donations, the BCBS was able to purchase the two-hundred-year-old farmhouse that now serves as its main building. The mission of the BCBS is to bring teachers, scholars, practitioners, and students together to study the teachings and lineages of the various Buddhist traditions in their original settings and in new cultural contexts in the West. In addition, the BCBS seeks to bridge the gap between scholarly investigation and meditative insight. To accomplish these goals, the BCBS offers an extensive variety of lectures, classes, seminars, workshops, research opportunities, conferences, independent study programs, and retreats. But the focus of these efforts is always on the interpenetration of study and practice.

The executive director of the BCBS is Andrew Olendzki. He has a Ph.D. from the University of Lancaster in England, and has also studied at Harvard University and the University of Sri Lanka. He is assisted by the director of the BCBS, Mu Soeng, for many years a Zen monk, and an acknowledged authority on the topic of the Korean Zen tradition. The BCBS draws its faculty from the many Buddhist communities in the area; a sampling of the faculty includes Sylvia Boorstein, George Bowman, Rev. Issho Fujito, Trudy Goodman, Paula Green, Ron Leifer, Daeja Napier, Geshe Michael Roach, Lama Surya Das, and Thanissaro Bhikkhu. The ecumenical composition of the faculty is immediately apparent as well. George Bowman is a lineage holder in the Korean Zen tradition, and serves as the resident teacher of the Cambridge Buddhist Association, where Trudy Goodman also teaches. Rev. Issho Fujito is the resident priest of the Valley Zendo in Charlemont, Massachusetts. Paula Green serves on the board of directors of the Buddhist Peace Fellowship. Geshe Michael Roach was the first Westerner to qualify for the *geshe* degree at Sera Monastery in India, while Lama Surya Das completed extensive training in the Dzogchen tradition, and is founder of the Dzogchen Foundation. Thanissaro Bhikkhu has been a Theravāda monk for more than twenty years, and serves as abbot of the Metta Forest Monastery in California. Because of its strategic location, the BCBS has also been able to enhance its agenda by attracting visiting faculty from local colleges and universities. Some of these scholars include Charles Hallisey, Diana Eck, and Christopher Queen from Harvard University; Georges Dreyfus from Williams College; Janet Gyatso from Amherst College; and Susan Murcott from M.I.T.

The BCBS also offers an exceedingly interesting special program known as the Nalanda Program of Buddhist Studies. Modeled on Nalanda Buddhist University in ancient India, it has been able to bring together groups of about fifteen students for two-week periods, during which group members sit together in the morning and evening, while filling the remainder of their day with lectures, reading, and discussion. In the evening, they meet together in seminars with visiting faculty and Dharma teachers. In some respects, the program is quite similar to the one described at the outset of this chapter, held in 1975 during the second summer of Naropa Institute. Andrew Olendzki and Mu Soeng serve as core faculty members for the program, which spends two weeks each on Theravāda Studies, Mahāyāna Studies, and Buddhist Studies. In addition, the BCBS also offers a year-round self-study program that is integrated into the other activities of the center, not the least of which is the production of a twice-yearly newsletter called *Insight* that is jointly published with the Insight Meditation Society. Since fall 1996 the newsletter has offered an online version that includes, in addition to the current retreat schedule at IMS and course schedule at the BCBS, interviews with well-known Dharma teachers and other articles and features.

Not long ago, in collecting material for this chapter, I reread a 1993 interview by *Tricycle* editor Helen Tworkov entitled "Empty Phenomena Rolling On: An Interview with Joe Goldstein." Tworkov's second question followed up on Goldstein's initial remark that it is always energizing to reconnect to what the Buddha's teaching is all about. She queried, "What *is* it all about?" Goldstein responded:

> For me the Buddha's teaching is about freedom and the qualities that come from freedom, like kindness and compassion. I see those situations where my mind is open and spacious and responsive, and the times when my mind contracts around something. The difference between those two experiences is so clear. The possibility of freedom, though, is contingent on seeing when the mind contracts or gets distracted and lost in the story.[89]

For Goldstein, and for most of the *vipassanā* teachers in North America, freedom is exactly what it is all about. It permeates their writing, especially so with Goldstein. Earlier that year, in *Insight Meditation: The Path of Freedom,* he stated almost at the outset, "We practice the Dharma in order . . . to be free."[90]

American *vipassanā* students pursue this-life goals, ones that inform their daily experience of the world and offer pragmatic results. No doubt many of those aspirations seem far removed from the Asian Buddhist emphasis on ending rebirth in *saṃsāra.* Later in the *Tricycle* interview, Tworkov asked whether the American Buddhist householder's life can be made comparable in power and practice to the traditional monastic life. Goldstein hedged not a bit:

> There have been cases of great enlightened masters as householders. But it's not common. As householders we're busy and we have a lot of responsibilities, and the work of dharma takes time. The view that it's as perfect a

vehicle as monasticism doesn't accord with what the Buddha taught. He was very clear in the original teachings that the household life is "full of dust." But since we don't have a monastic culture in America, the great challenge is how to achieve liberation as laypeople.[91]

One doesn't have to read too much Joe Goldstein to conclude that he believes we don't have a minute to lose in the pursuit.

Many years ago, in trying to find a dramatic way to convey to my students this sense of the immediacy of choice, to shake the foundations of their academic and personal lethargy, I found a documentary video of Alvin Toffler's 1970 book *Future Shock.* That it was narrated by Orson Welles made it all the more compelling. Toffler's notion of technology run wild, of the superimposition of the future onto the present, wouldn't seem so shocking today. Nonetheless, one segment of the video showed a series of young hitchhikers, at various points of the Coast Highway as it winds its way through Big Sur in California. Each had a sign pointing to the desired destination: "Santa Monica"; "Los Angeles"; "San Diego." At the end of the line was one not so memorable character, holding a sign that read simply: "ANYWHERE BUT HERE!" Maybe the millennial *vipassanā* rewrite would be: "EVERYWHERE IS HERE!" Or, as the title of Jon Kabat-Zinn's book tells us, *Wherever You Go, There You Are.*

When I met Joe Goldstein in 1974, I didn't realize how many similarities there were between us. We were both born in 1944. He began learning insight meditation in 1967; I started meditation practice a year earlier. As a practitioner-scholar, he learned from the leading *vipassanā* innovator of his time: Mahāsi Sayādaw. As a scholar-practitioner, I learned from the leading Buddhist Studies innovator of his time: Richard Robinson. We both served as faculty members during the initial summer of Naropa Institute in 1974. I went back in 1975 but not since; Joe has gone back many times. Our paths haven't crossed very many times in the intervening years, but when they have, he's always been smiling. It appears he hasn't wasted much time.

Shambhala International

In *American Buddhism* I committed almost twice as much space to Vajradhatu and the Nalanda Foundation as to any of the seven other American Buddhist communities included in that volume. Although the *sangha* of Chögyam Trungpa Rinpoche was undoubtedly the most complex and highly organized American Buddhist community of that time, a major factor in my decision to spend so many pages on this community was the huge impact that Chögyam Trungpa had made on the American Buddhist landscape. Of the approximately twenty pages in that chapter, about 25 percent of them were devoted to Trungpa's fascinating biography, and I included a short reminiscence of my first meeting with him in mid-June 1974, shortly before the beginning session of Naropa Institute's first momentous summer. At that time, I wrote:

> At once he is powerful and perceptive with his rather opaque, dark eyes that reveal very little, while at the same time he conveys a sense of pliability, of softness, hardly consistent with his role as director of this growing empire . . . He presents a contagious and genuine warmth, offered freely and openly. He also makes no apologies for his behavior (which is not always exemplary). He makes no promises that he cannot fulfill and does his best to promote a strong sense of equanimity in his community.[92]

Despite the chaos of that early attempt at a Buddhist approach to education, few who attended that beginning session have anything but warm memories. Even my children occasionally reflect on the wonderful times they had at the Naropa Institute day-care center, where they frolicked along with the other faculty kids, including Trungpa's.

Chögyam Trungpa has been dead more than a decade, but his important legacy for American Buddhism lives on in the developing communities that now thrive and prosper under the direction of his son. As one of the so-called Buddhologists at the initial session of Naropa Institute, I was regarded with more than a little suspicion, as I revealed at the outset of this chapter. But I had my suspicions, too. Trungpa's well-publicized reputation and unpredictability seemed to require at least a bit of caution from all who had not known him previously. Within a day of the episode described in the above passage from *American Buddhism,* I was offered a chance for a formal interview with Chögyam Trungpa, in his office at 1111 Pearl Street in Boulder, just down the block from the "New York Deli" made famous by the *Mork and Mindy* television series. My interview was scheduled for the following Monday afternoon, promptly at 4 P.M. At the time, I didn't know what "promptly" meant in the Vajradhatu community, but I surely didn't want to be late for my first "real" meeting with this important man. Trungpa saw me at just before

6 P.M., and since it didn't seem that anyone had entered or left his office while I waited, I couldn't understand the delay. I should have known I was on Trungpa time. I was told I could have five minutes with him, and given my displeasure for having waited so long, I thought it was perhaps twice as much as I wanted.

As soon as we began to talk, everything changed. Apart from his warm and friendly demeanor, and his very kind hospitality, he seemed to know everything about me, but not the sort of information he could have easily read on my professional vita. He knew about my more personal life, or what one might call my "Buddhist history." Within sixty seconds of my being seated, he began to engage me in a discussion of my "practice." At no time did he ever suggest that I should become *his* student, but rather that he wanted to share some things that he indicated he had observed initially in our meeting. For the next thirty minutes we dissected what was at that point nearly a decade of sitting practice. Never before, and never since, have I had a clearer, more succinct, and more accurate description of what I needed to do to move forward from a position of stalemate with myself that nobody had previously seemed to notice, except me . . . and then him! It was the best Buddhist diagnosis I had ever received, and the prescription, while quite astounding in all respects, was miraculous. We continued to talk for another ninety minutes, discussing his community, his students, and some of his seemingly troubling behavior patterns. He withheld nothing, and astonished me with his utter forthrightness. When I finally left, I extended my hand for a good-bye handshake, but when he grasped my hand, he pulled me forward and gave me one of the warmest hugs I could ever remember. And he said: "I'm so very glad you came. I do hope you will return next summer as well." In addition to my surprise at the length of our interview, which lasted far longer than the five minutes I had expected, I also learned to better appreciate the truth of Buddha's famous sermon in which he advises the Kālāmas to accept nothing on hearsay.

Amy Lavine has recently remarked that Chögyam Trungpa's North American *sangha* represents a "comprehensive attempt to merge the religious worldview of American Vajrayāna with all other aspects of American life."[93] Moreover, she says Trungpa

> sought to create a vision of "enlightened society" in North America. The concrete building blocks of that society include: a preschool, an elementary school, an accredited college bestowing undergraduate and graduate degrees,

a credit union, bookstores, a "secular" meditation program called Shambhala Training, and numerous for-profit businesses covering a wide range of interests and services. All of these institutions are operated with the idea of encouraging Tibetan Buddhist values.[94]

During his lifetime, the institutional organization of Trungpa's *sangha* revolved around the twin spires of Vajradhatu and the Nalanda Foundation, his religious and secular organizations, respectively. Now, under the direction of his eldest son, Sakyong Mipham Jampal Trinley Dradül Rinpoche (or simply Mipham Rinpoche), these communities have been reorganized under the title Shambhala International, which is further subdivided into three "gates": Vajradhatu, Shambhala Training, and Nalanda. The "Shambhala Vision" suggests: "Throughout history, men and women have aspired to create societies that express the dignity of human experience. Joining spiritual vision with practicality, such an 'enlightened society' provides a context for meaningful individual life within a flourishing culture."[95] Reflective of that vision, the Vajradhatu component involves the implementation of the Buddhist meditational path and Buddhist study through an extensive network of local centers called Dharmadhatus. The gate of Shambhala Training consists of a secular path of spiritual training, offered to practitioners of other spiritual traditions or those who have not chosen a particular spiritual tradition. Finally, the Nalanda gate provides training in a series of disciplines that includes the arts, health, education, and business, emphasizing specific instruction in poetics, visual art, archery (*kyūdō*), flower arranging (*ikebana*), and the tea ceremony.

The meditational path taught at the various Dharmadhatus was developed by Chögyam Trungpa as a means of integrating practice and study into the daily lives of practitioners. As such, it does not require a traditional, monastic approach. Moreover, it is somewhat ecumenical, incorporating both Zen and Theravāda elements into the practice—most particularly, the emphasis on *samatha* and *vipassanā* training. Vajradhatu oversees all aspects of the meditation and study programs, including the training of meditation instructors and teachers. The training is presented in a gradual, systematic fashion that allows not only for student individuality, but also for accommodating the American cultural heritage and lifestyle.

Shambhala Training is also referred to as the Sacred Path of the Warrior, and seeks to utilize the experience of modern societal complexity as an occasion to cultivate contemplative practice. It fosters the basic sanity that Chögyam Trungpa felt was necessary in order for us to fully experience our daily lives in a direct and meaningful way. The combination of mindfulness and awareness taught in Shambhala Training is designed to produce openness to all experiences on a moment-to-moment basis, yet without undermining the insights of other contemplative traditions or major religions. The program begins with a training known as the Heart of Warriorship, a series of weekend "levels" in which the practitioner establishes a personal meditational practice in an effort to discover what are called "the basic principles of warriorship" in daily life. There are five levels:

> *Level One: The Art of Being Human.* Experiencing the world as sacred and seeing basic goodness in your birthright.
>
> *Level Two: Birth of the Warrior.* Recognizing your habitual patterns and discovering fearlessness.
>
> *Level Three: Warrior in the World.* Developing confidence in all aspects of your daily life.
>
> *Level Four: Awakened Heart.* Allowing your heart and intuition to open so that you can communicate fully with the world.
>
> *Level Five: The Open Sky.* Trusting who you are and genuinely caring for others.[96]

Upon completion of the above program, the practitioner takes part in an additional six weekend levels known as the Sacred Path of the Warrior, followed by a two-week residential program called Warrior Assembly. Finally, a three-week residential "Shambhala Training Seminary" completes the program.

The Nalanda program is subtitled "Culture and Art in Everyday Life." It is designed to integrate art and culture into everyday life in a fulfilling and enriching fashion. Modeled on an eleventh-century Indian Buddhist university, Nalanda groups activities into four major categories (although not all Shambhala Centers offer all Nalanda programs): the arts, health, education, and business. The arts component includes *gagaku* and *bugaku,* the ancient music and dance of the Japanese imperial court; calligraphy; *chadō* (the tea ceremony); dance/movement; Dharma art; horsemanship and dressage; *ikebana* (flower arranging); *kyūdō* (archery); photography; music; poetics; visual art; and Mudra Space Awareness, an awareness program based on the various postures and movements of the traditional

Tibetan monastic dance. The health component includes contemplative psychotherapy; home care; palliative care; addiction programs; Maitri Space Awareness, a series of postures based on the principles of the five "Buddha families" and designed to create personal openness; and a collective known as the Amara Health Professionals. The education component includes, in addition to the well-known Naropa Institute and Nalanda Translation Committee, programs on early-childhood education and contemplative education. Finally, the business component includes a leadership training program and the Shambhala Guild Society (offering right-livelihood programs).

The creative vision that has fueled the community's thirty-year history in North America derives from Chögyam Trungpa and his two chief successors: first, Vajra Regent Ösel Tendzin (Thomas F. Rich); and now Chögyam Trungpa's eldest son, Mipham Rinpoche. Often referred to as the Vidyadhara, Chögyam Trungpa was the eleventh *tulku,* or incarnate descendent, in the Trungpa line. Trained in both the Kagyu and Nyingma lineages, he also was an adherent of the *ri-me,* or nonsectarian, ecumenical movement in Tibetan Buddhism. He was born in 1939, recognized as a *tulku* early, and installed as abbot of Surmang Monasteries in eastern Tibet well before he completed his Buddhist training. Fleeing Tibet in 1959, he stayed in India from 1959 to 1963 as a spiritual adviser at the Young Lamas Home School in Dalhousie. In 1963 he was awarded a Spaulding Fellowship, which enabled him to study at Oxford University. In 1967 he moved to Scotland and founded Samyê Ling, a meditation center. Following a car accident that left him partially paralyzed, he relinquished his monastic vows and began his work as a Buddhist lay teacher. His first book, *Meditation in Action,* was published in 1969, one year before he married Diana Pybus and moved to the United States to reside at a meditation center in Barnet, Vermont, established by a number of his students. Initially called Tail of the Tiger, it was eventually renamed Karmê-Chöling.

In the following decade Trungpa traveled widely, offering many seminars and lectures under the auspices of Vajradhatu, the revenue from which supported the growth and development of his expanding community. Between 1970 and 1980 he wrote six successful books, began three meditation communities, and founded Naropa Institute, which was the first major unit formed under the secular umbrella organization known as the Nalanda Foundation (begun in 1974). He led six Vajradhatu

Seminaries, three-month residential programs combining intensive meditation practice and study. During this decade he also developed the Shambhala Training program. In addition, upon Trungpa's invitation, Gyalwa Karmapa, the head of the Kagyu lineage, visited the United States for the first time. Following his yearlong retreat, Chögyam Trungpa began the decade of the 1980s by founding a monastery in Nova Scotia, where he eventually moved. Shortly thereafter, in April 1987, Chöygam Trungpa Rinpoche died after a debilitating illness. His celebratory cremation was held on a mountaintop above Karmê-Chöling, attended by several thousand people and reported on by nearly all the major media in North America.

Little more than ten years prior to his death, on 22 August 1976, Chögyam Trungpa empowered Thomas F. Rich as his "Vajra Regent" and gave him the name Ösel Tendzin. In 1977 Gyalwa Karmapa confirmed Tendzin's appointment as the first Western student to be empowered in this fashion. As Thomas Rich, he had worked in physical therapy after graduating from Fordham University. He met Chögyam Trungpa in Boulder in 1971, and by 1973 had been appointed to the first-ever board of directors of Vajradhatu, eventually becoming executive vice president of Vajradhatu and the Nalanda Foundation. Ösel Tendzin led the communities of Chögyam Trungpa during Trungpa's yearlong retreat and thereafter. He contracted AIDS in 1988 and died on 25 August 1990. His widow, Lila Rich, now resides in Ojai, California, where some of his students continue his work.

During Ösel Tendzin's illness, many of Trungpa's students turned to one of their teacher's teachers, Dilgo Khyentse Rinpoche, head of the Nyingma lineage, for advice. That advice, given in 1990, was to entrust Trungpa's eldest son, Mipham Rinpoche, with the continuation of his father's mission. Born Ösel Rangdröl Mukpo in 1962, he eventually went to live with his father at Samyê Ling, and moved to Boulder, Colorado, in 1971 to live with his father and his stepmother, Diana Mukpo. He was given the title Sawang, or "Earth Lord," in 1978 and empowered as Trungpa's heir. As a result of his anticipated role, the Sawang studied under many Kagyu and Nyingma teachers, both in North America and in Asia. From 1987 onward, he lived with Khyentse Rinpoche in Nepal, but was advised to return to the West following the death of Ösel Tendzin. In 1992 he consolidated the many programs of his father and renamed the organization Shambhala International. Three years later, in May 1995, he was installed as "Sakyong," or leader, of both the religious and secular components of Shambhala International. It was during his enthronement ceremony, led by Penor Rinpoche, that he was identified as Mipham Rinpoche, an incarnation of the nineteenth-century teacher Mipham Jamyang Namgyal. He continues as head of Shambhala International.

There are currently more than one hundred Shambhala Centers throughout the world, consolidated under the central administration of Shambhala International in Halifax, Nova Scotia. The main administration consists of an executive council (including a director of Shambhala, and officers in charge of the Office of the President, Vajradhatu, Communications, Shambhala Training, Finance and Development, and Shambhala Europe) and an administrative staff (which expands the executive council and provides a more complete division of labor). These administrators, along with members of the Shambhala Council, Dharmadhatu Executive Committee members, and Shambhala Training Executive Committee members, maintain an E-mail forum called "center-talk," which promotes communication and discussion on topics related to Shambhala International, and assist Mipham Rinpoche in his efforts on behalf of the organization.

Shambhala International maintains six main residential contemplative communities: (1) Karmê-Chöling in Vermont; (2) Rocky Mountain Shambhala Center in Colorado; (3) Dorje Khyung Dzong in Colorado; (4) Gampo Abbey in Nova Scotia; (5) Dorje Denma Ling in Nova Scotia; and (6) Dechen-Chöling in France. Karmê-Chöling, the earliest U.S. center, founded in 1970, is on a site surrounded by over five hundred acres of New England meadows and woods. It is about an hour's drive from White River Junction, Vermont, and is readily accessible from New York and Boston. The main house has six shrine rooms and a meditation hall that seats around two hundred people, and houses forty-five staff members. Karmê-Chöling also offers retreat cabins, a center-run store, and an outdoor target range and shrine for Zen archery. It maintains year-round programs in each of the three "gates," as well as meditation sessions ranging from two days to a month. In addition to its various programs for adults, it offers organized activities for children aged three to eleven and for young adults aged twelve to seventeen. The daily schedule of Karmê-Chöling includes five hours of meditation, three and a half hours of work, and study time; these are collectively referred to as "turning the three wheels of Dharma." Although both beginning and advanced students are invited to participate in the programs of the center, only those who have had a beginning-level training program at one of the Shambhala International centers, or have taken Shambhala Training Level One, can be admitted to the residency program. There is a rich and varied series of programs, and visitors are invited upon request.

Also among the earliest centers are the Rocky Mountain Shambhala Center and Dorje Khyung Dzong, both in Colorado. The Rocky Mountain Shambhala Center is at eight thousand feet in Red Feather Lakes, Colorado, and was the second residential center founded by Trungpa. It was the site of early Vajradhatu Seminaries, as well as more recent Shambhala Training Seminaries and the Shambhala Training Warrior's Assembly. Dorje Khyung Dzong rises even higher, to eighty-five hundred feet, and has seven retreat cabins on Mount Greenhorn in the Sangre de Cristo Range near Gardner, Colorado.

The two Canadian centers are the most recent of Trungpa's communities in North America. Gampo Abbey was established in 1984 as a monastic center housing those who chose to follow the monastic lifestyle on a temporary or permanent basis. Located on 230 acres overlooking the Gulf of St. Lawrence on Cape Breton Island, the abbey is led by one of Trungpa's senior students, an American-born nun, Pema Chödrön, who was also recently named one of nine acharyas (an Indian Buddhist designation for a respected teacher). Residents may take temporary ordination, for six months or a year, while living at the abbey. In addition, the abbey has instituted a special variation of the three-year retreat in which participants alternate retreat periods of six months to a year with equal periods in the world. On more gentle meadowland terrain is Dorje Denma Ling, in Tatamagouche, Nova Scotia. It was established in 1991 to serve the many community members in Nova Scotia. It holds both monthlong meditation retreats and shorter programs. Dechen-Chöling is the newest center, established in the summer of 1994.

Two of the most interesting programs in the Nalanda gate are Naropa Institute and the Nalanda Translation Committee. Today's Naropa Institute seems almost a world apart from the slapdash, frenzied environment of 1974 and 1975 that I described above. Named for the abbot of Nalanda University, it now occupies a 3.7-acre campus in Boulder, adjacent to the foothills of the Rocky Mountains. Accredited by the North Central Association of Schools and Colleges, in fall 1995 it had 680 degree candidates. It also registers about one thousand individuals through its new continuing-education program. It currently enrolls students from about three dozen states and half that many countries. It is still faithful to its original mission of promoting intellectual intimacy, and classes rarely have more than thirty students. Naropa Institute offers what it calls "contemplative education":

> A Naropa education initiates a lifelong process of creative personal development that extends beyond the college experience. Learning is a rigorous and joyful journey at The Naropa Institute. As a member of our community, you train wholeheartedly in your fields of study, gaining knowledge from a perspective that fosters precision, gentleness, and spontaneity. This approach is called "contemplative education," and is based on a deep respect for tradition and the intelligence within each person. It emphasizes intellectual acumen and intuitive understanding. The basic principles of this approach are:
>
> - Offering educational programs that cultivate awareness of the present moment through intellectual, artistic, and meditational disciplines.
> - Fostering a learning community that uncovers wisdom and heart.
> - Cultivating openness and communication, sharpening critical intellect, enhancing resourcefulness and developing effective action in all disciplines.
> - Exemplifying the principles grounded in the Naropa Institute's Buddhist educational heritage.
> - Encouraging the integration of world wisdom traditions with modern culture.
> - Nonsectarian and open to all.[97]

Although Naropa Institute is a private university, costs are no higher than at most other private liberal arts colleges, and approximately 75 percent of its students receive some form of financial aid. Moreover, Naropa Institute offers an extensive and unique series of options for study abroad.

The core of Naropa Institute's curriculum resides in its B.A., M.A., and M.F.A. programs. In the B.A. program, students may major in Early Childhood Education, Environmental Studies, InterArts (i.e., dance, movement, theater), Interdisciplinary Studies, Contemplative Psychology, Traditional Eastern Arts, Visual Arts, and Writing and Literature. At the M.A. level, major foci are Environmental Leadership, Gerontology and Long-Term Health Care Management, Somatic Psychology, Transpersonal Counseling Psychology, and Buddhist Studies. The M.F.A. centers on Writing and Poetics. This latter program is the ongoing development of the approach begun in 1974 by Allen Ginsberg and Anne Waldman as the "Jack Kerouac School of Disembodied Poetics." Additionally, continuing-education courses are offered in Arts and Creativity; Community, Culture, and Environment; Health, Healing, and Psychology; and World Wisdom Traditions. From its innovative and hectic beginning, Naropa Institute has evolved into perhaps the premier institution of its kind in the Buddhist world of North America.

The work of the Nalanda Translation Committee responds to Chögyam Trungpa's fervent desire that students be able to practice Buddhism in their own language, without being required to learn Sanskrit or Tibetan in order to have access to accurately rendered Buddhist teachings. The committee was founded in 1975 and, until his death in 1994, had nearly two decades of valuable input and guidance from Lama Ugyen Shenpen. The collaboration was an interesting and challenging one, because initially most of the Western students involved in the translation committee had little or no training in Sanskrit or Tibetan, while Lama Ugyen Shenpen knew only a little English. The committee began modestly, translating the daily chants and the Karma Kagyu "foundation practices," or *ngöndro,* expanding only as their acumen and language facility grew. When doing translations for certain levels of Vajrayāna and Shambhala practice, they have taken on a new name: the Vajravairochana Translation Committee.

Nonetheless, just as Naropa Institute offered its own creative definition of contemplative education, the Nalanda Translation Committee offers a fivefold statement of its own service for practicing and studying the Buddhadharma and Shambhala teachings:

- Creating fresh and authentic translations of Tibetan practice texts and commentaries in English and other Western languages.
- Translating from a variety of other genres of Tibetan Buddhist literature, including biographies, songs of realization, philosophy and culture.
- Assisting in the publication of those texts to ensure quality and consistency.
- Teaching and transmitting practices, to increase students' understanding of their significance and cultural background.
- Helping with the presentation of Buddhist and Shambhala ceremonies and practices.[98]

Currently, in addition to Executive Director Larry Mermelstein, the Nalanda Translation Committee has a staff of approximately twenty-five members, many of whom hold professorial positions at universities. The work of the committee has been enhanced considerably by the technical work of Tony Duff and Gerry Wiener, who have produced word-processing programs for Tibetan typeface and romanized Sanskrit with diacritics. They are currently at work on a variety of projects, including computerized dictionaries and glossaries. The publications of the Nalanda Translation Committee are available from the committee's office in Halifax, Nova Scotia, and at a variety of Shambhala International community sites.

Shambhala International also has a media service known as Kalapa Recordings, which sells videotapes and audiotapes of Chögyam Trungpa, Ösel Tendzin, and Mipham Rinpoche, as well as a few other individuals. Two of Trungpa's videos—*The Tantric Journey* and *Meditation: The Way of the Buddha*—are currently available, but there is a video recovery program under way that is attempting to preserve more than two hundred black-and-white video recordings made by Trungpa at Naropa Institute and other locations. Mipham Rinpoche is captured in *Shambhala: The Way of Meditation* and *Fearless in Meditation*. The audiotapes are too numerous to cite. Additionally, more than five thousand audio recordings of Chögyam Trungpa are housed in the Vajradhatu Archives. Finally, Trungpa was the author of fourteen books, all of which are now available from Shambhala Publications in Boston, a publishing company started more than a quarter century ago by community member Sam Bercholz, who has also been elevated to the status of acharya.

Until recently, there was little interaction or relationship between practitioners of American Vajrayāna and ethnic Tibetan communities. In 1991, however, the Tibetan Resettlement Project (TRP) began, and as a result of its efforts, over one thousand Tibetans were allowed to enter the United States. For many of the American Vajrayāna practitioners, most of whom come from Euro-American backgrounds, this was their very first contact with Tibetans who were not *geshes* or *tulkus* or lamas. As the TRP continues, and more Tibetans find their way into the United States illegally, a number of ethnic Tibetan communities have developed in large American cities. Members of these communities have only recently begun to attend talks by the famous teachers. It will be interesting to see what kind of interaction develops between the Shambhala International community and these ethnic Tibetan practitioners, as well as the interaction among their children.

As indicated above, I returned to Naropa Institute for its 1975 summer session. Many of the faculty members from the initial summer were back, and it was a fine opportunity to renew some familiar and growing friendships. High on my agenda, however, was to meet with Trungpa again and continue the discussions we had begun the previous year. The success of Naropa Institute, and the ongoing development Trungpa's many communities, however, were an enormous responsibility for him, and although he fulfilled all his duties with his usual flair and humor, he not only looked continually tired, but was far less accessible than before. To his credit, many people no doubt did not notice the change. When he later announced that he would be beginning a one-year retreat in March 1977, I was not surprised, but I was certainly pleased that he was finally taking the opportunity to recharge himself.

Without the anticipated opportunity for continued discussions with Trungpa, I was freer to pursue more detailed discussions with my module teaching partner, Reggie Ray. A remarkable young scholar, having been trained at the University of Chicago as one of Mircea Eliade's last group of students, Ray left a teaching position at Indiana University to become a permanent faculty member of Naropa Institute. Due to the tenuous, uncertain status of the institution in its early days, this was no small sacrifice in terms of both salary and security. Nonetheless, Ray was committed to the philosophy of Naropa Institute, and he put his career on the line to demonstrate that commitment. Some of my fondest memories of that summer revolve around our marathon discussions about which topics to cover in our module, and how much bibliographic material to include. Occasionally, these deliberations included Jan Nattier, a former student of Ray's with whom I was then collaborating on an article on Buddhist sectarianism. To my way of thinking, our furious give-and-take was precisely what the academic life was supposed to be: free exchanges, sometimes heated, always filled with friendship, and, although sometimes punctuated by lots of laughter or yelling, the best learning experience imaginable for young scholars. Similar experiences didn't happen for me at Penn State, or in the other academic settings in which I functioned, and I concluded that the environment we shared as Buddhists was the critical factor that energized our intellectual intimacy, although we rarely discussed our personal practice.

I also spent much time that summer with Larry Mermelstein. He was one of a few people in Trungpa's *sangha* that could be counted on to know everything, and to do anything that needed to be done. Not only was he a fledgling, if informal, Buddhologist (and budding Sanskritist who would later become executive director of the Nalanda Translation Committee), but he was also a great cook! While my discussions with Reggie Ray were almost always academic, my discussions with Larry Mermelstein were almost exclusively about Buddhist practice, and about practicing Buddhism in a rapidly changing American religious climate. While he cooked and we ate, we talked and talked and talked. And I learned.

Reggie Ray still lives in Boulder, where he continues on the faculty of Naropa Institute and also teaches at the University of Colorado. His recent book *Buddhist Saints in India* is perhaps the foremost new study on Buddhist hagiography. Larry Mermelstein now lives in the Shambhala community in Halifax, Nova Scotia, and continues to contribute to the *sangha* in a myriad of ways. Each has recently been named an acharya by Mipham Rinpoche. More importantly, I still communicate with each on scholarship matters, and for friendship and advice. To my mind, one of Chögyam Trungpa's most amazing contributions to American Buddhism was his ability to bring people together in sharing their Buddhism and their humanity. That his son continues the endeavor improves the flavor.

Briefly Looking Back

At the beginning of this chapter, I referred to the selection of American Buddhist groups for inclusion in *American Buddhism* as having been an extremely difficult task. Obviously, making the seven choices included here was equally difficult. There are more than one thousand Buddhist centers in the United States, many of which have a long and distinguished history. In making the above choices, I was reminded of Bob Seger's well-known song "Against the Wind," in which he laments the problem of continually deciding what to leave in and what to leave out. I have tried to select American Buddhist groups with a stable history—in most cases, one of at least twenty years, and in some cases very much longer. I have tried to strike a balance between ethnic American Buddhist communities, Euro-American Buddhist communities, and communities that are racially mixed. I have tried to include both monastic and lay communities of practitioners. And I have tried to span the various trainings that are manifested in American Buddhist communities, including a variety of meditational practices, devotional expressions, and chanting and ritual activities. Finally, I have attempted to strike a balance between groups I had studied previously and groups I would be visiting or considering for the first time.

What emerges from the above pages is a rich diversity in American Buddhism. Yet despite that diversity, the communities included in this study do seem to have an inordinate number of common features, the aggregate of which may well explain why they have all succeeded and thrived on the American scene. Most obviously, at the heart of each community is the practice tradition it maintains, irrespective of the nature of that practice. In addition, each community emphasizes the importance of Buddhist family life, and the ethical foundation in precepts that supports it. Each community offers a way to bring Buddhism into dialogue with daily life by placing a powerful emphasis on active social engagement, broadly defined. To facilitate these activities, each community understands the necessity of Buddhist education, manifested either by a formal university or by some other method of delivery that promotes an interpenetration of study and practice. In most cases, the educational program is assisted by a creative publication program that affords its community members, and others, an opportunity to bring the Dharma into their homes and to learn from professionally prepared books, audiotapes, and videotapes. Each community has evolved a highly developed organizational structure that promotes the smooth running of the community, both internally and externally, as it engages in Buddhist outreach activities. All of the communities have training programs for individuals who intend to become teachers and staff members in order to provide their *sanghas* with the next generation of American Buddhist teachers. Moreover, in their forward-looking conversation with others engaged in interreligious dialogue, each utilizes the most sophisticated tools of information exchange technology to make its histories, teachings, activities, schedules, and resources available to all who are interested. And as we shall see in chapter 6, the number of "Western" Buddhists is substantial, both in the United States and elsewhere.

CHAPTER 4

The Silent *Sangha*

Buddhism in the Academy

Virtually everyone who begins an academic career in Buddhist Studies eventually pores through Étienne Lamotte's exciting volume *Histoire de bouddhisme indien des origines à l'ère Śaka,* either in the original French or in Sara Webb-Boin's admirable English translation.[1] That Lamotte was a Catholic priest seems not to have influenced either his understanding of, or respect for, the Buddhist tradition, although he did worry a bit from time to time about the reaction of the Vatican to his work. Edward Conze, arguably one of the most colorful Buddhist scholars of this century, once remarked of Lamotte: "When I last saw him, he had risen to the rank of Monseigneur and worried about how his 'Histoire' had been received at the Vatican. '*Mon professeur,* do you think they will regard the book as *hérétique?*' They obviously did not. His religious views showed the delightful mixture of absurdity and rationality which is one of the hallmarks of a true believer."[2] Although there have been only a few scholarly studies chronicling the academic investigation of Buddhism by Western researchers, and, until quite recently, fewer studies still of the academic discipline known as Buddhist Studies, the issue of the religious affiliation of the researcher has not been part of the mix. Almost exclusively, the founding mothers and fathers of Buddhist Studies in the West have had personal religious commitments entirely separate from Buddhism.

As a novice graduate student in the prestigious Buddhist Studies program at the University of Wisconsin in the fall of 1967, I heard my very first "in-group" story from the senior students; it was about the recent visit of Edward Conze, conclusively acknowledged as the world's foremost scholar of that complicated form of Mahāyāna literature known as *prajñāpāramitā.* The narrative, however, had nothing whatsoever to do with Professor Conze's great scholarly passion. Instead, it concerned a question playfully put to the rather blunt and outspoken scholar during a seminar session: "Dr. Conze, do *you* actually meditate?" Conze's simple reply: "Yes." But the student pressed on: "Ever *get* anywhere?" The brusque response: "First trance state." The dialogue abruptly ceased and the issue was never broached again. Upon hearing that story as a naïve fledgling Buddhologist, I was utterly and absolutely astounded to learn that *any scholar* of Buddhism actually *did* anything Buddhist. Now, barely a quarter century later, it is rather commonplace for individuals teaching Buddhist Studies at universities throughout the world to be "scholar-practitioners," involved in the practice of trainings associated with various Buddhist traditions and sects. The back cover of Georges Dreyfus's recent book *Recognizing Reality: Dharmakīrti's Philosophy and Its Tibetan Interpretations,* for example, mentions his academic affiliation *and* the fact that he earned the monastic *geshe* degree following fifteen years of study in Tibetan Buddhist monasteries in India.[3] Nonetheless, it is not always easy for these academics to reveal their religious orientation in an environment that is not uniformly supportive of such choices. Thus this chapter will serve the dual purpose of describing not only the *development* of the academic study of Buddhism in America, but also some of the ways in which that development has affected the personal lives of those scholars who have made formal religious commitments to the Buddhist tradition.

European Antecedents

Recently, the important volume *Curators of the Buddha: The Study of Buddhism under Colonialism,* edited by Donald S. Lopez, Jr., has attracted much attention.[4] It was the topic of a panel at the 1995 annual meeting of the American Academy of Religion and the subject of a review article, "Buddhist Studies in the Post-Colonial Age," by Jan Nattier.[5] The book is a careful exercise in self-reflection, and Nattier is correct when she begins her article by observing, "This is a provocative book in many senses of the word. By exploring not just the ideas but the attitudes conveyed in the writings of several founding fathers of Buddhist Studies in the West . . . *Curators of the Buddha* will provoke its readers into seeing these figures in a new light."[6] However, the book is not the first attempt to contextualize and comment upon the discipline of Buddhist Studies in the West.

Although there was very little reliable information in the West pertaining to Buddhism prior to the nineteenth century, Henri de Lubac's *La rencontre du bouddhisme et de l'occident,* published in 1952, is especially useful in summarizing this early literature.[7] Of course one can find such landmark works as Simon de la Loubère's *Du royaume de Siam,* published in 1691,[8] but it was not until the early nineteenth century, with the appearance of Michel François Ozeray's *Recherches sur Buddhou* (1817),[9] that the picture began to brighten. Soon the pioneering efforts of Henry Thomas Colebrooke, Brian Houghton Hodgson, Alexander Csoma de Körös, and Eugène Burnouf, followed by the work of their intellectual heirs, brought the reliable study of Buddhism to Europe.

Despite the fact that the primary focus of this volume is on North America rather than Europe, it is nonetheless imperative to at least sample the flavor of the Buddhist studies that caught the fancy of the intellectual forebears of American scholars of Buddhism. To a large extent, this interest in Buddhism was philological, converging on the increasing availability of Sanskrit and Pali manuscripts that were appearing on the European continent. Perhaps the most thorough examination of this development is Russell Webb's "Pali Buddhist Studies in the West," serialized in the now defunct *Pali Buddhist Review.*[10] There Webb systematically reviews the developments of Pali and Buddhist Studies in virtually all European countries, as well as Canada and the United States. Webb continues this work, having updated these early studies, in his essay "Contemporary European Scholarship on Buddhism," published in 1989.[11] But the interested scholar should also examine William Peiris's *The Western Contribution to Buddhism,* which contains much historical detail and interesting character sketches of the early scholars of Buddhism.[12] Jan W. de Jong's *A Brief History of Buddhist Studies in Europe and America* also offers valuable information, although America is virtually absent from the volume despite its title.[13]

Perhaps the only conclusions that might be drawn from the above, insofar as conclusions are possible, is that several distinctions appear obvious from an examination of these sources. First, geographic associations seem to identify at least two "schools" of Buddhology: the Anglo-German and the Franco-Belgian. The former (and older) was led by Thomas W. Rhys Davids and Hermann Oldenberg, while the latter included primarily Louis de La Vallée Poussin, Jean Przyluski, Sylvain Lévi, Paul Demiéville, and Étienne Lamotte. To these schools Edward Conze, quite reasonably, adds a third: the Leningrad school, including Stcherbatsky, Rosenberg, and Obermiller.[14] The Anglo-German school almost exclusively emphasized the Pali literary tradition, while the Franco-Belgian school utilized the Sanskritic materials, along with their corresponding translations and commentaries in Chinese and Tibetan. The Leningrad school is clearly closer to the Franco-Belgian school than the Anglo-German. These are general classifications, but they nonetheless capture the style of the traditions as they have been maintained over the last century.

Early Buddhist Studies in America

Thomas Tweed's *The American Encounter with Buddhism, 1844–1912: Victorian Culture and the Limits of Dissent* is a wonderful and complete introduction to the early pioneers of the American Buddhist movement.[15] For those unwilling to wade through the more than two hundred pages of Tweed's meticulous prose, a pleasant narrative can be found in the chapter titled "The Restless Pioneers" in Rick Fields's *How the Swans Came to the Lake*.[16] Unfortunately, there are no such books or chapters documenting the development of the discipline of Buddhist Studies in America,[17] and the existence of such work remains a desideratum. Here we can only begin to sketch a very short overview of Buddhist Studies in America.

Although some might consider Eugène Burnouf to be the founding father of Buddhist Studies as a discipline,[18] the beginning of Buddhist Studies in the United States seems inextricably bound to three primary individuals: Paul Carus, Henry Clarke Warren, and Charles Rockwell Lanman. Carus arrived in America in the 1880s with a Ph.D. from Tübingen University, eventually becoming the editor of *Open Court* journal and later of Open Court Publishing Company. His career, and his relationship to American Buddhist Studies, are chronicled in a recent essay by Martin Verhoeven, "Americanizing the Buddha: Paul Carus and the

Transformation of Asian Thought."[19] Although he wrote more than a dozen books of his own, including the still widely read *Gospel of Buddhism* (1894), Carus is probably best known for bringing D. T. Suzuki to America and employing him at Open Court for many years.

Henry Clarke Warren and Charles Rockwell Lanman were more scholarly in their approach than Carus, and worked diligently to establish the Buddhist literary tradition in America. Lanman had studied Sanskrit under William Dwight Whitney, earning his doctorate at Yale in 1875 before moving on to Johns Hopkins, and eventually becoming a professor of Sanskrit at Harvard University in 1880. Warren, though horribly deformed as the result of a childhood accident, had studied Sanskrit with Lanman at Johns Hopkins, and followed his learned master back to Harvard, where the two struck up an alliance that culminated in the creation of a new publication series known as the Harvard Oriental Series. Hendrik Kern's edition of the *Jātakamālā,* a collection of Buddhist birth stories, was the first volume in the series, with Warren's famous *Buddhism in Translations* becoming the third in 1896.

Following Warren's death in 1899, and with Lanman moving on to other studies in the Indic tradition, the development of Buddhist Studies was left to others. One of these early trailblazers was Eugene Watson Burlingame, who had studied with Lanman at Harvard before shifting to Yale, where he worked industriously on a variety of Pali texts. By 1921 he had published a three-volume translation of the *Dhammapada* commentary in the Harvard Oriental Series. Burlingame was followed by W. Y. Evans-Wentz, a 1907 Stanford graduate, who studied extensively in Europe and is best known for his collaborative compiling of the translations of his teacher, Kazi Dawa-Sandup. By the time of Evans-Wentz's death in 1965, a new group of Buddhological scholars had developed on the American scene, including such committed educators as Winston King, Richard Gard, and Kenneth K. S. Ch'en.

Despite the work of these early scholars, it was not until after 1960 that Buddhist Studies began to emerge as a significant discipline in the American university system and publishing industry. During the Vietnam War years and immediately thereafter, Buddhist Studies was to enjoy a boom, largely through the efforts of such leading professors as Richard Hugh Robinson at the University of Wisconsin, Masatoshi Nagatomi at Harvard University, and Alex Wayman at Columbia University. No doubt there were many reasons for the increased development of

Buddhist Studies, not the least of which were the increase in Area Studies programs in American universities, growing government interest in things Asian, the immense social anomie that permeated American culture in the 1960s, and the growing dissatisfaction with (and perhaps rejection of) traditional religion. During the 1960s a formal graduate program was instituted at the University of Wisconsin offering both an M.A. and a Ph.D. in Buddhist Studies. Interdisciplinary programs emphasizing the study of Buddhism were soon available at Berkeley and Columbia as well. As other programs arose—such as the program at the Center for the Study of World Religions at Harvard University, and the history of religions program at the University of Chicago—it became possible to gain sophisticated training in all aspects of the Buddhist tradition, and in all Buddhist canonical languages as well. As a result, a new generation of young Buddhologists was born, appearing rapidly on the campuses of many American universities and rivaling their overseas peers in both training and insight.

This picture of expanding American Buddhology is perhaps not so rosy as one might at first think, rapid growth notwithstanding. As interest grew, funding for graduate education did not keep pace, and would-be Buddhologists no longer had the luxury of being able to spend six or eight or even ten *fully-funded years* in preparation for the Ph.D. As a result, the breadth and scope of their training was compromised, resulting in an accelerated urgency for specialization. The consequence was that very few new Buddhologists were appearing with the complete philological training and geographical comprehensiveness of their teachers. Thus it became usual to find individuals focusing on *one tradition,* such as Indian or Tibetan or Chinese or Japanese Buddhism, but rarely *all* of the traditions. And if the distinctions that characterize the Anglo-German, Franco-Belgian, and Leningrad schools, mentioned above, are accurate, the "American" school is equally divided within itself.

Current Buddhist Studies

More than fifteen years ago, I titled a review article on recent Buddhist literature "Buddhist Studies American Style: A Shot in the Dark," explaining at the outset that the conjured image of Inspector Clouseau "falling through banisters, walking into walls, crashing out of windows, and somehow miraculously getting the job done with the assistance of his loyal Oriental servant," was not an accidental choice on my part, that the path of Buddhist Studies in America was just as erratic as that of poor Clouseau.[20]

Lately, as noted above, Buddhist Studies in America has begun to engage in the useful process of self-reflection, and the results of that inquiry are fruitful and inspiring. Following the publication of David Seyfort Ruegg's insightful article "Some Observations on the Present and Future of Buddhist Studies,"[21] the *Journal of the International Association of Buddhist Studies* devoted an entire issue (winter 1995) to the topic "On Method," providing the occasion for scholars to reflect on various aspects of the discipline. José Cabezón, in a careful, brilliant article, summarizes the critical question:

> Although the academic study of Buddhism is much older than the International Association of Buddhist Studies and the journal to which it gave rise, the founding of the latter, which represents a significant—perhaps pivotal—step in the institutionalization of the field, is something that occurred less than twenty years ago. Nonetheless, whether a true discipline or not—whether or not Buddhist Studies has already achieved disciplinary status, whether it is proto-disciplinary or superdisciplinary—there is an apparent integrity to Buddhist Studies that at the very least calls for an analysis of the field in holistic terms.[22]

One must be aware, too, that there is a vast chasm between Buddhist Studies and other disciplinary studies in religion, such as Christian Studies. In the same forum, Luis Gómez notes:

> The difference between Christian and Buddhist Studies is perhaps in part explained by the fact that Buddhist Studies continues to be a Western enterprise about a non-Western cultural product, a discourse about Buddhism taking place in a non-Buddhist context for a non-Buddhist audience of super-specialists, whose intellectual work persists in isolation from the mainstream of Western literature, art, and philosophy, and occasionally even from the mainstream of contemporary Buddhist doctrinal reflection. The audience to which Christian Studies speaks shares with the Judeo-Christian tradition a more or less common language. It is possible, if not natural, for members of the audience to accept the conceit that they belong to the tradition and the tradition belongs to them . . . Furthermore, whereas Christianity and Christian Studies as we know them are the fruit of a continuous interaction with Western secularism, rationalism, and the modern and postmodern

Western self, most of our Buddhist materials and many of our Asian informants belong to a very different cultural tradition. The methods and expectations of our scholarship and our audiences have been shaped by a cultural history very different from that of Buddhist traditions.[23]

The homogeneity that a "common pattern of institutional support provides" is simply lacking in Buddhist studies, as Buddhologists invariably find their academic homes in Religious Studies departments, Area Studies centers, language institutes, and even schools of theology, as Cabezón straightforwardly points out.[24] Thus when he goes on to identify Buddhist Studies as a "hodge-podge," signaling its *heterogeneity,* this is no surprise. Nor should it surprise us when he proclaims, "Now that the cat of difference is out of the bag, what will guarantee the stability and longevity of the discipline is not the *insistence on homogeneity,* which in any case can now only be achieved through force, but instead by *embracing heterogeneity.*"[25]

To this point, what has also been ostensibly lacking in the discussion is a consideration of that portion of the community of North American Buddhologists that falls into a category that is most properly labeled "scholar-practitioner." Of the 106 respondents to a survey I did in 1995 (whose results will be reported below), *at least* 25 percent are openly Buddhist (although religious affiliation was *not* one of the items queried). It is my best estimate that *at least* another 25 percent remain silent about their Buddhist practice, for reasons that will become apparent. In many respects, these "silent Buddhists" are known to each other, but not to the larger community. During my early years at the Pennsylvania State University, my Buddhist Studies predecessor, Garma Chen-chi Chang, often invited me into his home for morning discussion. On these days he frequently met me in completely informal attire, and made green tea for us to share as we sat on the floor of his living room. Never did this discussion address my progress in my new position in the Religious Studies Department. Never did this discussion address my research progress or predicaments. Instead, it always concerned my own Buddhist practice, and the utterly compassionate advice of an older, and wiser, long-standing practitioner. My colleague worried not at all about my professional growth, which he assumed would develop properly, but about my spiritual health in a new and challenging environment. It was a discussion we shared with each other and never with non-Buddhists. Later, I learned why. In 1972, after a short research trip to Riverside, California, to work briefly with Professor Francis (Dojun) Cook, a fine scholar and a serious

Zen practitioner who was contributing several chapters to my forthcoming book *Buddhism: A Modern Perspective,* and who was more at ease with his personal commitment to Buddhism than any other Westerner I had ever met, I finally summoned the strength to declare to one of my Penn State colleagues that I was indeed Buddhist. His immediate response, knowing my Jewish heritage, was to say, "Oh, now you've become *Buddhish.*" It wasn't a joke, and I always wondered if it colored his future estimates of my scholarship.

In an interesting article entitled "The Ghost at the Table: On the Study of Buddhism and the Study of Religion," Malcolm David Eckel writes in his conclusion:

> It is not just students who are attracted to religious studies because they "want to know what it is to be human and humane, and intuit that religion deals with such things." There are at least a few scholars of Buddhism who feel the same way. For me the biggest unsettled question in the study of Buddhism is not whether Buddhism is religious or even whether the study of Buddhism is religious; it is whether scholars in this field can find a voice that does justice to their own religious concerns and can demonstrate to the academy why their kind of knowledge is worth having.[26]

Later in this chapter we shall examine with much specificity *how* the academic study of Buddhism in America now proceeds, but even the question of *where* to study Buddhism has been gaining greater, and continued, attention, and not only in scholarly sources. In a recent issue of *Tricycle: The Buddhist Review,* Duncan Ryūken Williams, an ordained Sōtō Zen priest and Ph.D. candidate at Harvard University, compiled a short list of institutions that offer graduate study in Buddhism. Although Williams's listing includes the expected sorts of categories ("Most Comprehensive Programs," "Institutions with Strength in Indo-Tibetan Buddhist Studies," etc.), he also includes a category called "Practitioner-Friendly Institutions." About these he says:

> Nevertheless, there are a number of degree programs that encourage or support Buddhist practice and scholarship among students. These "practitioner-friendly" programs generally offer one of three things: the ability to pursue a degree in the context of Buddhist priestly training, courses in the practice of Buddhism that complement academic study, or an emphasis on Buddhism from a normative point of view.[27]

Williams comes right to the edge of the scholar-practitioner pond when he notes, "At most universities, faculty members in Buddhist studies tend to be far fewer in number than their Christian or Jewish counterparts,"[28] but he chooses not to jump into the issue. Cabezón and Gómez elect to take the leap, both dramatically and insightfully. In advancing his comprehensive discussion of the discipline of Buddhist Studies, Cabezón suggests:

> One of the best entries into the identification of the variant kinds of scholarship is not through their sympathetic depiction, but through their caricature in stereotypes. These stereotypes are associated with specific racial/ethnic, national, religious and gender characteristics. Like all stereotypes, they are falsehoods: racist, sexist, and generally exhibiting the type of intolerance to which we as human beings are unfortunately heir. But exist they do.[29]

While Cabezón lists nine specific stereotypes, each of which is interesting in its own right, it is the first of those that informs this enterprise:

> Critical distance from the object of intellectual analysis is necessary. Buddhists, by virtue of their religious commitment, lack such critical distance from Buddhism. Hence, Buddhists are *never* good buddhologists. Or, alternatively, those who take any aspect of Buddhist doctrine seriously (whether pro or con) are scientifically suspect by virtue of allowing their individual beliefs to affect their scholarship. Good scholarship is neutral as regards questions of truth. Hence, evaluative/normative scholarship falls outside the purview of Buddhist Studies.[30]

Without undervaluing the critical goals implicit in all Buddhological scholarship, Gómez adds yet another dimension to the conversation, arguably the most critical. He says:

> Contemporary Buddhists, wherever they might be, are also an audience for our scholarship . . . They can be a source (however maligned and deprived of authority they may sometimes appear) because, inevitably, they speak to us and make demands on us . . . But in our field the object is also a voice that speaks to us and hears us. It is present not only as object but as a set of voices that demands something from us. In fact our "object" has had a biographic presence in all of our lives—*especially on those of us who can remember moments in our life narratives in which we have "felt Buddhists" or "have been Buddhists" or have "practiced," as the contemporary English expression has it.* I would venture more, even for those who at one time or another have seen in some fragment of Buddhist tradition a particle of inspiration or an atom of insight, Buddhism is an object that makes claims on their lives. For those who have failed even to experience this last form of interaction with the object, there must have been at least moments of minimal encounters with

seeking students or, after a dry and erudite lecture, one of those emotional questions from the audience that makes all scholars nervous.[31]

Of course the above places the contemporary Buddhologist squarely between the proverbial rock and hard place. If one acknowledges a personal commitment to the tradition being studied, the suspicion Cabezón cites so clearly is immediately voiced; but if one remains silent, how can the demands Gómez outlines be fairly confronted? These are issues not confronted by the American scholar of Judaism or Christianity, and they are a powerful impetus for the silence among Buddhologists alluded to in the chapter title.

The Academic Study of Buddhism in America: A Current Analysis

This chapter has made references to the perceptive reflections on the field of Buddhist Studies by Cabezón, Conze, de Jong, Gómez, Lopez, Peiris, and Ruegg, among others. What each of the above studies has lacked is a statistical component; and of course the need for data that a survey might provide is not, as I have indicated elsewhere,[32] without current precedent.

In the winter 1991 issue of the *Journal of the American Academy of Religion,* former editor Ray L. Hart was afforded 112 pages to present the results of a survey he had taken. Entitled "Religious and Theological Studies in American Higher Education: A Pilot Study,"[33] his "report" consisted of thirty-five pages of statistical evidence gleaned from a questionnaire distributed to 678 faculty members at eleven types of institutions, with the rest of the space devoted to Hart's interpretive narrative. Interestingly, he devotes an entire section of that narrative to a consideration of the key questions: "What is the relation between the *study* of religion and theology and the *practice* of religion?" and "What should the relation be?" Perhaps as expected, he could find only one statement on which all faculty everywhere agree: "One who practices religion needs to study it."[34] This of course begs the larger question, and Hart tries to clarify the three obvious positions he elicited:

1. The first view is that the study of religion and the practice of religion are two integral "terms"; each has its "site" and the two are not internally related.

2. The second view is that "the relation is completely open."
3. The third view will by now be obvious: the study of religion presupposes practice, and is undertaken to prepare for and enhance practice.[35]

Hart's findings have already been widely utilized in the discipline, clearly reflecting the perceived importance of self-definition and self-recognition within the broad field of Religious Studies.

Curiously, Hart's findings were nearly chronologically coincident with a five-year administrative review of the Buddhism Section of the American Academy of Religion, arguably the largest academic arena for Buddhologists in North America (if not the entire world). AAR's external evaluator for that review, Professor Malcolm David Eckel of Boston University, noted in his December 1991 report:

> The most important achievement of the Buddhism Group and Section at the AAR in the last 10 years has been to create a safe and reliable forum for Buddhist scholars who represent a wide variety of approaches, disciplines, and geographical orientations to exchange views and build bonds of cooperation and understanding that create an active and imaginative scholarly community.[36]

In a later article Eckel reveals that in the five years between 1986 and 1991, the attendance at the Buddhism Section's annual business meeting grew from 60 to 140, and the mailing list expanded from 106 to 600![37]

With interest piqued by the data included in Hart's report and the suppositions inherent in Eckel's, in October 1992 I set out to gather materials from the North American community of Buddhologists that would afford this community data similar to Hart's upon which to conduct a second level of self-reflection. It was clear from the outset that the six-hundred-member mailing list mentioned above contained, in addition to so-called Buddhologists, a large number of scholars of other Asian religions, many nonspecialist comparativists, and a profusion of "others." After careful sorting and synthesis, a list of 125 scholars whose primary teaching and research work fell within the discipline of Buddhist Studies was compiled, and these individuals were sent requests soliciting both data and narrative statements about the discipline. Following two additional requests, and with a rather surprising response rate of 69.6 percent (compared with Hart's 64 percent), the received material was collated. The preliminary results were presented in a paper at the 1993 AAR annual meeting in Washington, D.C., and published in the fledgling electronic journal *Gassho,* with the full results appearing slightly later in *Religion,* jointly published in England and the United States.[38]

For this current chapter, a second survey was conducted, beginning in fall 1995. In the intervening years the list was updated, revised, and refined, reflecting the arrival of new scholars into the Buddhological community, the death of others, and shifting interests. Thus the initial list of scholars in the new survey numbered 140, with 106 responses received (or 75.7 percent). On an individual level, the results collected provide an ample look at the demographics of Buddhist Studies in America. With regard to individual training, I am able to document the gender, educational background, language facility, and the like for those polled. Institutionally, I have tracked the respective academic rank of the respondents, the type of university in which they teach, and the specific department that employs each. I have collected data on memberships in professional organizations, editorships held, geographical area(s) of specialization, grants and fellowships received, professional papers presented, honors awarded, and various categories of publications (including books, refereed articles, and book reviews). From the narratives included with many of the responses, I have been able to determine a sense of the sample's collective perception of those issues deemed critical to the continuing development and advancement of the discipline. It was also possible to compile information on universities with extensive resources for the study of Buddhism. In presenting the results of my two surveys, the remainder of this chapter provides documentation for the most recent, and productive, generation of Buddhologists in America.

Individual Results

Regarding basic demographics, in Hart's survey 85.4 percent of the respondents were male, 14.4 percent female, with 0.2 percent not answering (p. 796). In my latest sample, 83 percent were male and 17 percent female, representing a small increase in percentage of females from my previous investigation (85.1 percent male, 14.9 percent female). Hart's survey revealed 90 percent of the respondents with one or more doctoral degrees, 9 percent with no doctoral degree, and 1 percent expecting the doctoral degree (p. 800). In my sample, 99.1 percent (105 of 106) had a Ph.D./Th.D. This was quite consistent with my previous survey, which revealed a 98.8 percent rate for doctoral degrees. However, my most recent sample seems to suggest a slightly younger discipline overall than several years ago: my earlier sample yielded 1975.9 as the average year for the granting of the terminal degree, whereas the newer sample shows 1980.0 as the average year. The earliest doctoral degree recorded was 1948, and the most recent 1996. Table 4 shows the breakdown in decades.

Table 4 *Decades in Which Respondents Received Doctorates (1995 Survey)*

Decade	Number of respondents who received Ph.D./Th.D.
1990s	21
1980s	45
1970s	25
1960s	12
1950s	1
1940s	1

The majority of the respondents in my studies earned their doctorates as shown in table 5.

Table 5 *Universities at Which Respondents Received Doctorates*

University	1993 survey	1995 survey
University of Chicago	8	14
University of Wisconsin	10	12
Harvard University	10	10
Columbia University	5	10
Yale University	6	7
University of Virginia	7	7
Stanford University	0	6
University of California (Berkeley)	4	5
Princeton University	3	4
Temple University	5	4
Northwestern University	3	3
University of Michigan	0	3
University of Washington	0	2
Tokyo University	0	2

In my 1993 survey, 44.9 percent of those responding taught in various public institutions, while 55.1 percent were employed by private institutions. The 1995 sample closely mirrors that result, with 44.4 percent of those responding teaching in various public institutions, 52.8 percent employed by private institutions, and 2.8 percent employed in other professional settings. Regarding rank, the results shown in table 6 were obtained.

Table 6 *Academic Rank of Respondents*

Rank	1993 survey	1995 survey
Emeritus	—	2.8%
Full professor	36.0%	33.0%
Associate professor	31.4%	33.0%
Assistant professor	22.1%	22.7%
Lecturer	—	3.8%
Other	10.5%	4.7%

In the 1993 survey, the emeritus and lecturer ranks were combined with adjunct professor, dean, and acting dean into the category "Other." In 1995, separate categories for "Emeritus" and "Lecturer" were listed.

In terms of specialization, any comparison between samples would be incongruous because for the 1993 sample only one primary specialization was recorded, while in the 1995 sample it became clear that in many cases multiple specializations were emphasized. For example, in 1993, 37.0 percent of the sample reported specializing in Japan/East Asia; 29.6 percent, India/South Asia; 23.5 percent, Tibet/Inner Asia; 6.2 percent, China/East Asia; 2.5 percent, Korea/East Asia; and 1.2 percent, other areas. Bearing in mind that multiple listings were allowed in the 1995 sample, yielding a total in excess of 100 percent, that survey showed the results set out in table 7.

Table 7 *Specializations of Respondents (1995 Survey)*

Area	Number of respondents	Percent of total respondents
Japan/East Asia	39	36.8
India/South Asia	37	34.9
Tibet/Inner Asia	22	20.8
China/East Asia	16	15.1
Korea/East Asia	2	1.9
Other areas	3	2.8

Language facility seems to be rather consistent with area specialization, taking into account the fact that many scholars develop a multiplicity of language skills and that Sanskrit appears to be the consistent foundation language from which other language studies related to Buddhism proceed. Table 8 gives the breakdown of language skills among respondents to the 1995 survey.

Table 8 *Language Skills among Respondents (1995 Survey)*

Language	Number of respondents
Sanskrit	59
Japanese	49
Pali/Prakrit	43
Chinese	37
Tibetan	33
Korean	2

Other languages cited include Hindi, Sinhalese, Nepali, Thai, Mongolian, Sogdian, and Vietnamese.

With regard to membership in professional and learned societies, Hart's study (p. 809) produced extremely surprising results, considering the nature of his sample. Of the seven most populated professional organizations, *four* had traditionally Asian constituencies: the Association for Asian Studies (which ranked second, at 22 percent), American Oriental Society (fourth; 17 percent), International Association of Buddhist Studies (tied for sixth; 8 percent), and the Society for Asian and Comparative Philosophy (tied for sixth; 8 percent). Not unexpectedly, the American Academy of Religion topped the list with 67 percent, while the Society of Biblical Literature was third with 19 percent. In my Buddhist Studies samples, a wide variety of professional societies was noted. Table 9 (see p. 189) presents a comparison of the 1993 and 1995 results.

Other societies garnering multiple mention by the respondents, in decreasing order, included the Buddhist Peace Fellowship, the Tibet Society, the International Association for the History of Religion, the T'ang Studies Society, and the International Association of Tibetan Studies. As expected, most respondents reported multiple, and often many, memberships. Many respondents in the most recent Buddhist Studies sample

Table 9 *Professional Organizations to Which Respondents Belonged*

Organization	Percent (and number) of respondents: 1993 survey	1995 survey
American Academy of Religion	75.9% (66)	87.7% (93)
Association for Asian Studies	57.5% (50)	57.8% (61)
International Assn. of Buddhist Studies	43.7% (38)	47.2% (50)
Society for Buddhist-Christian Studies	19.5% (17)	20.8% (22)
Society for Asian and Comp. Philosophy	17.2% (15)	15.1% (16)
American Oriental Society	16.1% (14)	12.3% (13)
Society for the Study of Japanese Religions	10.3% (9)	11.3% (12)
Society for the Study of Chinese Religions	8.0% (7)	11.3% (12)
Society for Tantric Studies	0	9.4% (10)
International Assn. of Shin Buddhist Studies	6.9% (6)	8.5% (9)
Pali Text Society	6.9% (6)	4.7% (5)

reported significant offices and administrative positions in the above societies.[39]

The 1995 sample has shown a remarkably high level of activity in presenting scholarly papers at the annual meetings of the professional societies listed above. Additionally, those sampled have been very active in presenting scholarly papers (not simply "lectures") in other professional settings such as international conferences, regional professional meetings, and thematic conferences sponsored by various institutions. Adjusting the results to reflect those who did not respond with information on this item, the findings show:

Papers at annual meeting	4.4 per respondent
Other scholarly papers	12.2 per respondent

Thus the average respondent has made 16.6 professional presentations during his or her academic career. That this figure is slightly lower than the 19.8 figure reported in the 1993 sample reflects the supposition, expressed above, that the 1995 sample is slightly junior to the previous group of respondents.

Both Buddhist Studies samples presented a high magnitude of success in grant and fellowship acquisition, both during graduate training and after the granting of the Ph.D. Again adjusting for those who did not respond with information in this category of inquiry, the 1995 sample reported 2.2 grants per respondent at the graduate school level. This figure included such items as National Defense Education Act fellowships, Fulbright awards, and the like, but not assistantships of any kind. With Ph.D. in hand, the samples went on to receive grants as summarized in table 10.

Table 10 *Awards Received by Respondents*

	Number of awards	
Grant/fellowship agency	1993 sample	1995 sample
National Endowment for the Humanities	57	73
Fulbright	35	24
American Council of Learned Societies	14	24
Japan Foundation	13	17
Social Science Research Council	8	8
American Academy of Religion	0	5
Lilly Foundation	0	4
Pew Charitable Trusts	0	4

In addition, grants from the Ford Foundation, Mellon Foundation, Danforth Foundation, and Rockefeller Foundation were cited, along with hundreds of grants internally administered by the various faculty members' host institutions. National and international grants yielded 2.1 awards per respondent, while internal university grants totaled 2.4 awards per respondent. Thus this sample reports a total of 6.7 awards per respondent across the scope of their activity in the discipline.

Just as the Buddhist Studies samples presented highly active involvement in professional societies, and significant success in grant and fellowship acquisition, they also demonstrated a high degree of accomplishment in securing meaningful editorial positions with leading academic presses and journals. Of the 1995 sample, no less than six individuals are editors for book series with university presses, while another ten sit on university press editorial boards. Presses represented in this group include Oxford University Press, Indiana University Press, University of California Press, University of Michigan Press, Princeton University Press, University of Virginia Press, and the State University of New York Press. Additionally, nineteen respondents edit book series for commercial/trade publishers, while another seven are editorial board members. Some of the presses cited in this category include Snow Lion, Shambhala, Motilal Banarsidass,

Curzon Press, Wadsworth, Buddhica Britannica, the Kuroda Institute Series (published by the University of Hawaii Press), and the AAR Monograph and AAR Texts & Translations Series (both published by Scholars Press).

Many respondents to the 1995 survey report major editorial positions with journals, as shown in table 11.

Table 11 *Journals at Which Respondents Hold Editorial Positions (1995 Survey)*

Editor in chief/coeditor (14)	Associate/assistant editor (9)
Buddhist-Christian Studies	*Critical Review of Books in Religion*
Buddhist and Tibetan Studies	*The Eastern Buddhist*
Critical Review of Books in Religion	*History of Religions*
History of Religions	*Journal of Asian Studies*
Indo-Judaic Studies	*Journal of Ecumenical Studies*
Japanese Journal of Religious Studies	*Journal of Indian Philosophy*
Journal of Buddhist Ethics	*Journal of the Intl. Assoc. of Buddhist Studies*
Journal of Buddhist Literature	*Journal of Religious Ethics*
Journal of the International Association of Buddhist Studies	
Korean Culture	
Pacific World	

Also, nine individuals hold or have held the position of book review editor at *Buddhist-Christian Studies, Journal of Chinese Philosophy, Pacific World, Philosophy East and West,* and *Religious Studies Review.* Another two have held positions as guest editor at *Cahiers d'Extrême-Asie* and *Journal of Religious Ethics.* Finally, forty-five respondents cited positions on the editorial boards of many of the journals listed above, as well as the *Chung-Hwa Buddhist Studies Journal, Garuda, Gender and World Religion, Journal of Asian Philosophy, Journal of the American Academy of Religion, Journal of Chinese Religions, Journal of Comparative Sociology and Religion, Journal of Feminist Studies in Religion, Numen, Soundings, Studies in Central and East Asian Religion, T'ang Studies,* and the *Tibet Journal.*

Although it has never been clear how to report scholarly publication data with precision, Ray Hart's study utilizes three publication categories: (1) books; (2) articles, essays, and chapters; and (3) book reviews. Hart is concerned only with the period of the past five years. In other words, Hart presents no career publication data—a statistic that may well be more revealing than his five-year information. Thus in this study I have confined myself to presenting *only* career data. The categories are at once problematic in that Hart does not distinguish between refereed and nonrefereed publications, a distinction now made at virtually all colleges and universities. Equally, Hart makes no distinction between books authored and books edited, another distinction that is part of the politically correct protocol of the American system of higher education.

In an attempt to address the exigencies of that system, I have sought to refine Hart's categories somewhat in favor of presenting more meaningful statistics. In so doing, I have separated the book category into two subcategories: (1) books authored/coauthored; and (2) books edited/coedited. I have also pared Hart's "articles, essays, and chapters" category down to refereed articles and chapters (taking the stand, not shared in all university evaluations, that chapters are indeed refereed, often bringing to bear a higher standard than many refereed journals). In my schema, I obtained the career results summarized in table 12.

Table 12 *Scholarly-Publication Data for Respondents*

	Average per respondent (and total for all respondents)	
Category of publication	1993 sample	1995 sample
Books authored/coauthored	2.4 (209)	2.3 (239)
Books edited/coedited	1.7 (148)	1.1 (116)
Refereed articles[a]	16.8 (1462)	7.3 (769)
Refereed chapters	—	6.5 (689)
Book reviews	12.7 (1105)	12.9 (962)[b]

[a] This category was combined with the following one (refereed chapters) in the first survey.

[b] Only 72 respondents said they had written book reviews, and this fact is reflected in the statistical average.

Allowing adjustment of the sample to reflect career duration, the two sets of results are remarkably similar. Further, by refining the data collection in the 1995 sample it was possible to determine that 126 of the 355 books reported as having been written were published with university presses.

Allowing for multiple authorship/editorship, it was possible to name and rank those book publishers most often utilized as publication avenues for Buddhist Studies. Table 13 offers a ranked list of those publishers.[40]

Table 13 *Publishers of Buddhist Studies*

University presses	Trade/commercial presses
1. State University of New York Press	1. Snow Lion
2. University of Hawaii Press	2. Prentice-Hall
3. Princeton University Press	3. E. J. Brill (tie)
4. University of California Press	3. Motilal Banarsidass (tie)
5. Oxford University Press	5. Tungta (tie)
6. University of Chicago Press	5. Wisdom Publications (tie)
7. Columbia University Press	7. Shambhala (tie)
8. Cambridge University Press	7. Greenwood Press (tie)
9. Penn State University Press (tie)	7. Orbis (tie)
9. University of S. Carolina Press (tie)	7. Asian Humanities Press (tie)

It is also possible to determine a ranked list of refereed journals most often utilized as a publication outlet by the overall sample:[41]

1. *History of Religions*
2. *Buddhist-Christian Studies*
3. *Journal of the International Association of Buddhist Studies*
4. *Philosophy East and West*
5. *Eastern Buddhist*
6. *Journal of the American Academy of Religion*
7. *Japanese Journal of Religious Studies*
8. *Journal of the American Oriental Society*
9. *Pacific World*
10. *Tibet Journal*
11. *Numen*
11. *Journal of Indian Philosophy*
13. *Journal of Asian Studies*
13. *Religion*
13. *Monumenta Nipponica*
13. *Journal of Religious Studies*
13. *Studia Missionalia*
13. *Journal of Chinese Philosophy*

Institutional Results

On the surface, it would appear that tracking institutional programs in Buddhist Studies should be quite easy. One might simply turn first to those universities, listed earlier, that produced the largest numbers of doctoral degrees among the 106 respondents to the individual portion of the 1995 survey. By cross-referencing those results with the latest *Directory of Departments and Programs of Religious Studies in North America* (edited by David G. Truemper), and with the appropriate portions of the World Wide Web pages maintained by these major universities, the results ought to be readily apparent. One could then add to the tracking process by following *where* the recipients of these doctoral degrees are currently employed. To some extent, that was how I compiled my 1993 results, although the World Wide Web was far less useful at that time.

In 1993 I reported that only two North American universities had more than three full-time faculty members whose work fell within the discipline of Buddhology: the University of Virginia and the University of Chicago. Additionally, I reported that Harvard University, Columbia University, the University of Michigan, Princeton University, and McMaster University each had three full-time Buddhist Studies faculty members; a much larger list of universities with two Buddhist Studies faculty was cited.

However, like all disciplines, Buddhist Studies is continually changing, primarily as a result of faculty relocation, altered interests, retirement, and new hires from the continually increasing pool of newly minted scholars entering the field. José Cabezón accurately points out that "for about a decade or so, buddhologists in North America have found employment in increasing numbers in departments of religious studies and schools of theology. Often this has meant that we have had to expand our pedagogical repertoire beyond courses in Buddhist Studies to accommodate the curricular need of these institutions."[42] After surveying a number of issues having impact on Buddhist Studies, Cabezón goes on to conclude:

> All of these factors have contributed to what we might call the diversification of the buddhologist: a movement away from classical Buddhist Studies based on the philological study of written texts, and toward the investigation of more general, comparative and often theoretical issues that have implications (and audiences) outside of Buddhist Studies. Some colleagues have resigned

themselves to this situation: a set of circumstances that must be tolerated for the sake of gainful employment. Others—and I count myself in this camp—have found the pressure to greater diversification intellectually stimulating, affording an opportunity to enter into broader conversations where Buddhist texts are one, but not the only, voice.[43]

Thus it is no longer completely clear what constitutes a full-time Buddhologist, and when one factors in the movement in the opposite direction—scholars from other disciplines incorporating Buddhist materials into their work—the entire issue of listing the number of full-time Buddhologists at any institution becomes quite murky.

One such attempt to at least begin the task of surveying institutions has been undertaken by Duncan Williams of Harvard University and cited above. Williams has devised a number of classificatory categories (with his choice of institutions appropriately placed):

Practitioner-Friendly Institutions

California Institute of Integral Studies
Graduate Theological Union
Hsi Lai University
Institute of Buddhist Studies
Naropa Institute

Most Comprehensive Programs

Harvard University
Indiana University
University of Chicago
University of Hawaii at Manoa
University of Michigan
University of Virginia

Institutions with Strength in East Asian Buddhist Studies

Princeton University
Stanford University
University of Arizona
University of California at Los Angeles
University of California at Santa Barbara
University of Pennsylvania
Yale University

Institutions with Strength in Indo-Tibetan Buddhist Studies

Harvard University

University of Michigan

University of Virginia

University of Washington

Institutions with Strength in Southeast Asian Buddhist Studies

Harvard University

University of Chicago

Other Noteworthy Programs

Columbia University

University of California at Berkeley

University of Texas at Austin

University of Wisconsin[44]

While the attempt is admirable, the results reflect precisely the kind of dilemma of uncertainty suggested by Cabezón: what to include and what not to include, and who counts where? For example, it might be possible to argue that Nyingma Institute and Barre Center for Buddhist Studies each have far more developed Buddhist Studies programs than the more academically diversified Graduate Theological Union (whose faculty listing contains the phrase "Access to professors at The Institute of Buddhist Studies"—hardly an endorsement for inclusion in this list) or California Institute of Integral Studies. In some cases, Williams's choices appear rather arbitrary as well.[45]

Conclusions

In the years between 1972 and 1978, while I was doing fieldwork for *American Buddhism,* I visited more American Buddhist groups than I can now remember, and although such educational enterprises as Nyingma Institute (founded in 1973) and Naropa Institute (founded in 1974) were still young and sparse on the American Buddhist landscape, there was scarcely a group I visited that didn't aggressively emphasize the relationship between, and need for, *both* study and practice. In an experiential age, with religious antinomianism of virtually all kinds rampant, this insistence on study along with practice startled me.

Stories reflecting the tension between study and practice in Buddhism are abundant in both the primary and secondary literature on the subject. Walpola Rahula's *History of Buddhism in Ceylon* provides a good summary of the issue.[46] During the first century B.C.E., in the midst of potential foreign invasion and a severe famine, Sri Lankan monks feared that the Buddhist Tripiṭaka, preserved only in oral tradition, might be lost. Thus the scriptures were committed to writing for the first time. Nonetheless, in the aftermath of the entire dilemma, a new question arose: What is the basis of the "teaching" (i.e., *sāsana*), learning or practice? A clear difference of opinion resulted in the development of two groups: the Dhammakathikas, who claimed that learning was the basis of the *sāsana*, and the Paṃsukūlikas, who argued for practice as the basis. The Dhammakathikas apparently won out, as is attested to by several commentarial statements quoted by Rahula.[47]

The two vocations described above came to be known as *gantha-dhura*, or the "vocation of books," and *vipassanā-dhura*, or the "vocation of meditation," with the *former* being regarded as the superior training (because surely meditation would not be possible if the teachings were lost). Rahula points out that *gantha-dhura* originally referred *only* to the learning and the teaching of the Tripiṭaka, but that in time it came to refer also to "languages, grammar, history, logic, medicine, and other fields of study."[48] Eventually, the *vipassanā-dhura* monks began to live in the forest, where they could best pursue their vocation undisturbed, while the *gantha-dhura* monks began to dwell in villages and towns. As such, the *gantha-dhura* monks began to play a significant role in Buddhist and even secular education. Peter Harvey, for example, notes: "The *Sangha* has also been active in education. In the lands of Southern and Northern Buddhism, monasteries were the major, or sole, source of education until modern times. This is reflected in the fact that the most common Burmese term for a monastery, *kyaung*, means 'school.' "[49] Rahula says as much, quoting R. K. Mookerji's *Ancient Indian Education*: "The history of the Buddhist system of education is practically that of the Buddhist Order or Sangha . . . The Buddhist world did not offer any educational opportunities apart from or independently of its monasteries. All education, sacred as well as secular, was in the hands of the monks."[50] In view of the above, it would probably not be going too far to refer to the *gantha-dhura* monks as "scholar-monks." These "scholar-monks" would largely fulfill the role of "settled monastic renunciant" in Reginald Ray's creative three-tiered model for Buddhist practitioners (contrasted with the "forest renunciant" and "layperson").[51]

Why is this distinction so important? It is significant for at least two reasons. First, and most obviously, it reveals why the tradition of study in Buddhism, so long minimized in popular and scholarly investigations of the American Buddhist tradition, has had such an impact on that same tradition, and has resulted in the rapid development of American Buddhist schools and institutes of higher learning in the latter quarter of this century. Furthermore, it explains why the American Buddhist movement has encouraged a high level of "Buddhist literacy" among its practitioners. However, it also highlights the fact that the American Buddhist movement has been almost exclusively a *lay* movement. While many leaders of various American Buddhist groups may have had formal monastic training (irrespective of whether they continue to lead monastic lifestyles), the vast majority of their disciples have not. Thus the educational model on which American Buddhists pattern their behavior is contrary to traditional Asian Buddhism. It is, in fact, the *converse* of the traditional model. Thus, at least with regard to Buddhist study and education, there is a leadership gap in the American Buddhist community, one largely not filled by an American *sangha* of "scholar-monks."

What has been the response to the gap in educational leadership on the part of American Buddhist communities? Again, I think the explanation is twofold. On the one hand, there is a movement in some American Buddhist communities to identify those individuals *within the community itself* who are best suited, and best trained, to serve the educational needs of the community, and to confer appropriate authority on those individuals in a formal way. Recently, Sakyong Mipham Rinpoche, son of Chögyam Trungpa and now head of the Shambhala International community, declared nine community members acharyas, or teachers. These nine individuals, one of whom holds a Ph.D. degree from the University of Chicago with specialization in Buddhism, were authorized to take on enhanced teaching and leadership roles in their community and beyond. In the words of one of the nine:

> We all felt a commitment to deepen the understanding in the West of Kagyu, Nyingma, and Shambhala traditions. There was also a common feeling that we could take a lead in looking outward beyond our community to engage in creative and open-minded dialogue with other spiritual traditions, and to explore the many forms of contemporary and traditional wisdom.[52]

There are a few communities in the United States where monks or nuns are in residence and the traditional Asian model is maintained, such as Hsi Lai Temple. However, most American Buddhist communities are bound by necessity to follow the procedure utilized by Shambhala International. Unlike many Asian countries where "Buddhist Studies finds consistent institutional support from religious circles,"[53] American scholars are not likely to benefit from enterprises that enhance the opportunities of their Asian counterparts, such as Sōka University in Japan.[54] There is, however, another alternative, where the American Buddhological scholar-practitioner is vital in the ongoing development of the American Buddhist tradition.

Above, it was noted that in Asia the monastic renunciants were almost exclusively responsible for the religious education of the lay *sangha*. On the other hand, virtually everyone who writes on American Buddhism sees it almost exclusively as a lay movement, devoid of a *significant* monastic component. Emma Layman, one of the earliest researchers in the field, says as much: "In general, American Buddhists are expected to lead their lives within the lay community rather than in a monastic setting."[55] Later, Rick Fields echoed the same sentiment: "Generalization of any kind seems to dissolve in the face of such cultural and religious diversity. And yet it does seem safe to suggest that lay practice is the real heart and koan of American Buddhism."[56] In the absence of the traditional "scholar-monks" so prevalent in Asia, it may well be that the "scholar-practitioners" of today's American Buddhism will fulfill the role of "quasi monastics," or at of least treasure troves of Buddhist literacy and information, functioning as guides through whom one's understanding of the Dharma may be sharpened. In this way individual practice might once again be balanced with individual study so that Buddhist study deepens one's practice while Buddhist practice informs one's study. Obviously, such a suggestion spawns two further questions: (1) Are there sufficient scholar-practitioners currently active in American Buddhism to make such an impact? and (2) Are they actually making that impact?

With regard to the former question, much of the information reported above is necessarily anecdotal. By simply making mental notes at the various conferences attended by American Buddhologists, based on discussions of individual practice, one can develop a roster of scholar-practitioners who are openly Buddhist; and while such a roster is not publishable in a survey that guarantees anonymity, the number is quite clearly *at least* 25 percent. I first became aware of ways in which personal study and practice interpenetrated during my initial summer at Naropa Institute in 1974, when at least one individual showed me the arrangement of his academic study and personal shrine, side by side in the same room. And it was not unusual for Buddhologists to teach their academic classes immediately preceding or following a shared session of meditation practice. When the American Academy of Religion last held its annual meeting in Kansas City, I attended a dinner with seven other academic Buddhologists, all of whom were Buddhists. One of my favorite memories of Calgary revolves around my first visit to the home of Professor A. W. Barber. Not only was his hospitality superb, but his Buddhist shrine was elegant, *and it was the first thing he showed me in his home.* To be sure, the descriptions that might be offered are plentiful. My best estimate is that *at least* another 25 percent of scholars surveyed are almost certainly Buddhist, but are very careful not to make public expressions of their religiosity, for fear of professional reprisal, keenly felt or perceived.

The second question is perhaps not so difficult to assess as the first. As one surveys the vast corpus of literature that surrounds the academic programs sponsored by numerous American Buddhist groups, the names of academic scholars of Buddhism have begun to dominate the roster of invited presenters, and these individuals are almost exclusively Buddhists. At a recent conference on Buddhism in America, held in Boston in January 1997, one practitioner playfully confided that he wondered if such occasions as this might be thought of as a "pro tour for Buddhologists" as he clamored off to hear Professor Robert Thurman deliver a keynote address titled "Toward American Buddhism." In other words, many American Buddhist masters have come to acknowledge and incorporate the professional contributions of these American Buddhist scholar-practitioners into the religious life of their communities, recognizing the unique and vital role they fulfill.

This is a new and emerging phenomenon as well. In 1977, I attended a well-planned and carefully executed conference at Syracuse University, devoted to the ambitious theme "The Flowering of Buddhism in America." Despite the academic-sounding titles of many of the presentations, nearly all of the papers had been prepared by nonacademic practitioners. Seventeen years later, when the Institute of Buddhist Studies in Berkeley, California, sponsored a semester-long symposium called "Buddhisms in America: An Expanding Frontier," every single participant had impressive academic credentials, and more than two-thirds of the nearly twenty presenters were Buddhist practitioners.

Ray Hart concludes in his investigation of religious and theological studies in American higher education that the data "cannot be reported in a form that is statistically meaningful" (p. 763). I would argue, instead, that the data in my surveys are absolutely meaningful in evaluating how the discipline defines itself. In collating the data in my surveys, and evaluating the narrative statements submitted, two clear sentiments emerged. The first, which was quite obvious, reflected the number of colleagues who came to the study of Buddhism, and to academe, as a result of their strong personal commitment to Buddhism as a religious tradition; or those who cultivated a commitment to the personal practice of Buddhism as a result of their academic endeavors. For many in this first group, this circumstance has created a powerful tension between scholarship and religious commitment, between Buddhology and personal faith. The second sentiment seemed to signal a shift away from Buddhist texts and philosophy (the Buddhist "theology" that some of us have been accused of propagating) and toward an investigation of Buddhism's contextual relationship with culture. Or, as José Cabezón puts it:

> There is today a call for the increased investigation of alternative semiotic forms—oral and vernacular traditions, epigraphy, ritual, patterns of social and institutional evolution, gender, lay and folk traditions, arts, archaeology, and architecture . . . The critique is really a call for greater balance and holism within the field; it is not only a demand that equal recognition be given to new areas of research, but a call for an integrated and mutually interpenetrating research program aimed at the understanding of Buddhism as a multifaceted entity.[57]

At the outset of this chapter, reference was made to the book *Curators of the Buddha,* along with a number of comments about it from a review article by Jan Nattier. To be sure, Nattier is correct when she outlines some of the issues still lacking in the volume: a consideration of the difference in outlook and methodology between specialists in Tibetan Buddhism and those in Chinese Buddhism; a consideration of variations in the training and perspective between Buddhist Studies scholars trained in Religious Studies departments and those who were trained in Area Studies programs; a consideration of those who have had a personal dialogue with a Buddhist community and those not so involved; and a consideration of the rifts in North American Buddhist Studies.[58] Yet, after praising Lopez, who in addition to editing the volume also wrote one of its essays, for his frankness and willingness, as an American Buddhologist, to discuss his own encounter with Buddhism, she concludes by saying, "If there are difficulties here, they are not with the keen and self-critical eye with which Lopez reflects on his own experience as a student of Buddhism but with the degree to which he generalizes from that experience to characterize prevailing attitudes in the Buddhist Studies field at large."[59] Whether these generalizations are correct or not remains to be seen. At least the question has now moved beyond Father Lamotte's concern with being *hérétique*.

CHAPTER 5

The Cybersangha

Virtual Communities

Although the two previous chapters were concerned with an examination of the American Buddhist *sangha,* the primary focus of each revealed two very different kinds of community. On the one hand, chapter 3 presented capsule studies of a number of practitioners' communities, selected on the basis of their integrity, longevity, and diversity. These multifaceted and complex *sanghas* were predominantly composed of a community of lay practitioners of both genders, under the guidance of one or more Buddhist teachers, and often of monks and/or nuns as well. On the other hand, chapter 4 considered the community of academic scholars of Buddhism, many of whom are also Buddhist practitioners. Both the practitioners' community and the scholars' community were shown to be instrumental in the growth and development of the American Buddhist tradition. This chapter considers yet another kind of Buddhist community, a *sangha* never imagined by the Buddha, but one that unites the practitioners and scholars into one potentially vast community: the cybersangha. The word "cybersangha" was coined in 1991 by Gary Ray as a generic term to describe the Buddhist community online. Its first appearance was in the "BodhiNet Bylaws," a document created by Ray and others in which they attempted to create a democratic Buddhist echomail network for bulletin-board systems. Ray and the others thus established a foundation through which the traditional fourfold *sangha* of monks, nuns, laymen, and laywomen might coalesce with and enhance a broader and more pervasive *sangha:* the *sangha* of the four quarters.

However, before exploring the term "cybersangha" in its various applications, we need to briefly examine the way in which the term *sangha* developed in the Buddhist tradition and came to have specialized applications to specific Buddhist communities.

Despite the fact that the term *sangha* is used today in a more extended and comprehensive fashion than originally, referring to almost any community or group loosely associated with Buddhism, in the time of the Buddha the term was used in a radically different fashion. The Sanskrit word *sangha* simply connotes a society or company, or a number of people living together for a certain purpose. Akira Hirakawa points out that political groups and trade guilds, as well as religious orders, were called *sanghas*.[1] In the midst of many religious *sanghas* in the general wanderers' (*parivrājaka*) community, the Buddha's followers appropriated the term in a rather distinct fashion—one that gave their fledgling community a clear and unique identity. While outsiders may have referred to the Buddha's first disciples as *Śākyaputrīya-śramaṇas,* or "mendicants who follow the Buddha," the original community referred to itself as the *bhikṣu-sangha.* Later, when the order of nuns was founded, they became known as the *bhikṣuṇī-sangha,* and the two units were collectively known as the *ubhay-ato-sangha,* the "twofold community." In Theravāda countries, this quite narrow usage of the term *sangha* has remained the predominant meaning of the word, as is pointed out by most modern scholars writing on the Buddhist community. Richard Gombrich, for example, says:

> The Sangha consists of all those ordained, both monks and nuns. In fact in the Theravāda Buddhist countries (Sri Lanka and most of continental South-east Asia) the Order of nuns in the strict sense has died out. There are women in those countries who lead cloistered lives and behave like nuns, but for lack of a valid ordination tradition they remain outside the Sangha in the usual, strict sense. In those countries, therefore, the term Sangha is generally understood to refer only to monks and male novices.[2]

Occasionally, in the early literature, the Buddha uses the term *cāturdisa-sangha* or the "*sangha* of the four quarters,"[3] but it seems clear from his usage that he means the *monastic sangha.* Sukumar Dutt says as much, suggesting:

> The exact import and implication of the phrase is somewhat obscure, but is indicative of the growth of a sense of unity in the scattered body of the Lord's Bhikkhu followers—a unity of ideal and purpose, though perhaps no union

of corporate life and activity yet. The expression, "Sangha of the Four Quarters," became canonical; it is taken in donatory inscriptions of later ages to connote a conceptual and ideal confraternity.[4]

Eventually, however, as the eremitical lifestyle deteriorated in favor of settled monasticism, the term "*sangha* of the four quarters" took on a new meaning. As Akira Hirakawa explains:

A present order was governed by the precepts of the *vinaya,* but did not have the right to alter those precepts. The *vinaya* transcended the rights and interests of any single order. Moreover, although a present order had the right to use the monastery and its buildings, it did not have the right to sell them. To explain this situation, the existence of a higher level of the *sangha* was posited. It was called "the order of the four quarters" or the "universal order" (*cāturdisa-sangha*) and consisted of all the disciples of the Buddha. It transcended time and place and included all the monks of the past, present, and future; it encompassed all geographical areas; it continued forever.[5]

Despite the fact that Hirakawa's statement greatly expands the temporal and geographic scope of the phrase *cāturdisa-sangha,* it is clear enough that *only* the Buddhist monastic assemblies are its constituent members.

Yet early Buddhist history records that the Buddha also admitted lay members into his community, and that they eventually became a vital, symbiotic part of that community. Nevertheless, the lay community was initially considered distinct from, and even autonomous from, the monastic community. Thus, "the four groups of Buddhists were not referred to collectively as a single order (*saṅgha*)."[6] How did this transformation from two distinct and autonomous groups (i.e., monastic and lay members) to a "fourfold *sangha*" of *bhikṣus, bhikṣuṇīs, upāsakas,* and *upāsikās* evolve? Reginald Ray, in his explanation of the so-called two-tiered model of Buddhist practitioners, is quite clear about the role of the laity in the early Buddhist tradition:

On the one hand is the Buddhism of the founder, the Buddhism of the monks, marked by renunciation of the world and entry into the monastic *saṃgha,* decorous behavior as defined by the *vinaya,* the pursuit of the vocation of texts and scholarship, and the goal of nirvāṇa. On the other hand is the Buddhism of the laity, characterized by virtuous behavior and generosity toward monastics as well as by participation in the cults of the stūpa and of local deities. The laity practiced a compromised Buddhism and, in so doing, acted as a kind of buffer between the authentic Buddhism of the monks and the non-Buddhist environment of larger India.[7]

The importance of this role for the laity, or what Ray calls "the second normative lifestyle" of Indian Buddhism,[8] cannot be minimized. Although the goal of the lay Buddhist is *puṇya,* or "merit," while the monastics' goal is arhantship, or "liberation," the two communities are clearly interdependent. To think otherwise, and especially so in the West, would be incorrect, as Gombrich notes: "Buddhism is sometimes presented in the West as if the religion of the laity on the one hand and of the clergy on the other were discontinuous, completely separate. That is wrong."[9] It is not hard to see, then, how the fourfold *sangha* of monks, nuns, laymen, and laywomen came to interpenetrate and become coincident with the *sangha* of the four quarters. In other words, it is possible to use the word *sangha,* in the broadest sense, to include all Buddhists. Étienne Lamotte summarizes both the result and process:

> The Saṃgha or Buddhist community consists of four assemblies (*pariṣad*): mendicant monks (*bhikṣu*), nuns (*bhikṣuṇī*), laymen (*upāsaka*), and laywomen (*upāsikā*). The religious are distinguishable from the lay followers through their robes, discipline, and ideal and religious prerogatives . . . Although both the sons of the Śākya, the monks and the layman represent divergent tendencies which, without coming into direct opposition, were to be asserted with increasing explicitness: on the one hand the ideal of renunciation and personal holiness and, on the other, active virtues and altruistic preoccupations.[10]

It was once simple to determine just *who* was a Buddhist. A Buddhist was anyone who took refuge in the Three Jewels: Buddha, Dharma, and *sangha.* In chapter 3, as we surveyed various Buddhist communities, we saw that the issue has become much more complicated now that Buddhism has grown into a worldwide religion. In light of the above it does not seem too far an intellectual or pragmatic stretch to suggest that the phrase "*sangha* of the four quarters," so important for the earliest Buddhist community of monastics in India, now might be usefully applied to the whole of the fourfold Buddhist *sangha,* irrespective of sectarian affiliation, geographic location, or method of practice. What remains is to see just what the cybersangha is, and how it might play a role in helping to generate or even complete the "harmonious order" (*samagra-saṅgha*) referred to in Buddhist texts.

For more than two decades the International Association of Buddhist Studies has been the primary professional organization for scholars engaged in the enterprise that has come to be known as Buddhology. The brainchild of A. K. Narain, it was launched at an international conference on the history of Buddhism held in August 1976. More than thirty scholars of Buddhism, from nearly as many countries, met together to present scholarly papers and create an ongoing forum and global professional society.

Following the presentation of an especially enthralling paper (which was later published in a major professional journal), one hand in the audience immediately sprang up with a question. The hand belonged to Leon Hurvitz, who could most kindly be described as a curmudgeon. Professor Hurvitz said that although he had no fault with the quality or content of the paper (which elicited a sigh of relief from the presenter), the author had made reference to a reconstructed Sanskrit title of a text that likely existed in Chinese but *never* in Sanskrit. "Why did you do that?" chided Hurvitz. "Because we *all* work in or make reference to Sanskrit," offered the respondent, "while not everyone here knows Chinese." More politely than usual, Hurvitz responded, "Well, please don't do that anymore," and the discussion moved on to more substantive questions about the presentation.

Hours later, as a number of scholars participating in the conference shared a lunchtime conversation, one of them said, "Wouldn't it be great if we could program a computer with all the rules of Sanskrit grammar, the unique grammatical variants of Buddhist Sanskrit, and the totality of the several best Sanskrit dictionaries? Then we could feed in Sanskrit texts and just sit back as the computer printed out the translations, while we minimally emended them where necessary. Maybe we could even do the same for Chinese and Tibetan and Japanese, so we could have multilingual, comparative translations, all nicely cross-referenced." Everyone laughed, and the author of the above statement confessed that he knew he was only dreaming about the impossible. In fact, although it would now be impossible to document, there was every reason to believe that none of the individuals present during that discussion had ever touched a computer. It was simply one of those engaging but frivolous conversations that everyone knew would never lead to anything substantial. Now, barely two decades later, everyone who participated in that discussion spends a significant portion of every day sitting in front of a computer terminal, composing electronic mail to share with colleagues around the world, and creating scholarship that includes many of the Sanskrit and Chinese and Tibetan and Japanese scripts and characters they had dreamed of previously. In addition, the International Association of Buddhist Studies now maintains a page on the World Wide Web through which news and information about the society can be shared instantly and globally.

Early Internet Resources: Discussion Forums, Databases, Electronic Journals

In the earliest general, comprehensive books on Buddhism in America, not a single word is written about the role of computer technology in the development of American Buddhism.[11] Even more recent, case-specific studies, such as Martin Baumann's brilliant 1993 volume *Deutsche Buddhisten: Geschichte und Gemeinschaften,* do not mention the role of electronic communication in the study of Western Buddhism. The earliest formal interest in the application of computer technology to Buddhism seems to have occurred when the International Association of Buddhist Studies formed a "Committee on Buddhist Studies and Computers" at its 1983 meeting in Tokyo.[12] Jamie Hubbard, in his amusing and highly significant article "Upping the Ante: budstud@millenium.end.edu," points out: "The three major aspects of computer technology that most visibly have taken over older technologies are word processing, electronic communication, and the development of large scale archives of both text and visual materials."[13] Hubbard goes on to relate his first experiences with IndraNet, an online discussion forum sponsored by the International Association of Buddhist Studies, begun in the mid-1980s and comanaged by Hubbard and Bruce Burrill, with equipment donated by Burrill. Apart from a small cadre of faithful participants, there was little interest in the forum and it died a largely unnoticed death within two years. Nonetheless, of the three impact-laden items cited by Hubbard, it was clearly electronic communication that was to have the most important and continuing consequences for the development of American (and worldwide) Buddhist communities.

Early in the 1990s, a profusion of online discussion forums (or E-mail discussion lists), similar in nature to the one described above, began to proliferate and thrive on the Internet. Although these forums were global in scope, the vast majority of subscribers and participants were from North America. One of the very first of these, called "Buddhist," was founded by Yoshiyuki Kawazoe, who was associated with the computer center at Tohoku University in Japan. Although the traffic on the list was often frenetic, and messages were sometimes delivered as late as six months after they were composed, it was an exciting beginning. Because the list was unmoderated, and most often concerned with various aspects of Buddhist practice and popular issues within modern Buddhism, the number of postings eventually became sufficiently unwieldy that Kawazoe decided to bequeath the list to a new owner-manager, Paul Bellan-Boyer, and the list was moved to McGill University in Canada, where it currently resides. The list is now comanaged by Chris Fynn in England.

During one of the periods in which the "Buddhist" list had broken down, Richard Hayes, a professor on the Faculty of Religious Studies at McGill University, surveyed a number of subscribers to the list and discovered that many of them favored beginning a separate list that was not only restricted to academic discussions of Buddhism but moderated as well. In collaboration with James Cocks, who works in the computer center at the University of Louisville, a new discussion forum called "Buddha-L" was created, initially monitored by Cocks under guidelines composed by Hayes. The forum considered scholarly discussions of virtually all aspects of Buddhism, as well as issues related to teaching Buddhism at the university level and occasional postings of employment opportunities in academe. Hayes confesses that, because of the narrow, academic nature of the forum, his expectation was for a small but dedicated number of subscribers. Within a year, however, the group had over one thousand subscribers. For the past several years, following careful purging of inactive subscribers, the list has had a steady subscriber base of approximately six hundred people, generating approximately fifty messages per week.[14]

In addition to the groups mentioned above, a number of other discussion groups built an early but substantial following among Buddhists on the Internet. Perhaps the best known of these additional groups is "ZenBuddhism-L," founded in August 1993 at the Australian National University by Dr. T. Matthew Ciolek, head of the Internet Publications Bureau of the Research School of Pacific and Asian Studies at the Australian National University. This group provides a worldwide forum for the exchange of scholarly information on all aspects of Zen Buddhism (in its Chinese, Japanese, Korean, *and Western* forms). The list has recently been renamed "ZenBuddhism," and as of June 1997 had 370 subscribers. Also devoted to discussions of Zen is "Universal Zendo," founded by Mikael Cardell, intended to offer discussions of Zen practice, and now owned by Debora A. Orf.

Lists devoted to discussions of Tibetan Buddhism, and to Tibet in general, also became active on the Internet. These include "Tibet-L," jointly owned by Conrad Richter of the University of Toronto and Lauran Ruth Hartley of the University of Indiana; "WTN-L," owned by Conrad Richter; and "Tibetan-Studies-L," established by the Australian National University in 1995, which is intended *only* for scholarly exchange and which eschews all political propaganda. Tibet-L subscribers tend to be academics with a predominantly scholarly interest in Tibet, while WTN-L tends to be devoted to news about Tibet, especially focusing on its struggle for freedom and the reestablishment of full human rights for its inhabitants. Also associated with this latter topic, although clearly not limited to Tibet, is the forum of the Buddhist Peace Fellowship/International Network of Engaged Buddhists, owned by Alan Senauke of Berkeley, California. For discussions of Buddhist practice, one finds "Insight-L," started by John Bullitt in 1994 as an open forum and now owned by Jim Lassen-Willems and Ellen O'Sullivan, which entertains conversations about Theravāda Buddhist practice and insight meditation. Its subscribers are almost exclusively practitioners of meditation who utilize the forum to discuss their Buddhist practice in a compassionate, supportive community of online listeners.[15]

Closely related to the online forums is an extensive network of Usenet newsgroups that provide online discussion on a wide variety of Buddhist topics. A small sampling of these groups includes, for example:[16]

alt.philosophy.zen

alt.religion.buddhism.nichiren

alt.religion.buddhism.nichiren.shoshu.news

alt.religion.buddhism.tibetan

alt.zen

alt.zen+budo

talk.religion.buddhism

talk.religion.buddhism.nichiren

uk.religion.buddhist

There are also a series of chat opportunities such as "Buddhist Chat," "Zen Chat," and "ZenMOO," whereby seekers can share their experiences, questions, and discussions on a more immediate basis.

In February 1992, an "Electronic Buddhist Archive" was established by the Coombs Computing Unit of the Australian National University.[17] Under the direction of T. Matthew Ciolek, it was positioned as a subsection of the Coombspapers FTP Social Sciences/Asian Studies research archive, which had been initiated several months earlier. It contained over 320 original documents in ASCII (plain text) format, including bibliographies, biographies, directories, Buddhist electronic texts, poetry, and the like. It also offered a unique collection of previously unpublished transcripts of teachings and sermons by many famous twentieth-century Zen masters such as Robert Aitken Rōshi, Taizan Maezumi Rōshi, Hakuun Yasutani Rōshi, and others.[18]

In addition to FTP retrieval, two other document retrieval systems were utilized by the Australian National University for accessing materials: "Gopher" and "WAIS." Gopher is a computer protocol that originated at the University of Minnesota, whose varsity sports teams are known as the Golden Gophers; hence the nickname. A Gopher is a series of hierarchically arranged menus from which particular items on a Gopher "server" can be accessed by utilizing a Gopher "client." WAIS is an acronym for "Wide Area Information Server." A WAIS contains an index of all documents residing on that server, and responds to searches by a keyword or short phrase, providing a listing of all documents on that server that contain those words. By June 1992, the Coombs Buddhist Databases had been initiated using Gopher and WAIS technology. These databases included:

1. ANU-Asian-Religions (June 1992): Bibliographic references to selected but mainly Buddhist religions.

2. ANU-ZenBuddhism-Calendar (July 1993): A database of dates, anniversaries, and festivals of Zen Buddhism.

3. ANU-ZenBuddhism-L (August 1993): An archive of the communications and exchanges submitted to the electronic forum of the same name. This database closed in October 1996 when the mailing list was moved from the Coombs Computing Unit to another address.

4. ANU-*Dhammapada*-Verses (November 1993): A complete anthology of the 423 verses of the text, translated from Pali by John Richards.

5. ANU-*Cheng-Tao-Ko*-Verses (November 1993): A Collection of 64 verses attributed to the Chinese Zen master Yung-chia Hsuan-chueh (Yongjia Xuanjue) of the T'ang Dynasty, translated from Japanese by Robert Aitken Rōshi.
6. ANU-Tibetan-ACIP-Catalog (December 1993): A list of titles input by the Asian Classics Input Project (ACIP) as of November 1993.
7. ANU-ZenBuddhism-Poetry (November 1994): A collection of poetry to mark the thirty-fifth anniversary of the founding of the Diamond Sangha in Honolulu and the twentieth anniversary of Robert Aitken having received permission to teach Zen from Koun Yamada Rōshi in Honolulu.

A "Buddhist Studies Facility" was established in July 1993 as a subsection of the Coombs Gopher system that integrated access not only to the materials in the Electronic Buddhist Archives and Coombs Buddhist Databases, but also to the growing number of online Buddhist resources *at other sites.* This portion of the Gopher system was closed in January 1997. With the advent of the World Wide Web (see below), much of the above material was consolidated into two new sites: the "Buddhist Studies WWW Virtual Library," established in September 1994, and "Tibetan Studies WWW Virtual Library," established in January 1995. As early as the summer of 1992, Ciolek's organizational work was identified as "the ultimate guide to Buddhism on the Net."[19]

E-mail discussion forums and Buddhist databases were not the only form of early Buddhist activity on the Internet. As early as 1993, the first electronic Buddhist journal made its appearance. Called *Gassho,* it was edited by its founder, Barry Kapke, who operated it and other enterprises under an umbrella organization known as DharmaNet International, founded in 1991. According to Kapke, *Gassho* was published "as a service to the international Buddhist community, inclusive of all Buddhist traditions." He goes on:

> *Gassho* was the prototype Buddhist e-journal, exploring applications of electronic technologies to reach a global audience across a wide array of computer platforms and capabilities, and setting many of the standards and conventions that later e-journals, Buddhist and otherwise, would follow (and further improve upon). It was the first e-journal to offer peer-reviewed articles for the

Buddhist Studies academic community, in concert with *practice*-oriented articles from both lay and monastic teachers. It combined news shorts with compiled listings of Buddhist resources—sitting groups, publishers, mailing lists, etc.[20]

Kapke uses the past tense in the above description because *Gassho* went on hiatus following the May-June 1994 issue. Quite simply, its rapid growth exceeded the capability of its entirely volunteer staff to keep up. Just as a new issue was nearly completed for December 1996, both Kapke's home computer and its Internet server crashed, resulting in a loss of all materials for that issue. Although no new issues have followed this devastating loss, it was clear from the first issue, in November-December 1993 (available in both online and hard-copy versions), that *Gassho* presented a vision of a new kind of Buddhist community. Its masthead refers to it as an "Electronic Journal of DharmaNet International and the Global Online Sangha."

The phrase "Global Online Sangha" captures precisely the same mood and spirit as Gary Ray's slightly flashier term "cybersangha." Ray describes "cybersangha" in the following way:

"There's nothing lonelier than a Buddhist in Alabama" is the kind of comment I hear from many Buddhists who live in the outlying regions of North America where their sangha is small or nonexistent and information about Buddhist practice and philosophy is scarce. By tapping into computer networks, however, geographic isolation can be overcome. This rapidly expanding "cybersangha" provides support and community for Buddhists around the world.[21]

The similarity between the projects of Kapke and Ray is no accident. Before Ray founded the Tiger Team Buddhist Information Network in the early 1990s, he and Kapke were close associates, although they now work separately while continuing to address common goals.

It wasn't long before the term cybersangha began to take on a remarkably expanded meaning. In 1995 Jamie Hubbard wrote:

The network explosion is nowhere more visible than in the growth of the "cybersangha," the online communities of Buddhist practitioners. Sometimes representative of one or another traditional communities but more often than not virtual communities existing only in cyberspace, most every sort of discussion group and resource can now be located online . . . Because these online communities are almost exclusively Euro-American in constitution and provide a forum for Buddhists outside of the academy, they are also immensely fascinating to anybody interested in the transmission of Buddhism to the West.[22]

Gassho and Tiger Team Buddhist Information Network notwithstanding, another online electronic journal would eventually provide the occasion for an immensely rapid, and continued, growth in the cybersangha by exploiting yet another electronic medium for the dissemination of information: the World Wide Web.

The *Journal of Buddhist Ethics* was born in July 1994. It was originally planned as a traditional, hard-copy scholarly journal by its editors, who quickly learned that potential publishers had little interest in a highly specialized, purely academic journal that was not likely to turn a profit. One of the coeditors, Damien Keown, suggested publishing the journal online, where there would be no expenses, and where the journal could provide a useful service to its constituent community, however tiny it might be. Once a technical editor was added to the staff (bringing the total to three), plans rapidly moved ahead, and the journal became available via the World Wide Web, as well as through FTP and Gopher retrieval. The journal went "online" on 1 July 1994, with no articles, but with a WWW page outlining the aims of the journal and listing its editorial board members. It advertised its presence on a small number of electronic newsgroups, and within a week had one hundred subscribers. The journal's first call for papers was made after Labor Day, and by the end of 1994 it had over four hundred subscribers in twenty-six countries, managed by a listserv created by the technical editor. It had grown to more than fifteen hundred subscribers (slightly over one thousand of whom are in the United States) in over fifty countries by June 1997. Early in the journal's development, the editorial board recognized what an incredibly potent medium the World Wide Web was for expanding the availability of both scholarly and nonacademic information on Buddhism. Careful use of the Web's resources could greatly expand access to Buddhist resources.

Along with other new features added to the journal's basic emphasis on scholarly articles devoted to Buddhist ethics, the journal began a new section called "Global Resources for Buddhist Studies." Rather quickly, the editors discovered that many communities of Buddhist practitioners began requesting that "links" to their own developing World Wide Web pages be listed with the *Journal of Buddhist Ethics.* In other words, it became clear that the World Wide Web in general was indeed growing immensely and quickly, furnishing a unique opportunity for communication that Buddhist communities had never known before. Although it was by no means unique in its establishment of a jumping-off point for the exploration of additional Buddhist resources of all kinds on the Web, along with DharmaNet International and the WWW Virtual Libraries at the Australian National Universities, the *Journal of Buddhist Ethics* provided a new way of thinking about Buddhist communities, one that augmented Gary Ray's cybersangha and Barry Kapke's global online *sangha.*

Buddhist Resources on the World Wide Web

It is quite commonly known that the World Wide Web (or WWW), and much of the technology that supports it, originated in Geneva, Switzerland, at the European Particle Physics Laboratory (CERN). It was largely the work of Tim Berners-Lee, an Oxford University graduate, who wanted to create a "hypertext" system for communication among researchers linked by a computer network, in order for them to collaborate on a multiplicity of projects in real time rather than through publications read long after the projects were completed. Hypertext, or "non-sequential writing," as it was dubbed by its 1960s founder, Ted Nelson, was used for locating, reading, and also creating information.[23]

Tim Berners-Lee

used hypertext technology to link together a web of documents that could be traversed in any manner to seek out information. The web does not imply a hierarchical tree, the structure of most books, or a simple ordered list. In essence, it allows many possible relations between any individual document and others. Tim implemented hypertext as a navigational system, allowing users to move freely from one document to another on the Net, regardless of where the documents are located.[24]

WWW browsers, such as Netscape, "are clients that connect to servers on the Internet using a mutually agreed-upon computer language and which interpret the content found there for display on a user's screen."[25] Because all the specifications utilized by the WWW are free, virtually anyone can create a client or server. Once one becomes familiar with the three most important terms in navigating the WWW ("Uniform Resource Locator" or URL, "HyperText Transfer Protocol" or HTTP, and "HyperText Markup Language" or HTML), the process by which the Web works is really not at all hard to understand:

A URL is the address of a document on a network server. If a user clicks on a link in a document that contains a URL, the client interprets the URL and then initiates a session with the specified server. HTTP is the protocol, a fixed set of messages and replies, that both the client and server understand. Thus, the client sends a message to the server requesting a document and the server returns it. The document itself is coded in HTML, and the browser interprets the HTML to identify the elements of the document and to render it. The use of HTML allows documents to be formatted for presentation using fonts and line justification appropriate for the system on which it is displayed.[26]

Thus, WWW "pages" are written in HTML, and as Patrick Durusau explains in *High Places in Cyberspace,* "The use of HTML allows the author to construct a page that may include hypertext links to other portions of the page, such as footnotes, or links to other relevant sources on that server or a server located on another continent."[27]

About the same time that the *Journal of Buddhist Ethics* was implementing its section called "Global Resources in Buddhist Studies," with links to other Buddhist sites and resources on the still-infant Web, Hsuan Peng, a graduate student in mechanical engineering at Cornell University, was compiling a similar list of resources for posting on "Buddha-L." Hsuan Peng's initial list, posted in November 1994, had fewer than twenty entries. By the time of Hsuan Peng's graduation and return to Taiwan in 1996, the file had grown to over one hundred sixty listings. One year prior to his departure, Connie Neal created a WWW version of the file (in June 1995), and has continued to diligently maintain the WWW version of the "Buddhist Resource File" on an almost daily basis.[28] It is the most clearly organized and comprehensive record of Buddhist resources on the WWW, and will be discussed below.

Obviously, the growth of the World Wide Web has been astronomical in the latter half of the 1990s, and the listings of Buddhist communities and resources have been no less dramatic. Thus it has been extremely difficult not only to keep track of this huge growth in Buddhist Web pages, but also to organize the various *categories* of pages into a user-friendly environment. In fact, while most groups routinely link to other

Buddhist resources on the Web, very few sites make any attempt whatsoever to explain the logic of their own linking procedure, or the criteria that govern their choices for inclusion. Even the *Journal of Buddhist Ethics,* which began the process in 1994 and had links to approximately 150 WWW sites in June 1997, has not created an organizational framework or classification scheme for these listings.

Of the few sites that do offer an organizational pattern for the presentation of links to various Buddhist resources, three stand out above the rest: DharmaNet International, created and maintained by Barry Kapke; the Buddhist Studies and Tibetan Studies WWW Virtual Libraries, created and maintained by Dr. T. Matthew Ciolek; and the Buddhist Resource File, created by Hsuan Peng but now maintained by Connie Neal. Each has a unique approach to managing and presenting Buddhist resources in cyberspace, as will become apparent as we explore each resource.

Dharmanet International (Gateways to Buddhism)

Barry Kapke is a long-standing Buddhist practitioner who has been able to use his computer skills to support his fervent desire to spread information and compassion throughout the American Buddhist community. Never intended as a commercial enterprise, DharmaNet International has survived on Kapke's own contributions and the support of others, freely donated. As such, it has remained a free service to all who are interested. Kapke describes what he calls "Gateways to Buddhism" as "an online clearinghouse for Buddhist Study and practice resources."

Gateways to Buddhism is organized around eighteen distinct categories, structured not in a hierarchical framework, but rather as "a centralized clearinghouse for Buddhist information, online and offline."[29] The categories are as follows:

What's New at DharmaNet/DEFA (Dharma Electronic Files Archive)

Contacting DharmaNet

Buddhist InfoWeb: Dharma Centers & Practice Groups
Interlinks: Buddhist Studies Resources

Personal Pages

Online Dharma Libraries: *Texts, Art, & Multimedia*

Gassho & Dharma Newsstand

Meditation Retreats Calendar

Buddhist E-mail Directory

DharmaBase: Buddhist Data Libraries

Dharma Dialogue: *Newsgroups, Lists, & Chat*

Dharma Teachers: *Who's Who*

Engaged Buddhism & Dana Opportunities

Community Bulletin Board

Dharma Marketplace

DharmaNet

How You Can Help . . .

Circle of Friends

Each italicized item above links to another "page" that provides information on the topic listed, and often to many more pages extending further into cyberspace. The section on contacting DharmaNet presents the International Board of Advisors, the vast majority of whom are based in the United States. Significantly, this group of advisers contains an evenly balanced mix of Buddhist practitioners and scholars of Buddhism, and almost without exception the scholars fall into the category of "scholar-practitioner" discussed in the previous chapter.

The most extensive section of DharmaNet's listings falls under the heading "Buddhist InfoWeb." This section comprises two major divisions. First, Kapke offers "General Directories: Buddhist Centers and Practice Groups." This is a listing of WWW links to about thirty various directories and centers, mostly outside the United States, each of which provides further links to the individual groups falling into the domain of that particular topic. Links in this category include, for example, Buddhism in Mexico, Buddhism in Toronto, Buddhists in Germany, Zen Centers of the World, and Buddhist Temples in Canada. The second major division in this section is devoted to Online Buddhist Centers and Information, and is internally subdivided into separate listings for the Theravāda, Tibetan/Vajrayāna, Zen/Ch'an, and Jōdo Shinshū/Pure Land traditions, as well as a listing for other traditions. As of June 1997, this section had slightly more than two hundred listings linked to the WWW pages of the organizations cited.[30]

The Interlinks section on Buddhist Studies Resources is also subdivided into three sections: (1) "Buddhist Databases & Input Projects," citing such items as the Asian Classics Input Project; (2) "Buddhist Studies Academic Resources," including widely diverse resources like the huge complex of materials at the Center for Buddhist Studies at the National Taiwan University and the Numata Center for Buddhist Translation & Research in Berkeley, California; and (3) "Non-Academic Buddhist Study Resources," linking to sites like the *Journal of Buddhist Ethics*'s online conference on Buddhism and human rights. Approximately seventy-five WWW sites are currently listed under Interlinks.

The remaining sections deliver essentially just what each section title indicates, but it is worth noting that Kapke cites nearly two dozen online journals of general Buddhist interest, and another half dozen purely academic journals. In chapter 2 we saw that an increasingly important aspect of current American Buddhism was the movement that has been identified as "socially engaged Buddhism." In the section titled "Engaged Buddhism & Dana Opportunities," Kapke provides links to about three dozen groups involved in various aspects of social engagement, half of which focus on Tibet. He also provides links to the International Network of Engaged Buddhists and the important Buddhist Peace Fellowship, based in the United States. Also of much value are the Dharma Marketplace links to an impressive array of Buddhist-oriented publishers (including Dharma Communications, Parallax Press, Shambhala Publications, Snow Lion Publications, and others), as well as sites where audiotapes, videotapes, and an assortment of Buddhist meditation supplies can be purchased online.

DharmaNet International also provides three other categories of links to what it calls "Other Spiritual Resources" (e.g., religion and spirituality, martial arts, yoga, etc.), "Miscellaneous Tools & Resources" (listing a variety of so-called search engines such as Yahoo), and "Body Dharma Online" (linking to resources on acupuncture, fitness training, alternative medicine, lifestyle and sexuality issues, and the like). One can see that DharmaNet International's site is comprehensive, stimulating, and thoroughly infused with the passion and compassion of its founder. It is enormously popular, too, having recorded more than sixty thousand "hits" in the first half of 1997.

Buddhist Studies–Tibetan Studies WWW Virtual Libraries

As noted above, the Buddhist Studies WWW Virtual Library was established in September 1994. It is updated almost daily, and as of June 1997 it was linked to approximately 190 facilities worldwide. Not only are prospective links evaluated prior to inclusion on the main site, but sites whose quality has not been maintained are periodically removed. In other words, the facility exercises rigorous quality control, using the computer skills of T. Matthew Ciolek and his two primary virtual librarians from within the field of Buddhist Studies: Professor John C. Powers (of the Australian National University) and Professor Joe Bransford Wilson (of the University of North Carolina at Wilmington).

The Buddhist Studies WWW Virtual Library is organized into nine primary areas, each of which is further subdivided through additional WWW links:

Buddhism Internet Resources: Meta-Register
Buddhism Major WWW Sites
Buddhist Texts Input/Translations Projects
Buddhism Gopher, FTP, Mailing Lists & Chat-Rooms Resources
Buddhism & Buddhist Studies Databases
Buddhism/Buddhist Electronic Newsletters & Journals
Buddhist Organisations
Buddhist Art
Other Religions' Networked Resources

While there is an obvious similarity between this table of contents and that of DharmaNet International, the differing emphases of the two enterprises are almost immediately apparent upon a cursory exploration of the individual areas. The Meta-Register, for example, leans far more heavily toward the academic study of Buddhism, listing—among less than ten offerings—a Buddhist Studies academic site at the University of Washington, a resource for Buddhist Studies and the arts, the U.K. Association for Buddhist Studies Web site, and Web resources for the study of Buddhism, Confucianism, and Taoism.

As the virtual library moves on to listing major WWW sites, it offers two major subdivisions: (1) "Buddhist Studies–Academic WWW Servers"; and (2) Buddhism sites. While the academic servers—including the Berkeley Buddhist Research Center, the Buddhist Studies Centre at the University of Bristol, the Center for Buddhist Studies at the National Taiwan University, and a "Web Guide to Graduate Studies in Asian Philosophy and Religion" (housed at Toyo Gakuen University in Japan)—reveal clearly what their names imply, the Buddhism sites are less practitioner-oriented and more scholar-oriented than one might expect. The second major subdivision is broken down into a seemingly tradition-based series of sites (general, Chinese, early Buddhism, Korean, Nichiren, Pure Land, Shingon, Tendai, Theravāda, Vajrayāna, Vietnamese, Yogācāra, and Zen-Ch'an-Son-Thien), but many of the links in that tradition-based series are to academic or scholarly resources such as the Buddhist Publications Society in Sri Lanka and the homepage of the Nichiren Shū for the United States, Canada, and Europe.

The section titled "Buddhist Texts Input/Translations Projects" has been administered by Charles Patton II since January 1997. It includes general information sites regarding Buddhist texts, such as the Classical Sanskrit Fonts Project at the University of Virginia; input projects and online archives, like the Electronic Buddhist Text Initiative of Hanazono University in Japan; translation projects, like the WWW Buddhist Canon Translation Project at Ohio State University; and citations of the many Buddhist texts available online.

The sections titled "Buddhism Gopher, FTP, Mailing Lists & Chat-Rooms Resources," "Buddhism & Buddhist Studies Databases," and "Buddhism/Buddhist Electronic Newsletters & Journals" are almost identical to those of DharmaNet International. But the section on Buddhist organizations, administered since April 1996 by Dharman Craig Presson, is quite different. It is vastly shorter, containing only about three dozen links, and is focused primarily on sites *outside the United States*. The Buddhist Studies WWW Virtual Library then moves quickly to its section on Buddhist art, listing half a dozen sites, almost exclusively in the United States, and housed on a server provided by the Huntington Archive of Buddhist and Related Arts at the Ohio State University (and maintained since May 1997 by Janice M. Glowski). The virtual library closes with a series titled "Other Religions' Networked Resources," again quite similar to that presented by DharmaNet International.

A somewhat smaller "Tibetan Studies WWW Virtual Library,"

established in January 1995 and mirroring the Buddhist Studies site, is also maintained by the team of virtual librarians listed above. It focuses on Tibet and Tibetan culture generally, along with a section on religion, with additional focus on Tibetan language and literature, Tibetan medicine, travel and tourism, politics, human-rights issues, electronic publications, and other similar items.

Although perhaps less comprehensive than DharmaNet International, the Buddhist Studies–Tibetan Studies WWW Virtual Libraries are almost certainly the site of choice for scholars and those in the academic community, who will be able to find links to almost every online resource for Buddhist Studies that is available throughout the world.

Buddhist Resource File

If Buddhist Web surfers find DharmaNet International or the Buddhist Studies–Tibetan Studies WWW Virtual Libraries confusing or inconvenient, that can only be because of the sites' chosen perspectives or their somewhat eclectic methods of organizing the immense amount of material collected. The Buddhist Resource File, begun by Hsuan Peng in November 1994 and maintained by Connie Neal since June 1995, provides the perfect solution to all problems of perspective and organizational methodology. When Neal assumed the responsibility for continually updating the Buddhist Resource File, her first efforts involved inserting the proper HTML codes in each entry. Eventually, she was able to employ a technology package developed by Bryan O'Sullivan, called Bibliography Mode, that automatically converts bibliography files to HTML files and allows keyword searching that produces highly restricted and stylized returns of the applicable records. The keywords that are available for searching are organized into four main categories:

1. General (untitled)
2. Traditions
3. Languages
4. Books and Supplies

Within the first three main categories there are extensive and alphabetically arranged subdivisions, yielding an easy navigable path for any searcher:

1. *General*

Bibliography	Texts
Biography	University
Chat	Usenet-Groups
Dictionaries	Women
Directory	
E-Magazines	
Humanitarian	
Images	
Listservs	
Sound-Files	

2. *Traditions*

Ch'an	Tibetan
Dhammakaya	Tibetan-Gelugpa
FWBO[31]	Tibetan-Gelugpa-FPMT[32]
Jōdo Shinshū	Tibetan-Kagyudpa
Nichiren	Tibetan–New Kadampa
Nondenominational	Tibetan-Nyingmapa
Pure Land	Tibetan-Sagyapa
Shin	Zen
Sōka Gakkai	Zen-Kwan-Um
Tendai	Zen-Rinzai
Theravāda	Zen-Sōtō

3. *Languages*

Chinese	Korean
Dutch	Norwegian
Finnish	Spanish
French	Swedish
German	Thai
Japanese	Vietnamese

4. *Books and Supplies*

Each keyword search within any subdivision yields an alphabetical listing for the information requested. Further, each individual listing offers a description of the site if applicable, its Internet location (either E-mail, Web URL, or both), and the date of the latest update verification. In some cases, contact persons, mailing addresses, and telephone numbers or fax numbers are provided. At the end of each subdivision a list of references is provided, citing the names of individuals who assisted in the development and updating of that subdivision. As of June 1997, the Buddhist Resource File contained more than 350 listings. In addition, there are separate files for locating additions made during the previous two months.

It would undoubtedly be redundant to survey the Buddhist Resource File as we did previously for DharmaNet International and the Buddhist Studies–Tibetan Studies WWW Virtual Libraries, but it is worth noting that the "Bibliography" keyword yields an alphabetical listing of *all sites* in the entire file. The Buddhist Resource File offers an admirable balance between academic or scholarly sites and those of practitioner communities. And because this site presents materials in twelve foreign languages, computer-literate Buddhist immigrants can also navigate their way to valuable materials in their own language. Moreover, the fourth main category, "Books and Supplies," provides a far more extensive list of citations than any of the sources noted previously. The second main category, "Traditions," is the only area in which the searcher encounters some surprises. Although the vast majority of links for practitioner communities point to sites in the United States, there is an overwhelming dearth of Zen groups listed, the reason for which is not apparent.

Irrespective of which World Wide Web search engine or resource file one uses, including the many not mentioned above, the possibility exists for any Internet-linked American Buddhist to connect with the enormous richness of the Buddhist tradition, both in North America and throughout the world. By navigating through cyberspace, the practitioner can remain an active part of a Buddhist community in which he or she does not reside—as we saw in chapter 3 with members of the Zen Mountain Monastery community of John Daido Loori. Equally important, the scholar of Buddhism can access indispensable research materials on the other side of the globe without ever leaving the computer keyboard. And the scholar-practitioner can do both of the above easily and effortlessly. Yet there is another important application for the technology described in this chapter: it can provide for some practitioners a Buddhist community *without location in real space,* either as a means of intellectual or other kind of communication, or as a means of providing an opportunity for learning and practicing with the pragmatic intention of deepening one's Buddhist practice. It is worth examining some of these landmark efforts aimed at redefining Buddhism in an important new way.

Some Buddhist Cyber-Communities

There seem to be at least three major types of online Buddhist practitioner-oriented communities. First, there are WWW pages created by many traditional American Buddhist groups as a communication tool and convenience for their members. Some of these latter communities have created enormously complex pages, which, if all the linked resources were actually printed in hard copy, would extend to hundreds of pages of documents. Second, there are virtual temples created by traditional *sanghas* as an *addition* to their existing programs. Third, there are a number of communities that exist nowhere except in cyberspace; that is, they have no actual home in geographic space anywhere. Because the latter two kinds of *sanghas* have no geographic home in real space, they are the communities we will consider here. In addition, a number of publications have emerged that target and attract these online communities, and we shall consider one of those as well. It should be noted at the outset that not all of these online communities and publications are as yet well developed or complete. Clearly the development of virtual communities remains in its infancy. Nonetheless, if the growth of American Buddhist virtual communities duplicates even a small portion of the growth of general Buddhist resources on the Internet, they will soon present a formidable presence in cyberspace.

The True Freedom Cyber-Temple

It is hard to imagine a Buddhist community with no location in real space: no buildings, no shrine, no supportive lay community of believers, no ritual practices or meditation. Yet in early March 1996 a truly formless community, to be called the "True Freedom Cyber-Temple," was proposed by the American monk Suwattano.

Suwattano was ordained in Thailand after having served (as Todd Robinson) in the Gulf War as a specialist in nuclear, biological, and chemical defense. Prior to returning to the United States, he worked with the U.S. Navy Chaplain Corps in Okinawa, Japan, and studied Rinzai Zen.

Upon returning to this country he created the Cyber-Temple on a 386DX33 computer that had been donated to the project in mid-April 1996. The Web page went online on a limited basis later that month, and made its official debut on 31 May 1996.

In early November 1996 Suwattano moved from Michigan to Denver, where he took up residence at the Wat Buddhawararam Thai temple. At that time, he continued to build the Internet Web site of the Cyber-Temple while serving the Vipassana Dhura Meditation Society of Denver. In January 1997 Suwattano moved to the Vipassana Towers, from where he continues to run his cybersangha.

The World Wide Web main page of the True Freedom Cyber-Temple includes information about all of the resources available to the community. There are links to information about the teacher; a welcome to the temple, offering bits of past, present, and future history; and a clear statement about the meaning and importance of the "Three Jewels," revealed by clicking on a link entitled "First & Foremost." The heart of the resources of the Cyber-Temple is the "communications platforms" of the community: two-hour Cyber-Temple Dharma-Chat sessions based on "Internet Relay Chat" (IRC) technology Past Dharma discussions on IRCNet are archived and accessible to the cybersangha community. An "Audio Cyber-Temple" access is also available via Pow Wow, a Windows program that allows up to nine people to chat, transfer files, and navigate the WWW together. An "Ask the Teacher" link is provided whereby E-mail questions and comments may be directed to Suwattano's E-mail address. There is also a link to the Cyber-Temple community that as of June 1997 listed eight individuals in addition to Suwattano. The main page offers a rather extensive "Library" that connects to a series of electronic editions of Zen and Theravāda books, as well as Zen *kōan* studies, electronic Zen texts, and a series of extracts from the *Vinaya Piṭaka* and *Sutta Piṭaka* of the Theravāda scriptures (although these extracts are from translations done by other individuals such as Thanissaro Bhikkhu). The site also contains a small number of links to other Buddhist sites, most notably Zen Mountain Monastery, the Electronic Bodhidharma, Access to Insight, DharmaNet, The Tricycle Hub (the Web site of *Tricycle: The Buddhist Review*), and the *Journal of Buddhist Ethics*, as well as a brief statement of future plans to develop a practice center in the mountains of Colorado.

One of the most interesting features of the True Freedom Cyber-

Temple is a short discourse of Suwattano, first presented in 1996 and updated in March 1997, entitled "Mindfulness and Insight on the Internet." It casts exploring the Internet, with its "clicking," "looking," and "moving," in the classic language of Theravāda *satipaṭṭhāna* meditation, moving gradually toward the realization that no permanent self is to be found anywhere. Although envisioning Internet exploration as a vehicle of traditional Buddhist meditation might seem at first rather eccentric, it reminded me of a conversation (reported in chapter 3) that I had in the summer of 1995 during a walk through the woods in Mt. Tremper, New York, with Abbot John Daido Loori, in which he explained that while his interest in using computer technology for the advancement of his Zen Mountain Monastery community at first blew away his students' notions of Zen romanticism, they gradually came to see using computers in the same way as they viewed any activity: as an opportunity for awareness.

The White Path Temple

The White Path Temple describes itself as "a virtual Shin Buddhist Temple in the Cyberspace." It was created by Claude Huss, but is supported by the general Shin Buddhist community, and links directly to the Shin Buddhist Resource Center, Shin Buddhist Network, Enmanji Buddhist Temple, and San Jose Buddhist Church Betsuin. It is far more complete than the True Freedom Cyber-Temple, offering an extensive "navigator" at the beginning of its main page. The navigator offers a series of clickable links to the sixteen subpages in the temple's WWW site, including a subpage that explains how the White Path Temple took its name. The most extensive of these subpages is entitled "Introduction to Buddhism?" and includes many explanations of various aspects of Buddhism in general and Shin Buddhism in particular. This section is cross-linked to the "Beginner's Homepage" to familiarize visitors with the main doctrines of the parent organization of the virtual temple. There is a virtual temple that can be toured in either English or Japanese, and a library with extensive holdings of English-, Chinese-, and Japanese-language materials. Included in the English-language materials are entries by Alfred Bloom and Taitetsu Unno, two of the world's foremost authorities on Shin Buddhism.

The main page also offers links to a Shin virtual art gallery containing a wonderful series of JPEG images, a "Visit Kyoto" subpage that has GIF images of such items as the garden in Byodo Temple and the Shinran statue in the Nishi Otani Masoleum, and a series of Shin mandalas. A link to a fine series of online Buddhist dictionaries prepared by Professor Charles Muller at Toyo Gakuen University in Chiba, Japan, is also provided. The main page furnishes a number of places where visitors can sign the "Guestbook" or ask E-mail questions of the tour guide, identified as "Mida Buddy." In addition, online visitors can link to two online bookstores—the Buddhist Bookstore in San Francisco and the Buddhist Study Center Press in Honolulu—and to the Shin Buddhist Resource Center or Shin Buddhist Network.

To create online dialogue, there are instructions for subscribing to the Shin Buddhist Forum (sponsored by the Shin Buddhist Resource Center), as well as a Usenet newsgroup (tnn.religion.buddhism.shinshu). There is also a general discussion area, and a Shin Buddhism Frequently Asked Questions (FAQ) file. Like the True Freedom Cyber- Temple, the White Path Temple is international in scope, and although it is somewhat more complete than the former group, one must realize that it has support from and the resources of an extensive network of Shin Buddhist groups, whereas Suwattano has for the most part been a solitary pioneer.

Cybersangha: The Buddhist Alternative Journal

Summer 1995 marked the appearance of a new kind of Buddhist publication, under the editorship of Gary Ray. Known as *CyberSangha* and subtitled *The Buddhist Alternative Journal,* it was to have significant and continuing impact on the growing electronic Buddhist community. The mission of *CyberSangha* is stated clearly enough:

> *CyberSangha* is . . . dedicated to exploring alternative methods of Buddhist practice, especially electronic means such as the Internet. There appears to be three main arenas of discussion regarding Buddhism in America: Buddhist practice centers, academia and the Internet . . . *CyberSangha* is dedicated to exploring that arena and all that happens there that is related to Buddhism.[33]

It is perhaps somewhat anomalous that a journal focusing primarily on the cyberspace community of Buddhists would publish initially in print, and only later post its back issues on its WWW site, but with an extensive staff and a hopeful eye toward expansion, revenue is necessary to sustain the publication. Its debut issue focused on the theme "Is the Digital Age a Dharma Destroyer?" and contained three articles on various aspects of Buddhism and technology and another titled "Buddhist Modernism and the American Buddhist Lineage." One of the technology articles, "The Perception of 'Karma-Free' CyberZones" (by Richard P. Hayes), warns that the Internet is not so "environmentally friendly, economical, democratic, and egalitarian" as one may think. The author notes: "Even here in cyberspace we have to think carefully about the consequences of our actions."[34] Although the second (fall 1995) issue more than doubled the number of articles, the theme of optimism for the expanding role of the cybersangha tempered by responsibility persisted. Rev. Heng Sure describes the meaning of the word *sangha* in traditional Buddhism in "New Electronic Community: Ancient Spiritual Roots," but then goes on to say: "If we expand the meaning of the sangha to include Tiger Team's CyberSangha . . . then you've got an American definition." He continues: "If the orthodox sangha can go online and swap files with scholars and computer users, then there is still hope for a better tomorrow."[35] In the same issue Joachim Steingrubner echoes that sentiment: "The possibilities of electronic media empower the members of the CyberSangha with tools that, wisely used, can help to make the difference between surrendering to the wheel of life or transcending it."[36]

Given its optimistic approach to Buddhist communities online, it should not be surprising that *CyberSangha*'s list of advertisers includes such Internet-aware clients as *Tricycle: The Buddhist Review,* Snow Lion Expeditions, Dharma Communications, Big Sur Tapes, the Kanzeon Zen Center, the Dzogchen Foundation, and others. Moreover, in its "Editorial Guidelines," some of the story ideas suggested to prospective authors embrace such specific topics as "What do contemporary Buddhist teachers think of the Internet as a medium for Buddhist expression?" and "Is the online medium perpetuating the elitism that is present in contemporary American Buddhism?"

The *CyberSangha* WWW page contains, in addition to the features noted above, a link to "The Buddhist Library"—a useful series of texts, artwork, sound files, and miscellaneous materials, and additional HTML links. In order to constantly promote the responsible exercise of its mission statement, *CyberSangha* began a program (in spring 1996) referred to as "*CyberSangha's* Web Watch," in which eight Buddhist Web sites are selected each quarter for citation by the journal. Selection is based on an impressive and demanding series of criteria: contribution to the tradition, quality of information, simplicity of design, functionality, content, balance between text and graphics, interactivity, and links to other sites. Winners are entitled to portray a special *CyberSangha* Web Watch logo on their WWW page.

While *CyberSangha* presents a different kind of attraction than the two other Buddhist electronic communities briefly described above, its value as a widely available forum for discussing the present and future of Western Buddhism cannot be overstated. The dialogue it facilitates helps to bring together all the various applications of the term *sangha* that have been explored in this chapter.

Completing the *Sangha*

At the outset of this chapter we discussed the traditional meanings of the term *sangha.* We learned that in its initial, and strictest, use, the term *sangha* referred to the community of ordained Buddhist monks and nuns, later called the "*sangha* of the four quarters" and extending beyond mere geographic space. Eventually, in utilizing a wider application of the term, *sangha* came to mean the entire fourfold community of monks, nuns, laymen, and laywomen, and we suggested that this latter usage might be subsumed under the former meaning so that the phrase "*sangha* of the four quarters" would truly transcend geographical, temporal, and sectarian boundaries.

Now we have learned that if the "*sangha* of the four quarters" is to be a fully comprehensive term, it must also include the "cybersangha" in its various meanings as the entire Buddhist community online and/or the specific Buddhist *sangha* of a particular, spatially located, community.[37] Joachim Steingrubner says as much:

> The CyberSangha can be seen as a subset of the all-encompassing Sangha, a community of persons who actively scout their way to truth; who have, as an additional gift, the ability to communicate instantly without regard for their geographical proximities—an ability which would have been considered a siddhi, a magical power, just a couple of decades ago.[38]

More than a decade ago, the 1987 Conference on World Buddhism in North America, held at the University of Michigan, affirmed a "Statement of Consensus":

1. To create the conditions necessary for tolerance and understanding among Buddhists and non-Buddhists alike.

2. To initiate a dialogue among Buddhists in North America in order to further mutual understanding, growth in understanding, and cooperation.
3. To increase our sense of community by recognizing and understanding our differences as well as our common beliefs and practices.
4. To cultivate thoughts and actions of friendliness towards others, whether they accept our beliefs or not, and in so doing approach the world as the proper field of Dharma, not as a sphere of conduct irreconcilable with the practice of Dharma.[39]

Certainly it is the inclusion of the cybersangha as a new constituent of the *sangha* of the four quarters that further enables and more deeply enhances the still profound consensus affirmed above. Nor should we lose sight of the fact that it is the *sangha* that completes and empowers the "Three Jewels." Yet we should also not lose sight of the fact that it is possible to construe the cybersangha as a true sign of the cold, rational, contemporary world in which communication is faceless and even impersonal. For many, the loss of face-to-face encounter, personal support, and shared practice in real space may be a strong liability that undermines the potential value of the cybersangha.[40]

An Afterthought on Sanghas

On a delightful spring day in 1968, I was sitting in a restaurant in Madison, Wisconsin, with Professor Richard H. Robinson, mastermind of the highly successful Buddhist Studies program at the University of Wisconsin. Soon to become my mentor and friend, he was munching his way through his third bratwurst sandwich as he outlined the work he expected me to do as his newly appointed research assistant. In the midst of outlining what seemed like a huge and unmanageable list of duties, he abruptly stopped, and leaned across the table with a broad grin on his face. Knowing his reputation for ferocity and even rudeness with students, I imagined the worst, and found myself almost instinctively sliding back from the table. "Chuck," he said with a little laugh, "I am now going to tell you how to have a long and prosperous career in Buddhist Studies." His advice seemed bizarre at the time, reminding me of the one-word career *kōan* uttered to Dustin Hoffman's character, Benjamin, in the 1967 film *The Graduate:* "Plastics!" Robinson said, simply, "*Sangha!*" Stunned and clueless, I beseeched him to explain his presumably sage but seemingly impenetrable advice. Noticing my discomfort, he went on as he finished his third beer, "Choose a specialty that nobody is interested in and you will essentially be guaranteed safe and continuous employment by virtue of being the world's only authority on the topic." Before I could recover, or even ask him what his suggestions for pursuing this curious specialty might be, he concluded this surrealistic episode by saying, "I, in fact, am the world's foremost authority on Lithuanian flute music . . . although nobody knows it." While I never did find out about the Lithuanian flute music, I eventually did learn that the erstwhile professor was totally serious in his advice to me.

Upon returning to the university in the fall of 1968, I found that my very first assignment from him was to prepare a lesson on the *sangha* for a seminar he was conducting called "The Foundations of Buddhology." Just as I was beginning to realize that he really *was* serious about his advice, he further confused me by remarking one day that he was sorry everyone always associated his research with the Mādhyamika school of Buddhism and overlooked his serious interest in other topics, not the least of which was the above-mentioned Lithuanian flute music. Nevertheless, he was relentless in his passion for me to learn everything about the *sangha,* and, fueled by frequent doses of his ferocity and rudeness, I tried. I learned all I could about the historical aspects of the *sangha*'s foundation, the textual tradition associated with its disciplinary regulation, its expansion and development throughout India and beyond, and its eventual separation into sectarian divisions. Although Richard Robinson died before my degree work at the university was completed, his peculiar advice, offered over bratwurst and beer, has continued to be the skillful means guiding my work. Investigating the *sangha,* in all its manifestations, remains the thread that knits together the various themes of my research into one ideally harmonious fabric. But Robinson was wrong: far from being a topic of no interest to scholars and practitioners, the *sangha* has become one of the most exciting and intriguing topics of research and investigation. Perhaps the most consequential impact of the aggressive spread of Buddhism into cyberspace, along with the creation of a new kind of American Buddhist *sangha* never imagined by the Buddha, is the uniting of all the Buddhist communities or *sanghas* described above into one universal *sangha* that can communicate effectively in an attempt to eliminate the suffering of individuals throughout the world.

CHAPTER 6

The Future of the American *Sangha*

On 17–19 January 1997, a "Buddhism in America Conference" was held at the Boston Park Plaza Hotel. To be sure, this was no ordinary conference. The promotional brochure distributed by the conference's producer, Al Rapaport, subtitled the event "A Landmark Conference on the Future of Buddhist Meditative Practices in the West." In addition to the various keynote addresses, preconference workshops, and panels, there was a cornucopia of American Buddhist activities available for all to experience. Throughout the weekend, the Drepung Loseling Tibetan monks were creating a Medicine Buddha Sand Mandala, and on Saturday evening nine lamas from the Drepung Loseling Monastery performed their world-famous multiphonic singing; there was morning meditation and tai chi; and audiocassettes of the various sessions were immediately available for purchase on-site. There were almost two dozen commercial exhibitors, consisting of booksellers, distributors of Dharma-ware, and vendors of other Buddhist items. Charles E. Tuttle Publishing even produced a book to commemorate the conference, noting in its announcement: "This book is destined to be considered a classic in Buddhist publishing."

Fortuitously, a research trip of mine that been previously postponed was now rescheduled to coincide with this conference, enabling me to drop in from time to time and attend some of the events. In his opening welcome address, Al Rapaport commented that during the months preceding the conference he had received many inquiries about the event, and even an E-mail message from a professor who wondered why there were so very few scholars participating in the conference.[1] His remark brought an instant, collective laugh from the large audience. Rapaport went on to suggest that this was a conference not for academic scholars, but for Buddhist practitioners in America. And he proceeded rather directly thereafter to introduce the first speaker of the evening, Peter Muryo Matthiessen, who was to deliver a keynote address entitled "The Coming of Age of American Zen."

Since nobody in the audience knew that I was the author of the E-mail that Al Rapaport thought was so funny, there was neither any visible embarrassment on my part nor any necessity to explain that my inquiry had been thoroughly misunderstood. Yet as I surveyed the program of the weekend's extensive events, I was extremely disappointed to learn not only that scholar-practitioners had been almost completely excluded from this conference, but also that the various and important ethnic Buddhist communities in America had not been included, nor had the practitioners of the Sōka Gakkai tradition. Of course, it could be argued that this was a conference about *meditative traditions* in American Buddhism, and that the ethnic Buddhist communities and Sōka Gakkai largely did not engage in meditative practices. However, a significant number of the presentations at the conference had nothing whatsoever to do with meditative practices or their future, so the exclusion of some groups was, I think, an unfortunate but revealing choice on the part of the conference organizer.

During the weekend I noticed a few black, Hispanic, and Asian American faces in the audience, but for the most part I saw Euro-American Buddhists congregating to share and discuss their views and understanding of Buddhist practice in North America. I was reminded again and again of two recent magazine articles on American Buddhism. The first, "800,000 Hands Clapping," was written by Jerry Adler for the 13 June 1994 issue of *Newsweek*. It was subtitled "Religion: America May Be on the Verge of Buddhadharma." The title's reference to 800,000 Buddhists—the total counted by Seymour Lachman and Barry Kosmin and cited in their book *One Nation under God: Religion in Contemporary American Society*, and a figure that I believe is off by as many as several million—was of little interest to me. More interesting, though, was the focus of the article: John Daido Loori, a well-educated, charming, and serious Zen practitioner who is the abbot of Zen Mountain Monastery, and who is trying to help shape an American Buddhist tradition that is, as Adler points out in his article, technologically aware, egalitarian, and "sophisticated about the ways of power in American life." The second article was Rodger Kamenetz's profile of Robert Thurman in the *New York Times Magazine* of 5 May 1996, titled "Robert Thurman Doesn't *Look* Buddhist." Quite apart from acknowledging Thurman's current high-profile image as president of Tibet House—where he regularly consults with such popular icons as Richard Gere, Michael Stipe, and Natalie Merchant, a fact that caused his friend and colleague Jeffrey Hopkins of the University of Virginia to refer to him as "the Red Skelton of Tibetan Buddhism"—Kamenetz captures the serious, academic side of Thurman in his role as Jey Tsong Khapa Professor of Indo-Tibetan Buddhist Studies at Columbia University. But the powerful images evoked by these two magazines articles seemed continually juxtaposed against two other, equally powerful portraits: those of the Washington Buddhist Vihara and of the Berkeley Buddhist Church, two institutions that I had visited in December 1996. These are quiet ethnic-Buddhist temples, one Theravāda and the other Jōdo Shinshū, which simply go about the important business of offering a Buddhist religious center for their respective communities of families.

Is it possible to make any sense out of these seemingly conflicting sketches of American Buddhism at the turn of the millennium? We noted earlier that the first general, comprehensive book on American Buddhism was Emma Layman's *Buddhism in America,* published in 1976. In other words, there has been only a quarter century of systematic investigation of the American Buddhist movement. Kenneth Tanaka says as much. In the very first words of his epilogue to *The Faces of Buddhism in America* he notes that "the study of Buddhism in America is still in its infancy."[2] Perhaps the most reasonable way to have a prospective look at the American Buddhism that is likely to develop in the next century is to briefly compare, and evaluate for accuracy, the future-looking evaluations of the earliest researchers of American Buddhism, move ahead to the futuristic ruminations of American Buddhists made approximately halfway between 1975 and 2000, and then examine some of the current suggestions and expectations voiced by various influential members of the Buddhist community.

First Conclusions

Although I had read Layman's *Buddhism in America* long before I wrote even the first word of my now horribly outdated *American Buddhism,* I confessed in my introduction that I considered Layman's initial question about Buddhism in America to be fundamental to both our inquiries: "Is there a characteristically American style of Buddhism?"[3] It was clear that *something* Buddhist was happening in America, but those who undertook all of the preliminary investigations of this phenomenon seemed at a loss in trying to understand or explain it. It was this resulting frustration and confusion that led to my beginning part one of my book with a line from Bob Dylan's "Ballad of a Thin Man": "Something is happening here, but you don't know what it is, do you, Mr. Jones?" Nothing could have been more accurate in describing the American Buddhism we were trying so hard to comprehend.

At that time, the closest thing to an *early* book devoted entirely to Buddhism in a Western context that I could find was Christmas Humphreys's *Zen Comes West: The Present and Future of Zen Buddhism in Britain,* published in London by George Allen & Unwin in 1960. Eight years later the Buddhist Society in London published Humphreys's follow-up volume: *Sixty Years of Buddhism in England (1907–1967).*[4] But that was England, and it was American Buddhism I was trying to understand. For my purposes, the first text of choice was Louise Hunter's *Buddhism in Hawaii: Its Impact on a Yankee Community,* published in 1971, but Hunter devoted less than two pages to future considerations, most of those being confined to rather perfunctory remarks about the Jōdo Shinshū tradition. Shortly after Layman's landmark publication, Tetsuden Kashima published his well-researched and extremely useful study *Buddhism in America: The Social Organization of an Ethnic Religious Institution,* but like Hunter's volume, Kashima's focused only on the Jōdo Shinshū tradition. Kashima's focus, however, didn't lessen the impact of his chapter on the future. Amid a clearly stated awareness of the uncertainty ahead, Kashima was able to identify three major themes that he believed would affect Buddhist Churches of America: "Protestantism," interreligiosity, and pluralism.[5] Furthermore, he considered some possible futures influenced by five factors:

1. decreasing and changing membership;
2. the ethnic character of the membership;

3. economic problems at many churches, especially at headquarters;
4. the proper techniques for teaching Buddhism; and
5. interrelated problems with the ministry concerning number, composition, and finances.[6]

Layman's short chapter titled "What Future for Buddhism in America?" is much different from the above sources. Before listing and describing what she refers to as "contingency variables"[7] that will determine the future of Buddhism, she contextually locates her discussion in the midst of the work of two scholars who had studied the process by which religions transform themselves: Donald Swearer and Jacob Needleman. Swearer has extensively studied modern Buddhism in Thailand, and Layman draws from his insights in *Buddhism in Transition,* noting, "When society is undergoing change, religion may respond in three ways: it may remain unchanged and rigid, isolating itself from the culture; it may adapt itself creatively to conditions existing within the society while at the same time retaining its basic values and character; it may undergo such radical changes that it is no longer recognizable for what it was."[8] In an unpublished 1972 paper entitled "Three Modes of Buddhism," Swearer identifies three ways in which Buddhism can influence the West: appropriation, transformation, and dialogue. By "dialogue" Swearer means the interreligious conversations between Buddhists and non-Buddhists, aimed at mutual enrichment and understanding. "Transformation" is that process by which one adopts certain Buddhist ideas and practices into one's life without actually becoming Buddhist. Twenty-five years later, Thomas Tweed would refer to people experiencing transformation as "night stand Buddhists,"[9] and Jon Kabat-Zinn has even extended this methodology into his medical practice, utilizing *vipassanā* meditation as a stress-reduction technique. Finally, "appropriation" occurs when a person actually becomes Buddhist, by whatever process. These issues inform Layman's judgment as a prognosticator of Buddhism's future. Also having impact on her ability to objectively look ahead into Buddhism's American development is her acceptance of Buddhism as a "new religion," as described by Needleman—a point we shall return to below. Needleman warns against overstating the value of purely numerical growth in new religions: "To take only one example: ordinarily, we tend to think of the growth of a movement in terms of numbers of adherents. But are we capable of judging between those who merely adopt the terminology of a new teaching without changing anything essential in their inner lives, and those who are struggling to live by the teaching?" Needleman goes on, with specificity for Buddhism: "Thus, if someone were to predict that in ten or fifty years, twenty million Americans would be Buddhists, it would by itself mean nothing. If twenty million Americans became real Buddhists, that of course would be extraordinary."[10] While both Layman and Needleman muse a bit about precisely what constitutes a *real* Buddhist, Needleman seems far more suspicious than Layman about what has taken root in American soil when he says, "From where we stand, there is still the possibility that nothing at all will grow, or that what does grow will be twisted and barren."[11]

Layman tabulates six contingency variables that she believes will determine the future of Buddhism in America: (1) economic, social, political, ideational, and technological factors within society; (2) methods of propagating the Dharma and modifications within Buddhism itself; (3) developments within Judaism and the Christian church; (4) meditational movements and techniques of a secular nature; (5) continued success of meditational approaches to psychotherapy; and (6) growth of the movements of humanistic and transpersonal psychology. Each of these contingency variables emerges from more extensive discussions of the topics listed in previous chapters of *Buddhism in America*.

In identifying factors within society, Layman avoids actually discussing any of them. Instead, she cites the emergence of the 1960s counterculture as a generic, but comprehensive, expression of the social anomie resulting from problems in the factors listed above, positing Buddhism as a potential spiritual remedy for the ills of society. Under methods and modifications within Buddhism, she briefly considers Buddhist missionary efforts, the Westernization of Buddhist practices, and the development of an American *sangha*. In the period immediately prior to, and during, Layman's research, many Asian Buddhist groups expanded their missionary activity into North America. Layman suggests that this is a fruitful approach, speculating that urban areas and university communities might remain fertile areas for expansion. For Layman, the Westernization of Buddhist practices means essentially three things: (1) adjusting meditational techniques to an American lifestyle; (2) providing more English-language material for American adherents; and (3) minimizing what she calls the "Oriental trappings" of Buddhism. Since most of her suggestions target the Euro-American community, it appears that Layman sees only a minimal role for Asian Americans in the American Buddhism she envisions.

In developing an American *sangha,* she suggests an increasing role for "Western" leaders (i.e, ministers, Zen masters, monks, nuns, and lamas). She mentions the American Buddhist innovation of a quasi-monastic or intermediate lifestyle for married *sangha* members, but chooses not to develop the idea.

Layman's discussion of developments within Judaism and the Christian church does not, as might be expected, address the situation of how these groups might compete with other religions in a time of declining church attendance and growing secularism and pluralism, but rather suggests that interfaith dialogue might *detract* from continuing interest in Buddhism as Jewish and Christian groups begin to incorporate meditational training into their traditional religious practice. To support her supposition, she cites the popularity of books by Father Thomas Merton, Dom Aelred Graham, and Father William Johnston. She also wonders whether secular meditational movements such as transcendental meditation will advance or hinder further growth in Buddhism.

Layman's final two concerns reflect her background as a retired psychology professor at Iowa Wesleyan University. As an example of the relationship between meditation and psychotherapy, she references a group of sixty psychological practitioners who enrolled in a "Human Development Training Program" at Nyingma Institute during the summer of 1973. She notes that most who enrolled had had previous and beneficial experiences with various forms of meditation, and that approximately one-third of the group had incorporated meditation as a therapeutic tool into their professional practices. Finally, she observes that the various meditational traditions of Buddhism in America have always attracted an extremely high number of professional people (she specifically cites teachers, social workers, lawyers, priests, psychologists, and psychiatrists). Although she offers no supporting data, Layman argues that psychologists have shown the highest rate of increase in recent years. Thus it seems logical—at least to Layman—to conclude that as the disciplines of humanistic and transpersonal psychology grow, so also will interest in Buddhism.

How do Layman's observations translate into speculations about the future of American Buddhism? Here she is extremely brief and quite cautious. In general terms she remarks, "Indications are that there will be an acceleration of interest in Buddhism for a few more years, followed by a period of slower growth."[12] One is sorely tempted to criticize

Layman for her unwillingness to be more aggressive or specific in her assertion. However, in an environment almost totally lacking in empirical data, there is little she might have added with any sense of certainty. For Layman in 1976, and for Buddhism at the turn of the millennium, there are no reliable, *comprehensive* figures. Layman's estimates of the total number of Buddhists reflect a problem addressed earlier in this book: how is status as a Buddhist determined? She uses a sliding scale. If the yardstick for measurement is "taking refuge," her guess is 50,000; if some *other* kind of expression of Buddhist commitment is included, she increases her estimate to 300,000; if participation in some form of Buddhist practice is a criterion, she suggests 500,000 or more. But the operative word for Layman was "guess," and it still is today.

Layman forecasts continued, mushrooming growth in the meditational forms of Buddhism, followed by slower growth, except in the Tibetan groups, which for no explicable reason she presumes will continue growing rapidly. Thus she anticipates continued interest in Zen, Theravāda, and Tibetan meditation, along with a change in the nature of membership, which she expects to reflect greater involvement on the part of intellectuals. Her anticipation of growing numbers of intellectuals in the movement reflects her conclusion that Buddhism is gradually moving away from what she considered its faddish attraction for many refugees from the drug culture of the 1960s. She believes that Japanese American Buddhist groups (which she refers to as "church types") will lose membership among third- and fourth-generation Japanese Americans, and will have little chance of gaining membership from non-Asian Americans unless meditational practices are incorporated into the liturgy. Finally, she is reluctant to predict the future of Nichiren Shōshū of America. She sees an inevitable slowing of recruitment within this group, and a lag of interest from college students, and presumably from college-educated people in general. Regarding the three modes of Buddhist influence proposed by Swearer, Layman concludes:

> The likelihood that seriously committed Buddhists will ever approach the number of Christians and Jews in America is so slight as to be almost nonexistent. Also, there seems little probability that there will be many Buddhists in the deep South or the rural Midwest in the foreseeable future. Yet it is almost certain that Americans will continue to "take the refuge" and that Buddhist groups will continue on American soil, although how many and in what sects may be uncertain.[13]

History has shown that, for the most part, Layman's conclusions are wrong. By the time her book was published, growth in what she calls the meditational forms of Buddhism was already slowing considerably. On the other hand, following the passage of the 1965 Immigration and Nationality Act, which reversed the governmental policy of Asian exclusion dating back to the Chinese Immigration Exclusion Act of 1882, the number of U.S. residents from Theravāda countries rose enormously in the 1970s and 1980s. Paul Numrich proposes "a conservative estimate of between one-half and three-quarters of a million immigrant Theravada Buddhists in the United States in 1990," and he counted 142 immigrant Theravāda temples.[14] Although she was reluctant to comment extensively on the future of Nichiren Shōshū of America, Layman envisioned both a declining recruitment and a loss of literate followers. Jane Hurst, in "Nichiren Shōshū and Sōka Gakkai in America: The Pioneer Spirit," has estimated that SGI-USA (as it is now called) has more than 300,000 members; it maintains a strong membership base among minority groups (chiefly African American and Hispanic American), and is also a highly literate group, as evidenced, for example, by the important work of the Boston Research Center for the 21st Century, directed by Virginia Straus.[15] Layman imagined that the number of seriously committed Buddhists in America would never "approach the number of Christians and Jews in America," but Martin Baumann has recently cited between 3 and 4 million Buddhists in America,[16] certainly approaching at least half of the Jewish population, and exceeding the membership of several Protestant denominations. Moreover, irrespective of whether one consults the various Internet guides to Dharma centers mentioned in chapter 5 or Don Morreale's now revised and expanded *Complete Guide to Buddhist America,* both the deep South and rural Midwest are rich in Dharma centers.

What seems to be lurking in the background of Layman's concerns for the future of Buddhism in America is her inability to reconcile the largely isolated Buddhism of Asian American immigrants with the highly visible, literate Buddhism of its Euro-American converts. For Layman, and for most early researchers of American Buddhism, these groups represented two distinct Buddhisms in America, and although this typology has recently been challenged, success was generally measured by the degree to which Buddhist groups acculturated to American values and forms. It was an incorrect standard of measurement, I think, but one to which I also subscribed, as we shall see below.[17]

The concluding chapter of my 1979 book *American Buddhism* shares with Layman's *Buddhism in America* an abiding acknowledgment that the topic of our respective volumes most properly belongs under the rubric "new religions," although I'm not sure I would make a similar argument today. Identifying American Buddhism as a new religion did not come without a struggle. As a participant in the National Conference on the Study of New Religious Movements in America, held at the Graduate Theological Union in Berkeley in June 1977, and used as the launching platform for GTU's innovative Program for the Study of New Religious Movements in America, I found myself immediately at odds with Jacob Needleman. While Langdon Gilkey awoke early to play tennis and Harvey Cox went off to chant with the local Hare Krishna group, I went running in the Berkeley hills as I mentally rehearsed speeches to convince the learned convener of the conference that what I perceived as his inherent suspicion of the authenticity of the American Buddhist movement was wrong. Eventually I convinced myself that probably he was less suspicious than I had imagined, and my speeches were more convincing than I had expected. Nonetheless, when the conference proceedings were published, Needleman confirmed my worst fears when he wrote rather directly in the book's preface:

> The present influx of Asian religious teachings into America allows us direct witness to a process that has been going on in the West for at least a hundred and fifty years. Anyone who has observed the new religious movement at close hand cannot but conclude that in many cases what we are seeing is a drama in which ideas and methods that in their original setting required extensive moral, social, and psychological preparation before being given out are now being made available to anyone simply for the asking. As a result, the question has arisen whether these ideas and methods are in fact being used for purposes that are even antithetical to the purposes for which they were originally intended.[18]

Thus, convincing me that American Buddhism was a new religion was not an easy task in view of what I think is Needleman's misunderstanding of Buddhism in America *and* in Asia.

Why was it so important to identify American Buddhism as a new religious movement (NRM)? More than anything else, for me it was an early tactical maneuver designed to accentuate the legitimacy and enhance the visibility of the American Buddhist movement. Lots of nonscholarly books on popular aspects of Buddhism in America were beginning to appear in the trade market, many of them poorly written and highly inaccurate, and I feared that they would detract from the overall integrity of American Buddhism and the important contribution it could make to the American religious landscape. By identifying American Buddhism as an NRM, it was possible for scholars interested in this phenomenon to consult with and learn from the best minds in American religion. This was important, too, because at that time there were no scholars with *dual training* in American religions and Buddhist Studies. A partial roster of that first GTU conference illustrates the potential for constructive cross-fertilization of disciplines. Well-known historians of American religion participated, such as Sydney Ahlstrom and John Dillenberger; early proponents of the NRM attended, including Dick Anthony, Thomas Robbins, and Robert Wuthnow; theologians and others, like Harvey Cox and Theodore Roszak, added their input; and Asianists Robert Ellwood and I also attended. An important dividend for the American Buddhist movement emerged from this early association: a fruitful dialogue began that yielded important and influential multidisciplinary studies from both sides of the equation, thus dramatically enhancing our understanding of the American Buddhist movement. In the process, literature on the American Buddhist movement found an initial, scholarly home.

The development of this early identification of American Buddhism as an NRM came with a price, although many of us did not realize it at the time. The most strident, and accurate, critique of this identification comes from Paul Numrich, who says:

> Since the 1960s, interpreters of trends in American religion have devoted a great deal of time to studying so-called new religious movements (NRMs), that is, recently established, marginal religious groups that have drawn converts away from the traditional religions of Christianity and Judaism. Buddhism, though certainly not a "new" religion worldwide, became a new interest among non-Asian Americans beginning in the 1960s, thereby entering the field of vision of NRM studies. Due to their focus on the American-convert experience, NRM studies as a rule bracket out considerations of immigrant expressions of a religion.[19]

Numrich points out that *every book-length treatment* of American Buddhism (e.g., Layman's *Buddhism in America,* my *American Buddhism,* Fields's *How the Swans Came to the Lake,* Boucher's *Turning the Wheel: American Women Creating the New Buddhism,* and Morreale's *Buddhist America: Centers, Retreats, Practices*) minimizes the role ascribed to Asian Americans in forging a distinctly "American" Buddhism. Apart from building what Numrich believes is an incorrect designation of Euro-American converts as the most important part of American Buddhism, this minimization does something equally improper:

> It also has created typologically strange bedfellows for Buddhism as observers of American religious history seek to make sense of increasing religious pluralism in this country. Buddhism as a whole, despite its ethnic-Asian majority, often finds its way into a grab-bag category that can include Jonestown, the Unification Church, and the Self-Realization Fellowship.[20]

Numrich is right, and despite his focus on immigrant Theravāda groups, his critique is equally applicable to all other Asian American groups, and especially those in the newest wave of immigration that followed the passage of the 1965 Immigration and Nationality Act. He has a creative corrective too, one that potentially bridges the gap between the "two Buddhisms" referred to above. It is called "parallel congregations," and represents a phenomenon he observed in the two Theravāda temples he studied: "In such temples, under one roof and through the guidance of a shared clergy, two ethnic groups pursue largely separate and substantively distinct expressions of a common religious tradition."[21] Before 1960, this practice had been noted by Louise Hunter and other researchers in some Buddhist Churches of America temples in Hawaii and California, but it never became widespread, although Tetsuden Kashima and Alfred Bloom both suggest that the phenomenon may be reemerging.[22] Curiously, Numrich points out, this particular pattern of parallel congregations, as seen in Buddhism, appears not to be observable in other immigrant religious traditions.[23]

Ethnic acculturation aside, *American Buddhism* looked to the future with a series of issues and questions, more prescriptive than proscriptive, that might determine the shape of American Buddhism in the last two decades of this century. Because the role of the American Buddhist teacher is pivotal for preserving the integrity and enhancing the mission of each Buddhist community, I suggested that it would be critical for certification procedures for all clergy and lay instructors to be established. Corollary to the certification of teachers, the chapter anticipated an escalating number of senior, mature students being mainstreamed into leadership roles. The chapter emphasized the recognition for and continuation of all Buddhist lineages as a means of maintaining American Buddhism's contact with its own heritage.

Of course my chapter shared with Layman confusion and concern about the definition of Buddhist affiliation. Unlike Layman, however, I offered an unusual alternative. I suggested a Buddhist appropriation of Agehananda Bharati's definition of a mystic. For Buddhists, it would be: "A Buddhist is a person who says 'I am a Buddhist,' or words to that effect, consistently, when questioned about his/her most important pursuit." Thus issues of taking refuge, church attendance, monetary donation, meditation or other practices, and the like would be avoided in membership determinations.

The chapter acknowledged, as Layman's chapter does, that American Buddhism has made its greatest advances in the human sciences, and particularly in psychology. But it went further, suggesting that American Buddhism would need to confront modernity by advancing in the physical sciences as well. By extension, advancing in the physical sciences would provide the gateway for effective utilization of the new technology, irrespective of whether it produced better means of communication or heightened awareness of our ecological dialogue with the planet. And there was a clear recognition that American Buddhism was essentially a city movement and was likely to remain so. Coincident with American Buddhism's attempt to confront its situation in the modern world is the realization that the style and method of membership are different in American Buddhism than they have been in its Asian counterpart. While the ideal type remains the monk or nun for many American Buddhist groups, the chapter argued that recognition of the reality of a primarily lay lifestyle would be necessary for a meaningful experience in American culture. Along with a primarily lay lifestyle must be the recognition that traditional Buddhist ethical guidelines, both monastic and lay-oriented, were primarily postulated for sixth-century B.C.E. India. Thus *American Buddhism* called for the creation of American Buddhist commentaries, a new *Vinaya* and *śīla* for the modern world, ones that would include social ethics as a major component.

Because the decade of the 1970s presented such a vast proliferation of Buddhist cultures and sectarian groups in America, the chapter argued for ecumenicism and a recognition of the necessity for mutual sharing, addressing rather than neglecting the difficult question of how to be Buddhist *and* American. The chapter suggested pervasive optimism and an evolutionary viewpoint as attitudes that might unite rather than divide American Buddhists. And it expressed hope for sacred centers that would capture an American weltanschauung. Finally, the chapter suggested active participation in Buddhist practice, irrespective of its specific style, for all members.

Although many of the above suggestions, offered in 1979, seem to have been correct, certainly an equal number of the underlying assumptions were wrong. Most of these wrong assumptions surrounded an unfortunate sense of urgency on my part for the acculturation of all Buddhist groups to an American framework, without proper understanding of and accommodation to the integrity of their own ethnic heritage, and an urgency to find ways, as Numrich has suggested, of properly addressing this issue. Yet the chapter was most clearly wrong about the future when it proclaimed:

> Throughout this study, I have made much of the fact that there is a singular relationship between Buddhism's degree of acculturation in its new American environment and its potential future role in American religious life. To my way of thinking, there is a clear yardstick by which acculturative growth may be measured, namely, the extent to which American Buddhist groups begin to identify with American civil religion.[24]

To the best of my knowledge, not a single Buddhist group has done that. So perhaps that yardstick might serve as my personal *kōan,* best understood when broken over my head.

Emma Layman's *Buddhism in America* and my *American Buddhism,* however, were not the only comprehensive books of that early period. Rick Fields's *How the Swans Came to the Lake* was published in 1981, and continues now in its third edition, published in 1992. It is remarkably easy to read and fun throughout, and Fields is a far more gifted writer than Layman or I might ever hope to be. But in his first edition Fields makes no attempt to confront the future. It is pure narrative, with no evaluative materials. Some concerns for the future do appear in Fields's chapter titled "The Changing of the Guard," but that was not inserted until the third edition, and by that time Fields had already contributed much important material elsewhere on the future of American Buddhism, as we shall see below.

Some Midcourse Corrections

Early in his 1988 essay "Recent Developments in North American Zen," Kenneth Kraft remarks that "as it entered the 1980s, North American

Zen suffered a recession."[25] Although no figures exist that might document Kraft's suspicion, most people writing on American Buddhism acknowledge that the 1980s marked a period of slower growth for Buddhism. It also was a period of internal upheaval for many Buddhist centers, as Kraft also observes. And, acknowledging the growing role of women in American Buddhism, the development of a new generation of teachers, and an aggressive concern for social engagement on the part of American Buddhists, Kraft calls American Buddhism "a tradition in transition" and suggests that the future is "difficult to foresee."[26]

While American Buddhism experienced a period of more modest growth than previously, popular and scholarly literature on the subject proliferated, offering those interested in the topic an enormous amount of provocative reading. Much of the popular literature appeared in the journals or newsletters of various Dharma centers and special-interest groups, and the majority of the articles focused on a particular issue or lineage. A number of important, influential topical books were published as well, especially in the latter half of the 1980s and the early 1990s. In 1987, a full decade after Kashima's seminal study, Donald R. Tuck published *Buddhist Churches of America: Jodo Shinshu.* Useful for its wealth of data, Tuck's book unfortunately draws virtually no conclusions about the American Buddhist movement. In the following year Dharmachari Vessantara issued an interesting volume entitled *The Friends of the Western Buddhist Order,* focusing on Sangharakshita's influential and growing movement. The first edition of Helen Tworkov's useful portrait of a number of American Zen teachers was published as *Zen in America* in 1989, and eventually reissued in an expanded edition in 1994. And in 1992 Jane Hurst gave us a glimpse of yet another Buddhist tradition in *Nichiren Shoshu Buddhism and the Soka Gakkai in America: The Ethos of a New Religious Movement.* Some of these topical studies offered important insights. Lenore Friedman's *Meetings with Remarkable Women: Buddhist Teachers in America,* although intended as a celebration of the role of women in American Buddhism, also offers a sentiment similar to Kraft's:

> Buddhism in the United States may in fact be at a crossroads. The emergence of influential women seems to be coinciding with what might be termed American Buddhism's incipient coming of age . . . So Buddhism has been transplanted to American soil. It has been watered and fertilized by rich, ancient Asian traditions that have helped strengthen its roots and young

stems. But the terrain and climate here are different, and different nourishment seems needed now. For Buddhism to become truly established in America, it will need to move away from reliance on inherited forms and to look instead at the very ground on which it is growing . . . This is the stage we have arrived at now. American Buddhism is in the process of finding its own nature.[27]

Two books with a more general scope did appear in 1992: Joseph B. Tamney's *American Society in the Buddhist Mirror* and Thomas Tweed's *American Encounter with Buddhism, 1844–1912: Victorian Culture and the Limits of Dissent.* Although Tweed's book offers only five pages of "postscript" regarding Buddhism in America after 1912, he does outline two major themes that seem to color the way in which Buddhism continues to be perceived by Americans: optimism and activism. Tweed remarks:

I have noted some of the ways in which mid-Victorian American interpreters of all perspectives affirmed optimism and activism and struggled with Western accounts that challenged those affirmations. These convictions and attitudes continued to be an important part of Victorian culture in the United States as Buddhist interest intensified (1879–1912).[28]

Many of the scholars and critics of the time, according to Tweed, argued that Buddhism contradicted these values, evoking a strong and contrary response from Buddhism's Euro-American supporters. Apparently the former opinion won out, as Tweed reveals in a quote from a letter written by Anagarika Dharmapala to Mary Carus in 1921: "At one time there was some kind of activity in certain parts of the U.S. where some people took interest in Buddhism; but I see none of that now."[29] But the sentiment remains, and, for some scholars, still plays a role in shaping considerations of the future of American Buddhism. Kenneth Tanaka, for example, concludes his epilogue to *The Faces of Buddhism in America* with a reference to Tweed's typology:

Within this period of social and religious changes, the earlier labels of pessimism and passivity have weakened and given way to optimism and activism, the very qualities that many found lacking a century earlier. Activism, as defined by Tweed, reveals itself most notably in the "engaged Buddhism" which seeks to take Buddhist ideals beyond the inner spiritual concerns and into the social arena and the home. Optimism, as understood by Tweed, saw humans, the world, and history as fundamentally good or capable of becoming good. Nowhere was this sense of optimism expressed more poignantly than in the manner in which American Buddhists regard practice. They practice, largely in the form of meditation and chanting, in the belief that through self-discipline they can transform themselves and the world . . . And out of these transformative and empowering human experiences, the Buddhist insights of nonduality and interdependence contribute a distinctive dimension to the face of optimism and activism in American religiosity.[30]

To be sure, Tanaka highlights many other themes in his epilogue (ethnicity, democratization, practice, engagement, and adaptation), but it is optimism and activism that he sees as the ingredients that integrate these themes into a meaningful whole.

I would contend that it is not in the books cited above that we find the most useful so-called midcourse corrections, but rather in two small articles often overlooked by many American Buddhists of the 1980s. The first is Jack Kornfield's "Is Buddhism Changing North America?" published as one of three short introductions to Don Morreale's *Buddhist America: Centers, Retreats, Practices,* while the second is Rick Fields's "Future of American Buddhism," published in the October-November 1987 issue of the *Vajradhatu Sun*.

Jack Kornfield was instrumental in founding the Insight Meditation Society in Barre, Massachusetts, and later, Spirit Rock Center (or Insight Meditation West) in Marin County, California. Both of these enterprises reflect Kornfield's long personal involvement with Theravāda Buddhism, first as a monk in Asia and later as a layman and teacher of *vipassanā* in America. In other words, Kornfield understands well the tension between adherence to a long-standing tradition and the need to be practical. He states this rather directly:

Historically, all major religions, including Buddhism, have contained a basic tension—one which persists as Buddhism comes to America. This is the tension between tradition or orthodoxy and adaptation or modernization. Many people involved in Buddhism see it as their purpose and their duty to preserve and sustain the *sutras,* the tradition, the practices just as they were handed down from the time of the Buddha. Other people have found it important to try to adapt Buddhist practice to new cultures, finding skillful means of allowing access to and understanding of the great wisdom of Buddhism, without presenting it in old, ungainly, and inaccessible forms. This tension has been present since the time of the Buddha himself.[31]

Kornfield's attempt to resolve that tension is apparent when one observes the differences between the early Insight Meditation Society, which was devoted almost exclusively to traditional meditation retreat practice, and Spirit Rock Center, which includes an emphasis on study, Buddhist peace work, ecology, and family considerations, as well as traditional meditation practice.

Cognizant that North American Buddhism was not likely to ever stress the traditional monastic practice that was the staple of Asian Buddhism, Kornfield focuses on three key themes that he believes lie at the heart of Buddhism's ability to have a lasting and meaningful future in America: democratization, feminization, and integration. Democratization involves a movement away from the hierarchical and authoritarian model of Asian Buddhism. It suggests what Kornfield calls "a structure of mutual support and appreciation," one in which there is community participation in all decision making. The community empowerment resulting from democratization has allowed a number of Buddhist communities to safely traverse the upheavals of the 1980s, noted above by Kenneth Kraft. In 1983, for example, Katy Butler wrote: "Last spring we became the first new American religious community to effectively tell its leader to stop. It has been painful, but I think that the way the people of Zen Center have faced this crisis could be an encouragement to other religious communities facing similar problems."[32] Perhaps it has. Several years after Richard Baker resigned his position at San Francisco Zen Center in December 1983, the center chose a new abbot, but limited the position to four years. Other examples of community-based decision making, precipitated by less extreme circumstances, can now be cited throughout the American Buddhist tradition. This style may well become the normative mode of operation in the majority of American Buddhist communities, one that Kornfield sees as a "great vitalizing factor."

Feminization is identified as perhaps the most important of Kornfield's three themes. Contrary to the patriarchal institutional development of Buddhism in Asia, American Buddhism is working diligently to develop gender equality. The entire issue had been summarized very well by Joanna Macy in 1986: "As American women opening to the Dharma, we are participating in something beyond our own little scenarios. We find ourselves reclaiming the equality of the sexes in the Buddha-Dharma. We are participating in a balancing of Buddhism that has great historic significance."[33] In addition, the publication of Lenore Friedman's *Meetings with Remarkable Women* and Sandy Boucher's *Turning the Wheel: American Women Creating the New Buddhism* (first published in 1988, but updated and expanded in 1993) made a great impact on American Buddhism in the 1980s. Boucher drew compelling literary sketches of about fifty prominent American Buddhist women, highlighting their roles in leading Buddhist centers, working toward positive changes in Buddhism, breaking the silence on abuses of power by male teachers, and finding ways to integrate Buddhist practice into their professional and private lives. Thus, by the time that Rita Gross's influential and much debated *Buddhism after Patriarchy: A Feminist History, Analysis, and Reconstruction of Buddhism* was published in 1993, the discussion of what Gross calls a "feminist revalorization of Buddhism" was already well under way. This literary tradition has continued in such works as Karma Lekshe Tsomo's edited volume *Buddhism through American Women's Eyes* (1995).

The final item in Kornfield's tripartite structure is integration. For Kornfield, integration involves moving away from the otherworldly model of world renunciation that he encountered in Asia, and replacing it with a world-affirming application of Buddhist practice to daily life in the world of family people. In many respects, integration is the fulfillment of the previous two themes—a process that demands courage in confronting the many difficult areas of cultural dissonance that affect the possibility of developing a wholesome American Buddhist lifestyle. Although I have criticized Kornfield elsewhere for his less than subtle insinuation that meditation is the only *real* practice of the Buddha, and that American Buddhists do not want to simply make merit by offering gifts or hearing a weekly sermon, his emphasis on the above three themes and the necessity for cross-fertilization among the various Buddhist traditions offers a sane and optimistic methodology for American Buddhism as it enters the future, one that provides for both self-reflection and productive change.[34]

Rick Fields's article, although published a year before Kornfield's essay, went much further and offered much more specificity.[35] Fields's thoughts crystallized while he was attending two events within a three-week period in May 1987. The first was called "Engaging American Buddhism: A Retreat and Experiment for Artists with Thich Nhat Hanh," and the second was the cremation ceremony for Fields's teacher, Ven. Chögyam Trungpa Rinpoche. At the former event, Thich Nhat Hanh suggested that the many artists present try their collective hand at designing some forms for American Buddhism, and much discussion about those American forms took place in the last seven days of the ten-day retreat.

The latter event was a study in contrasts as many American students trained by Trungpa Rinpoche converged on the mountaintop above Karmê-Chöling in Barnet, Vermont, to participate in his cremation with many Tibetan Buddhist monks who now lived in Nepal, Sikkim, and Bhutan. Fields points out that while the Tibetan monks performed their own liturgy in Tibetan, Trungpa's American students performed theirs in English. The Tibetans were virtually all monks except for a few high-ranking lay practitioners, while the Americans were almost all lay practitioners except for a few monks and nuns. The Tibetans were almost all men, while among the Americans, men and women were present in almost equal numbers.

Prior to actually presenting his thinking about the future of American Buddhism, Fields reflects a bit on the impact of these two events. He organizes his thoughts into two categories: (1) "American Buddhist Pluralism"; and (2) "Four Strategies for Continuity." Regarding American Buddhist pluralism, he sees America as a preserve for threatened Buddhist lineages in Asia, and the American coexistence of all forms of Asian Buddhism as a major consequence for American Buddhism. However, rather than seeing America as a melting pot of Asian Buddhism, combining all forms into one eclectic mix, he sees a pluralistic Buddhism in which the meditational traditions and devotional traditions will exist in an atmosphere of dialogue and exchange. His four strategies for continuity involve: (1) the monastic *sangha;* (2) Dharma transmission; (3) the *tulku* tradition; and (4) organizations.

Fields begins his discussion of the monastic *sangha* by recollecting the Buddhist tradition that argues that Buddhism cannot be said to have become established in a country until there are sufficient native-born monks and nuns to have a valid ordination lineage. When he wrote the article, only the Gold Mountain Monastery had established that valid ordination lineage, so by traditional Buddhist standards one could not say that Buddhism had become established in America. Fields also discusses the Japanese Sōtō lineage, which has married priests, and the American attempt to create what he calls a "quasi-monastic sangha," with men and women living halfway between the lay and monastic ideal.[36] He concludes by wondering whether, as the baby-boomer Buddhists age, the monastic *sangha* might become a more attractive avenue for American Buddhists.

The issue of Dharma transmission is what Fields fancifully calls the "Tag-You're-It" strategy. And while he acknowledges that a number of American students, particularly in the Zen and Vajrayāna lineages, had been "tagged," he did not see this as sufficient to ensure continuity in American Buddhism. He takes a straightforward wait-and-see attitude on this issue. He is more optimistic about the *tulku* tradition of reincarnate lamas, not only because it is the strategy of choice in the tradition to which he belongs, but also because a number of *tulkus* appear to have been reborn in North America. (The 25 January 1996 issue of *USA Today* even ran a feature story on *tulkus,* noting that as many as twenty of them had been recognized in the West, not all depicted as in the movie *Little Buddha.*) Fields's last point focuses on institutional strategy for continuity. He sees, within various Buddhist communities, a network of rural retreat centers associated with parent organizations in urban areas. These rural locales, according to Fields, can serve as grassroots organizations for meditation practice, irrespective of whether any particular center has a certified teacher currently in residence.

Having offered his speculative suggestions for maintaining continuity in American Buddhism, Fields next shares his vision of the future. It focuses on eight specific features:[37]

1. American Buddhism will be a practice-oriented tradition.
2. American Buddhism will be essentially a lay-oriented tradition. How one maintains one's practice amid the potential pitfalls of lay life, and how right livelihood can be maintained, are issues of concern.
3. Feminism will greatly affect American Buddhism. Fields considers two particular issues especially noteworthy: a critique of Buddhist practice from the standpoint of what he calls "women's spirituality," emphasizing those forms of practice more expressive of women's issues; and the strong movement to reestablish the nuns' or *bhikṣuṇī* lineage.
4. American Buddhism will continue its already fruitful dialogue with Western psychology, resulting in an "American Buddhist Abhidharma" that classifies therapies in accordance with Buddhist ideals.
5. American Buddhism will continue its growing societal concern, emphasizing the implementation of Buddhist values such as compassion. Fields sees an important role for the Buddhist Peace Fellowship and continuing Buddhist-Christian dialogue.
6. American Buddhism will develop a democratic form of governance that supports and is conducive to Buddhist practice. Fields does not

see formal "voting" procedures for American Buddhists in each *sangha,* but rather a continued multiplicity of choices regarding teachers, practices, and so forth.

7. The issue of democracy may extend into considerations of hierarchy and spiritual authority in the various American Buddhist communities. Issues such as competency of the teacher, the teacher's role, and the relationship between student and teacher will be considered. Fields believes that working through the problematic issues that emerged in these areas in the 1980s will strengthen and mature the American Buddhism of the future.
8. American Buddhism, as a largely lay religious tradition, will reflect an emphasis on Buddhism's life-affirming features. Fields sees Buddhist ethics, as manifested in precepts and the like, being applied to everyday problems. And he calls for a *Vinaya* for laypeople.[38]

When Fields added a chapter titled "The Changing of the Guard" to the third edition (1992) of his *How the Swans Came to the Lake,* many of the above issues were included. In his chapter "Divided Dharma: White Buddhists, Ethnic Buddhists, and Racism," included in *The Faces of Buddhism in America* in 1998, he was still using many of the themes addressed in his 1987 article. One might suppose that in frequently revisiting these issues, Fields remains convinced of their accuracy. Irrespective of whether one agrees with or challenges Fields's conclusions about the future of American Buddhism, there can be no dispute whatsoever that he has offered a clear and comprehensive accounting of the obvious and not-so-obvious possibilities for the tradition as it approaches the last decade of the century. What remains ahead is a consideration of the last wave of reflections on the development of American Buddhism at the turn of the millennium, and for that we must return to Boston, where this chapter began, and visit Berkeley, where so many American Buddhist developments have occurred.

At the Millennium

By the mid-1990s, the practice and study of Buddhism in America had penetrated virtually every aspect of American culture, from its popular press to its cuisine. Well-known sports figures, such as Phil Jackson, the cerebral coach of the world champion Chicago Bulls professional basketball team, openly embraced Buddhism. In the acknowledgments to his best-selling book *Sacred Hoops,* Jackson even thanks Helen Tworkov and Carole Tonkinson at *Tricycle* for providing the suggestion that germinated into the book project, and expresses gratitude to Zen practitioners Richard Baker and Charlotte Joko Beck for their important contributions to the book. Stories on American Buddhism and American Buddhists were not uncommon in the *New York Times,* the *Wall Street Journal,* and other major newspapers; they could even be found in *Newsweek* and *Christianity Today.*

When *ABC Nightly News with Peter Jennings* presented a major multi-evening feature on American Buddhism in 1994, it was no longer satisfactory to simply identify well-known American Buddhists as "celebrity Buddhists." In its 6 June 1994 issue, *New York Magazine* put an entirely new spin on classifications of popular American Buddhists. Sallie Dinkel's story "In with the Om Crowd" identified twelve categories of highly visible American Buddhists:

Beat Buddhists—including Anne Waldman, Allen Ginsberg, Gary Snyder, Philip Whalen, and Michael McClure

Celluloid Buddhists—including Richard Gere, Oliver Stone, and Willem Dafoe

Art Buddhists—including Milton Glaser, Francesco Clemente, and Robert Moskowitz

Power Buddhists—including Jerry Brown

Benefit Buddhists—including Porter McCray and Bokara Legendre

Philanthropic Buddhists—including Lawrence Shainberg, Steven Rockefeller, Henry Luce III, and John and Jodie Eastman

Jazz and Classical Buddhists—including Philip Glass, Herbie Hancock, and Meredith Monk

Rock-and-Roll Buddhists—including Suzanne Vega, Adam Yauch, Marianne Faithfull, Lou Reed, Jerry Garcia, Tina Turner, Natalie Merchant, Edie Brickell, and Leonard Cohen

Theatrical Buddhists—including Merce Cunningham, Laurie Anderson, and Spalding Gray

Cyber-Buddhists—including Mitch Kapor, Jaron Lanier, and Thomas Zimmerman

Jock Buddhists—including Orlando Cepeda and Phil Jackson

Literary Buddhists—including Helen Tworkov, John Avedon, Kate Wheeler, Pico Iyer, Peter Muryo Matthiessen, and Robert Thurman.

There seems to be no end to the media attention, and with its increased visibility, American Buddhism continues to grow and thrive.

I first began teaching courses on American Buddhism in the mid-1970s, and quite often my students asked me how they could find Buddhist groups to visit as they traveled throughout America. At that time, for lack of other sources, I relied on the carefully networked resources I had developed as I prepared my book *American Buddhism.* Now I tell them to look in both the Yellow Pages, under "Churches: Buddhist," and *Tricycle.* Still, the two questions I am most frequently asked are: (1) How many Buddhists are there now in America? and (2) Why are there so many? To the former question, there is a safe and easy answer: We don't know! When Peter Jennings's researchers contacted me to solicit my estimate of the number of American Buddhists, I asked them why they had contacted *me.* They said that Robert Thurman had referred them to me, as a means of verifying *his* estimate of 5 to 6 million. I told them that I thought Thurman was wrong, and that I would be very surprised if there were more than 3 or 4 million Buddhists in America. Needless to say, they asked me how I arrived at that figure. My response: "I got that figure the same way Thurman got his. I guessed." The second question is harder, but I am continually convinced that Peter Berger was correct when he said, about religion in general, more than thirty years ago: "Secularization brings about a de-monopolization of religious traditions and thus, *ipso facto,* leads to a pluralistic situation."[39] Berger went on to say: "The key characteristic of all pluralistic situations, whatever the details of their historical background, is that monopolies can no longer take for granted the allegiance of their client populations . . . The pluralistic situation is, above all, a *market situation.*"[40] American Buddhism has simply done an outstanding job of marketing its product.

In each of the subsections of this chapter, I have emphasized that books devoted to American Buddhism increased significantly over time. By the mid-1990s they were growing almost exponentially, and publishing companies like Snow Lion, Wisdom Publications, and Shambhala were using the World Wide Web as a means of reaching an even larger Buddhist clientele. Moreover, a number of Buddhist periodical publications were becoming increasingly popular on the national scene. *Tricycle: The Buddhist Review* was launched in the fall of 1991, and by middecade had a faithful, devoted readership. Additionally, in September 1992 the *Vajradhatu Sun* was transformed into the *Shambhala Sun,* bringing a new focus to the magazine that has enabled it to extend far beyond its original mission as an expression of the communities founded by Chögyam Trungpa Rinpoche. And the journals and newsletters of individual *sanghas* continue to proliferate. DharmaNet International lists more than two dozen online publications, and it is quite likely more than twice that number of communities offer *sangha*-specific print publications. Scholarly books are making an important contribution as well. Paul Numrich's *Old Wisdom in the New World: Americanization in Two Immigrant Theravada Buddhist Temples* is one of the most frequently reviewed new books in Buddhist Studies, and Stephen Prothero's *White Buddhist: The Asian Odyssey of Henry Steel Olcott* paints an exciting portrait of an early American Buddhist pioneer. Two recent anthologies are equally important: *The Faces of Buddhism in America,* edited by Kenneth Tanaka and myself; and *American Buddhism: Methods and Findings in Recent Scholarship,* edited by Duncan Ryūken Williams and Christopher S. Queen.

In chapter 4, I referred to an early but important national conference, "The Flowering of Buddhism in America," held at Syracuse University in 1977. While small, local conferences have periodically been sponsored by various individual Buddhist communities over the past two decades, national conferences devoted to the development of American Buddhism have begun to emerge in the 1990s as a vehicle for scholarly, institutional, and even ecumenical communication. The first of these, also referred to in chapter 4, was held at the Institute of Buddhist Studies (IBS) at Berkeley in 1994. Each year the IBS sponsors the Numata Lecture Series, named in honor of Yehan Numata, a Japanese industrialist who founded Mitutoyo Manufacturing Company, and who sponsored many Buddhist programs all over the world, including the one at the IBS. The 1994 series, organized by Kenneth Tanaka, was titled "Buddhisms in America: An Expanding Frontier" and spanned a three-month period between September and December. The topics fell into one of two major areas of inquiry: (1) discussions of particular American Buddhist traditions; and (2) considerations of critical issues in the development of American Buddhism. With the exception of Rick Fields, each lecturer was an academic professor. Because the nucleus of each lecture was a highly specific subject, there was little opportunity for any of the participating scholars to address the general issue of the future of American Buddhism, although the presentation of each certainly highlighted items that would invariably have an impact on that future.

When the presented papers were collected for publication, Tanaka, as convener of the series, wrote an important epilogue, subtitled "The Colors and Contours of American Buddhism," in which he carefully extracted the common themes of the papers and framed them in a forward-looking perspective. As noted above, Tanaka isolated five major issues from the conference: ethnicity, democratization, practice, engagement, and adaptation.

In discussing ethnicity, Tanaka points out: "Ethnic temples serve not only the spiritual but the cultural and social needs of their members, particularly among the most recent of the immigrant population," whereas "most observers note that the Euro-American groups focus primarily on the spiritual."[41] He confronts squarely the suggestion of Tworkov and others that Asian American Buddhists have not contributed significantly to the developing "American" form of Buddhism, but questions the accuracy of such a sharp dichotomy and points instead to the cooperative activities of regional Buddhist councils such as those found in New York, southern California, northern California, Hawaii, and other locations.

Although Tanaka's treatment of democratization has much in common with Kornfield's, he sees the currently prominent role of women in American Buddhism as a proper manifestation of democratization, especially in a markedly lay tradition that is increasingly nonhierarchical. He believes that this trend was hastened by the various accusations of sexual misconduct on the part of some Buddhist teachers beginning in the 1980s. He also sees a future enhanced by what Rita Gross has called "natural hierarchy," in which American Buddhist institutions manifest neither authoritarian nor egalitarian approaches, as well as an expanded role for gay and lesbian practitioners in the *sangha*.

Regarding modes of practice, Tanaka acknowledges that meditation, and to a lesser extent chanting, are of primary import to American Buddhist converts. He makes an important connection between modes of meditation such as *vipassanā* and their strong association with Western psychotherapy, citing the famous first verse of the *Dhammapada* in which mind is cited as chief, the forerunner of all. And he sees a future American

Buddhism in which the rich and varied forms of practice spawn communities of self-reliant, energetic, spiritually healthy individuals.

In emphasizing the role of social engagement in the future of American Buddhism, Tanaka notes that the Buddhist Peace Fellowship, with more than four thousand members nationally, is the most socially visible Buddhist organization on the North American continent. But he also points out the growing number of projects undertaken by individual communities, such as the AIDS hospice of the San Francisco Zen Center and the "Street Zen" program of Bernard Glassman Rōshi in New York. Tanaka sees a future in which American Buddhist social engagement, grounded in the Buddhist doctrines of interconnectedness and nonduality, provides a therapeutic methodology for such areas as conflict resolution, environmental awareness, and right livelihood. This area of Buddhist endeavor has become sufficiently important that Christopher Queen has privately, if not publicly, suggested that social engagement might well become the "fourth yāna," or vehicle, of future Buddhism.

"Adaptation" is Tanaka's term for what many before him have called acculturation. While he recognizes that the process of adaptation took place in Buddhism's transmission into every culture in Asia, he points out additional items: first, that "the pace and fervor of emphasis on adaptation in modern America are unprecedented," and second, that this is the first time Buddhism has been transmitted from less-developed societies to a highly developed society.[42] These are critically important issues, exacerbated by the fact that although Buddhism was able to make important inroads in America's pluralistic society, various American Buddhist groups find themselves competing with other American Buddhist groups in the same community for members—something that rarely happened in Asia. Thus, according to Tanaka, the future of American Buddhism may well become more consumer-oriented than previously. This consumer orientation may also yield members with "diffuse affiliations" or commitments to more than one religious tradition. Such a diffuse affiliation may manifest itself in a person's holding concurrent multiple affiliations in various Buddhist groups, or in cross-traditional linkages, such as the Jewish-Buddhist amalgam Rodger Kamenetz calls "JUBU."[43] In the end Tanaka has postulated an American Buddhism for the twenty-first century, united under the twin categories of optimism and activism, that will look very much different from the Buddhism of a quarter century earlier.

Slightly more than two years after the IBS Numata Lecture Series concluded, the Buddhism in America Conference cited at the outset of this chapter convened. Of the nearly three dozen presenters at the conference, only two (Robert Thurman and Miranda Shaw) held traditional academic positions in American universities. One other held an academic appointment outside the United States (John Stevens), and a few (like Stephen Batchelor) held positions in nontraditional but still somewhat academic settings. Also unlike the Berkeley conference, this Boston meeting was commercially planned and marketed by its organizer. Those interested in getting a head start on their weekend of conference participation could choose from seven "Pre-conference Workshops," for a $95 fee. The conference itself carried a $315 price tag, but the "Early Bird" shoppers could register for $275, while late registration was $335. With all the commercial exhibitors selling everything from books to meditation harnesses (designed quite literally to hold one in meditative posture with back and leg support), the weekend took on something of a carnival atmosphere. Nonetheless, despite the glitz, the vast majority of the planned sessions were remarkably interesting, and the presenters had impressive credentials. In fact, many of the participants were the *subjects* of the newspaper and magazine articles referred to earlier in this chapter. The only link in presenters between this conference and the one held earlier at Berkeley was Rick Fields, who participated in both.

Although I had much personal interest in many of the sessions, because of the requirements of my research I was able to attend only those presentations that coincided with my professional concerns, ones that would affect the preparation of this book. Three events were on my "must attend" list: keynote addresses by Robert Thurman (called "Toward American Buddhism") and Lama Surya Das (called "Emergent Trends in Western Dharma"), and a talk by Bernard Glassman Rōshi called "Instructions to the Cook: Zen Lessons in Living a Life That Matters." The title of Glassman's presentation does not reveal its allure, but the printed description does:

> This "cooking" class will offer recipes for the "supreme meal," the life lived fully and completely. Tetsugen Roshi will discuss the five main "courses" of a complete meal that sustains and nourishes life: spirituality, study, livelihood, social action, and relationship/community. Aimed at those who wish to explore the role of Zen Buddhist teaching in the world of business and social action.[44]

Considering the remarkable, important work in social action carried out by this primary Dharma heir of Maezumi Rōshi, and the presumed topics to be discussed, I expected fertile insights that might help me better understand the future directions of American Buddhism. I found nothing of the kind. After spending five minutes wrestling with the table at which he sat, and another five adjusting the seating arrangements for the perhaps two hundred avid listeners, Glassman explained his methodology for the two-hour session. At the outset he would allow people in the audience to offer a series of short questions, which he would then fashion into a little discourse that would he hoped make some sense out of their enterprise as American Buddhists. After his discourse, he would allow further questions. I was reminded of some of my professor colleagues who utilize this technique when they are not prepared to lecture. But this was Bernard Glassman Rōshi! Who was I to question his methodology? At the conclusion of the two hours, I felt that very little, if anything, described in the program had been delivered. Questions were avoided, and audience participants were treated rudely, in a fashion that could not be construed as even a Zen form of compassion. To the rōshi's followers and devotees, he was probably brilliant; to the rest of us, he was disappointing. Near the end of the session, one audience member asked what advice Glassman might have for "cooking up" an American Buddhism that acknowledged its diversity and complexity, yet allowed American Buddhists to share common social causes and concerns; in other words, the classic social-engagement question, asked of one of the foremost socially engaged Buddhists in America. Glassman refused to answer, tossing the question right back at the questioner, advising him not to ask academic questions and to cook up his own answer.

The other sessions were better. That same evening Robert Thurman appeared, energetic as ever, to present his keynote address. After dropping out of Harvard University, Thurman became the first Western Tibetan Buddhist monk, and was ordained by the Dalai Lama himself in 1965. Thurman eventually returned to Harvard, finished his training, and went on to a productive career in Buddhology, a field he claims to have created.[45] It was hard to know in advance what to expect from Thurman, and apart from listing the tantalizing title, the program brochure said only: "A discussion of foundational insights and straightforward guidelines for the total life practice of Buddhism in contemporary and 21st century America." Following some clever introductory banter, Thurman outlined four areas for his presentation: (1) What is Buddhism? (2) What is it doing here or could it do here? (3) How will it do it? and (4) Will it do it? In the ensuing hour it was sometimes unclear where one item ceased and the next began, but Thurman's ruminations, enhanced by his style of presentation and quick wit, were both surprising and useful. As he continued, Thurman reassessed his overall thesis by remarking: "Buddhism will not actually be able to succeed in its mission here in America unless it is able to perform that mission without being Buddhism." He went on: "Buddhism has to go beyond being Buddhism in order to do the work that Buddhism wants to do wherever it is. OK, so it's Buddhism without Buddhism. That's my title." Then he looked up at Glassman Rōshi sitting in the balcony of the auditorium, chuckled, and said, "That's very Zen, don't you think, Rōshi?"

Early in his presentation, he reminded the audience that Buddhism's appearance in America should not be taken for granted, for just as it appeared, so also it can *disappear,* as it has largely done in the country of its birth. Thurman went on to explain that, rather than being a religion, "Buddhism is a therapy the Buddha elaborated for demented human beings." He further suggested that it was a therapy about "selfishness," and that the traditional four noble truths were a "therapeutic recipe." The main emphasis of his presentation was on Buddhism as a social revolution and a means for attaining human happiness. Thus it surprised nobody when he suggested that for America to become a mainstream Buddhist country, it would have to abandon its military. He even pondered the possibility of turning military bases into Dharma centers. At no time did he suggest that Americans should actually *become* Buddhists, but rather that they should seek Buddhist methodologies *within* their own traditional religious frameworks (his advice sounding very much like what Kenneth Tanaka called "diffuse affiliations"). As his talk became more fanciful, Thurman described Buddhism as an "evolutionary sport," picking up an earlier thread in his discussion in which he mused about the possibility of Buddhism being taught as a "sport" in public school. As the talk advanced toward its conclusion, it was clear that Thurman was serious about his proclamation that the future of Buddhism in America lay in "Buddhism without Buddhism." Before concluding, he recounted a story that described the visit of eminent Buddhologist Gadjin Nagao to the Mt. Baldy Zen Center about twenty years before, at which Professor Nagao argued that there were five "peaks" in Buddhist history. By the end of Nagao's description of the fourth peak, Thurman noted, the Zen students were falling asleep. But they awoke with a start when Nagao argued that there was *no fifth peak unless it happened here in America.* Thurman's talk ended on a positive note, suggesting, with Nagao, that Buddhist innovations in America might well reverberate throughout Asia.

The next evening Lama Surya Das gave the final speech of the conference. Surya Das is an interesting and engaging person. He had been given his name by the Hindu teacher Maharaj-ji many years before, and in his speech he joked that it is a fitting title, and that his girlfriend sometimes refers to him as "Serious" Das. He was born Jeffrey Miller in 1950, and graduated from the State University of New York at Buffalo in 1971. Between 1971 and 1976 he traveled extensively in India and Nepal, taking a year out in 1973–74 to live in Kyoto, Japan, where he studied Zen. He also practiced *vipassanā* with S. N. Goenka and A. Munindra. Eventually becoming a lama in the nonsectarian practice lineage of Tibetan Buddhism, he practiced under Kalu Rinpoche, Lama Thubten Yeshe, and others, and twice completed the traditional Tibetan three-year retreat. After returning to the United States, he founded the Dzogchen Foundation in Cambridge, Massachusetts.

Despite the fact that many members of the audience looked slightly tired from a weekend of virtually nonstop events, because of its provocative description in the program brochure, most were eager to hear Surya Das's presentation, whose printed description read:

> Throughout the ages, each time Buddhism has entered a new culture it has had to reinvent itself anew in order to remain applicable. Today we face a great challenge in helping to shape the emerging face of a liberating, autonomous and delightful American Buddhism. Lama Surya Das will discuss twelve trends he has identified as defining the emerging face of the Dharma in the West.

Actually, he described only *ten* trends, but they were carefully organized and useful, and they offered a vision for the twenty-first century that provided a more than fitting closure for the conference.

While everyone in the audience could readily acknowledge the accuracy of Surya Das's claim that America afforded the first occasion in history for every Buddhist school from each Asian tradition to be together in one place and at the same time, the audience was less than pleased when he noted that, to a large extent, the Three Jewels of American Buddhism were *Me, Myself,* and *I.* Nonetheless, he moved ahead quickly to a summary of the ten points that he believed would characterize the American Buddhism of the future, each of which he described briefly.[46] These included:

1. Dharma without dogma. Like other speakers before him (most notably Stephen Batchelor), he argued for a "Buddhism without belief."
2. A lay-oriented *sangha.* He acknowledged and supported the notion of *three* communities in American Buddhism: the traditional monastic *sangha,* the lay *sangha,* and what he referred to as "the in-between *sangha,*" with the latter reflecting the attempts by many men and women to maintain a monastic-oriented lifestyle while living a traditional family life.
3. A meditation-based and experiential tradition. He contrasted this feature with a study-based or academic Buddhism. There was no mention of nonmeditational practices, such as those utilized by the Pure Land tradition, or by Sōka Gakkai.
4. Gender equality. Surya Das noted that half of the Buddhist teachers in the West are women, and that the American Dharma needed to be an equal-opportunity enterprise.
5. A nonsectarian tradition. Surya Das stressed that the developing American Buddhism of the next century must be eclectic, ecumenical, and utterly equal.
6. An essentialized and simplified tradition. Here he maintained that American Buddhism needed to be demystified, and bypass technical jargon and foreign terminology. In reshaping the Dharma for the West, however, he also underscored the need to avoid New Age and pop psychology.
7. An egalitarian, democratic, and nonhierarchical tradition. The chief emphasis in this point was Surya Das's insistence that American Buddhism not be class-oriented or theocratic. He argued for supporting noninstitutionalized forms of American Buddhism.
8. A psychologically astute and rational tradition. Perhaps in an attempt to expand and clarify point 3 above, he restated his insistence on a practice-based American Buddhism, but here included faith and devotional practices as well. But he also argued for the tradition to be skeptical, practical, and acquiring. Nonetheless, he concluded this point by advocating self-help as a primary aspect of American Buddhism.
9. An experimental, innovating, inquiry-based tradition. Surya Das wants American Buddhism to be forward looking rather than

preservationist. He argued aggressively against preserving old wine in new bottles. Of special interest was his observation that we are now experiencing the "third wave" of teachers: Western teachers trained by *Western teachers*.

10. A socially informed and engaged tradition. As his final point, he accentuated an integrative rather than reclusive American Buddhism in which family life was included as part of the spiritual path. He further indicated the importance of hospice work, ethics and right livelihood, deep ecology, the performing arts, sports, social service, and interfaith dialogue as critical features of the socially engaged Buddhism of the future.

Surya Das closed the conference by inviting the entire audience to chant with him—perhaps a fitting way to bring everyone together into a practice that reflected the points he emphasized in his presentation.

Only a few months following the auspicious ending of what I heard some participants call the "American Buddhism Blowout," a few miles down the road, the annual Harvard Buddhist Studies Forum sponsored a very different kind of American Buddhism conference, called "Buddhism in America: Methods and Findings in Recent Scholarship," carefully planned by Christopher S. Queen and Duncan Ryūken Williams. Slightly more than a dozen scholars congregated for a weekend in May to discuss many of the same issues as noted immediately above, but from a very different perspective. Unlike the IBS conference, in which most of the participants were scholar-practitioners, or the Boston conference, in which *all* the participants were practicing Buddhists, the Harvard conference boasted only a few scholar-practitioners, and perhaps a smattering of members belonging to what I referred to in chapter 4 as the "silent *sangha*." It was a conference to talk *about* American Buddhism, and there was very little consideration of the future of American Buddhism, apart from the sparse reflections on that topic in a few of the papers, which, despite their lack of a forward-looking perspective, were extremely interesting and discerning.

At the opening session of the conference—a conference at which Diana Eck would preview her CD-ROM *On Common Ground: World Religions in America* and present a paper titled "American Religious Pluralism and the Study of Buddhism"—Duncan Williams remarked that as we approached the turn of the millennium, it was now simply not possible to earn a degree in Buddhist Studies without paying proper attention to its newest subdiscipline: American Buddhism. Later, once the conference was over and the papers were being solicited for publication, Christopher Queen organized the proposed volume into four distinct parts: (1) "Asian American Buddhist Identities"; (2) "Profiling the New Buddhism"; (3) "Modes of Dharma Transmission"; and (4) "The Scholar's Place in American Buddhist Studies." It all seemed so neat and tidy and clear-cut. Yet one still wonders if there are any ways in which American Buddhist practitioners, scholars of American Buddhism, and American Buddhist scholar-practitioners can meaningfully engage in a dialogue that will prove instrumental in understanding the common themes that are emerging in the American Buddhism that will soon witness the turn of the millennium.

Common Themes

Harvey Cox wrote: "Few faiths ever escape modification when they collide or interact with others. Most profit from such encounters."[47] Buddhism has made a long journey from its homeland in India in the sixth century B.C.E. to virtually every country on the globe by the dawn of the twenty-first century C.E. There is now a vast and important literature that documents Buddhism's growth throughout Asia, and helps us understand the process by which Buddhism was able to acculturate in each place, becoming distinctly Chinese, or Tibetan, or Korean. Now we are trying to understand how Buddhism might be American, and with a healthy dose of presumptuous impatience, we somehow expect the process to be already complete. Yet the places we have visited in this volume, and the viewpoints we have examined, suggest that American Buddhism is still growing, changing, and adapting. The most astute contributors to the new commentarial literature that is emerging in American Buddhism counsel that it is in the process itself that acculturation or adaptation occurs.

In reviewing the forward-looking suggestions of researchers during the previous twenty-five year period, it is possible to isolate a number of common, internal variables in the American Buddhist movement, and there is virtually unanimous agreement among these researchers that the development of American Buddhism in the next century will depend on the unfolding of these internal variables. Broadly defined, they include the nature and definition of the *sangha,* democratization within the entire tradition, ethnicity, gender equality, practice orientation, social engagement, and sectarian issues as the challenges of the future.

Although there seems little doubt that American Buddhism will continue to be a mostly lay-oriented movement, more and more successful monastic communities—such as Gampo Abbey on Cape Breton Island, in Nova Scotia—are beginning to appear on the landscape that provide various kinds of monastic living experiences for members of the American Buddhist *sangha.* Contextually, it is within the expanding inclusiveness of the American *sangha* that new and evolving experiments in self-governance are emerging that provide exciting possibilities for American Buddhists living in both urban and rural settings. Further, these attempts at a rationally conceived democratization of the *sangha* include thoughtful considerations of how to successfully implement gender equality, respect for the full spectrum of Buddhist practices and practitioners within both the Asian-immigrant and American-convert communities, and a keen awareness that social engagement is the most profound expression of Buddhism's life-affirming attitude. Nurtured in an environment of concern for a proper application of Buddhist ethics, implemented in a modern and global Buddhist community, and with an renewed sense of inquiry into the nature, quality, and requirements of spiritual authority, the American Buddhism of the next millennium will gain from the above factors an active and positive agenda.

Nonetheless, each of the above topics includes a host of variables that will act and react in an interdependent fashion, yielding an almost endless set of possible permutations for the future of American Buddhism. In addition to these internal variables, there are many external ones as well, relating to the changing face of American religious life.[48] Not the least of these will be the way in which the expanding role of information-exchange technology opens new modes of communication in the various American Buddhist *sanghas,* as we saw in chapters 3 and 5. American Buddhism, once studied primarily by historians of American religion and Buddhologists, may well benefit from renewed interest in the scientific study of religion, and the manner in which American Buddhism addresses religious change. Books such as *Tradition in Contact and Change,* edited by Peter Slater and Donald Wiebe,[49] and *Innovation in Religious Tradition: Essays in the Interpretation of Religious Change,* edited by Michael William,

Collett Cox, and Martin Jaffee,[50] will prove helpful in understanding the American Buddhism of the next century. Too, one should not lose sight of the fact that ethnic Buddhists represent only one of the various religious diasporas of this century, and that much can be learned from studying others. Ninian Smart, for example, remarks about Hinduism and Buddhism that "during the Global Period [from the 1960s onward] there is a tendency toward the consolidation of world religions, however dispersed."[51]

Further, there is an "evolution of a kind of ecumenical Buddhism . . . [and] a new feeling of identity, since Buddhism perceives itself as a world religion."[52] The importance of the development of an ecumenical American Buddhism cannot be stressed strongly enough, for it provides perhaps the best potential for American Buddhist unity in the next century. One scholar who has studied the impact of Buddhist ecumenicism says:

> This new ecumenical self-understanding has also brought about a new perception of now neighboring Buddhist traditions. In Asia, the many different schools and traditions had virtually no contact with each other for hundreds of years. In the West . . . these various schools have all become settled in comparatively small regions such as, for example, the Netherlands, Austria or Southern California. Intra-Buddhist activities and a Buddhist ecumenicalism have availed themselves of this geographical proximity. A rapid increase in inter-traditional relations has emerged, transforming disdain into mutual respect. In consequence, this has brought to the fore new concepts such as a joint Buddhist Confession in Germany, national and international umbrella organisations or an international Network of Western Buddhist Teachers.[53]

In other words, in looking for innovative and creative methodologies for successfully negotiating the future, American Buddhism and American Buddhists might well look beyond the North American borders and learn from the experiences of other Western Buddhists. Part of that learning experience must necessarily be to understand the process of transplantation and adaptation.[54]

One of those modes of adaptation is the Buddhist Confession referred to above. German Buddhists are quick to point out that they are the only Buddhists in the world to have a Buddhist Confession (*Buddhistisches Bekenntnis*),[55] which is acceptable to all German Buddhists irrespective of tradition or school. It involves an affirmation of (1) the three refuges (Buddha, Dharma, *Sangha*), followed by (2) the four noble truths. These principles are applied to daily life in (3) ethical conduct, specifically manifested by (4) the five precepts. All who follow these principles and practices should develop (5) the four sublime states (love, compassion, sympathetic joy, and equanimity).[56] Almost unanimously passed in 1985 by the German Buddhism community, this confession not only standardizes German Buddhism to some degree, but also distinguishes German Buddhists from proponents of other religions. Whether similar measures would be effective in American Buddhism is unclear, but the cooperation and ecumenicism necessary to effect such goals are already apparent in some regional American Buddhist councils.

The potential importance of national and international umbrella organizations should also not be overlooked. The European Buddhist Union (EBU), founded in 1975, was very useful for its attempt "to unite national Buddhist umbrella organisations and Buddhist institutions, i.e., orders or centres with a Europe-wide distribution. Members are the national umbrella organisations from Great Britain, France, Italy, Austria, Switzerland, Belgium, Germany and The Netherlands."[57] In addition, independent Buddhist assemblies like Vajradhatu, the FWBO, Zen and Shin groups, and others were included as well. The EBU has held major congresses in Paris (in 1979 and 1988), Turin (in 1984), and Berlin (in 1992). The major result has been valuable dialogue between the various European Buddhist groups. By 1991, the EBU had thirty member groups from eleven countries, but it has not been a complete success, as most ethnic-Asian Buddhist organizations and Sōka Gakkai rarely participate, causing Baumann to speculate, "It is difficult to imagine that a unified, jointly practised 'European Buddhism' will emerge in the next century."[58] Nevertheless, a similar structure on the North American continent might allow American Buddhism to move sanely into the next century, emphasizing a shared Buddhist mission and mutual respect. And it is perhaps still too soon to predict how NEWBUT (Network of Western Buddhist Teachers), established at the 1993 conference of Western Buddhist teachers with the Dalai Lama in Dharamsala, will fare. An "integrative" Buddhism in North America is only one of many potential developments in our postmodern age. Nonetheless, irrespective of how the above issues invariably interpenetrate in the next century, it is at least clear that the globalization of Buddhism is surely at hand.

APPENDIX

A Postscript on North American Buddhism

In 1974, while I was writing *American Buddhism,* I was fortunate enough to meet John Maraldo during the first tumultuous summer at Naropa Institute in Boulder, Colorado. He pointed me to a book called *Buddhism in the Modern World,* originally published in German but soon to appear in English translation. Maraldo had served as associate editor on the project, working under the well-known scholar Heinrich Dumoulin (who was the general editor). Maraldo thought I might find the book interesting in that it contained sections on Buddhism in each of the various countries of Asia. The sections were prepared by an eminent list of scholars, including Hajime Nakamura, Winston King, Donald Swearer, Holmes Welch, Heinz Bechert, Alex Wayman, David Snellgrove, Heinrich Dumoulin, and others. More importantly, the concluding chapter was Ernst Benz's "Buddhism in the Western World." When the book was eventually published in 1976, I was shocked and horrified to find that Benz covered the entirety of non-Asian Buddhism in seventeen pages! Nearly a decade later, Heinz Bechert's essay "Buddhist Revival in East and West," published in *The World of Buddhism,* which Bechert coedited with Richard Gombrich, and which had an equally eminent cast of authors, proved to be no better.

Although we have just concluded nearly three hundred pages of collecting and documenting historical data, reflecting on critical issues, examining sample Buddhist communities, considering the academic study of Buddhism, outlining the availability of resources on the Internet, and in the process trying to reach some meaningful overall conclusions—all with a sole focus on America—it would be an unfortunate mistake to imagine that American Buddhism can any longer be studied in isolation from the rest of "world Buddhism." For just as there are now many scholars and committed practitioners studying American Buddhism, an equal number of individuals are studying Buddhism in other Western countries. In addition, there is an increasing number of traveling teachers, from Asia and Europe alike, who have made a strong impact on American Buddhist communities.[1]

Recently, in a marvelously engaging article called "The Dharma Has Come West: A Survey of Recent Studies and Sources,"[2] Martin Baumann surveyed some of the literature devoted to Buddhism in Great Britain, France, Germany, Australia, and South Africa. In addition, he published a comprehensive bibliography, called "Buddhism in Europe: An Annotated Bibliography on Its Historical Developments and Contemporary States of Affairs," that is archived at a variety of Internet sites. If one tabulates the available data on Western Buddhism, some interesting and surprising results can be obtained, as summarized in table 14.

Table 14 *Buddhists and Buddhist Groups in the Mid-1990s*

Country	Buddhists	Euro-American Buddhists	Centers	Population	Percent of pop.
USA	3–4 million	800,000	500–800	261,000,000	1.6
Australia	140,000	14,000	150	18,000,000	0.8
South Africa	5,000	2,500	40	42,000,000	0.01
Great Britain	180.000	50,000	300	58,000,000	0.3
France	650,000	150,000	130	58,000,000	1.15
Germany	150,000	40,000	400	81,000,000	0.2
Italy	75,000	50,000	30	57,000,000	0.1
Switzerland	20–25,000	?	80	7,000,000	0.3
Netherlands	20,000	5,000	40	15,000,000	0.1
Denmark	8,000	5,000	32	5,000,000	0.16
Austria	13,000	5,000	25	8,000,000	0.16
Hungary	6,500	6,000	12	10,000,000	0.07
Czech Republic	2,100	2,000	15	10,000,000	0.02
Poland	4,500	4,000	15	38,000,000	0.01
Russia	1 million	40,000	100	149,000,000	0.7

SOURCE: *Journal of Buddhist Ethics* 4 (1997), p. 198. The category titles in this table were altered slightly for presentation here, but the data were not altered in any fashion.

Baumann argues aggressively for a mutual sharing of information and the "importance of both geographic, country-focused" and "global, general surveys" because "observations and insights won through the study of Buddhist history in one country may fruitfully be transferred to another, Western context."[3] In other words, Baumann is suggesting that as Western Buddhism creates new forms in its developmental process, these forms of world Buddhism beg for comparative analytical research. And, at least with regard to European Buddhism, he has begun to do that. His article "Creating a European Path to Nirvâna: Historical and Contemporary Developments of Buddhism in Europe"[4] is both comparative and forward-looking.

Although Baumann is right when he surmises that no one monograph can sufficiently cover Buddhism in the Western World, perhaps it is not unrealistic to hope that when the next team of enterprising scholars seek to once again update the work of Dumoulin and Maraldo, or of Bechert and Gombrich, they will be able to include current, comprehensive studies on Buddhism as practiced throughout the world.

Notes

Chapter 1. American Buddhism: A Brief History

1. Thomas Tweed, *The American Encounter with Buddhism, 1844–1912: Victorian Culture and the Limits of Dissent* (Bloomington: Indiana University Press, 1992), xix, 2.

2. Rick Fields, *How the Swans Came to the Lake: A Narrative History of Buddhism in America,* 3d ed., rev. and updated (Boston: Shambhala, 1992), 70–71.

3. Tweed, *American Encounter,* 13.

4. Louise Hunter, *Buddhism in Hawaii* (Honolulu: University of Hawaii Press, 1971), 32.

5. Ibid., 33.

6. The above story is thoroughly detailed in Fields, *How the Swans Came to the Lake,* 76–82.

7. See Theosophical Society, *The Theosophical Movement, 1875–1950* (Los Angeles: Cunningham Press, 1957), 44.

8. Stephen Prothero's important book *The White Buddhist: The Asian Odyssey of Henry Steel Olcott* (Bloomington: Indian University Press, 1996) provides a wealth of data and insight on the work of Olcott.

9. For important reading on the World Parliament of Religions, consult Richard H. Seager, *The World's Parliament of Religions: The East-West Encounter, Chicago, 1893* (Bloomington: Indiana University Press, 1995).

10. Fields, *How the Swans Came to the Lake,* 120.

11. Anagarika Dharmapala, "Opening Address," cited in John Henry Barrows, ed., *The World's Parliament of Religions: An Illustrated and Popular Story of the World's First Parliament of Religions, Held in Chicago in Connection with the Columbian Exposition of 1893,* 2 vols. (Chicago: Parliament Publishing Company, 1893), 95–96.

12. For more on Paul Carus, see Martin Verhoeven, "Americanizing the Buddha: Paul Carus and the Transformation of Asian Thought," in *The Faces of Buddhism in America,* ed. Charles S. Prebish and Kenneth K. Tanaka (Berkeley: University of California Press, 1998), 207–27.

13. Fields, *How the Swans Came to the Lake,* 129.

14. Kenneth K. Tanaka, "Epilogue: The Colors and Contours of American Buddhism," in Prebish and Tanaka, *Faces of Buddhism,* 297. Also see Tweed, *American Encounter,* 133–56.

15. Sigetsu Sasaki Rōshi, "Excerpts from *Our Lineage,*" *Wind Bell* 8, nos. 1–2 (fall 1969), 8.

16. This quote is widely reported in the literature. See, for example, John Snelling, *The Buddhist Handbook: A Complete Guide to Buddhist Schools, Teaching, Practice, and History* (Rochester, Vt.: Inner Traditions, 1991), 235.

17. Louis Nordstrom, ed., *Namu Dai Bosa: A Transmission of Zen Buddhism to America* (New York: Theatre Arts Books, 1976), xix–xx.

18. Mary Farkas, "Footsteps in the Invisible Wind," *Wind Bell* 8, nos. 1–2 (fall 1969), 18.

19. Helen Tworkov, *Zen in America: Five Teachers and the Search for an American Buddhism,* new ed. (New York: Kodansha International, 1984), 155.

20. Ibid., 156.

21. Charles S. Prebish, *American Buddhism* (North Scituate, Mass.: Duxbury Press, 1979), 22.

22. Theodore Roszak, *The Making of a Counter Culture* (Garden City, N.Y.: Anchor Books, 1969), 134.

23. Fields, *How the Swans Came to the Lake,* 243.

24. Tworkov, *Zen in America,* 18.

25. Ibid., 227.

26. Fields, *How the Swans Came to the Lake,* 234.

27. From "Reflections on the Book of Equanimity," *ZCLA Journal* (Yasutani Roshi Memorial Issue), summer-fall 1973, 10–11.

28. See Robert H. Sharf, "Sanbokyodan: Zen and the Way of the New Religions," *Japanese Journal of Religious Studies* 22, nos. 3–4 (fall 1995), 417–58.

29. Fields, *How the Swans Came to the Lake,* 241. If one takes into account Eugen Herrigel's *Zen in the Art of Archery,* published in German in 1948, Fields's claim is not entirely correct.

30. Some of the material presented in this section has been abbreviated because the community in question receives extensive treatment in chapter 3 below.

31. Tetsuden Kashima, *Buddhism in America: The Social Organization of an Ethnic Religious Institution* (Westport, Conn.: Greenwood Press, 1977), 5. For a detailed history of the Japanese Canadian Buddhist church, see Terry Watada, *Bukkyō Tozen* (Toronto: Toronto Buddhist Church, 1996).

32. An excellent source for historical information on Buddhist Churches of America is Donald Tuck's *Buddhist Churches of America: Jodo Shinshu* (Lewiston, N.Y.: Edwin Mellen Press, 1987).

33. See Kashima, *Buddhism in America,* 38–44.

34. Tuck, *Buddhist Churches of America,* 13. This information is also presented as a useful table in Kashima, *Buddhism in America,* 53.

35. Similar conclusions can be found in the Japanese Canadian Buddhist church. See, for example, Janet McLellan's chapter titled "Japanese Canadians and Toronto Buddhist Church" in her unpublished 1977 manuscript "Many Petals of the Lotus: Asian Buddhist Communities in Toronto."

36. Some of the material presented in this section has been abbreviated because the community in question receives extensive treatment in chapter 3 below.

37. Emma Layman, *Buddhism in America* (Chicago: Nelson-Hall, 1976), 125.

38. See the 9 January 1970 issue of *Life* magazine.

39. See Jane Hurst, "Nichiren Shōshū and Sōka Gakkai in America: The Pioneer Spirit," in Prebish and Tanaka, *Faces of Buddhism,* 81.

40. A good organizational schematic chart is found in Layman, *Buddhism in America,* 128.

41. See Prebish, *American Buddhism,* 76.

42. Ibid., 76–77.

43. Hurst, "Nichiren Shōshū," 96.

44. Stuart Chandler, "Chinese Buddhism in America: Identity and Practice," in Prebish and Tanaka, *Faces of Buddhism,* 16.

45. Department of Commerce, Bureau of the Census, *Statistical Abstract of the United States* (Washington, D.C.: GPO, 1994), table 55.

46. Irene Lin, "Journey to the Far West: Chinese Buddhism in America," *Amerasia Journal* 22, no. 1 (1996), 108.

47. Chandler, "Chinese Buddhism in America," 17 and n. 13.

48. Lin, "Journey to the Far West," 107.

49. Bhikṣuṇī Heng Yin, translator's introduction to *Records of the Life of the Venerable Master Hsüan Hua,* vol. 1 (San Francisco: Sino-American Buddhist Association, 1973), xiii.

50. Ibid.

51. Some of the material presented in this section has been abbreviated because the community in question receives extensive treatment in chapter 3 below.

52. See Lin, "Journey to the Far West," 122.

53. Chandler, "Chinese Buddhism in America," 30. Here he is drawing on Robert Michaelson's notion that a religious organization can achieve long-term survival only insofar as it successfully balances the tension between spontaneity and control, spirituality and practicality, ecstasy and action, grace and morality, virtue and power, and individuality and community. See Robert Michaelson, *The American Search for Soul* (Baton Rouge: Louisiana State University Press, 1975), 27–28.

54. Fields, *How the Swans Came to the Lake,* 353.

55. Mu Soeng, "Korean Buddhism in America: A New Style of Zen," in Prebish and Tanaka, *Faces of Buddhism,* 121.

56. See his autobiography in *Zen Lotus Society Handbook* (Toronto: Zen Lotus Society, 1986).

57. Ibid., 36.

58. See A. W. Barber and Cuong T. Nguyen, "Vietnamese Buddhism in North America: Tradition and Acculturation," in Prebish and Tanaka, *Faces of Buddhism,* 131.

59. Ibid., 141.

60. Layman, *Buddhism in America,* 180.

61. Ibid.

62. In 1983 Ven. Gunaratana went on to found the successful Bhavana Society, a monastic and lay community in West Virginia.

63. Paul Numrich, *Old Wisdom in the New World: Americanization in Two Immigrant Theravada Buddhist Temples* (Knoxville: University of Tennessee Press, 1996), xviii. Numrich's source is Department of Commerce, Bureau of the Census, *Statistical Abstract of the United States* (Washington, D.C.: GPO, 1993), tables 8 and 9.

64. Numrich, *Old Wisdom,* xix–xx.

65. See Numrich, *Old Wisdom,* 142; and Don Morreale, comp. and ed., *The Complete Guide to Buddhist America* (Boston: Shambhala, 1998).

66. Some of this material is presented in John Dart's informative newspaper article "45 American Buddhist Groups Convene, Form National Unit," *Los Angeles Times,* 14 November 1987, pt. II, 6.

67. BSCSC newsletter, Vaisakha 1990, 1.

68. Some of the material presented in this section has been abbreviated because the community in question receives extensive treatment in chapter 3 below.

69. An extremely use source of information on Tibetan Buddhism in the West is Graham Coleman, ed., *A Handbook of Tibetan Culture: A Guide to Tibetan Centres and Resources throughout the World* (London: Rider, 1993). See especially pp. 179–204 (on centers), 207–74 (on biographies), 159–63 (on foundations), and 177–78 (on publishers).

70. Some of the material presented in this section has been abbreviated because the community in question receives extensive treatment in chapter 3 below.

71. See http://shell.rmi.net/~buddamer for the data capsulized here.

Chapter 2. Shaping the *Sangha:* Developmental Issues in American Buddhism

1. Over the ensuing two decades, I have lost touch with two of the five students who participated in that refuge ceremony, but the other three continue to practice Buddhism in a serious, ongoing fashion.

2. Layman, *Buddhism in America,* 251–63.

3. Barry A. Kosmin and Seymour P. Lachman, *One Nation under God: Religion in Contemporary American Society* (New York: Harmony Books, 1993), 3.

4. Jan Nattier, "Who Is a Buddhist? Charting the Landscape of Buddhist America," in Prebish and Tanaka, *Faces of Buddhism,* 184–85.

5. Ibid., 185. Also see Rodney Stark and William Sims Bainbridge, *The Future of Religion* (Berkeley: University of California Press, 1985), and especially Chapter 2, where they develop the typology referred to by Nattier.

6. Nattier, "Who Is a Buddhist?" 187.

7. Martin Baumann, E-mail correspondence with author, 29 January 1997; in this correspondence Baumann was commenting on a variety of issues in a broader context.

8. Agehananda Bharati, *The Light at the Center* (Santa Barbara, Calif.: Ross-Erikson, 1976), 25.

9. Prebish, *American Buddhism,* 188.

10. Martin Baumann, "The Dharma Has Come West: A Survey of Recent Studies and Sources," *Journal of Buddhist Ethics* 4 (1997), 198.

11. Tanaka, "Epilogue," 288.

12. Helen Tworkov, "Many Is More," *Tricycle: The Buddhist Review* 1, no. 2 (winter 1991), 4.

13. Ibid.

14. *Sangha Newsletter,* no. 7 (summer 1994), 2–10.

15. See Charles S. Prebish, "Two Buddhisms Reconsidered," *Buddhist Studies Review* 10, no. 1 (1993), 187–206.

16. See Prebish, *American Buddhism,* 51.

17. Prebish, "Two Buddhisms Reconsidered," 189.

18. Ibid., 192–93. Although not cited there, Williams makes it clear that "export religions" also often include active missionary enterprises on the part of the Asian religions themselves.

19. Rick Fields, "Divided Dharma: White Buddhists, Ethnic Buddhists, and Racism," in Tanaka and Prebish, *Faces of Buddhism,* 197.

20. Ibid., 206.

21. See Jan Nattier, "Visible and Invisible: The Politics of Representation in Buddhist America," *Tricycle: The Buddhist Review* 5, no. 1 (fall 1995), 42–49.

22. Nattier, "Who Is a Buddhist?" 189.

23. Ibid., 190.

24. Numrich, *Old Wisdom,* 64.

25. Ibid.

26. Ibid., 63 and 161 n. 1. His reference is to Jan Nattier, "History, Subjectivity, and the Study of Buddhism," review of *The Vision of Buddhism,* by Roger Corless, *Journal of the American Academy of Religion* 55 (1992), 525–36. The quote is from p. 532 n. 5.

27. Numrich, *Old Wisdom,* 144.

28. Diana Eck, "Two Buddhisms or One?" in *On Common Ground CD-ROM* (New York: Columbia University Press, 1997).

29. Jack Kornfield, "Is Buddhism Changing North America?" in *Buddhist America: Centers, Retreats, Practices,* ed. Don Morreale (Santa Fe, N.Mex.: John Muir Publications, 1988), xxv.

30. Ryo Imamura to *Tricycle,* 10 January 1993; although Imamura's letter never appeared in *Tricycle,* it was eventually published in *Sangha Newsletter* 7 (summer 1994), 2–10.

31. Stephen Batchelor, "The Future Is in Our Hands," in *Engaged Buddhist Reader,* ed. Arnold Kotler (Berkeley: Parallax Press, 1996), 243.

32. Ibid.

33. I. B. Horner, trans., *The Book of the Discipline,* 6 vols. (London: Luzac & Company, 1938–1966), vol. 1, xviii.

34. Charles S. Prebish, "Text and Tradition in the Study of Buddhist Ethics," *Pacific World,* n.s., 9 (1993), 51.

35. For a survey of these texts, see Charles S. Prebish, *A Survey of Vinaya Literature* (Taipei: Jin Luen Publishing House, 1994; now published by Curzon Press), 46–125.

36. Prebish, *American Buddhism,* 46.

37. Numrich, *Old Wisdom,* 52–53.

38. *Changing Faces of Buddhism in America: The Dalai Lama Meets the Buddhist Sangha Council of Southern California* (Los Angeles: Buddhist Sangha Council of Southern California, n.d.), 18.

39. Harold Coward, "The Role of Scripture in the Self-Definition of Hinduism and Buddhism in India," *Studies in Religion* 21, no. 2 (1992), 143.

40. David Van Biema, "Buddhism in America," *Time,* 13 October 1997, 80.

41. Prebish, *American Buddhism,* 36.

42. Charles S. Prebish, "Ethics and Integration in American Buddhism," *Journal of Buddhist Ethics* 2 (1995), 135.

43. Rick Fields, "The Future of American Buddhism," *Vajradhatu Sun* 9, no. 1 (October-November 1987), 26.

44. Jack Kornfield, "Is Buddhism Changing North America?" xv.

45. Van Biema, "Buddhism in America," 80.

46. Helen Tworkov, "The Formless Field of Buddhism," *Tricycle: The Buddhist Review* 1, no. 3 (spring 1992), 4.

47. Shunryu Suzuki, *Zen Mind, Beginner's Mind* (New York: John Weatherhill, 1970), 133.

48. Numrich, *Old Wisdom,* 125–26.

49. Fields, "Future of American Buddhism," 24.

50. Harvey Cox, *The Seduction of the Spirit* (New York: Simon and Schuster, 1973), 56.

51. Rita Gross, *Buddhism after Patriarchy: A Feminist History, Analysis, and Reconstruction of Buddhism* (Albany: State University of New York Press, 1993), 240–41.

52. Ibid., 226.

53. Rita Gross, "Helping the Iron Bird Fly: Western Buddhist Women and Issues of Authority in the Late 1990s," in Prebish and Tanaka, *Faces of Buddhism,* 248.

54. See "Bibliography: Women and the Female in Buddhism," at http://members.tripod.com/~Lhamo/8bibli.htm.

55. Fields, "Future of American Buddhism," 26.

56. See Peter Harvey, *An Introduction to Buddhism: Teachings, History, and Practices* (Cambridge: Cambridge University Press, 1990), 224; and Gross, *Buddhism after Patriarchy,* 243.

57. Thubten Chodron, "You're Becoming a What? Living as a Western Buddhist Nun," in *Buddhist Women on the Edge: Contemporary Perspectives from the Western Frontier,* ed. Marianne Dresser (Berkeley: North Atlantic Books, 1996), 232–33.

58. Gross, *Buddhism after Patriarchy,* 242.

59. Gross, "Helping the Iron Bird Fly," 251.

60. Sandy Boucher, *Opening the Lotus: A Women's Guide to Buddhism* (Boston: Beacon Press, 1997), 42–44.

61. Ibid., 43–44.

62. Lenore Friedman, *Meetings with Remarkable Women: Buddhist Teachers in America* (Boston: Shambhala, 1987), 33–34.

63. Boucher, *Opening the Lotus,* 50–52.

64. In *Buddhism, Sexuality, and Gender,* ed. José Cabezón (Albany: State University of New York Press, 1992), 203–214.

65. In *Homosexuality and World Religions,* ed. Arlene Swidler (Valley Forge, Pa.: Trinity Press International, 1993), 81–101.

66. Published by Shambhala in 1993.

67. In Prebish and Tanaka, *Faces of Buddhism,* 253–65.

68. Reported in "In the News," *Tricycle: The Buddhist Review* 7, no. 1 (fall 1997), 116. See also *Turning Wheel: Journal of the Buddhist Peace Fellowship,* fall 1997, 25–26.

69. "In the News," 117.

70. Ibid., 118.

71. Roger Corless, "Coming Out in the *Sangha:* Queer Community in American Buddhism," in Prebish and Tanaka, *Faces of Buddhism,* 256.

72. Ibid., 264.

73. Kenneth Kraft, "Prospects of a Socially Engaged Buddhism," in *Inner Peace, World Peace: Essays on Buddhism and Nonviolence,* ed. Kenneth Kraft (Albany: State University of New York Press, 1992), 12.

74. Cited in Catherine Ingram, *In the Footsteps of Gandhi: Conversations with Spiritual Social Activists* (Berkeley: Parallax Press, 1990), 161.

75. See Tweed, *American Encounter,* 133–56.

76. See Donald Rothberg, "Responding to the Cries of the World: Socially Engaged Buddhism in North America," in Prebish and Tanaka, *Faces of Buddhism,* 273.

77. Ibid., 272.

78. Kraft, "Socially Engaged Buddhism," 21. These principles are excerpted by Kraft from Nhat Hanh's *Interbeing: Commentaries on the Tiep Hien Precepts* (Berkeley: Parallax Press, 1987), 27–57.

79. Layman, *Buddhism in America,* xiii, xvi.

80. Ibid., 279.

81. Prebish, *American Buddhism,* xvii.

82. Nattier, "Who Is a Buddhist?" 192.

83. Tanaka, "Epilogue," 294.

84. Prebish, *American Buddhism,* 192.

85. See, for example, Suwanda H. J. Sugunasiri, "Buddhism in Metropolitan Toronto: A Preliminary Overview," *Canadian Ethnic Studies* 21, no. 2 (1989), 83–103.

86. Friedman, *Meetings with Remarkable Women,* 23–24.

87. For the former article, see *Tricycle: The Buddhist Review* 4, no. 1 (fall 1994), 48–52; the latter article is included in Prebish and Tanaka, *Faces of Buddhism,* 49–78.

88. Victor Sōgen Hori, "Japanese Zen in America: Americanizing the Face in the Mirror," in Prebish and Tanaka, *Faces of Buddhism,* 77.

89. Tanaka, "Epilogue," 295.

90. See Peter Berger, *Sacred Canopy: Elements of a Sociological Theory of Religion* (Garden City, N.Y. Doubleday, 1966), 134, 137, 140–47.

91. See chapter 5 below for the full text of the "Statement of Consensus."

92. Layman, *Buddhism in America,* 203.

Chapter 3. Seeking American Buddhist *Sanghas:* North American Buddhist Communities

1. A new edition of this catalogue has been compiled, with groups being able to utilize the Internet in order to register themselves in Morreale's database.

2. The name of the order is taken from Dōgen Zenji's *Mountains and Rivers Sūtra,* a text of continuing importance for Abbot John Daido Loori.

3. These include the Zen Center of Los Angeles; Zen Mountain Center in Mountain Center, California; Zen Community of New York; Kanzeon Zen Centers of Salt Lake City and Europe; and Zen Mountain Monastery in Mt. Tremper, New York.

4. Bernard Tetsugen Glassman Rōshi was the first president of the White Plum Sangha, and Dennis Genpo Merzel Rōshi is the current president.

5. Community members in the White Plum Sangha include the Zen Center of Los Angeles, Zen Community of New York, the Village Zendo, Zen Mountain Monastery, White Cliff Sangha, Dragon Gate Sangha, Hidden Mountain Zen Center, Zen Community of Oregon, Zen Mountain Center, New River Zen Community, Zen Center of Hawaii, Clare Zendo, Great Mountain Zen Center, Sagaponack Zendo, Three Treasures Zen Community, and Kanzeon Zen Center. It is also noteworthy that Maezumi Rōshi ordained sixty-eight Zen priests and gave lay precepts to over five hundred people. Moreover, his twelve Dharma successors have "transmitted" nine additional (now second-generation) successors.

6. Jerry Adler, "800,000 Hands Clapping," *Newsweek,* 13 June 1994, 47.

7. More recently, an American Rinzai priest, Kobutsu Malone, has gained notoriety for establishing the Dharma Song Zendo in New York's Sing Sing Prison in 1992. He now serves this *zendō* as prison chaplain, and cofounded the Engaged Zen Foundation to support spiritual life in prisons.

8. See Prebish, *American Buddhism,* 38–40, 83–85.

9. The two passages quotes here are taken from "Precepts and Environment," by Abbot John Daido Loori, posted on the World Wide Web site of Zen Mountain Monastery at http://www.zen-mtn.org/zmm/teisho3.htm.

10. Quoted from the "BPF Statement of Purpose," http://www.bpf.org/bpf.

11. Ibid.

12. Quoted from http://www.bpf.org/bpf/ineb.html.

13. See http://www.bpf.org/bpf/think.html.

14. The training and retreat components are quoted from the BPF BASE project description at http://www.bpf.org/bpf/base.html.

15. See Hurst, "Nichiren Shōshū," 83–84. The chart is adapted from a 1976 *NSA Study Booklet,* 17. Hurst notes that the chart represents the point of view of the Nichiren Shōshū Priesthood, studied by believers as such.

16. Ibid., 81.

17. Masayasa Sadanaga's name change is interesting in that it is the converse of the practice, popular during the 1970s, in which Euro-American converts to American Buddhist groups took Asian Buddhist "Dharma names," most usually in the Tibetan and Zen traditions.

18. Bryan Wilson and Karel Dobbelaere, *A Time to Chant: The Sōka Gakkai in Britain* (Oxford; Clarendon Press, 1994), 30–31.

19. Ibid., 148.

20. See the short biography of Daisaku Ikeda at http://sgi-usa.org/ikedabio.html.

21. See http://sgi-usa.org/aboutsgi.html.

22. Wilson and Dobbelaere, *A Time to Chant,* 239. This book presents a complete and interesting explanation of this issue in its appendix A, "The 1990–1991 Schism of Nichiren Shōshū and Sōka Gakkai," 232–45.

23. Hurst, "Nichiren Shōshū," 93.

24. See http://sgi-usa.org/getinvolved.html.

25. Hurst, "Nichiren Shōshū," 95.

26. Wilson and Dobbelaere, *A Time to Chant,* 63.

27. Soka University in Japan is a private, nondenominational liberal arts college and graduate school, located in Hachioji (about an hour's drive from downtown Tokyo). It was founded in 1971 and currently has about seven thousand students. To some extent, its approach is based on Tsunesaburo Makiguchi's *Theory of Value Creating Education,* published in 1930.

28. White and Dobbelaere, *A Time to Chant,* 22, 24, 25. The quoted passage within the citation is from Richard Causton, *Nichiren Shōshū Buddhism: An Introduction* (London: Rider, 1988), 182.

29. Ibid., 177.

30. Sandy McIntosh, "As American As Apple Pie? An Insider's View of Nichiren Shoshu," *Tricycle: The Buddhist Review* 2, no. 2 (winter 1992), 24.

31. Ibid., 25.

32. Kornfield, "Is Buddhism Changing North America?" xxv.

33. Helen Tworkov, "Many Is More," *Tricycle: The Buddhist Review* 1, no. 2 (winter 1991), 4.

34. The letter was shared with me in a personal correspondence from Ryo Imamura dated 10 January 1993. It was subsequently published in my article "Two Buddhisms Reconsidered," 190–91.

35. Rick Fields, "Confessions of a White Buddhist," *Tricycle: the Buddhist Review* 4, no. 1 (fall 1994), 56.

36. Donald Tuck's *Buddhist Churches in America: Jodo Shinshu* (Lewiston, N.Y.: Edwin Mellen Press, 1987) does a very thorough if not interpretive job of documenting the American development of Buddhist Churches of America. Tetsuden Kashima's *Buddhism in America: The Social Organization of an Ethnic Religious Institution* (Westport, Conn.: Greenwood Press, 1977), while perhaps even more thorough than Tuck's book, is extremely helpful in its willingness to interpret, clarify, and even decode a complex historical evolution, albeit from Buddhist Churches of America's perspective.

37. For data on Japanese immigration figures, see Robert A. Wilson and Bill Hosokawa, *East to America: A History of Japanese in the United States* (New York: Morrow, 1980), 28–36.

38. Kashima, *Buddhism in America,* 12.

39. Ibid., 44.

40. See Alfred Bloom, "Shin Buddhism in the American Context," http://www.aloha.net/~albloom/shinstudy/unit08.htm.

41. Ibid. At the time BCA was divided into eight "districts." These included: District I—Bay District, California; District II—Central California; District III—California Coast; District IV—Eastern United States; District V—Mountain United States; District VI—Northern California; District VII—Northwest United States; District VIII—Southern California and Arizona. See Prebish, *American Buddhism,* 61–62; or Kashima, *Buddhism in America,* 190–91.

42. Kashima, *Buddhism in America,* 60–61.

43. Ibid., 142. Kashima has gleaned his data from a variety of sources, each of which is documented at the above cited location.

44. Alfred Bloom, "Shin Buddhism in America: A Social Perspective," in Prebish and Tanaka, *Faces of Buddhism,* 40. Bloom's figures for 1977 are taken from Tuck, *Buddhist Churches of America,* 79, 96, while his 1995 numbers are taken from *BCA Annual Report,* 1995, 45.

45. Bloom, "Shin Buddhism in America," 40–41.

46. Adapted from Kashima, *Buddhism in America,* 176–77.

47. See Kashima, *Buddhism in America,* 69–112, 113–65, 167–96.

48. Bloom, "Shin Buddhism in America," 38–40.

49. Gordon L. Fung and Gregory Fung, "Adapting the Jōdo-Shinshū Teaching for the West: An Approach Based on the American Work Ethic," *Pacific World,* n.s., 9 (fall 1993), 24–31.

50. Ibid., 28–30.

51. Ibid., 31.

52. Prebish, *American Buddhism,* 67.

53. See Tetsuden Kashima, "The Buddhist Churches of America: Challenges for Change in the Twenty-First Century," *Pacific World,* n.s., 6 (fall 1990), 28–40.

54. Robert N. Bellah, "American Civil Religion in the 1970s," in *American Civil Religion,* ed. Donald G. Jones and Russell E. Richey (New York: Harper & Row, 1974), 258.

55. Kashima, "Buddhist Churches of America," 39.

56. Alfred Bloom, "Buddhism in a New Age," http://www.aloha.net/~rtbloom/shinran/abloom/new-age.txt.

57. *BCA Annual Report,* 1985, 101.

58. See Lin, "Journey to the Far West," 108.

59. See Chandler, "Chinese Buddhism in America," 17.

60. See Department of Commerce, Bureau of the Census, *Historical Statistics of the United States, Colonial Times to 1970,* pt. 1 (Washington, D.C.: GPO, 1976), 108.

61. Ibid., 14.

62. Department of Commerce, *Statistical Abstract* (1994), table 55.

63. Peter Kwong, *The New Chinatown* (New York: Hill and Wang, 1987), 22.

64. Ronald Takaki, *Strangers from a Different Shore* (New York: Penguin Books, 1989), 425.

65. Lin, "Journey to the Far West," 108.

66. See, for example, the article in the *Los Angeles Times,* 10 January 1988.

67. Lin, "Journey to the Far West," 126 n. 10.

68. See http://www.ibps.org/page1.htm and http://www.ibps.org/etable.htm.

69. Lin, "Journey to the Far West," 111.

70. See http://www.blia.org/blia2.html.

71. Chandler, "Chinese Buddhism in America," 18–19. Chandler also maintains that meditation classes in Chinese Buddhist organizations are patronized almost exclusively by Euro-Americans and not Chinese Americans.

72. Lin, "Journey to the Far West," 119.

73. See http://hlu.edu.

74. Ibid.

75. Chandler, "Chinese Buddhism in America," 25–26.

76. Evelyn Kallen, *The Western Samoan Kinship Bridge: A Study in Migration, Social Change, and New Ethnicity* (Leiden: E. J. Brill, 1982), 30.

77. Ibid.

78. Lin, "Journey to the Far West," 118.

79. Chandler, "Chinese Buddhism in America," 19.

80. Lin, "Journey to the Far West," 116.

81. Gil Fronsdal, "Insight Meditation in America: Life, Liberty, and the Pursuit of Happiness," in Prebish and Tanaka, *Faces of Buddhism,* 167.

82. Robert Greenfield, *The Spiritual Supermarket* (New York: E. P. Dutton, 1975), 212.

83. Published as an appendix to Jack Kornfield's *A Path with Heart: A Guide through the Perils of Spiritual Life* (New York: Bantam Books, 1993), 340–43.

84. Fronsdal, "Insight Meditation in America," 167.

85. See *Inquiring Mind* 2, no. 1 (summer 1985), 7.

86. Jack Kornfield, "Meditation and Psychotherapy: A Plea for Integration," *Inquiring Mind* 5, no. 1 (summer 1988).

87. See http://www.spiritrock.org/about/vision.html.

88. Fronsdal, "Insight Meditation in America," 177.

89. Helen Tworkov, "Empty Phenomena Rolling On: An Interview with Joe Goldstein," *Tricycle: The Buddhist Review* 3, no. 2 (winter 1993), 13.

90. Joseph Goldstein, *Insight Meditation: The Path of Freedom* (Boston: Shambhala, 1993), 3.

91. Tworkov, "Empty Phenomena Rolling On," 15.

92. Prebish, *American Buddhism,* 147.

93. Amy Lavine, "Tibetan Buddhism in America: The Development of American Vajrayāna," in Prebish and Tanaka, *Faces of Buddhism,* 103.

94. Ibid.

95. See http://www.shambhala.org/int/vision.html.

96. See http://www.shambhala.org/st/index.html.

97. Although Naropa Institute is no longer listed at this URL, this 1996 description was posted at http://www.trịadcom.com/naropa. A newer and shorter description is to be found at http://www.naropa.edu.

98. See http://www.shambhala.org/ntc/who.html.

Chapter 4. The Silent *Sangha:* Buddhism in the Academy

1. Both Lamotte's original volume and Sara Webb-Boin's translation were published by the Institut Orientaliste of the University of Louvain, in 1958 and 1988, respectively.

2. Edward Conze, *The Memoirs of a Modern Gnostic,* pt. 2 (Sherborne, England: Samizdat Publishing Company, 1979), 43.

3. See Georges B. J. Dreyfus, *Recognizing Reality: Dharmakīrti's Philosophy and Its Tibetan Interpretations* (Albany: State University of New York Press, 1997). It is interesting to note that Dreyfus lists his *lharampa geshe* degree (earned in 1985) on his curriculum vitae along with his M.A. (1987) and Ph.D. (1991) from the University of Virginia.

4. See Donald S. Lopez, Jr., ed., *Curators of the Buddha: The Study of Buddhism under Colonialism* (Chicago: University of Chicago Press), 1995.

5. Jan Nattier, "Buddhist Studies in the Post-Colonial Age," *Journal of the American Academy of Religion* 65, no. 2 (summer 1997), 469–85.

6. Ibid., 469.

7. Henri de Lubac, *La rencontre du bouddhisme et de l'occident* (Paris: Aubier, 1952).

8. See Simon de la Loubère, *Du royaume de Siam* (Paris, 1952).

9. See Michel François Ozeray, *Recherches sur Buddhou* (Paris, 1817).

10. See Russell Webb, "Pali Buddhist Studies in the West," *Pali Buddhist Review* 1, no. 3 (1976), 169–80; 2, no. 1 (1977), 55–62; 2, no. 2 (1977), 114–22; 2, no. 3 (1977), 162–67; 3, no. 1 (1978), 35–36; 3, no. 2 (1978), 84–87; 3, no. 3 (1978), 146–53; 4, nos. 1–2 (1979), 28–31; 4, no. 4 (1979), 86–90; 5, nos. 1–2 (1980), 39–41; 5, no. 3 (1980), 89–92.

11. Russell Webb, "Contemporary European Scholarship on Buddhism," in *The Buddhist Heritage,* ed. Tadeusz Skorupski, vol. 1 of *Buddhica Britannica* (Tring, U.K.: Institute of Buddhist Studies, 1989), 247–76.

12. See William Peiris, *The Western Contribution to Buddhism* (Delhi: Motilal Banarsidass, 1973).

13. Jan W. de Jong's *Brief History of Buddhist Studies in Europe and America,* 2d ed., rev. and enlarged (Delhi: Sri Satguru Publications, 1987), originally appeared as two articles in the *Eastern Buddhist.* The first carried the same title as the eventual book and appeared in *Eastern Buddhist,* n.s., 7 (1974); the second was titled "Recent Buddhist Studies in Europe and America, 1973–83" and appeared in *Eastern Buddhist,* n.s., 17 (1984). It is curious that of the roughly four hundred individuals listed in the index under "Names of Scholars," less than 5 percent are primarily associated with North America. Like nearly all of de Jong's publications, this one bristles with his trenchant editorializing and brutal evaluations. In the foreword, he mentions Guy Welbon's engaging *Buddhist Nirvāṇa and Its Western Interpreters* (Chicago: University of Chicago Press, 1968), based on Welbon's doctoral dissertation at the University of Chicago, concluding that "the usefulness of his book is diminished by the fact that the author was not sufficiently equipped for this difficult task" (p. 2), and giving a reference to his even more acerbic review in the *Journal of Indian Philosophy.*

14. Edward Conze, "Recent Progress in Buddhist Studies," *Middle Way* 34 (1959), 6–14; 34 (1960), 144–50; 35 (1960), 93–98, 110. Conze's article was later included in *Thirty Years of Buddhist Studies: Selected Essays by Edward Conze* (Columbia: University of South Carolina Press, 1968), 1–32. Conze maintains the terminology utilized by C. Regamey.

15. See Tweed, *American Encounter.*

16. See Fields, *How the Swans Came to the Lake,* 54–69.

17. I am not the only one to make this point. José Cabezón, in "Buddhist Studies as a Discipline and the Role of Theory," *Journal of the International Association of Buddhist Studies* 18, no. 2 (winter 1995), says as much: "No comprehensive history of Buddhist Studies as a discipline exists" (p. 236 n. 8).

18. See, for example, Luis Gómez, "Unspoken Paradigms: Meanderings through the Metaphors of a Field," *Journal of the International Association of Buddhist Studies* 18, no. 2 (winter 1995), 193 n. 8.

19. In Prebish and Tanaka, *Faces of Buddhism,* 207–27.

20. See Charles S. Prebish, "Buddhist Studies American Style: A Shot in the Dark," *Religious Studies Review* 9, no. 4 (October 1983), 323–30.

21. In *Journal of the International Association of Buddhist Studies* 15, no. 1 (summer 1992), 104–17.

22. Cabezón, "Buddhist Studies," 236.

23. Gómez, "Unspoken Paradigms," 190.

24. See Cabezón, "Buddhist Studies," 236–38. The quoted phrase is Cabezón's as well.

25. Ibid., 236, 240.

26. Malcolm David Eckel, "The Ghost at the Table: On the Study of Buddhism and the Study of Religion," *Journal of the American Academy of Religion* 62, no. 4 (winter 1994), 1107–8.

27. Duncan Ryūken Williams, "Where to Study?" *Tricycle: The Buddhist Review* 6, no. 3 (spring 1997), 68.

28. Ibid.

29. Cabezón, "Buddhist Studies," 243.

30. Ibid. To his credit, Cabezón cites Jacques May's alternative view in "Études bouddhiques: Domaine, disciplines, perspectives," *Études de lettres* (Lausanne), 3d ser., 6, no. 4 (1973), 18.

31. Gómez, "Unspoken Paradigms," 214–15. The italics are mine.

32. See Charles S. Prebish, "The Academic Study of Buddhism in America: A Current Analysis," *Religion* 24 (1994), 271–78.

33. See Ray L. Hart, "Religious and Theological Studies in American Higher Education: A Pilot Study," *Journal of the American Academy of Religion* 59, no. 4 (winter 1991), 715–827.

34. Hart, "Religious and Theological Studies," 779.

35. Ibid., 780–81.

36. Malcolm David Eckel, "Review and Evaluation of the Buddhism Section of the American Academy of Religion" (1991, photocopy), 2.

37. Eckel, "Ghost at the Table," 1088.

38. The *Gassho* article, "The Academic Study of Buddhism in America: A Current Analysis," appeared in vol. 1, no. 2 (January-February 1994), while the *Religion* article, "The Academic Study of Buddhism in the United States: A Current Analysis," appeared in vol. 24 (1994), 271–78.

39. Offices and administrative positions include:

American Academy of Religion

President (1)
Board of Directors (1)
Chair/Cochair:

Buddhism Group/Section (5)
Japanese Religions Group (3)
Comparative Studies in Religion Section (3)
Tantric Studies Seminar (2)
Asian Religions/History of Religion Section (2)
Electronic Publications Committee (2)
Publications Committee (2)
Himalayan & Tibetan Religions Consultation (1)
Program Committee (1)
Religion & Ecology Group (1)

Steering Committee

Buddhism Group/Section (9)
Japanese Religions Group (5)
Ritual Studies Group (3)
Himalayan & Tibetan Religions Consultation (3)
Tantric Studies Seminar (2)
Korean Religions Group (2)
Religion & Ecology Group (1)
Mysticism Group (1)
East Asian Religions Consultation (1)
Asian Religions/History of Religion Section (1)
Comparative Study in Hinduism & Judaism Consultation (1)

Association for Asian Studies

Buddhist Studies Steering Committee (4)
Board of Directors (2)
Program Committee (1)
Korean Studies Chair (1)
South Asia Council (1)
Northeast Asia Council (1)

International Association of Buddhist Studies

Board of Directors (4)
General Secretary (2)
Secretary (1)
Associate Secretary (1)
Treasurer (1)

Society for Buddhist-Christian Studies

Board of Directors (5)
President (2)
Vice President (2)
Secretary (1)

Society for the Study of Japanese Religions

President (3)

Society for the Study of Chinese Religions

President (1)
Secretary-Treasurer (1)
Board of Directors (1)

International Association of Shin Buddhist Studies

Vice President (3)
Steering Committee (2)
Board of Directors (1)

In addition, respondents reported one executive director and five members of the board of directors with the Kuroda Institute, and at least one reported administrative position in the Pali Text Society, the American Oriental Society, the Tibet Society, the Mongolian Society, the Society for Asian and Comparative Philosophy, and the Buddhist Peace Fellowship.

40. To some extent, with regard to trade/commercial publishers, the publishers listed here reflect the personal preferences of a number of prolific authors. For example, the citations for Prentice-Hall and Tungta reflect the publications of Robert Ellwood and Charles Fu, respectively. Other university presses mentioned include Indiana University Press, University of Virginia Press, Stanford University Press, and the University of Michigan Press. Other trade publishers mentioned frequently include Allen & Unwin, Harper & Row, M. D. Gunasena, Peter Lang, St. Martin's Press, Curzon Press, HarperCollins, Beacon, Wadsworth, Scholars Press, Anima, Eerdmans, Munshiram Manoharlal, Mellen Press, Westminster, and Mouton.

41. In at least two cases, journals cited reflect the personal favorites of two prolific scholars: *Journal of Chinese Philosophy* (for Charles Fu) and *Studia Missionalia* (for Alex Wayman). Other journals receiving a significant numbers of citations include *Cahiers d'Extrême-Asie, Religious Studies Review, Journal of Indian and Buddhist Studies, Journal of the Pali Text Society, Journal of Feminist Studies of Religion, Indo-Iranian Journal, Journal of Buddhist Ethics, Journal of Religious Ethics, Buddhist Studies Review,* and *Korean Culture.*

42. Cabezón, "Buddhist Studies," 255.

43. Ibid., 255–56.

44. Williams, "Where to Study?" 68–69, 115–17.

45. When Williams's list was published, the University of Wisconsin, which is one of only two universities in the United States to offer a Ph.D. in Buddhist Studies, was omitted from the "Most Comprehensive Programs" list and cited only under "Other Noteworthy Programs." Impending or recent retirements notwithstanding, the University of Wisconsin continues to offer a complete and

comprehensive curriculum in Buddhist Studies with three primary faculty (Minoru Kiyota, Geshe Sopa, and Gudrun Buhnemann) and at least three other ancillary faculty (André Wink, Gautam Vajracharya, and Tongchai Winchakul). In some cases, an institution is listed on the basis of one very strong scholar (e.g., Gregory Schopen at the University of Texas at Austin), while others are omitted despite several strong scholars (Carleton College, with Roger Jackson, Mark Unno, and Bardwell Smith, *emeritus*). There are omissions, too. Indiana University's listing does not include Stephen Bokenkamp and Robert Campany, each of whom deserves a place on the roster. Finally, it is clear that when Williams uses the term "America," he actually means "United States," as no mention at all is made of Canadian universities, a number of which boast strong Buddhist Studies faculties. McMaster University, for example, has a faculty that includes Phyllis Granoff, Graeme MacQueen, K. Shinohara, and Yun-hua Jan, *emeritus*. The University of Calgary could easily have been included as well (with Leslie Kawamura, A. W. Barber, X. J. Yang, and regular visiting appointments through the Numata Chair in Buddhist Studies). The above critique should by no means be construed as demeaning. Rather, it merely highlights that the problem of identifying and classifying the Buddhist Studies academic landscape is significantly more difficult than first meets the eye.

Despite the fact that there is no easy way to synthesize faculty size with the comprehensiveness of any given Buddhist Studies curriculum, materials available in 1997 have enabled me to provide a listing that attempts to harmonize—at least for that time period—the two above factors, and thus augments and ideally enhances that of Duncan Williams. As such, the following listing proceeds from the most complete programs in Buddhist Studies to the least complete (and includes all faculty who make a substantial contribution to that program).

Harvard University

Galen Amstutz
Charles Hallisey
Helen Hardacre
Christopher Queen
Oktor Skjaervo
Stanley Tambiah
Leonard van der Kuijp
Masatoshi Nagatomi (*emeritus*)

University of Hawaii

Helen Baroni
David Chappell
David Kalupahana
Steve Odin
Graham Parkes
George Tanabe
Willa Tanabe
Oung Thwin

Indiana University

Stephen Bokenkamp
Robert Campany
John McRae
Jan Nattier
Eliot Sperling
Michael Walter

University of Wisconsin

Gudrun Buhnemann
Minoru Kiyota
Geshe Sopa
Gautam Vajracharya
Tongchai Winchakul
André Wink

Princeton University

Martin Collcutt
Gananath Obeyesekere
Soho Machida
Jacqueline Stone
Stephen Teiser

University of Virginia

David Germano
Paul Groner
Jeffrey Hopkins
Karen Lang
H. L. Seneviratne

University of Toronto

Janet McLellan
Neil McMullin
Leonard Priestley
David Waterhouse
A. K. Warder (*emeritus*)

University of Chicago

Steven Collins
Paul Griffiths
Matthew Kapstein
Frank Reynolds

University of Washington

Collett Cox
Ter Ellingson
Charles Keyes
Richard Salomon

McMaster University

Phyllis Granoff
Graeme MacQueen
K. Shinohara
Yun-hua Jan (*emeritus*)

University of Colorado

Robert Lester
Reginald Ray
Eric Reinders

University of Michigan

Luis Gómez
Donald Lopez
Robert Sharf

Columbia University

Ryuich Abé
Robert Thurman
Alex Wayman (*emeritus)*

Carleton College

Roger Jackson
Mark Unno
Bardwell Smith (*emeritus*)

University of Saskatchewan

James Mullens
Braj Sinha Leslie
Julian Pas (*emeritus*)

University of Calgary

A. W. Barber
Kawamura
X. J. Yang

In addition to the above, a number of other North American universities have at least two faculty members whose work falls primarily within the discipline of Buddhist Studies: Florida State University (Tessa Bartholomuesz, Daniel Lusthaus), McGill University (Richard Hayes, Arvind Sharma), Pennsylvania State University (Steven Heine, Charles Prebish), Smith College (Jamie Hubbard, Taitetsu Unno), State University of New York at Stony Brook (Sung Taek Cho, Sung Bae Park), the University of California at Berkeley (Padmanabh Jaini, Lewis Lancaster), and the University of California at Los Angeles (Robert Buswell, William Bodiford).

46. See Walpola Rahula, *History of Buddhism in Ceylon,* 2d ed. (Colombo: M. D. Gunasena, 1966), 157–63.

47. Ibid., 158–59: "Even if there be a hundred thousand bhikkhus practicing *vipassanā* (meditation), there will be no realization of the Noble Path if there is no learning (doctrine, *pariyatti*)" (from the commentary on the *Aṅguttara Nikāya*). Commentaries from the *Dīgha Nikāya, Majjhima Nikāya,* and *Vibhaṅga* echo the same sentiment.

48. Ibid., 161.

49. Peter Harvey, *An Introduction to Buddhism: Teachings, History, and Practices* (Cambridge: Cambridge University Press, 1990), 242.

50. Rahula, *History of Buddhism in Ceylon,* 287.

51. See Reginald Ray, *Buddhist Saints in India: A Study in Buddhist Values and Orientations* (New York: Oxford University Press, 1994), 433–47.

52. Jeremy Hayward, "Acharyas Define Teaching Role," *Shambhala Sun* 5, no. 4 (March 1997), "Shambhala News Section," 1.

53. Cabezón, "Buddhist Studies," 237.

54. See, for example, Daniel Metraux, *The History and Theology of Soka Gakkai: A Japanese New Religion* (Lewiston, N.Y.: Edwin Mellen Press, 1988), 126–28.

55. Layman, *Buddhism in America,* 18.

56. Fields, *How the Swans Came to the Lake,* 371.

57. Cabezón, "Buddhist Studies," 262–63.

58. Nattier, "Buddhist Studies," 484.

59. Ibid., 480.

Chapter 5. The Cybersangha: Virtual Communities

1. Akira Hirakawa, *A History of Indian Buddhism: From Śākyamuni to Early Mahāyāna,* trans. and ed. Paul Groner (Honolulu: University of Hawaii Press, 1990), 62.

2. Richard Gombrich, "Introduction: The Buddhist Way," in *The World of Buddhism: Buddhist Monks and Nuns in Society and Culture,* ed. Heinz Bechert and Richard Gombrich (New York: Pacts on File Publications, 1984), 13.

3. See, for example, Hermann Oldenberg, ed., *The Vinaya Piṭakaṃ,* 5 vols. (reprint, London: Luzac & Company, 1964), vol. 1, 305; vol. 2, 147.

4. Sukumar Dutt, *The Buddha and Five After Centuries* (London: Luzac & Company, 1957), 60–61. Also see the discussion in Sukumar Dutt, *Early Buddhist Monachism* (London: Kegan Paul, Trench, Trübner and Company, 1924), 83 ff.

5. Hirakawa, *History of Indian Buddhism,* 64.

6. Ibid., 60.

7. Ray, *Buddhist Saints in India,* 21.

8. Ibid., 19.

9. Gombrich, "Introduction," 14.

10. Étienne Lamotte, *History of Indian Buddhism: From the Origins to the Śaka*

Era, trans. Sara Webb-Boin (Louvain: Institute Orientaliste de l'Université Catholique de Louvain, 1988), 54.

11. It must be understood from the outset that the Buddhist resources on the Internet cited in this chapter are not intended to represent a comprehensive listing. Such an attempt is probably not desirable in a book of this nature, nor is it a realistic possibility due to the transient, ephemeral nature of many Internet resources, and the occasional changing of Internet addresses. Thus in most cases all but the most stable Internet addresses are excluded. To locate the resources cited in this chapter, one can consult any of the traditional search engines currently utilized on the World Wide Web. These include, but are not limited to, Yahoo (http://www.yahoo.com), Infoseek (http://www.infoseek.com), Excite (http://www.excite.com), and Lycos (http://www.lycos.com). In addition, a very useful Internet guide, with specific application to Religious Studies (as well as several other disciplines), is Patrick Durusau's *High Places in Cyberspace* (Atlanta: Scholars Press, 1996). This book is also available online, with periodic updates, at the following URL: http://scholar.cc.emory.edu/scripts/high-places.html.

12. Jamie Hubbard, "Upping the Ante: budstud@millenium.end.edu," *Journal of the International Association of Buddhist Studies* 18, no. 2 (winter 1995), 310.

13. Ibid., 309.

14. At the time of this writing, Buddha-L was being jointly monitored by Hayes, Chris Fynn, and Peter Junger of Case Western Reserve University. Richard P. Hayes, e-mail correspondence with author, 10 June 1997.

15. There are many E-mail discussions forums, and it is not possible to list them all. I have simply chosen to cite those that I believe, in my own idiosyncratic fashion, are the most important ones. Others include the "Forum on Jodo Shinshu Buddhism," "Forum on Buddhist Philosophy," "Forum on Eastern American/East Asian Buddhism," "Forum on Shin Buddhism," and "Tantra."

16. Again, this list is by no means intended to be complete or comprehensive, but merely a sampling of what is available to interested inquirers.

17. I am deeply indebted to Dr. T. Matthew Ciolek for providing a most lucid account of the development of the vast array of electronic materials devoted to Buddhism at the Australian National University. All information on the Coombs Computing Unit of the Australian National University derives from his kind assistance.

18. These valuable and interesting documents remain accessible for electronic retrieval through FTP (File Transfer Protocol) at ftp://coombs.anu.edu.au/coombspapers.otherarchives/electronic-buddhist-archives.

19. See Gary Ray, "A Resource Roundup for the Cybersangha," *Tricycle: The Buddhist Review* 3, no. 4 (summer 1994), 61.

20. This information is taken from the description of *Gassho* at DharmaNet International's World Wide Web site at http://www.dharmanet.org/gassho.html

21. Ray, "Resource Roundup," 60.

22. Hubbard, "Upping the Ante," 313.

23. Dale Dougherty and Richard Koman, *The Mosaic Handbook* (Sebastapol, Calif.: O'Reilly & Associates, 1994), 9.

24. Ibid.

25. Durusau, *High Places in Cyberspace,* 77.

26. Dougherty and Koman, *Mosaic Handbook,* 10.

27. Durusau, *High Places in Cyberspace,* 77.

28. Connie Neal documented the history of the original database, and its ongoing development, in E-mail dated 16 June 1997.

29. Barry Kapke, E-mail correspondence to author, 23 June 1997.

30. There is a link here to "DharmaNet's Guide to Dharma Centers in the USA," which presents an alphabetical listing of the states, each one of which may be accessed to reveal Buddhist centers in that state, as well as Internet links to each group possessing an Internet connection.

31. FWBO refers to Friends of the Western Buddhist Order.

32. FPMT refers to the Foundation for the Preservation of the Mahāyāna tradition.

33. From "About CyberSangha," http://www.wenet.net/~csangha/aboutcs.htm.

34. See Richard P. Hayes, "The Perception of 'Karma-Free' CyberZones," *CyberSangha,* http://www.hooked.net/~csangha/hayessu95.htm.

35. See Rev. Heng Sure, "New Electronic Community: Ancient Spiritual Roots," *CyberSangha,* http://www.hooked.net/~csangha/suref95.htm.

36. See Joachim H. Steingrubner, "CyberSangha: Building Buddhist Community Online," *CyberSangha,* htpp://www.hooked.net/~csangha/steinf95.htm.

37. It is not my intention to suggest that further innovations in the *sangha* are not possible. Rather, in speaking of the cybersangha as the completion of the Buddhist community, I am arguing that all further considerations of the ongoing development of the Buddhist *sangha* must necessarily include this important component of community life.

38. Steingrubner, "CyberSangha."

39. Cited in Eleanor Rosch, "World Buddhism in North America Today," *Vajradhatu Sun* 9, no. 1 (October-November 1987), 28.

40. Clearly, the cybersangha is an alternative form of Buddhist community, one that begs a fuller sociological analysis of the phenomenon. That analysis, however, goes well beyond the scope of what is possible here.

Chapter 6. The Future of the American *Sangha*

1. Of the nearly three dozen scheduled presenters, only three had traditional credentials in the Buddhist Studies academic community: Robert Thurman, Stephen Batchelor, and Miranda Shaw.

2. Tanaka, "Epilogue," 287.

3. Layman, *Buddhism in America,* xiii.

4. I didn't discover Humphreys's earlier work *The Development of Buddhism in England* (London: Buddhist Society, 1937) until much later.

5. Kashima, *Buddhism in America,* 212–20.

6. Ibid., 207.

7. Layman, *Buddhism in America,* 282.

8. Ibid., xv.

9. Thomas A. Tweed, "Night Stand Buddhists and Other Creatures: Sympathizers in the History of Buddhism in America," in *American Buddhism: Methods and Findings in Recent Scholarship,* ed. Christopher S. Queen and Duncan Ryūken Williams (Surrey, U.K.: Curzon Press, 1998), 71–90.

10. Jacob Needleman, *The New Religions* (Garden City, N.Y.: Doubleday, 1970), 227.

11. Ibid., 226.

12. Layman, *Buddhism in America,* 289.

13. Ibid.

14. Numrich, *Old Wisdom,* xix, xxi.

15. See Hurst, "Nichiren Shōshū," 80, 88.

16. Baumann, "The Dharma Has Come West," 198.

17. When I coined the term "two Buddhisms" in *American Buddhism,* my primary point of reference was *not* the Asian American and Euro-American Buddhist communities, but rather the kind of Buddhism each practiced. To the former group I attributed a traditional form of Buddhist practice grounded in canonical writings and normative doctrines, irrespective of the sectarian distinctions that might have been represented. To the latter group I attributed what I considered a less orthodox Buddhist practice, grounded in the exotic, "hip," flamboyant teachings of a few popular Buddhist teachers. Much later, I published "Two Buddhisms Reconsidered," in *Buddhist Studies Review* 10, no. 2 (1993), 187–206, as a response to a mild controversy involving *Tricycle: The Buddhist Review,* and it was at that point that the term "two Buddhisms" took on an expressly ethnic character. Jan Nattier, first in "Visible & Invisible" (*Tricycle: The Buddhist Review* 5, no. 1 [fall 1995], 42–49) and later in "Who Is a Buddhist? Charting the Landscape of Buddhist America" (in Prebish and Tanaka, *Faces of Buddhism,* 183–95), develops a threefold typology of "Elite or Import Buddhism," "Evangelical or Export Buddhism," and "Ethnic or Baggage Buddhism." Each of these views has its supporters and detractors, and the two typologies have stimulated a very lively and useful debate.

18. Jacob Needleman and George Baker, eds., *Understanding the New Religions* (New York: Seabury Press, 1978), xv.

19. Numrich, *Old Wisdom,* xxii.

20. Ibid.

21. Ibid., 144.

22. See Alfred Bloom, "The Unfolding of the Lotus: A Survey of Some Recent Developments in Shin Buddhism in the West," *Buddhist-Christian Studies* 10 (1990), 157–64; and Testuden Kashima, "The Buddhist Churches of America:

Challenges for Change in the Twenty-First Century," *Pacific World,* n.s., 6 (fall 1990), 28–40.

23. Numrich, *Old Wisdom,* 145.

24. Prebish, *American Buddhism,* 192.

25. Kenneth Kraft, "Recent Developments in North American Zen," in *Zen: Tradition and Transition,* ed. Kenneth Kraft (New York: Grove Press, 1988), 181.

26. Ibid., 183–98.

27. Lenore Friedman, *Meetings with Remarkable Women: Buddhist Teachers in America* (Boston: Shambhala, 1987), 23–24.

28. Tweed, *American Encounter,* 134.

29. Ibid., 157.

30. Tanaka, "Epilogue," 298.

31. Kornfield, "Is Buddhism Changing North America?" xxiii.

32. Katy Butler, "Events Are the Teacher," *CoEvolution Quarterly* 40 (winter 1983), 115.

33. Joanna Macy, "The Balancing of American Buddhism," *Primary Point* 3, no. 1 (February 1986), 6.

34. Prebish, "Ethics and Integration," 134.

35. It was the published version of a paper Fields gave at the "Buddhism and Christianity: Toward the Human Future" conference, held at the Graduate Theological Union on 10–15 August 1987. Interestingly, it was juxtaposed with Eleanor Rosch's article "World Buddhism in North America Today," which reported on the "World Buddhism in North America" conference (mentioned above). It hardly seemed an accident to present one article that highlighted the myriad Buddhist traditions now present, and another on the future of American Buddhism.

36. The idea of a quasi-monastic *sangha* has been affirmed by many American Buddhist teachers, Taizan Maezumi Rōshi and Shunryu Suzuki Rōshi among them. Suzuki Rōshi, for example, says on p. 133 of *Zen Mind, Beginner's Mind* (New York: John Weatherhill, 1985): "American students are not priests and yet not completely laymen. I understand it this way: that you are not priests is an easy matter, but that you are not exactly laymen is more difficult. I think you are special people and want some special practice that is not exactly priest's practice and not exactly layman's practice. You are on your way to discovering some appropriate way of life."

37. Fields, "Future of American Buddhism," 26.

38. This eighth factor is the only one in which Fields cites reliance on the work of others. Here he makes reference to Robert Aitken's 1984 book *The Mind of Clover: Essays in Zen Buddhist Ethics* and my article "Karma and Rebirth in the Land of the Earth-Eaters," published in Ron Neufeldt's edited volume *Karma and Rebirth: Post Classical Developments.*

39. Berger, *Sacred Canopy,* 134.

40. Ibid., 137.

41. Tanaka, "Epilogue," 287.

42. Ibid., 294–95.

43. Rodger Kamenetz, *The Jew in the Lotus* (San Francisco: Harper San Francisco, 1994), 7.

44. This description is taken from the conference program brochure. It also corresponds to material developed in Bernard Glassman and Rick Fields, *Instructions to the Cook: A Zen Master's Lessons in Living a Life That Matters* (New York: Bell Tower, 1996).

45. For this claim, see Rodger Kamenetz, "Robert Thurman Doesn't *Look* Buddhist," *New York Times Magazine,* 5 May 1996, 48–49.

46. In his book, *Awakening the Buddha Within: Tibetan Wisdom for the Western World,* published somewhat later (New York: Broadway Books, 1997), he presents a slightly different list of ten trends in Buddhism on pp. 383–86: (1) meditation-based and experientially oriented; (2) lay-oriented; (3) gender equal; (4) democratic and egalitarian; (5) essentialized, simplified, and demystified; (6) nonsectarian; (7) psychologically astute; (8) exploratory; (9) community oriented; and (10) socially and ecologically conscious.

47. Harvey Cox, *Seduction of the Spirit* (New York: Simon and Schuster, 1973), 121.

48. See Prebish, "Ethics and Integration," 128–29.

49. Waterloo, Ontario: Wilfred Laurier University Press, 1983.

50. New York: Mouton de Gruyter, 1992.

51. Ninian Smart, "The Importance of Diasporas," in *Gilgut,* ed. S. Shaked, D. Shulman, and G. G. Stroumsa (Leiden: Brill, 1987), 293.

52. Ibid.

53. Martin Baumann, "Buddhism in the West: Phases, Orders, and the Creation of an Integrative Buddhism," *Internationales Asienforum* 27, nos. 3–4 (1996), 361–62.

54. Having examined the process of Buddhism's growth in European countries for many years, Martin Baumann has identified five categories of what he calls "processive modes of transplantation." First there is "contact," or the geographic arrival of the foreign tradition into the new culture. Second comes "confrontation and conflict," in which the host society and foreign religion encounter each other, with the degree of tolerance in each direction determined by such factors as political, economic, social, and even legal factors. Third is "ambiguity and adaptation," of which Baumann notes that while ambiguities are virtually unavoidable when one religion is transplanted into a new sociocultural context, adaptation allows for a resolution of those ambiguities. "Recoupment" or "reorientation" is next, in which the various communities strive to retain their own identity while adjusting to the transition of adaptation. Finally comes "innovative self-development," in which new forms and innovations in the previously foreign religion occur. Baumann points out that these five processive modes need not follow each other successively, nor do they occur in each transplantation process. Nonetheless, the process was very helpful in understanding the development of German Buddhism. Baumann even offers a series of six strategies of adaptation,

based on Steven Kaplan's "six different modes of adaptation" and Klaus-Josef Notz's "actualization strategies" of acculturation. See Martin Baumann, "The Transplantation of Buddhism to Germany: Processive Modes and Strategies of Adaptation," *Method and Theory in the Study of Religion* 6, no. 1 (1994), 35–61.

55. Baumann, "Transplantation of Buddhism," 43–44.

56. The full text of the confession can be found in the German journal *Lotusblätter* 1 (spring 1987), 7. A commentary by Geshe Thubten Ngawang (of the Tibetan Center in Hamburg) appears on pp. 8–11. This confession was reprinted a number of times in later issues of *Lotusblätter* as well. Also see Martin Baumann, *Deutsche Buddhisten: Geschichte und Gemeinschaften* (Marburg: Diagonal-Verlag, 1993), 430. Baumann also points out that the Buddhist Confession was one of the legal requirements for the establishment of the "Buddhist Religious Community of Germany," the application for which was rejected ("Transplantation of Buddhism," 43).

57. Martin Baumann, "Creating a European Path to Nirvâna: Historical and Contemporary Developments of Buddhism in Europe," *Journal of Contemporary Religion* 10, no. 1 (1995), 65.

58. Ibid.

Appendix. A Postscript on North American Buddhism

1. Also see Stephen Batchelor, *The Awakening of the West: The Encounter of Buddhism and Western Culture* (Berkeley: Parallax Press, 1994), pp. 272–280.

2. See *Journal of Buddhist Ethics* 4 (1997), pp. 194–211.

3. Ibid., pp. 204–205.

4. In *Journal of Contemporary Religion* 10, no. 1 (1995), pp. 55–70.

Selected Bibliography on Buddhism in the West

Adam, Enid L., and Philip J. Hughes. *Religious Community Profiles: The Buddhists in Australia.* Canberra: Australian Government Publishing Service, 1996.

Akizuki, Ryōmin. *New Mahāyāna: Buddhism for a Post-Modern World.* Translated by James W. Heisig and Paul L. Swanson. Berkeley: Asian Humanities Press, 1990.

Almond, Philip C. *The British Discovery of Buddhism.* Cambridge: Cambridge University Press, 1988.

———. "The Buddha in the West: From Myth to History." *Religion* 16 (1986), 305–22.

Ames, Van Meter. *Zen and American Thought.* Honolulu: University of Hawaii Press, 1962.

Asai, Senryū, and Duncan Ryūken Williams, "Japanese American Zen Temples: Cultural Identity and Economics." In *American Buddhism: Methods and Findings in Recent Scholarship,* edited by Duncan Ryūken Williams and Christopher S. Queen, 20–35. Surrey, U.K.: Curzon Press, 1998.

Barber, A. W., and Cuong T. Nguyen. "Vietnamese Buddhism in America: Tradition and Acculturation." In *The Faces of Buddhism in America,* edited by Charles S. Prebish and Kenneth K. Tanaka, 129–46. Berkeley: University of California Press, 1998.

Batchelor, Stephen. *The Awakening of the West: The Encounter of Buddhism and Western Culture.* Berkeley: Parallax Press, 1994.

Baumann, Martin. "Buddhism in the West: Phases, Orders, and the Creation of an Integrative Buddhism." *Internationales Asienforum* 27, nos. 3–4 (1996), 345–362.

———. "Creating a European Path to Buddhism: Historical and Contemporary

Developments of Buddhism in Europe." *Journal of Contemporary Religion* 10, no. 1 (1995), 55–70.

———. "Culture Contact and Valuation: Early German Buddhists and the Creation of a 'Buddhism in Protestant Shape.' " *Numen* 44 (1997), 270–95.

———. *Deutsche Buddhisten: Geschichte und Gemeinschaften*. Marburg: Diagonal-Verlag, 1993; 2d ed., updated and enlarged, 1995.

———. "The Transplantation of Buddhism to Germany: Processive Modes and Strategies of Adaptation." *Method and Theory in the Study of Religion* 6, no. 1 (1994), 35–61.

Becker, Carl. "Japanese Pure Land Buddhism in Christian America." *Buddhist-Christian Studies* 10 (1990), 143–56.

Bell, Sandra. "Change and Identity in the Friends of the Western Buddhist Order." *Scottish Journal of Religious Studies* 17, no. 1 (1996), 87–107.

Bloom, Alfred. "Shin Buddhism in America: A Social Perspective." In *The Faces of Buddhism in America,* edited by Charles S. Prebish and Kenneth K. Tanaka, 31–47. Berkeley: University of California Press, 1998.

———. "The Unfolding of the Lotus: A Survey of Recent Developments in Shin Buddhism in the West." *Buddhist-Christian Studies* 10 (1990), 157–64.

Boucher, Sandy. *Opening the Lotus: A Women's Guide to Buddhism*. Boston: Beacon Press, 1997.

———. *Turning the Wheel: American Women Creating the New Buddhism*. Updated and expanded ed. Boston: Beacon Press, 1993.

Bridges, Hal. *American Mysticism from William James to Zen*. New York: Harper & Row, 1970.

Buddhist Churches of America. *Buddhist Churches of America: Seventy-Five Year History, 1899–1974*. 2 vols. Chicago: Nobart, 1974.

Butler, Katy. "Encountering the Shadow in Buddhist America." *Common Boundary* 8, no. 3 (May-June 1990), 14–22.

———. "Events Are the Teacher." *CoEvolution Quarterly* 40 (winter 1983), 112–23.

Cabezón, José. "Buddhist Studies as a Discipline and the Role of Theory." *Journal of the International Association of Buddhist Studies* 18, no. 2 (winter 1995), 231–68.

Causton, Richard. *The Buddha in Daily Life: An Introduction to the Buddhism of Nichiren Daishōnin*. London: Rider, 1995. (A later edition of *Nichiren Shōshū Buddhism*.)

———. *Nichiren Shōshū Buddhism: An Introduction*. London: Rider, 1988. (An earlier edition of *The Buddha in Daily Life*.)

Chandler, Stuart. "Chinese Buddhism in America: Identity and Practice." In *The Faces of Buddhism in America,* edited by Charles S. Prebish and Kenneth K. Tanaka, 13–30. Berkeley: University of California Press, 1998.

———. "Placing Palms Together: Religious Cultural Dimensions of the Hsi Lai Temple Political Donations Controversy." In *American Buddhism: Meth-*

ods and Findings in Recent Scholarship, edited by Duncan Ryūken Williams and Christopher S. Queen, 36–56. Surrey, U.K.: Curzon Press, 1998.

Coleman, Graham, ed. *A Handbook of Tibetan Culture: A Guide to Tibetan Centres and Resources throughout the World.* London: Rider, 1993.

Coleman, James William. "The New Buddhism: Some Empirical Findings." In *American Buddhism: Methods and Findings in Recent Scholarship,* edited by Duncan Ryūken Williams and Christopher S. Queen, 91–99. Surrey, U.K.: Curzon Press, 1998.

Collcutt, Martin. "Epilogue: Problems of Authority in Western Zen." In *Zen: Tradition and Transition,* edited by Kenneth Kraft, 199–207. New York: Grove Press, 1988

Conze, Edward. "Recent Progress in Buddhist Studies." In *Thirty Years of Buddhist Studies,* 1–32. Oxford: Bruno Cassirer, 1967.

Corless, Roger. "Coming Out in the *Sangha:* Queer Community in American Buddhism." In *The Faces of Buddhism in America,* edited by Charles S. Prebish and Kenneth K. Tanaka, 253–65. Berkeley: University of California Press, 1998.

Cox, Harvey. *Turning East: The Promise and Peril of the New Orientalism.* New York: Simon and Schuster, 1977.

Croucher, Paul. *A History of Buddhism in Australia: 1848–1988.* Kensington, Australia: New South Wales University Press, 1989.

Cush, Denise. "British Buddhism and the New Age." *Journal of Contemporary Religion* 11, no. 2 (1996), 195–208.

de Jong, J. W. *A Brief History of Buddhist Studies in Europe and America.* 2d rev. ed. Bibliotheca Indo-Buddhica, no. 33. Delhi: Sri Satguru, 1987.

Dresser, Marianne, ed. *Buddhist Women on the Edge: Contemporary Perspectives from the Western Frontier.* Berkeley: North Atlantic Books, 1996.

Dumoulin, Heinrich, and John Maraldo, eds. *The Cultural, Political, and Religious Significance of Buddhism in the Modern World.* New York: Collier Macmillan, 1976.

Eckel, Malcolm David. "The Ghost at the Table: On the Study of Buddhism and the Study of Religion." *Journal of the American Academy of Religion* 62, no. 4 (winter 1994), 1085–1110.

Ellwood, Robert S. *Alternative Altars: Unconventional and Eastern Spirituality in America.* Chicago: University of Chicago Press, 1979.

———. "Buddhism in the West." In *Encyclopedia of Religion,* edited by Mircea Eliade, vol. 2, 436–439. New York: Macmillan, 1987.

———. *The Eagle and the Rising Sun.* Philadelphia: Westminster Press, 1974.

Ellwood, Robert S., and Harry B. Partin. *Religious and Spiritual Groups in Modern America.* 2d ed. Englewood Cliffs, N.J.: Prentice-Hall, 1988.

Eppsteiner, Fred, ed. *The Path of Compassion: Writings on Socially Engaged Buddhism.* Berkeley: Parallax Press, 1988.

Farber, Don, and Rick Fields. *Taking Refuge in L.A.: Life in a Vietnamese Buddhist Temple.* New York: Aperture Foundation, 1987.

Farkas, Mary, ed. *The Zen Eye: A Collection of Zen Talks by Sokei-an.* Tokyo: Weatherhill, 1993.

Fields, Rick. "Confessions of a White Buddhist." *Tricycle: The Buddhist Review* 4, no. 1 (1994), 54–56.

———. "Divided Dharma: White Buddhists, Ethnic Buddhists, and Racism." In *The Faces of Buddhism in America,* edited by Charles S. Prebish and Kenneth K. Tanaka, 196–206. Berkeley: University of California Press, 1998.

———. "The Future of American Buddhism." *Vajradhatu Sun* 9, no. 1 (1987), 1, 22, 24–26.

———. *How the Swans Came to the Lake: A Narrative History of Buddhism in America.* 3d ed., rev. and updated. Boston: Shambhala, 1992.

Finney, Henry C. "American Zen's 'Japan Connection': A Critical Case Study of Zen Buddhism's Diffusion to the West." *Sociological Analysis* 52, no. 4 (1991), 379–96.

Friedman, Lenore. *Meetings with Remarkable Women: Buddhist Teachers in America.* Boston: Shambhala, 1987.

Fronsdal, Gil. "Insight Meditation in America: Life, Liberty, and the Pursuit of Happiness." In *The Faces of Buddhism in America,* edited by Charles S. Prebish and Kenneth K. Tanaka, 163–80. Berkeley: University of California Press, 1998.

Fung, Gordon L., and Gregory Fung. "Adapting Jōdo-Shinshū Teaching for the West: An Approach Based on the American Work Ethic." *Pacific World,* n.s., 9 (fall 1993), 24–31.

Gómez, Luis. "Unspoken Paradigms: Meanderings through the Metaphors of a Field." *Journal of the International Association of Buddhist Studies* 18, no. 2 (winter 1995), 183–230.

Goss, Robert E. "Buddhist Studies at Naropa: Sectarian or Academic?" In *American Buddhism: Methods and Findings in Recent Scholarship,* edited by Duncan Ryūken Williams and Christopher S. Queen, 215–37. Surrey, U.K.: Curzon Press, 1998.

Gross, Rita. *Buddhism after Patriarchy: A Feminist History, Analysis, and Reconstruction of Buddhism.* Albany: State University of New York Press, 1993.

———. "Helping the Iron Bird Fly: Western Buddhist Women and Issues of Authority in the Late 1990s." In *The Faces of Buddhism in America,* edited by Charles S. Prebish and Kenneth K. Tanaka, 238–52. Berkeley: University of California Press, 1998.

Gunter-Jones, Roger. *Buddhism and the West.* London: Lindsay Press, 1973.

Hammond, Phillip, and David Machacek. "Supply and Demand: The Appeal of American Buddhism." In *American Buddhism: Methods and Findings in Recent Scholarship,* edited by Duncan Ryūken Williams and Christopher S. Queen, 100–114. Surrey, U.K.: Curzon Press, 1998.

Hayes, Richard P. "The Internet as Window onto American Buddhism" In

American Buddhism: Methods and Findings in Recent Scholarship, edited by Duncan Ryūken Williams and Christopher S. Queen, 168–79. Surrey, U.K.: Curzon Press, 1998.

Hecker, Hellmuth. *Buddhismus in Deutschland: Eine Chronik.* 3d ed. Plochingen: Deutsche Buddhistische Union, 1985.

———. *Lebensbilder deutscher Buddhisten: Ein bio-bibliographisches Handbuch.* 2 vols. Constance: University of Constance, 1990 and 1992.

Henderson, Harold. *Catalyst for Controversy: Paul Carus of Open Court.* Carbondale: Southern Illinois University Press, 1993.

Hing, Bill Ong. *Making and Remaking Asian America through Immigration Policy, 1850–1990.* Stanford: Stanford University Press, 1993.

Hori, Victor Sōgen. "Japanese Zen in America: Americanizing the Face in the Mirror." In *The Faces of Buddhism in America,* edited by Charles S. Prebish and Kenneth K. Tanaka, 49–78. Berkeley: University of California Press, 1998.

———. "Sweet-and-Sour Buddhism." *Tricycle: The Buddhist Review,* 4, no. 1 (1994), 48–52.

Humphreys, Christmas. *The Development of Buddhism in England.* London: Buddhist Lodge, 1937.

———. *Sixty Years of Buddhism in England (1907–1967).* London: Buddhist Society, 1968.

———. *Zen Comes West: The Present and Future of Zen Buddhism in Britain.* London: George Allen & Unwin, 1960.

Hunter, Louise. *Buddhism in Hawaii.* Honolulu: University of Hawaii Press, 1971.

Hurst, Jane. "Nichiren Shōshū and Sōka Gakkai in America: The Pioneer Spirit." In *The Faces of Buddhism in America,* edited by Charles S. Prebish and Kenneth K. Tanaka, 79–97. Berkeley: University of California Press, 1998.

———. *Nichiren Shoshu Buddhism and the Soka Gakkai in America: The Ethos of a New Religious Movement.* New York: Garland Press, 1992.

Imamura, Ryo. "Buddhist and Western Psychotherapies: An Asian American Perspective." In *The Faces of Buddhism in America,* edited by Charles S. Prebish and Kenneth K. Tanaka, 228–37. Berkeley: University of California Press, 1998.

———. "A Comparative Study of Temple and Non-Temple Buddhist Ministers of the Jōdo Shin Sect Using Jungian Psychological Types." Ph.D. diss., University of San Francisco, 1986.

Jackson, Carl T. "The Influence of Asian upon American Thought: A Bibliographical Essay." *American Studies International* 22 (1984), 3–31.

———. "The Meeting of East and West: The Case of Paul Carus." *Journal of the History of Ideas* 29 (1968), 73–92.

———. *The Oriental Religions and American Thought.* Westport, Conn.: Greenwood Press, 1981.

Jones, Ken. *The Social Face of Buddhism: An Approach to Political and Social Activism.* London: Wisdom Publications, 1989.

Kashima, Tetsuden. *Buddhism in America: The Social Organization of an Ethnic Religious Institution.* Westport, Conn.: Greenwood Press, 1977.

———. "The Buddhist Churches of America: Challenges for a Change in the Twenty-First Century." *Pacific World,* n.s., 6 (fall 1990), 28–40.

Kitagawa, Joseph T. "Appendix: Buddhism in America." In *On Understanding Japanese Religion,* edited by Joseph T. Kitagawa, 311–328. Princeton: Princeton University Press, 1987

———. "Buddhism in America, with Special Reference to Zen." *Japanese Religions* 5 (1967), 32–57.

Kornfield, Jack. "Is Buddhism Changing North America." In *Buddhist America: Centers, Retreats, Practices,* edited by Don Morreale, xi–xxviii. Santa Fe, N.Mex.: John Muir Publications, 1988.

Kraft, Kenneth. "Recent Developments in North American Zen." In *Zen: Tradition and Transition,* edited by Kenneth Kraft, 178–198. New York: Grove Press, 1988.

Lachs, Stuart. "A Slice of Zen in America." *New Ch'an Forum* 10 (1994), 12–20.

Lancaster, Lewis R. "Buddhism in the United States: The Untold and Unfinished Story." *Shambhala Review* 5, nos. 1–2 (1976), 23–25.

Lavine, Amy. "Tibetan Buddhism in America: The Development of American Vajrayāna." In *The Faces of Buddhism in America,* edited by Charles S. Prebish and Kenneth K. Tanaka, 99–115. Berkeley: University of California Press, 1998.

Layman, Emma. *Buddhism in America.* Chicago: Nelson-Hall, 1976.

Lin, Irene. "Journey to the Far West: Chinese Buddhism in America." *Amerasia Journal* 22, no. 1 (1996), 107–32.

Lopez, Donald S., Jr., ed. *Curators of the Buddha.* Chicago: University of Chicago Press, 1995.

Lorie, Peter, and Hillary Foakes, eds. *The Buddhist Directory: The Total Buddhist Resource Guide.* Boston: Tuttle, 1997.

Macy, Joanna. "The Balancing of American Buddhism," *Primary Point* 3, no. 1 (February 1986).

Mann, Robert. *Buddhism in a Foreign Land: Essays on Meditation.* Bradford-on-Avon, U.K.: Aukana, 1996.

Mellor, Philip A. "Protestant Buddhism? The Cultural Translation of Buddhism in England." *Religion* 21 (1991), 73–92.

Metraux, Daniel. *The History and Theology of Soka Gakkai: A Japanese New Religion.* Lewiston, N.Y.: Edwin Mellen Press, 1988.

———. *The Lotus and the Maple Leaf: The Soka Gakkai Buddhist Movement in Canada.* Lewiston, N.Y.: University Press of America, 1996.

Morreale, Don, ed. *Buddhist America: Centers, Retreats, Practices.* Santa Fe, N.Mex.: John Muir Publications, 1988.

Mortland, Carol A. "Khmer Buddhists in the United States: Ultimate Questions." In *Cambodian Culture since 1975,* edited by May M. Ebihara and Judy Ledgerwood. Ithaca, N.Y.: Cornell University Press, 1984.

Nattier, Jan. "Buddhist Studies in the Post-Colonial Age." *Journal of the American Academy of Religion* 65, no. 2 (summer 1997), 469–85.

———. "Visible and Invisible." *Tricycle: The Buddhist Review* 5, no. 1 (1995), 42–49.

———. "Who Is a Buddhist? Charting the Landscape of Buddhist America." In *The Faces of Buddhism in America,* edited by Charles S. Prebish and Kenneth K. Tanaka, 183–95. Berkeley: University of California Press, 1998.

Needleman, Jacob. *The New Religions.* New York: E. P. Dutton, 1977.

Needleman, Jacob, and George Baker, eds. *Understanding the New Religions.* New York: Seabury Press, 1978.

Notz, Klaus-Josef. *Der Buddhismus in Deutschland in seinen Selbstdarstellungen: Eine Religionswissenschaftliche Untersuchung zur Religiösen Akkulturationproblematik.* Frankfurt am Main: Peter Lang, 1984.

Numrich, Paul David. "Local Inter-Buddhist Associations in North America." In *American Buddhism: Methods and Findings in Recent Scholarship,* edited by Duncan Ryūken Williams and Christopher S. Queen, 117–42. Surrey, U.K.: Curzon Press, 1998.

———. *Old Wisdom in the New World: Americanization in Two Immigrant Theravada Buddhist Temples.* Knoxville: University of Tennessee Press, 1996.

———. "Theravāda Buddhism in America: Prospect for the *Sangha.*" In *The Faces of Buddhism in America,* edited by Charles S. Prebish and Kenneth K. Tanaka, 147–61. Berkeley: University of California Press, 1998.

———. "*Vinaya* in Theravāda Temples in the United States." *Journal of Buddhist Ethics* 1 (1994), 23–32.

Oliver, Ian P. *Buddhism in Britain.* London: Rider, 1979.

Peiris, William. *The Western Contribution to Buddhism.* Delhi: Motilal Banarsidass, 1973.

Prebish, Charles. "The Academic Study of Buddhism in America: A Silent *Sangha.*" In *American Buddhism: Methods and Findings in Recent Scholarship,* edited by Duncan Ryūken Williams and Christopher S. Queen, 183–214. Surrey, U.K.: Curzon Press, 1998.

———. "The Academic Study of Buddhism in the United States: A Current Analysis." *Religion* 24 (1994), 271–278.

———. *American Buddhism.* North Scituate, Mass.: Duxbury Press, 1979.

———. "Buddhism." In *Encyclopedia of the American Religious Experience: Studies of Traditions and Movements,* edited by Charles H. Lippy and Peter W. Williams, vol. 2, 669–82. New York: Scribner's, 1988.

———. "Introduction." In *The Faces of Buddhism in America,* edited by Charles S. Prebish and Kenneth K. Tanaka, 1–10. Berkeley: University of California Press, 1998.

———. "Karma and Rebirth in the Land of the Earth-Eaters." In *Karma and Rebirth: Post Classical Development,* edited by Ronald W. Neufeldt, 325–38. Albany: State University of New York Press, 1986.

———. "Reflections of the Transmission of Buddhism to America." In *Understanding the New Religions,* edited by Jacob Needleman and George Baker, 153–72. New York: Seabury Press, 1978.

———. "Two Buddhisms Reconsidered." *Buddhist Studies Review* 10 (1993), 187–206.

Prebish, Charles S., and Kenneth K. Tanaka, eds. *The Faces of Buddhism in America.* Berkeley: University of California Press, 1998.

Prothero, Stephen. *The White Buddhist: The Asian Odyssey of Henry Steel Olcott.* Bloomington: Indiana University Press, 1996.

Rapaport, Al, ed. *Buddhism in America: The Official Record of the Landmark Conference on the Future of Buddhist Meditative Practices in the West.* Boston: Tuttle, 1997.

Rawlinson, Andrew. *The Book of Enlightened Masters: Western Teachers in Eastern Traditions.* Chicago and La Salle, Ill.: Open Court, 1997.

———. "The Transmission of Theravāda Buddhism to the West." In *Aspects of Religion: Essays in Honour of Ninian Smart,* edited by Peter Masefield and Donald Wiebe, Toronto Studies in Religion, vol. 18, 357–88. New York: Lang, 1994.

Rommeluere, Eric. *Le guide du Zen.* Paris: Editions de Livre de Poche, Collection les Guides Selene, 1997.

Rothberg, Donald. "Responding to the Cries of the World: Socially Engaged Buddhism in North America." In *The Faces of Buddhism in America,* edited by Charles S. Prebish and Kenneth K. Tanaka, 266–86. Berkeley: University of California Press, 1998.

Sangharakshita, Bhikshu. *New Currents in Western Buddhism.* Glasgow: Windhorse Publications, 1990.

Schneider, David. *Street Zen: The Life and Work of Issan Dorsey.* Boston: Shambhala, 1993.

Seager, Richard Hughes. "Buddhist Worlds in the U.S.A.: A Survey of the Territory." In *American Buddhism: Methods and Findings in Recent Scholarship,* edited by Duncan Ryūken Williams and Christopher S. Queen, 236–61. Surrey, U.K.: Curzon Press, 1998.

———. *The World's Parliament of Religions: The East-West Encounter, Chicago, 1893.* Bloomington: Indiana University Press, 1995.

Shimano, Ediō Tai, ed. *Endless Vow: The Zen Path of Nakagawa Soen.* Boston: Shambhala, 1996.

Sidor, Ellen S., ed. *A Gathering of Spirit: Women Teaching in American Buddhism.* Cumberland, R.I.: Primary Point Press, 1987.

Snelling, John. "Buddhism Comes West." In *The Buddhist Handbook: A Complete Guide to Buddhist Schools, Teaching, Practice, and History,* 194–256. Rochester, Vt.: Inner Traditions, 1991.

———. *Buddhism in Russia: The Story of Agvan Dorzhiev, Lhasa's Emissary to the Tsar.* Rockport, Mass.: Element, 1993.

———. *The Buddhist Handbook: A Complete Guide to Buddhist Schools, Teaching, Practice, and History.* Rochester, Vt.: Inner Traditions, 1991.

Snow, David A. "Organization, Ideology, and Mobilization: The Case of Nichiren Shōshū in America." In *The Future of New Religious Movements,* edited by David G. Bromley and Phillip E. Hammond, 153–72. Macon, Ga.: Mercer University Press, 1987.

Soeng, Mu. "Korean Buddhism in America: A New Style of Zen." In *The Faces of Buddhism in America,* edited by Charles S. Prebish and Kenneth K. Tanaka, 117–28. Berkeley: University of California Press, 1998.

Sponberg, Alan. "Green Buddhism and the Hierarchy of Compassion." *Western Buddhist Review* 1 (December 1994), 131–55.

Strain, Charles R. "The Pacific Buddha's Wild Practice: Gary Snyder's Environmental Ethic." In *American Buddhism: Methods and Findings in Recent Scholarship,* edited by Duncan Ryūken Williams and Christopher S. Queen, 143–67. Surrey, U.K.: Curzon Press, 1998.

Subhuti, Dharmacari (Alex Kennedy). *Buddhism for Today: A Portrait of a New Buddhist Movement.* 2d ed. Glasgow: Windhorse Publications, 1988.

———. *Sangharakshita: A New Voice in the Buddhist Tradition.* Glasgow: Windhorse Publications, 1994.

Sugunasiri, Suwanda H. J. "Buddhism in Metropolitan Toronto: A Preliminary Overview." *Canadaian Ethnic Studies* 21, no. 2 (1989), 83–103.

Surya Das, Lama. *Awakening the Buddha Within: Tibetan Wisdom for the Western World.* New York: Broadway Books, 1997.

Swick, David. *Thunder and Ocean: Shambhala and Buddhism in Nova Scotia.* Lawrencetown Beach, Nova Scotia: Pottersfield Press, 1996.

Tamney, Joseph B. *American Society in the Buddhist Mirror.* New York: Garland Publishing, 1992.

Tanaka, Kenneth K. "Epilogue: The Colors and Contours of American Buddhism." In *The Faces of Buddhism in America,* edited by Charles S. Prebish and Kenneth K. Tanaka, 287–98. Berkeley: University of California Press, 1998.

———. "Issues of Ethnicity in the Buddhist Churches of America." In *American Buddhism: Methods and Findings in Recent Scholarship,* edited by Duncan Ryūken Williams and Christopher S. Queen, 13–19. Surrey, U.K.: Curzon Press, 1998.

Tonkinson, Carole, ed. *Big Sky Mind: Buddhism and the Beat Generation.* New York: Riverhead Books, 1995.

Tsomo, Karma Lekshe, ed. *Buddhism through American Women's Eyes.* Ithaca, N.Y.: Snow Lion, 1995.

Tuck, Donald. *Buddhist Churches of America: Jodo Shinshu.* Studies in American Religion, vol. 28. Lewiston, N.Y.: Edwin Mellen Press, 1987.

Tweed, Thomas. *The American Encounter with Buddhism, 1844–1912: Victorian Culture and the Limits of Dissent.* Bloomington: Indiana University Press, 1992.

———. "Night Stand Buddhists and Other Creatures: Sympathizers, Adherents, and the Study of Religion." In *American Buddhism: Methods and Findings in Recent Scholarship,* edited by Duncan Ryūken Williams and Christopher S. Queen, 71–90. Surrey, U.K.: Curzon Press, 1998.

Tworkov, Helen. *Zen in America: Five Teachers and the Search for an American Buddhism.* New ed. New York: Kodansha International, 1994.

Van Esterik, Penny. "Ritual and the Performance of Buddhist Identity among Lao Buddhists in North America." In *American Buddhism: Methods and Findings in Recent Scholarship,* edited by Duncan Ryūken Williams and Christopher S. Queen, 57–68. Surrey, U.K.: Curzon Press, 1998.

van Gemert, Victor. *Boeddhisme in Nederland: Oversicht van boeddhistische stromingen in Nederland en Belgie.* Nijmegen: Zen-uitgeverij Theresiahoeve, 1990; updated 1993.

Verhoeven, Martin. "Americanizing the Buddha: Paul Carus and the Transformation of Asian Thought." In *The Faces of Buddhism in America,* edited by Charles S. Prebish and Kenneth K. Tanaka, 207–27. Berkeley: University of California Press, 1998.

Vessantara, Dharmachari. *The Friends of the Western Buddhist Order.* Glasgow: Windhorse Publications, 1988.

Webb, Russell. "Contemporary European Scholarship on Buddhism." In *The Buddhist Heritage,* edited by Tadeusz Skorupski, Buddhica Britannica, vol. 1, 247–76. Tring, U.K.: Institute for Buddhist Studies, 1989.

———. "Pali Buddhist Studies in the West." *Pali Buddhist Review* 1, no. 3 (1976), 169–80; 2, no. 1 (1977), 55–62; 2, no. 2 (1977), 114–22; 2, no. 3 (1977), 162–67; 3, no. 1 (1978), 35–36; 3, no. 2 (1978), 84–87; 3, no. 3 (1978), 146–53; 4, nos. 1–2 (1979), 28–31; 4, no. 4 (1979), 86–90; 5, nos. 1–2 (1980), 39–41; 5, no. 3 (1980), 89–92.

Wells, Mariann Kaye. *Chinese Temples in California.* Berkeley: University of California Press, 1962.

Williams, Duncan Ryūken. "Where to Study?" *Tricycle: The Buddhist Review* 6, no. 3 (spring 1997), 68–69, 115–17.

Williams, Duncan Ryūken, and Christopher S. Queen, eds. *American Buddhism: Methods and Findings in Recent Scholarship.* Surrey, U.K.: Curzon Press, 1998.

Wilson, Bryan, and Karel Dobbelaere. *A Time to Chant: The Sōka Gakkai Buddhists in Britain.* Oxford: Clarendon Press, 1994.

Wratten, Darrel. "Buddhism in South Africa: From Textual Imagination to Contextual Innovation." Ph.D. diss., Cape Town University, 1995.

Index